125

AIRCRAFT IN PROFILE

AIRCRAFT
IN
PROFILE

PROFILE
Nos. 25-48

GENERAL EDITOR
MARTIN C. WINDROW

WITH ILLUSTRATIONS BY

R. WARD

P. ENDSLEIGH CASTLE, A.R.Ae.S.

G. J. GOULDING

K. BROOMFIELD

K. G. RUSH

PUBLISHED BY

DOUBLEDAY AND COMPANY, INC.,

GARDEN CITY   NEW YORK.

Uniform with this Volume

Classic Cars in Profile, Vol. 1 (Nos.   1-24)
Classic Cars in Profile, Vol. 2 (Nos. 25-48)
Aircraft in Profile, Vol. 1   (Nos. 1-24)

DOUBLEDAY AND COMPANY INC.
Garden City, New York.

First Published in Great Britain (1965) by
PROFILE PUBLICATIONS LIMITED
P.O. Box 26, LEATHERHEAD, SURREY

Printed in 9 pt. Times New Roman 327
by George Falkner & Sons Ltd., for McCorquodale City Printing Division, London & Manchester, England

Profiles Printed on Clyde Continental and Invercarron Art Paper
Monotone and 4-colour half-tone blocks by Viaduct Process Engraving Co., London, England.

FOREWORD

In this, the second collection of Aircraft Profiles, the emphasis is still upon the military aeroplane for, despite the belief of many that "the warplane has been the prostitution of a recreation", the vast sums of money spent on air defence in times of war have undoubtedly accelerated the development of the flying machine. Necessity has certainly sired invention, and in no other field has invention been more spectacular than in aviation. World War II brought with it a greater advance in aerotechnology than any other equal period in the twentieth century.

Yet to present only military aircraft from World War II would be to recount an incomplete story and start it in the middle. Many traditions, upheld in Hitler's War, were born in the Kaiser's War and often nurtured in the teeth of military apathy during the intervening years of "peace". Squadrons were born, disbanded and later re-born; no one who has served in an élite Squadron would remain for long unaware of his Unit's traditions. Such historical associations would so often become manifest in unit liveries, insignias and other ex officio *identification.*

Turning from the purely military evolution of aviation, one can cite instances in which the air minded—active and passive—have nurtured their nation's heritage in the air in more peaceful pursuits. Air racing has always appealed to active peacetime flyers, and this book contains the Profile devoted to the graceful Supermarine Schneider Trophy winners. How Mitchell developed his Spitfire from his racing seaplanes is well-known history, but without the knowledge gained from them, perhaps this immortal aeroplane would have never been designed.

CONTENTS

ACKNOWLEDGEMENTS

The Authors, Artists and Publishers wish to acknowledge the kind assistance given by many learned bodies, societies, Government departments, armed services and individuals during the course of preparation of the various Profiles. Particular mention should be made of the following:

Mr. Harold Andrews
Sr. G. Apostolo
Mr. Richard Atkins
Mr. R. Besecker
Mr. C. A. Nepean Bishop
Mr. K. J. Blackston
Mr. D. W. Brown
Mr. R. B. Brown
Mr. John W. Caler
Mr. E. F. Cheeseman
Mr. D. C. Cooke
Miss R. Coombs (of the Imp. War Mus.)
Mr. H. Cunningham
Mr. E. J. Creek
Mr. d'E. C. Darby
Mr. R. De Leva
Mr. Jay Frank Dial
Mr. Fred C. Dickey, Jr.
S/Ldr. F. E. Dymond
Mr. E. Ferko
Mr. D. S. Glover
Mr. J. L. Golding (of the Imp. War Mus.)
Mr. Peter M. Grosz
M. Werner Gysin Jr.
Mr. D. F. Harris
Mr. Ronald W. Harrison
Herr G. W. Heumann
Mr. E. C. H. Hine (of the Imp. War Mus.)
Herr F. von Hippel
Mr. H. Hope
Mr. Jack Hospers
Mr. Alex Imrie
Mnhr. G. H. Kamphuis
Herr Egon Krueger
Mr. William T. Larkins
Mr. G. J. Letzer
Mr. Witold Liss
Mr. A. S. C. Lumsden
Wg. Cdr. Norman Macmillan, O.B.E., M.C., A.F.C., D.L., A.F.R.Ae.S.
Maj. M. E. McGuinn, U.S. Army
Mr. David W. Menard
Col. Cesar Milani
Mr. K. M. Molson
Mr. R. G. Moulton
Herr H. J. Nowarra
Mr. M. B. Passingham
Mr. Harald Penrose, O.B.E., F.R.Ae.S.
Mr. W. Puglisi
Mr. A. U. Schmidt
Mr. A. Schoeni
Mr. C. Schuler
Mr. A. G. Simmons
Lt.-Col. E. M. Sommerich, U.S.A.F.

Mr. John W. R. Taylor, F.R.Hist.S., A.R.Ae.S.
Mr. Charles D. Thompson
Mr. Pavel Vancura
Mr. Art Whitmer
Mr. Bo Widfeldt
Mr. Gordon S. Williams
Mr. B. R. Winbourne

H.M. Ministry of Defence (Air)
The Air Historical Branch (Ministry of Defence)
The Royal Aeronautical Society
The Royal Air Force
The Royal Australian Air Force
The Royal Canadian Air Force
The Canadian War Archives
The Finnish Air Force
The Swedish Air Force (*Flygvapnet*)
The United States Air Force
The United States Marine Corps
The United States Navy

The Imperial War Museum
La Musée de l' Air
The National Aviation Museum of Canada
The Science Museum (South Kensington)

Shipp Photo Collection
Air Britain
The American Aviation Historical Society
Cross and Cockade
The New Zealand Aviation Historical Society

Aer Macchi
The British Aircraft Corporation (All Divisions)
The Boeing Airplane Company
The Curtiss Aircraft Corporation
Fairey Aviation Co. Ltd.
Goodyear Aerospace Corporation
Hawker Siddeley Aviation Ltd. (All Divisions)
Ling-Temco-Vought Inc.
North American Aviation Inc.
Rolls-Royce Ltd.
Svenska Aeroplan A.B. (SAAB)

"Aeroplane"
"Aeromodeller"
"Air Pictorial"
"Aireview" (Tokyo)
"Flight International"

PROFILE
PUBLICATIONS

The
Fokker
D.VII

NUMBER 25

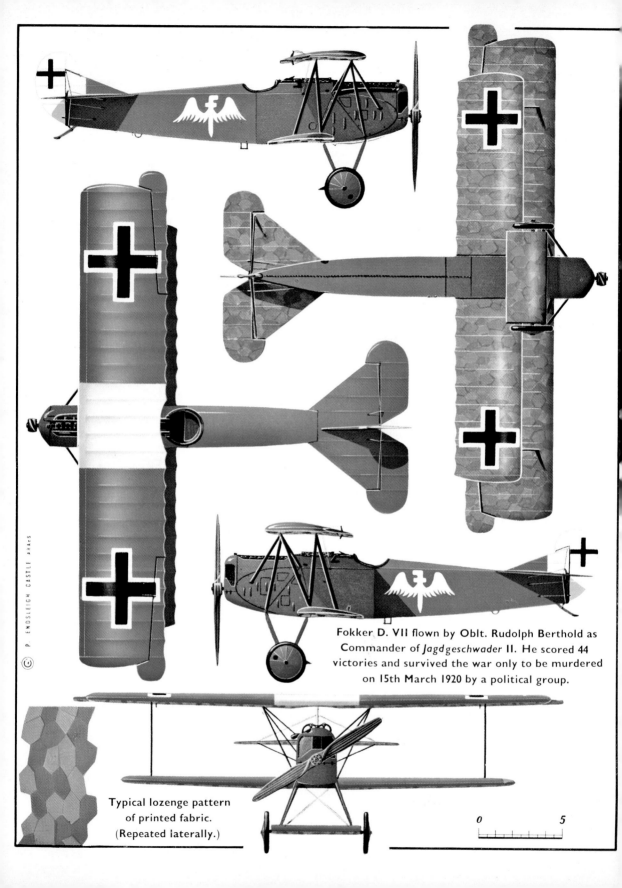

Fokker D. VII flown by Oblt. Rudolph Berthold as
Commander of *Jagdgeschwader* II. He scored 44
victories and survived the war only to be murdered
on 15th March 1920 by a political group.

Typical lozenge pattern
of printed fabric.
(Repeated laterally.)

© P. ENDSLEIGH CASTLE ᴬᴿᴬᴱˢ

0   5

The Fokker D.VII

by Peter L. Gray

Decorative—but unidentified Fokker D VII. (Photo: Egon Krueger)

The lush green turf of Cappy airfield, in the vigour of its early summer growth, suddenly bowed itself in the blast of slipstream as a Mercedes engine bellowed into life, shattering the silence of the dawn. Another; and another, motor spluttered, caught, then roared into life until seven machines were soon warming up with a rhythmical tick-over. A hand signal from the leader and the yellow-nosed biplanes began to trundle slowly over the resilient greensward to a far corner of the aerodrome where they turned into wind and, with a thundering roar, climbed swiftly into the western sky. In silhouette their shape was now more apparent, lean flanked, straight winged, as they formed into the loose stepped-up echelon in which they hunted. Fokker D VIIs! This was an element of *Jagdstaffel* 10 (of the Richthofen *Jagdgeschwader* I) first to be equipped with, and airborne at last in, this long awaited fighter machine. For the first time in many months they could meet their opposing S.E.5s, Camels and Spads on equal, if not superior terms. The distinctive straight-winged silhouette that was to strike anxiety, if not fear, into the hearts of Allied pilots as it began to appear in increasing numbers.

In an endeavour to find an aircraft to regain the ascendancy over the Allied fighters on the Western Front, the German authorities invited manufacturers, towards the end of 1917, to submit single-seat fighter prototypes utilising the 160-h.p. Mercedes D III power plant, for evaluation in a series of trials (D *Flugzeug Wettbewerb*). For several days the machines were to be put through their paces by pilots from combat units in addition to demonstration by the manufacturers. The first competition, it could be considered no less, was to be held in the latter part of January 1918 at Berlin's *Adlershof* airfield, and the machine adjudged to be the winner was to be awarded a production contract. All aircraft were assessed on an equal footing and were evaluated for general flying qualities, manœuvrability, diving ability, pilot's view, combat qualities, etc. There were also comparative test flight climbs to 5,000 m. (16,400 ft.) at which altitude speed trials were made. Speeds were

also compared at the 1,000 m. (3,280 ft.) level. All aircraft had to carry up to 100 kg. (approx. 220 lb.) useful load in addition to the pilot, and two barographs were installed in each machine.

Altogether thirty-one machines attended the trials, namely: A.E.G. D I; Albatros D Va (4 different aircraft); Aviatik D III; Fokker V 9, V 11, V 13 (two models), V 17, V 18, V 20, Dr I triplane (2 different aircraft); Kondor D II; Pfalz D IIIa (2 different aircraft), D VI, D VII; L.F.G. Roland D VI (2 different aircraft) D VII, D IX; Rumpler D (2 different models); Schütte-Lanz D III; Siemens Schuckert D III (4 different aircraft). (Not all these machines were Mercedes powered, many having rotary engines, but were included for comparative evaluation.) The eventual winner was adjudged to be the Fokker V 11. To speed production of the V 11 the fuselage and tail surfaces of the Fokker Dr I triplane were used, but this did not allow for the additional side area forward presented by the in-line engine now used, and in consequence it was found necessary to lengthen the fuselage to compensate for this factor. A vertical fin was also added before the machine went into production when, with the application of its military designation, it became the D VII. The prototype as it stood was over-sensitive and unstable in a dive and the modifications were largely made as a result of Manfred von Richthofen's criticisms. Testing the V 11

The redoubtable Fokker D VII in flight.

3

Fokker V 11. The first prototype which shows its unmistakable derivation from the Dr I triplane.

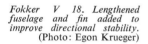

again after the alterations had been effected von Richthofen now found it easy to fly and no longer directionally unstable when diving; he was most enthusiastic about the aircraft and commended it especially to Klein and Loerzer to try.

Of his competitors Fokker considered the diminutive Rumpler to be the most serious rival but its design did not make for ease of mass production; he considered the Rolands had no visibility and the rest he dismissed as of little account! In the sham combats that were held the V 11 proved supreme and in particular it was its ability to retain its manœuv-

Fokker D VIIs (Alb) under construction at the Albatros-Werke, Johannisthal, *1918.* (Photo: Egon Krueger)

rability at altitude and "hang on its prop" that impressed the pilots from the *Jastas*. They were unanimous in their choice of this aeroplane.

THE D VII IS ORDERED

An order for 400 D VIIs to be put into immediate production at his Schwerin factory was awarded to Anthony Fokker and he was to receive 25,000 marks (approx. £1,250) for each aircraft. What pleased the pugnacious (his own adjective) Dutchman almost as much was the fact that his great rival, the Albatros company, was also ordered to undertake quantity manufacture of the D VII at both the *Johannisthal* and *Schneidemühl* plants. Albatros were to receive only 19,000 marks for the D VIIs they produced and on this figure a five per cent royalty was paid to Fokker. The fact that 6,000 marks more per aircraft was awarded to the designing company was in order to take into account their experimental and engineering costs.

Expert welding technicians from the Fokker firm were sent to the Albatros works to impart the technique of constructing the steel tube fuselages to the rival company's workmen, who were accustomed to wooden construction. No complete set of drawings existed at the Fokker factory, so a specimen machine was sent to each of the Albatros factories and they prepared their own drawings from it! As a result, although all the aircraft looked alike they differed in

Fokker D VII (O.A.W.) 4197/18 of Jasta *78. Note patchwork painting of motor hood panels to simulate camouflage pattern.*
(Photo: Egon Krueger)

A D VII in the former Dutch East Indies.
(Photo: Via G. H. Kamphuis)

detail (each firm applying its own standards) and not all components were interchangeable. As a safeguard against a shortage of steel the Albatros company built a D VII with a plywood skinned wooden fuselage (D VII Alb 541/18) but, in the event, circumstances did not necessitate its manufacture. Curiously this wooden D VII weighed out some 40 lb. heavier than the normal steel fuselaged machine.

With the coming of the Armistice, and consequent clipping of the German wings, the Fokker D VII was specifically mentioned in Article IV which detailed materials to be handed over to the Allies, i.e. ". . . in erster Linie alle Apparate D VII . . ." (especially all machines of D VII type). Although a singularly unique advertisement for Fokker the cost proved prohibitive as it meant the entire liquidation of his companies and the loss of a huge investment, nearly all of which was located in Germany where he had expected to continue in the manufacture of civil aircraft. In an endeavour to mitigate this loss the Dutchman managed to secrete some 220 aeroplanes and 400 engines in remote barns and other hiding places, away from the prying eyes of the Inter Allied Armistice Commission.

Eventually, after much bribery of various officials, no less than six trains, each of some sixty wagons, were organised and transported (smuggled would probably be a more apposite term) into Holland.

A hundred and twenty D VIIs and C Is in dismantled form, also the 400 engines and many wagon loads of spares and raw materials were shifted. During the civil strife which flared up in Germany towards the end of the war, Fokker had a D VII (V 38) specially modified with a second seat as early as September 1918, with tankage for a six hour flight. This would have enabled him to have flown with his fiancée Elizabeth (the daughter of General Kurt Ernst von Morgen) from Schwerin to Holland in a single hop. However, this measure did not prove possible in the end as the machine was put under guard by the revolutionary workmen and he returned to Amsterdam, most prosaically, by passenger train.

It has only become known in more recent years that the real designer of the later successful Fokker machines was Reinhold Platz, who endeavoured to make practical some of Anthony Fokker's often wild ideas. Until the death of Martin Kreutzer, who had been mainly responsible for the earlier types, D I to D IV, etc. Platz was chief welding engineer. However, after Kreutzer was killed in a flying accident Platz became responsible for design: it was he who pioneered the thick cantilever wing, first used in a production aeroplane in the Fokker Dr I triplane. Platz is only briefly mentioned twice in Fokker's autobiography, and through his somewhat retiring personality has

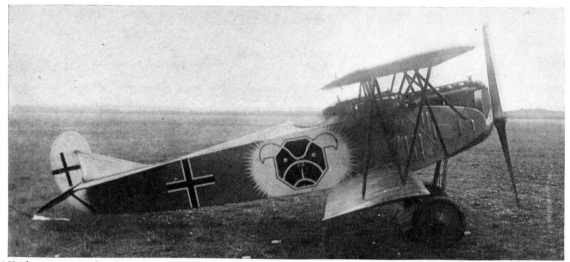

Used on post-war police duties (Polizerflieger staffel)—*a garishly marked D VII at Paderborn 1919–20.* (Photo: Egon Krueger)

O.A.W.-built aircraft flown by J. H. von Hippel when Commander Jasta 71. (Photo: Egon Krueger)

never received due credit for his work. Anthony Fokker, however, was undoubtedly a brilliant pilot and had an instinctive flair for diagnosing what modifications were required to improve a machine once it was flyable—as may be seen from his modifications to the V 11. It was through his flying ability too, that he was on such intimate terms with many of the leading fighter pilots from the *Jastas*.

THE D VII DESCRIBED

With its straight wings, uncluttered with any bracing cables, the Fokker D VII was, for its day, a remarkably clean, albeit somewhat sinister, looking aeroplane; in spite of its blunt nose, more reminiscent of British than German design. It was in fact the first operational German machine to feature a car-type honeycomb radiator, mounted on the nose in front of the Mercedes D III engine. A small central portion, about four inches wide, was flat and the outer parts were angled back. A small water header tank was mounted on top of the radiator. The fuselage was a slab sided, steel tube structure, the sides being parallel back to the cockpit, from which point they tapered to a vertical knife-edge at the sternpost. The steel tubes reduced in gauge and diameter from nose to tail and all joints were welded with a high degree of skill. At the junction of all vertical and cross members a small quadrant shaped "corner" tube was welded in to take the bracing cable, this was looped through and the ends joined in a single turnbuckle for tightening, the resultant structure being a rigid braced box-girder. Decking aft of the cockpit was in the form of a curved plywood panel over which the fabric was stretched.

The engine was borne on tubular bearers carried on a complex web of welded tubes. Metal panels punched with louvres and fitted with access doors extended back to the forward centre-section struts. Louvres

and doors differed from side to side. On the early D VIIs the exhaust manifold was ducted down inside the starboard nose panelling and ejected through a short exhaust pipe about the middle of the fuselage depth. On later aircraft the panelling was cut away level with the top of the cylinders and a simple collector manifold exhausted to starboard just aft of the rear cylinder. Of distinctive shape, with triangular fixed surfaces and large semi-circular balanced control surfaces, the entire empennage was also framed from steel tube. The tailplane was braced to the lower longerons with short struts.

Of wooden construction, the constant-chord wings were based on two box spars, the top and bottom flanges consisting of two laminations and not a single plank, the spars tapering (in front elevation) towards the tips. Ribs were built of solid webs of plywood with narrow flanges (cap strips) tacked all round both sides of the perimeter thus forming a sandwich with the rib as the "meat": they reduced in depth according to the taper of the spars. The leading-edge was of thin three-ply sheet extending back to the front spar where it was finished with a serrated edge the apex of which was tacked to the spar. Trailing-edge was

Left: *Rudolph Stark, Commander* (Staffel führer) *Jagdstaffel 35 with his O.A.W.* Schneidemühl-*built machine.*

Right: *Lt. Windisch, Commander* Jasta *66 in cockpit of his Fokker D VII emblazoned with leaping deer motif.*
(Photos: Egon Krueger)

in the form of a wire threaded through copper eyelets attached to the ends of the ribs (this imparted the characteristic scalloped profile when dope drew the fabric taut). Between the rear spar and the trailing-edge an additional, square-sectioned wooden stiffener ran through the wings. Between both spars and between trailing-edge the ribs were strengthened with tapes running alternatively under and over the ribs.

The lower wing was of considerably less chord than the upper, to afford improved downward vision, and was unusual in being a "one piece" structure. To accommodate this a "cut out" was arranged in the lower longerons to allow the wing spars to go right through the fuselage. The wing was bolted in place and a tubular frame bolted in to bridge the gap in the "cut out", and the whole covered with a metal panel. Ailerons, with overhung balances, were of steel tube framing. Their seemingly small area was in fact more than adequate and imparted a lively lateral control to the D VII.

Centre-section struts were of streamlined steel tube, the front pylon consisting of three struts: the foremost welded to the engine bearers, the middle and third to the lower and upper longeron respectively. A single strut connected the top rear spar to the lower longeron. Interplane struts were also of the same medium and of "N" format which obviated the need for any incidence bracing cables. A simple "vee" type undercarriage chassis with streamline steel struts was fitted. The upper ends of the struts terminated in balls which fitted into sockets welded to the fuselage members, and were retained by a short bolt. The lower ends were welded to a sheet steel box which was slotted to accommodate the travel of the axle on its coil spring shock absorbers. An alloy box spreader connected the apices of the Vees, forming the main spar of the aerofoil fairing which, it has been estimated, contributed enough lift to compensate for the weight of the undercarriage chassis. Standard 760×100 m. wheels were fitted. A stout ash tailskid was hinged adjacent to the tailpost and sprung with two coil springs connecting its upper end to the top longerons. With the exception of the metal nose panels and the plywood covering of the axle fairing the rest of the airframe was fabric covered.

Hermann Göring in his all-white Fokker D VIIF 5125/18, August 1918.

An unarmed Fokker D VII in post-war service of the Swiss Air Force. (Photo: Egon Krueger)

A mint product of the Ostdeutsche Albatros-Werke (O.A.W.) *at* Schneidemühl. *Fokker D VII (O.A.W.) 6376/18. Note ex-works white fin and rudder.* (Photo: Egon Krueger)

Intriguing chicken motif on a D VII of Jasta 74. *The Very pistol for firing signal cartridges, mounted on the centre-section cut-out is of interest, also the large rear view mirror.* (Photo: Egon Krueger)

(Photo: Egon Krueger)

Fokker D VIIs began to reach the Aircraft Parks (*Armeeflugpark*) during April 1918; initial allocations were to Richthofen's *Jagdgeschwader* No. I and Alloys Heldmann reports that *Jasta* 10 was one of the first of the component *Jastas* to receive the machine and that he himself used his in combat as early as the middle of the month. In accordance with the usual German practice new aircraft were issued to the "star" units first, and when received were allocated to pilots in order of seniority. Gradually the war weary Albatroses and Pfalz machines were replaced by the Fokker D VIIs, but it was a long time before many of the lesser known *Staffeln* were issued with this much wanted equipment. It was not until 24th August 1918 that *Jasta* 35 was informed that six D VIIs were awaiting collection at the Aircraft Park. *Staffel* Commander Rudolph Stark reports:

"Six Fokkers . . . great rejoicing throughout the *Staffel*. An Albatros, two Pfalz and three Rolands are wheeled out for exchange. Now comes the burning question, who is to fly the new machines— I decide the last to join the *Staffel* must be the ones to wait. I report to the Technical Officer who presents the necessary documents to make us the happy owners of six Fokkers which are waiting in the hangar. I climb into the cockpit which wears an unfamiliar aspect; the engine roars; the ground roars away from under me. Swiftly we rise, the machines climb wonderfully and answer to the slightest movement of the controls. We land and put our treasures safely away in the hangars. The painter marks them with the *Staffel* badge, the arrowhead on the wings, then paints the fuselages with the coloured bands that identify the individual pilots. He takes particular care with my machine embellishing my lilac stripe with narrow black edges. Only then do the machines really belong to us."

At one time difficulties with the overheating and pre-explosion of incendiary ammunition in the Fokker D VII gave rise to consternation as machines caught fire in the air and several fatal crashes occurred, including the death of Fritz Friedrichs. It was partly due to this factor that orders were given for supplies of the Pfalz D XII as a safeguard, but in the event the trouble was overcome with extra ventilation and a new type of incendiary bullet, and production continued. Later in the summer the B.M.W. engined D VIIf began to appear; this engine developed some 185 h.p. and was rated to give the power at altitude, where it was most needed, at upwards of 18,000 feet. It was this version of the Fokker that achieved a real superiority over its adversaries and could out-manoeuvre them all in the upper atmosphere.

Black and white striped machine of Jagdstaffel 6. *Note damaged upper wing.* (Photo: Egon Krueger)

An experimental D VII fitted with "rhino horn" type manifold exhausting over the top wing. (Photo: Egon Krueger)

Lt. O. von Beaulieu-Marconnay, Jasta 19, with his D VII which bore "branding iron" insignia related to his former cavalry unit. (Photo: Alex Imrie)

Georg Hantelmann's D VII (Jasta 15). This was the machine in which Wüsthoff was shot down by an S.E.5a on 17th June 1918.

Vzfw. Willi Gabriel, Jasta 11, with his orange and light blue tailed D VII, before painting of the orange stripe was continued along the rear decking. (Photo: Alex Imrie)

Oblt. Rudolph Berthold as Commander of Jagdgeschwader No. II, with his "winged sword" insignia.

THE D VII IN COMBAT

A graphic, and singularly unbiased, description of combat with these machines is given by Lt. John M. Grider of 85 Sqdn. R.A.F. who were flying S.E.5as:

"We got into a dogfight this morning with the new brand of Fokkers and they certainly were good. They had big red stripes on the fuselage diagonally so they must have been von Richthofen's old circus. There were five of us and we ran into five Fokkers at 15,000 feet. We both started climbing of course—and they outclimbed us. We climbed up to 20,500 feet and couldn't get any higher. We were practically stalled and these Fokkers went right over our heads and got between us and the lines. They didn't want to dogfight but tried to pick off our rear men. Inglis and Cal were getting a pretty good thrill when we turned back and caught one Hun napping. He half rolled slowly and we got on his tail. Gosh, its unpleasant fighting at that altitude. The slightest movement exhausts you. (N.B. It must be remembered that no oxygen equipment was carried. P.L.G.). Your engine has no pep and splutters; its hard to keep a decent formation, and you lose 500 feet on a turn. The Huns came in from above and it didn't take us long to fight down to 12,000 feet. We put up the best fight of our lives but these Huns were just too good for us. Cal got a shot in his radiator and went down and Webster had his tail-plane shot to bits and his elevator control shot away. He managed to land with his stabiliser wheel (trim wheel, with which S.E.s were fitted. P.L.G.) but cracked up. I don't know what would have happened if some Dolphins from 84 hadn't come up and the Huns beat it. I think we got one that went

Fokker D VII's of Jasta 11, Gabriel's machine is in the foreground. (Photo: Alex Imrie)

The wooden-fuselage D VII built by Albatros factory at Johannisthal.

down in a spin while Cal was shooting at it but we couldn't see it crash. I got to circling with one Hun, just he and I, and it didn't take me long to find out that I wasn't going to climb above this one. He began to gain on me and then did something I've never heard of before. He'd been circling with me and he'd pull around and point his nose at me and open fire and just hang there on his prop and follow me around with his tracer. All I could do was keep on turning the best I could. If I'd straightened out he'd have had me cold as he already had his sights on me. If I had tried to hang on my prop that way, I'd have gone right into a spin. But this fellow just hung right there and sprayed me with lead like he had a hose. All I could do was to watch his tracer and kick my rudder from one side to the other to throw his aim off. This war isn't what it used to be."

The reader will see from this that Grider himself was a very cool customer!

A list of *Jagdstaffeln* equipped with Fokker D VIIs will be found in the tabulated data, but it is doubtful if they were all completely equipped with the Fokker machine. During the last three months of the war many, if not most, units were operating with a depleted establishment of six or eight aircraft, due to a combined shortage of pilots, aircraft and fuel.

COLOUR SCHEMES

The early Fokker-built D VIIs had the fuselage covered with fabric finished with a streaky camouflage effect, the dark olive green dope seemingly being brushed out in places leaving the paleness of the plain linen fabric showing through. Wings were covered with lozenge fabric, pre-printed in two patterns, one consisting of a five-colour scheme and the other a four-colour scheme. Each pattern was printed in two types: darkish shades for the top and side surfaces and paler shades for the undersurfaces. The top surface shades were, approximately: indigo, blue-grey, deep mauve, sage green and beige. Under surfaces were: pale pink, cream, bright reddish pink, leaf green and pale cerulean blue. The fabric was fastened to the ribs with light blue rib tapes. Albatros and O.A.W. built D VIIs used lozenge fabric all over. Metal nose panelling and all struts were painted dark olive or dark grey-green "ex works": on O.A.W. built aircraft the panels were painted in a simulation of the fabric pattern and shades.

As may be seen from the illustrations, many and varied were the colour schemes applied by the *Jadgstaffeln*, combining both unit and individual identification of aircraft, and could well form a study in themselves. Sometimes markings were meticulously and artistically applied, sometimes they were quite crudely marked, according to the abilities of the unit "artist". In the application of large areas of paint—the blue rear fuselages of the illustrated JG II machines may be instanced—the national insignia crosses were often painted over and could be faintly discerned underneath the colour. Model makers wishing to achieve an authentic simulation could well apply cross transfers (decals) and then paint over them. When machines were transferred from one unit to another as sometimes happened, or from one pilot to another, the former owner's identity could often be noticed beneath the new paint.

It has proved difficult to pin down specific colour schemes as units changed their colour from time to time and no complete record of exactly detailed markings seems to have existed, or if it did, has not

Fokker D VII (O.A.W.) 2052/18 used by Karl Thom, displays pilot's initial, also two-colour (possibly black and white) fuselage band. (Photo: P. M. Grosz)

Fokker D VII built by Allgemeine Ungarische Maschinen Fabrik A.G. *(M.A.G.) of Budapest. It was fitted with 210-h.p. Austro Daimler engine and radiator similar to the type used on Austrian Berg D I fighter.* (Photo: Pavel Vancura)

survived. The only certain method of finding out what colour specific machines were painted has been the patient tracking down of pilots, and other *staffel* personnel, still alive and getting them to interpret the photographs if possible. This has been done by such diligent enthusiasts as Alex Imrie in Germany (who provided much data for the colour plates herein) and Don Hastings in America. Less detailed colour notes, culled from Intelligence Reports, combat reports, etc., may be of interest: *Jasta* 4, red nose, light blue tail (July 1918): *Jasta* 5, green tails outlined red: *Jasta* 7, black aircraft: *Jasta* 9, black fuselage, white radiator, white wings: *Jasta* 10, Yellow nose: *Jasta* 11, red nose, fuselage, various colour tails: *Jasta* 16, black and white stripes aft of cockpit: *Jasta* 27, yellow noses and under sides: *Jasta* 34, silver tail: *Jasta* 36, blue nose: *Jasta* 46, green and yellow striped tail: *Jasta* 71, red nose, white tail: *Jasta* 74, blue nose, white rear fuselage with various chicken motifs: *Jasta* 80, black tails with white stripes. Fritz Rumey of *Jasta* 5 was reported flying an all yellow D VII when shot down on 27th September 1918 by Lt. G. E. B. Lawson of 32 Sqdn. R.A.F. (S.E.5a). Hermann Göring flew a D VII with red nose and yellow rear fuselage when with JG I.

Towards the end of hostilities units were usually only too thankful to lay hands on D VIIs and wasted little, if any, time applying markings.

The black and white striped Fokker D VII used by Josef Mai, Jasta 5.

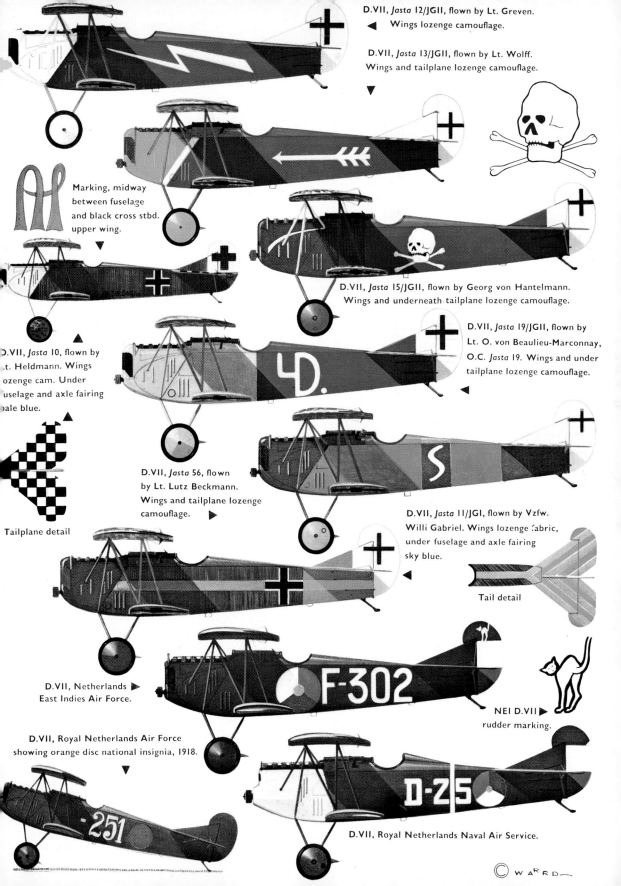

D.VII, *Jasta* 12/JGII, flown by Lt. Greven.
◄ Wings lozenge camouflage.

D.VII, *Jasta* 13/JGII, flown by Lt. Wolff.
Wings and tailplane lozenge camouflage.
▼

Marking, midway
between fuselage
and black cross stbd.
upper wing.
▼

D.VII, *Jasta* 15/JGII, flown by Georg von Hantelmann.
Wings and underneath tailplane lozenge camouflage.

D.VII, *Jasta* 10, flown by
Lt. Heldmann. Wings
lozenge cam. Under
fuselage and axle fairing
pale blue.
▲

D.VII, *Jasta* 19/JGII, flown by
Lt. O. von Beaulieu-Marconnay,
O.C. *Jasta* 19. Wings and under
tailplane lozenge camouflage.
◄

Tailplane detail

D.VII, *Jasta* 56, flown
by Lt. Lutz Beckmann.
Wings and tailplane lozenge
camouflage. ▶

D.VII, *Jasta* 11/JGI, flown by Vzfw.
Willi Gabriel. Wings lozenge fabric,
under fuselage and axle fairing
sky blue.
◄

Tail detail

D.VII, Netherlands ▶
East Indies Air Force.

NEI D.VII▶
rudder marking.

D.VII, Royal Netherlands Air Force
showing orange disc national insignia, 1918.
▼

D.VII, Royal Netherlands Naval Air Service.

© WARD

Ernst Udet with red fuselaged D VII bearing LO! monogram. This was complimentary to his fiancée Lola Zink whom he married after the war. (Photo: Egon Krueger)

Colourful Fokker D VII captured by 84 Sqdn. R.A.F. Unfortunately colour details are not known. (Photo: W. Puglisi)

A D VII of the L.V.A. in the Nederlands. (Photo: Via G. H. Kamphuis)

Captured Albatros-built D VII, No. 6839, of 1918, under test by Lt. Esca Coleman, R.F.C. (Photo: Via M. C. Windrow)

SPECIFICATION

Manufacturers: Fokker Flugzeug-Werke G.m.b.H. Schwerin (Fok.). Albatros-Werke G.m.b.H. Johannisthal (Alb.). Ostdeutsche Albatros-Werke. Schneidemühl (O.A.W.).

Powerplant: 160 h.p. Mercedes D III. 175 h.p. Mercedes D IIIa. 185 h.p. B.M.W. IIIa.

Dimensions: Span 8·9 m. (29 ft. 3½ in.). Length 6·954 m. (22 ft. 11½ in.). Height 2·75 m. (9 ft. 2¼ in.). Wing area 20·5 sq. m. (221·4 sq. ft.).

Weights: Empty 670 kg. (1,474 lb.). Loaded 960 kg. (2,112 lb.). Captured aircraft: Empty 1,622 lb. Loaded 1,936 lb.

Performance: *Mercedes D VIII—Max. speed 189 km. hr. (118·1 m.p.h.). (Captured aircraft—114 m.p.h. at 6,560 ft.). Climb 1,000 m. (3,280 ft.) in 4 min. 15 sec. 2,000 m. (6,560 ft.) in 8 min. 18 sec. 3,000 m. (9,840 ft.) in 13 min. 49 sec. 4,000 m. (13,120 ft.) in 22 min. 48 sec. 5,000 m. (16,400 ft.) in 38 min. 5 sec.

†B.M.W. D VII—Max. speed 200 km. hr. (125 m.p.h.). Climb 1,000 m. in 1·75 min. 2,000 m. in 4 min. 3,000 m. in 7 min. 4,000 m. in 10·25 min. 5,000 m. in 14 min. 6,000 m. in 18·75 min.

‡Udet's B.M.W. D VII—4253/18. Climb 2,000 m. in 6 min. 3,000 m. in 9 min. 4,000 m. in 12 min. 5,000 m. in 16 min. 6,000 m. in 21 min.

N.B. The vastly superior performance of the B.M.W. Fokker may be seen from the above figures. Also of interest is the comparison of factory figures and an actual service aircraft.

Armament: Twin fixed Spandau machine guns firing forward, each with 500 rounds of ammunition.

*In service use; from "Luftnachrichtenblatt" 1926.
†Factory figures; "Flugsport" 1919.
‡"Motor"; May/June 1919.

Staffeln equipped with Fokker D VII:
Geschwader I—Js 4, 6, 10 and 11. Geschwader II—Js 12, 13, 15 and 19. Geschwader III—Js 2, 26, 27 and 36. Jastas—5, 7, 8, 14, 16, 17, 20, 22, 23, 24, 28, 29, 30, 32, 35, 37, 40, 44, 46, 47, 48, 49, 51, 52, 53, 54, 56, 57, 58, 59, 66, 69, 71, 74, 79, 80.

Known Serial Numbers of Fokker D VII and D VIIF machines: D VII 230/18. D VII 208/18 (Jasta 11). D VII 244/18 (Heldmann Jasta 10). D VII 249/18 (Jasta 10). D VII 262/18 (Thuy Jasta 28). D VII 286/18 (Gabriel Jasta 11). D VIIF 294/18 (Göring Jasta 11). D VIIF 309/18 (Friedrichs Jasta 10). D VII 383/18. D VII 406/18 (Alb.) 461/18. D VII 507/18. D VII (Alb.) 527/18. D VII 541/18. D VII (Alb.) 677/18. D VII 773/18 (Buckler Jasta 17). D VII (Alb.) 804/18 (Jasta 17). D VII (Alb.) 805/18 (Jasta 17). D VII 817 (Alb.). D VII 871/18. D VII 1445/18. D VII 1450/18. D VII (OAW) 2009/18. D VII (OAW) 2010/18. D VII 2024/18. D VII 2063/18 (Bender Jasta 4). D VII 2319/18. D VII 2469 (Wüsthoff Jasta 15). D VII (Alb.) 2760/18. D VII (OAW) 4092/18. D VII 4253/18 (Udet Jasta 4). D VIIF 4264/18

(Heldmann Jasta 10). D VII (OAW) 4418/18. D VII (OAW) 4635/18 (Smithsonian Institute). D VII (OAW) 4488/18. D VIIF 5125/18 (Göring, all white). D VII 5202/18 (Jasta 17). D VII 5211/18 (Jasta 17). D VII 5216/18 (Jasta 17). D VII 5273/18. D VII (Alb.) 5327/18. D VII (Alb.) 5334/18. D VII (Alb.) 5341/18. D VII (Alb.) 5354/18. D VII (Alb.) 5356/18. D VII 5438/18 (Jasta 17). D VII 5454/18 (Jasta 17). D VII 5524/18. D VII 6329/18 (Jasta 17). D VII 6357/18. D VII (OAW) 6520/18. D VII 6587/18 (Jasta 17). D VII 6591/18. D VII 6592/18. D VII 6596/18 (Jasta 17). D Vil (Alb.) 6660/18. D VII (Alb.) 6666/18. D VII (Alb.) 6745/18. D VII (Alb.) 6796/18. D VII (Alb.) 6786/18. D VII (Alb.) 6810/18. D VII (Alb.) 6822/18. D VII 7705/18. D VII 7729/18. D VII 7755/18. D VII 7756/18. D VII 7772/18. D VIIF 7773/18. D VII 7774/18. D VII 7776/18. D VIIF 7795/18. D VIIF 7799/18. D VII 7800/18. D VII 8323/18. D VII 8348/18. D VII 8414/18. D VII (OAW) 8482/18. D VII (OAW) 8493/18. D VII (OAW) 8503/18. D VII (OAW) 8507/18. D VII (OAW) 8508/18. D VII (OAW) 8520/18. D VII (OAW) 8539/18. D VII (OAW) 8541/18.

PRINTED IN ENGLAND. © Profile Publications Ltd., P.O. Box 26, Leatherhead, Surrey, England, by George Falkner & Sons Ltd., for McCorquodale City Printing Division, London.

PROFILE
PUBLICATIONS

The
de Havilland
D.H.4

NUMBER 26

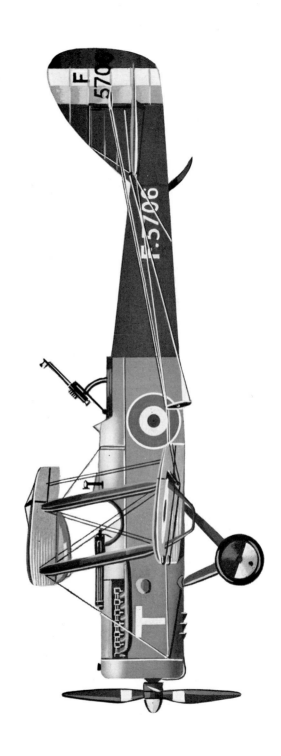

Late production D.H.4 (Rolls Royce
Eagle VIII) of No. 202 Squadron.

JAMES GOULDING ©

The de Havilland D.H.4
by J. M. Bruce

N5972 photographed at Yeovil. It had the twin Vickers guns and raised Scarff ring that characterised D.H.4s of the first Westland batch; no radiator shutters were fitted. A sister aircraft, N5960, was tested at Martlesham; the second Vickers gun reduced the speed at 10,000 ft. to 102 m.p.h.; the climb to that height took 18 mins. 18 secs. (Photo: Harald Penrose, O.B.E., F.R.Ae.S.)

At about the same time as Frank Barnwell was designing the Bristol R.2A as a two-seat reconnaissance aircraft intended to replace the B.E.2c and 2e, Captain (later Sir) Geoffrey de Havilland was working on the design of a generally similar two-seater, to which the Aircraft Manufacturing Co. had allotted the type number D.H.4. The D.H.4 was intended for reconnaissance and bombing duties, and was designed round the 160-h.p. Beardmore engine.

The prototype was nearing completion in the summer of 1916; so too was the first example of a new British aero-engine. This power unit was a water-cooled, six-cylinder in-line engine that had been designed by the young F. B. Halford. He had been greatly impressed by the aluminium monobloc construction of the Hispano-Suiza engine, and in his own first design he employed two aluminium monobloc muffs into each of which three steel liners, threaded over their entire length, were screwed; the cylinder heads were of cast iron, the water jackets of sheet steel.

Halford had first become associated with Sir William Beardmore and T. C. Pullinger, head of Arrol-Johnston Ltd. of Dumfries, when he modified the 120-h.p. Beardmore to give 160-h.p. They backed his new engine, which was made at the Arrol-Johnston works and was named the Beardmore-Halford-Pullinger or B.H.P. The first B.H.P. was running on the bench in June 1916; it delivered something over 200-h.p.

Several published references to the combination of this new engine with the first prototype D.H.4 air-frame imply that Halford wangled the installation, but it is doubtful whether much wangling would in fact be needed. The B.H.P. was of the same basic configuration as the Beardmore for which the D.H.4 was designed but offered at least 25 per cent more power. Clearly it was sensible to modify the aircraft to accommodate a promising and (for mid-1916) powerful engine.

The overall dimensions of the 160-h.p. Beardmore were: length 1,450 mm., width 506 mm., height 810 mm.; its dry weight was 615 lb. Corresponding values for the 200-h.p. B.H.P. were about 1,708 mm., 476 mm., 1,111 mm., and 690 lb. Because the B.H.P. was so much longer and taller than the Beardmore the nose of the first D.H.4 was somewhat longer than had been intended and the top decking immediately behind the engine cowling had to be given a sharp downward slope to the front of the pilot's cockpit. An oval radiator and four-blade airscrew were fitted; an exhaust manifold on the port side terminated in an upright stack that discharged above the upper wing.

The D.H.4 itself was a sturdy and well-proportioned two-bay biplane made of the conventional materials of its time. The fuselage was remarkable for having cross bracing only in the four bays immediately behind the rear cockpit. The entire forward fuselage and the portion under the tailplane were covered with 3 mm. plywood, producing a strong but light box structure that needed no other bracing. The main fuel tanks were installed immediately behind the pilot's seat, consequently the observer's cockpit was several feet farther aft. The pilot sat immediately under the

Left: The first prototype D.H.4, with 200-h.p. B.H.P. engine. The centre-section struts converged upwards in side elevation. (Photo: via K. M. Molson). *Right: The second prototype, with 250-h.p. Rolls-Royce engine.* (Photo: via K. M. Molson)

centre section, which was covered with transparent material to improve his upward view. The main flight surfaces were conventional; the fin and rudder had the characteristic graceful profile that became a distinctive feature of so many de Havilland designs.

Piloted by its designer, the D.H.4 made its first flight in mid-August 1916. Frank Halford was ill with influenza and was unable to be present, consequently the observer's cockpit was occupied by Major G. P. Bulman. Performance was excellent and the aircraft's handling qualities left nothing to be desired.

This was confirmed by the Testing Flight of the Central Flying School, where the D.H.4 prototype underwent official trials between 21st September and 12th October 1916. Its speed at 10,000 ft. was 113 m.p.h. at 2,946 lb. (without bomb load) and about 108 m.p.h. at 3,148 lb. (with one 262-lb. bomb and fuel for 7·3 hours); that altitude was reached in 16 mins. 20 secs. and 19 mins. respectively, these being the best of several recorded times in the series of tests. The C.F.S. report on the aircraft was enthusiastic:

"Stability: lateral very good; longitudinal very good; directional very good. Length of run to unstick 150 yds.; to pull up (engine stopped) 120 yds. Control: stick; dual for elevator and rudder. Machine is exceptionally comfortable to fly and very easy to land. Exceptionally light on controls. Tail adjusting gear enables pilot to fly or glide at any desired speed without effort. Length of time to prepare engine for starting, 2 mins. approx."

There was no provision at that time for large-scale production of the B.H.P. engine. It seems that further examples were made after its success in the D.H.4, but quantity production was not initiated. The D.H.4 was wanted, however: the first War Office contract, No. 87/A/496, dated 11th July 1916, was initially for fifty aircraft numbered *A2125–A2174*, to be built by the Aircraft Manufacturing Co., Ltd. The date suggests that the D.H.4 was ordered before the B.H.P.-powered prototype flew.

Most of the aircraft of the first Airco production batch were powered by the 250-h.p. Rolls-Royce engine; it is known that *A2129* had the 250-h.p. Rolls-Royce Mk III (later known as the Eagle III) and that the 250-h.p. Rolls-Royce Mk IV (Eagle IV) was installed in *A2166* (engine no. 4/250/138, W.D. 12152), *A2169* (No. 4/250/78, W.D.12160) and *A2170* (No. 4/250/130, W.D.12151). A second prototype

The second prototype at Orfordness with modified rear cockpit and Lewis gun on pillar mounting. The markings in the white stripe on the rudder are G X 04; this may not be the full inscription.

Also photographed at Orfordness, A2129 was the subject of the Martlesham trial report No. M.83. Its engine was a 250-h.p. Rolls-Royce Mk III (284-h.p. Eagle III), W.D.10071.

Westland-built D.H.4 with radiator shutters and taller under-carriage, of No. 5 Naval Squadron, Dunkerque.

D.H.4, fitted with a 250-h.p. Rolls-Royce engine, had been completed later in the summer of 1916. Apart from the inevitable differences in the engine and cowling, the second aircraft had a revised undercarriage with larger wheels, mounted farther forward than that of the first prototype; its centre-section struts were parallel in side elevation; the pilot's cockpit was farther aft; the shape of the observer's cockpit was altered to accommodate a ring mounting for a Lewis gun.

The D.H.4 Puma installation is here exemplified in D1773, which also has the two wind-driven fuel pumps that replaced the pressure-feed system of earlier D.H.4s. The taller undercarriage was fitted to all aircraft from D1769 onwards in this batch.
(Photo: Harald Penrose, O.B.E., F.R.Ae.S.)

Left: *Westland-built D.H.4 with square-section rear top decking, No. 5 Naval Squadron, Dunkerque.* Right: *The Galloway Adriatic installation did not differ significantly from that of the Puma. The form of the exhaust manifold was not an infallible means of distinguishing one engine from the other.* (Photo: Imp. War Mus.)

Left: B3957 *was one of the N-series Westland-built D.H.4s that were transferred to the R.F.C. It retained the two Vickers guns; in this photograph it is seen with twin Lewis guns on the Scarff mounting and two T.W.R. parachute flares on the under-wing bomb ribs.* Right: *Subject of Martlesham report M.92, A2168 had the R.A.F.3a engine. Its Scarff ring had been raised several inches above the upper longerons. This photograph was made at Martlesham Heath in April 1917.* (Photo: via E. F. Cheesman)

Left: *D.H.4 with Fiat A-12 engine, photographed at Wyton.* (Photo: D. S. Glover). Right: A2148 *with 300-h.p. Renault 12Fe engine.* (Photo: Musée de l'Air)

When it first appeared the prototype Rolls-Royce D.H.4 had no armament. It went to the experimental armament station at Orfordness, where it was flown with a Lewis gun on an experimental pillar-type mounting. At this time a coaming was added to the front of the observer's cockpit and the exhaust pipes had been extended by the addition of twin upright stacks.

The production D.H.4s began to appear early in 1917. They were substantially similar to the second prototype, but wing-tip skids were added under the lower wings and armament was fitted. A Scarff No. 2 ring mounting for the observer's Lewis gun was mounted directly on the upper longerons; the pilot had a fixed Vickers gun mounted externally on the top decking in front of his cockpit and offset to port. The Vickers gun was synchronised by the new Constantinesco hydraulic mechanism.

Many of the early D.H.4s were delivered to No. 55 Squadron, which was the first R.F.C. unit to be equipped with the type. The squadron flew to France on 6th March 1917, thus earning the minor distinction of being the first operational unit to go there with aircraft fitted with the Constantinesco gear as standard equipment.

The Admiralty also ordered the D.H.4 for the R.N.A.S. Serial numbers (3696–3697) were allotted for two Admiralty prototypes but it is doubtful whether the second was built. No. 3696 was still in service early in 1918: it was recorded as being "at Depot" at the R.N.A.S. station, Dunkerque, on 7th February. The first Admiralty production contract, C.P.100786 for fifty aircraft, N5960–N6009, was given to the Westland Aircraft Works of Yeovil; the Rolls-Royce engine was specified. Westland-built D.H.4s of this batch had twin Vickers guns for the pilot and, while retaining the rounded after top-decking, had their Scarff ring mountings raised to the level of the top of the fuselage. This improved the observer's handling of his Lewis gun. The first Westland-built D.H.4 was delivered on 29th March 1917.

Unfortunately for the D.H.4, production of its admirable Rolls-Royce engine had run into difficulties. The official history records the unhappy fact that "Of forty-two 250-h.p. Rolls-Royce engines promised for January 1917, only sixteen had been delivered". The activities of the Rolls-Royce company were seriously handicapped by the inability or unwillingness of the Air Board to take decisions relating to the firm's production facilities. Alternative engines had to be found for the D.H.4, for the War Office wanted to equip more squadrons with the type and the original Airco contract had been enlarged by a further 690 aircraft numbered A7401–A8089 and B1482.

In No. 202 Squadron, 'A' Flight was known as the Photographic Flight, 'B' Flight as the W/T Flight, 'C' Flight as the Escort Flight. This Eagle VIII D.H.4 of 'A' Flight had a fairing under the fuselage housing a large camera; several other D.H.4s of this unit had similar fairings. This D.H.4 was the aircraft usually flown by Captain Warne-Brown, D.S.C., and is here seen at Bergues.

Cockpits of an Eagle VIII D.H.4, at Martlesham Heath.
(Photo: via E. F. Cheesman)

The 200-h.p. B.H.P. engine that had powered the first prototype had, at the request of the Air Board, been studied by the internal combustion engine sub-committee of the Advisory Committee for Aeronautics in January 1917. The sub-committee considered the merits of the B.H.P., the Sunbeam Saracen and Arab, and the Hispano-Suiza with a view to deciding which of the four was most suitable for mass production. The choice fell, unhappily, on the Sunbeam Arab, and the sub-committee also recommended the B.H.P. as superior to the Saracen.

On the strength of this recommendation 2,000 B.H.P. engines were ordered from the Siddeley-Deasy Motor Car Co., Ltd. of Coventry. The Siddeley-Deasy company modified the engine extensively for mass production: J. D. Siddeley was personally responsible for replacing the B.H.P.'s cast-iron cylinder heads by aluminium heads into which open liners were screwed on short threads instead of being threaded over their full length and screwed into an aluminium muff. Aluminium water jackets were introduced in place of the original sheet-steel jackets. The re-designed engine was named the Siddeley Puma; unfortunately, several official documents do not distinguish it clearly from the B.H.P. and it is now virtually impossible to determine which engine was fitted to individual aircraft. It is safe to assume that references to a "200-h.p. B.H.P. Siddeley" engine indicated that a Puma was in fact installed.

Serious production difficulties beset the Puma and by the time it was in full production, in the spring of 1918, it was obsolete; in service it was not conspicuously reliable. Deliveries of Pumas had begun at the end of June 1917. A batch of the engines were delivered to the Aircraft Manufacturing Co. in July 1917 for installation in D.H.4s, but it was found that the Siddeley modifications has so altered the dimensions of the engine (1,775 mm. × 612 mm. × 1,108 mm.) that it would not fit the airframe. The

D.H.4s had to be modified to take the Pumas and their delivery was inevitably delayed.

The basic design of the B.H.P. engine was also put into production at the Dumfries works of the Galloway Engineering Co. later in 1917, presumably as a kind of insurance against total failure of the Puma. This version of the engine was named Galloway Adriatic; one was tested at Martlesham in the D.H.4 A7671 in November 1917. It seems that it was produced in comparatively small numbers only, for on 31st October 1918 the R.A.F. had no more than 89

Above, Right:
A7459, one of the two long-range D.H.4s (R.A.F. 3a engine) specially modified for the proposed reconnaissance of the Kiel area. After the abandonment of this project the aircraft was intended to be used in the anti-airship rôle, hence the two Lewis guns above the centre section.

Right:
The other long-range D.H.4, A7457, still with its fawn and blue camouflage, fitted with hydrovane, flotation gear and wing-tip floats, at the Isle of Grain, 28th January 1918.

A7457 *shortly after ditching, 29th March 1918.*

The single-surface hydrovane later fitted to the D1769. Photograph dated 16th August 1918.

The Puma D.H.4 D1769 with biplane hydrovane. (Below).

Adriatics on charge, all at home stations, whereas 3,255 Pumas were on charge on that date, 546 of them with the Expeditionary Forces and 287 at eastern stations.

In point of time, the first alternative engine to be tried in a D.H.4 was the 200-h.p. R.A.F.3a. This was a water-cooled V-12 that had been designed at the Royal Aircraft Factory in September 1914 as the R.A.F.3 with a bore of 4·3 inches. With a revised lubrication system and bore increased to 4·5 inches it was placed in production at the Acton works of D. Napier & Son. The first tests of the R.A.F.3a in a D.H.4, *A2168*, were made in March 1917. A frontal radiator was fitted and the installation could be distinguished by its single central exhaust stack.

Enough Rolls-Royce engines had been obtained to allow No. 57 Squadron, R.F.C., to be re-equipped with D.H.4s in May 1917; and No. 25 Squadron exchanged its F.E.2ds for the new type, also with Rolls-Royce engines, in the following July. On 26th June 1917 No. 18 Squadron had received the first of the D.H.4s that were to replace its gallant old F.E.2bs, but the D.H.4s that equipped this unit had the 200-h.p. R.A.F.3a engine.

Early operational experience with the R.A.F.3a was not happy. Writing in 1955,* Air Vice Marshal Sir Ranald Reid recorded this of No. 18 Squadron's D.H.4s:

"At last a replacement type of aircraft arrived. Everyone had been indulging in the new vogue of spinning F.Es for fun (quite a difficult feat), but this did not pay on the new D.H.4s, the first of which promptly lost its tail in the air after a spin; and the R.A.F. IIIA (*sic*) engine was appalling. In the hurry to get this replacement overseas some 57 modifications had not been incorporated and all these bugs came out in service. Poor Brooke-Popham, from R.F.C. H.Q., was often with us trying to help out. He was always met with some new engine horror—valves pounded into balls in the cylinders and shot out of some part of the brute's anatomy. It was a good aircraf otherwise, and later it did great work."

At a surprisingly early stage it was agreed to supply fifty D.H.4s to the Russian Government; it seems possible that the shortage of suitable aero-engines may have had something to do with Britain's willingness to part with the aircraft in September 1917. The Russian D.H.4s were to be powered by the 260-h.p. Fiat A-12, the engines to be provided by the Russian Government. But a British bombing offensive against Germany was hurriedly planned that September in retaliation for German bombing attacks on England, and the D.H.4s would make a useful addition to the British bomber force. Russia was asked to allow these D.H.4s to be diverted to R.F.C. squadrons on the understanding that they would be replaced by seventy-five aircraft in the spring of 1918. With winter close at hand, the Russian Government agreed readily.

*See Flight, 27th January 1956, p. 110.

A2168 *with 1½-pounder C.O.W. gun firing upwards through the centre section for anti-airship duties.*

A number of these Fiat-powered D.H.4s were used in France, a few of them by No. 49 Squadron. This unit arrived in France on 12th November 1917 equipped with R.A.F.3a D.H.4s, which version remained its standard equipment. Other Fiat-powered D.H.4s saw service in northern Russia in 1918, and some were used at training aerodromes in the United Kingdom. The Fiat installation was generally similar to that of the Puma in the D.H.9, having an underslung radiator. Official tests of a Fiat-powered D.H.4 had been conducted as early as July 1917; the subject aircraft was *A7532*.

During that summer an experimental installation of the 300-h.p. Renault 12Fe was made, in France, in the D.H.4 *A2148*. With this powerful engine performance was good, but no development ensued.

Several other experimental engine installations were made in D.H.4s. A 200-h.p. R.A.F.4d was fitted to *A7864*, which had originally had a 200-h.p. R.A.F.3a; and a 400-h.p. Sunbeam Matabele was installed in *A8083* in 1918. This D.H.4 was one of several that were transferred, engineless, to the R.N.A.S., and that service was responsible for fitting the Matabele.

Some doubt attaches to the connection between the D.H.4 and the 260-h.p. Ricardo-Halford Inverted Supercharger engine. The original B.H.P. Supercharger was running as early as July 1917. It was not supercharged by any form of blower, employing instead a system that introduced a stratum of inert exhaust gas and clean air to the crowns of the working pistons. This weakened the mixture strength at low altitudes, and it was only at heights between 10,000 ft. and 20,000 ft. that a fully effective mixture entered the cylinders.

The engine was unusually tall and threatened seriously to obstruct the pilot's forward view on any tractor aeroplane in which it might be installed. A solution was found by inverting the engine, but it was thought that it would be difficult to win acceptance for such a radical design. The artist F. Gordon Crosby was therefore commissioned to produce a painting of a D.H.4 fitted with the inverted engine. Speaking in 1959, the late J. L. P. Brodie said:

"The painting sold the design. Three of this engine and three of a 12-cylinder type R.H.A. (Ricardo-Halford-Armstrong) were made, but the end of the war brought about a cessation of their development."*

According to another source, however, an installation of a Ricardo-Halford Supercharger engine was made in a D.H.4. This may be a confusion with the Gordon-Crosby painting, or possibly even with the flight trials of the later R.H.A. engine which (contrary to Mr. Brodie's statement) had been installed in the D.H.9 *E630* by 9th January 1919 and was tested at the R.A.E. in the spring and summer of that year.

In July 1919 Martlesham tested a D.H.4 powered by an engine described as the Rolls-Royce Experimental 'G'. This power unit delivered 353-h.p. at 1,800 r.p.m. at sea level, but its precise nature has not yet been discovered.

In August 1917 an early specimen of the superb Rolls-Royce Eagle VIII engine was tested in the D.H.4 *A7446*. This was the finest combination of engine and airframe: without bombs the maximum speed was no less than 133·5 m.p.h. at 10,000 ft., which altitude was reached in nine minutes. The D.H.4 retained its manœuvrability, but the official report notes that it was "tail heavy at full speed and nose heavy with engine off except at extreme tail-plane adjustments". The test subject, *A7446*, was later used by No. 2 Squadron, R.N.A.S., at Bergues; in February 1918 it was on the strength of 'B' Flight of that unit.

The diameter of the airscrew fitted to the Eagle III of *A2129* was 8 ft. 9 in.; that of the double Integral airscrew of *A7446* was 10 ft. 2 in. Ground clearance

D1769 *with dummy load attached to stowed Guardian Angel parachute.*

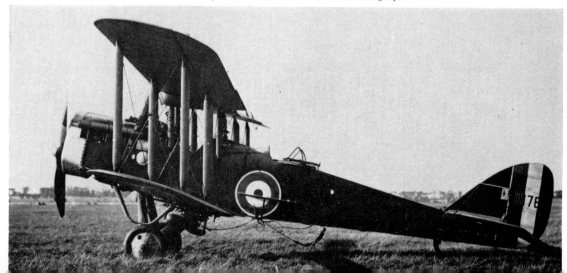

D.H.4 floatplane at Felixstowe. (Photo: Imp. War Mus.)

had been little enough with the smaller airscrew, consequently a taller undercarriage was designed and was fitted to all the later D.H.4s, regardless of the type of engine fitted. The appearance of the rear fuselage was altered by raising the observer's gun ring, much as on the Westland-built aircraft, and fitting a rectangular rear top-decking.

With the different marks of Rolls-Royce engine the radiators and engine cowling underwent detail changes. No shutters were fitted, originally at least, to the radiators of the 250-h.p. Mk III (Eagle III) engines; the early Westland-built D.H.4s likewise had no shutters. Later, certainly on the Eagles VI, VII and VIII, vertical shutters were fitted.

It was as a bomber that the D.H.4 began its operational career, and it is best remembered as the first successful high-performance day bomber. The D.H.4s of No. 55 Squadron were, like No. 48's Bristol F.2As, kept in reserve before the Battle of Arras in order to achieve the maximum surprise. Six D.H.4s of No. 55 Squadron bombed railway sidings at Valenciennes on 6th April 1917 and, says the official history, "a feature of their attack was the ease with which the de Havillands out-manœuvred and out-distanced enemy fighters which endeavoured to intercept them." The D.H.4s' high ceiling enabled them to operate without fighter escort at that time; nevertheless, in the intensive operations connected with Arras No. 55 suffered some losses. In October 1917 this squadron became the first day-bomber unit of the 41st Wing, R.F.C., the precursor of the Independent Force, R.A.F.

The first D.H.4s delivered to the R.N.A.S. went to No. 2 Naval Squadron at St. Pol in the spring of 1917; in July No. 5 Naval Squadron began to replace its Sopwith 1½-Strutters with the D.H.4. At various times aircraft ordered for the R.N.A.S. were transferred to the R.F.C. and vice versa. Seventeen of the first Westland-built R.N.A.S. batch went to the R.F.C. and were apparently renumbered B3954–B3970. It seems likely that well over 80 of the air-

craft ordered for the R.F.C. were either transferred to the R.N.A.S. or found their way to Naval squadrons.

The R.N.A.S. used its D.H.4s as general-purpose aircraft and they did much valuable photography, reconnaissance and gunnery spotting along the Belgian coast in addition to bombing. On 13th January 1918, No. 17 Naval Squadron was formed at Bergues for anti-submarine patrols; four of its D.H.4s sank the submarine U.B.12 on 12th August 1918. At about that time No. 217 Squadron (as No. 17 Naval had become on 1st April 1918) believed itself to be the only squadron to be entirely equipped with Eagle VIII D.H.4s. Doubtless this was because its work entailed long oversea flights.

An earlier project that would have demanded a long-distance flight over water was an Admiralty requirement for aerial photographs of German naval bases west of the Kiel Canal. Two D.H.4s, *A7457* and *A7459*, were fitted with additional tankage to increase their endurance to 14 hours and special cameras were installed. The crews (originally Sqn. Cdr. the Master of Sempill, Flt. Lt. F. S. Cotton, Lts. G. S. Trewin, D.S.C., and E. B. C. Betts) went to Hendon in June 1917 to train on their aircraft, which were given a special camouflage of matt fawn and sky blue. On 9th August the D.H.4s were flown to Bacton, whence they were to fly across the North Sea, photograph their objectives, and land at Dunkerque.

About mid-August the Admiralty apparently abandoned the Kiel project and decided that the D.H.4s should remain at Great Yarmouth for anti-airship operations in collaboration with flying boats. This decision may have been coloured by the unrelia-

Eagle D.H.4 with experimental camouflage, Isle of Grain, 1918.

Page 8: Journal of the Royal Aeronautical Society, April 1959, pp. 195–196: First Halford Memorial Lecture, 5th February 1959.

bility of the R.A.F.3a engines installed in the two D.H.4s. For its new duties *A7459* was given two fixed Lewis guns above the centre section. It may have been the Yarmouth D.H.4 flown by Flt. Lt. A. H. H. Gilligan and Trewin that, after attacking the Zeppelin L.44 on 5th September 1917, was forced down on the sea by engine failure. Its crew were picked up by the accompanying Curtiss H-12, No. *8666*, which was then unable to take off and drifted for three days.

Greater success attended the Yarmouth D.H.4 *A8032* which, flown by Major E. Cadbury, D.S.C., D.F.C., with Captain R. Leckie, D.S.O., D.S.C., D.F.C., as gunner, shot down the Zeppelin L.70 on 5th August 1918. This was the occasion of the last Zeppelin raid on the United Kingdom, but the evolution of anti-airship weapons went on. Two D.H.4s were experimentally armed with a Coventry Ordnance Works 1½-pounder gun mounted nearly upright between the cockpits, but the Armistice was signed before firing tests could be made. One of the aircraft was *A2168*, earlier the R.A.F.3a engine test subject.

Perhaps the most remarkable wartime development of the D.H.4 was the seaplane version that was tested at Felixstowe. The long floats were built in the experimental shed at Felixstowe and were based on the design of the floats of the German Brandenburg seaplanes. It was apparently hoped that the D.H.4 seaplane would prove to be an effective answer to the Brandenburgs, which were such a thorn in the side of the Felixstowe flying-boat crews. The D.H.4 floatplane was flown successfully but no development was undertaken because the Fairey IIIC was expected to meet operational requirements.

In November 1918 the Puma-powered D.H.4 *D1769*, which had earlier been a test vehicle for the Grain flotation gear, was used in experiments with Guardian Angel parachutes. Two were stowed in containers let into the underside of the fuselage. Preliminary trials with a bomb casing as a dummy load were followed by live drops made by Major Ordlees.

In France, Italy, Russia and in the Aegean the D.H.4 was flown until the end of the war; a few were used in Mesopotamia in 1918. Production had reached its peak early in 1918 but was revived again later that year, doubtless in consequence of the disappointing operational showing of the D.H.9. Late contracts were given to the Glendower Aircraft Co., Ltd., Palladium Autocars, Ltd., and Waring & Gillow, Ltd.

The D.H.4 was built in large numbers in the U.S.A. and was the only American-built British aircraft to see operational use. The American history of the D.H.4 will form the subject of a separate Profile.

After the Armistice the D.H.4 did not survive for long in the R.A.F. A few served with the Communication Wing during the 1919 peace conference; some of these were modified to have a two-seat passenger cabin and were redesignated D.H.4A. One of these, *F2664*, was regarded as General Seely's personal aircraft and was fitted with Conner silencers.

Some D.H.4s were sent to Commonwealth countries under the Imperial Gift Scheme. Twelve of the Glendower batch, *F2672*, *F2673* and *F2705–F2714*, went to Canada, where they entered service with the Canadian Air Force from October 1920 onwards. They were used for forest-fire patrol, photographic survey and mail-carrying duties; the eight survivors were finally written off in November 1928. During their service several had the positions of the pilot's cockpit and the fuel tanks reversed. In Canada the modified aircraft were sometimes called D.H.4B by

One of the so-called Canadian D.H.4Bs with the pilot's cockpit behind the wings, G-CYDM was used for photographic-survey work and is seen here with a camera port in the fuselage side. Originally F2706, this D.H.4 was taken on C.A.F. strength on 19th April 1921 and was not struck off until 30th November 1923. (Photo: via K. M. Molson)

analogy with the similarly modified American D.H.4B. One of the Canadian D.H.4s, *G-CYCW* (ex-*F2713*) was converted into a single-seater.

Two D.H.4s, *A7929* and *A7993*, went to New Zealand. Both had Eagle VIII engines and both were still in service in March 1927. South Africa also received a few, including *B7991*, in 1921.

Other countries using the D.H.4 included Belgium, Chile, Greece, Iran and Spain. Belgium bought a number of war-surplus aircraft in 1919–20 and fifteen were built by the SABCA in 1926; D.H.4s were used by six units of l'Aeronautique Militaire Belge and remained in service until 1932 Spain operated three squadrons of D.H.4s against the Riffs in Morocco from 1922 onwards.

In the field of post-war commercial aviation the D.H.4 did valuable work, mostly in its D.H.4A form. The year 1919 saw the D.H.4R, a racing single-seat conversion with clipped lower wings, powered by a 450-h.p. Napier Lion and capable of 150 m.p.h.

© *J. M. Bruce 1965.*

SPECIFICATION

Armament: One fixed 0·303 in. Vickers machine gun with Constantinesco C.C. synchronising gear, Aldis and ring-and-bead sights, Cox's 'D'-Type loading handle. One 0·303 in. Lewis machine gun on Scarff No. 2 ring mounting with Norman 100 m.p.h. sight. On *N5960–N6009* twin Vickers guns were fitted. Some R.N.A.S. D.H.4s had pillar mountings for two individual Lewis guns in the rear cockpit instead of the Scarff ring. The bomb load was two 230 lb. or 112 lb. bombs, or an equivalent weight of smaller bombs, carried in racks under the lower wings and fuselage; depth charges could be carried for anti-submarine work. Negative Lens bomb sight.

Service use—France: R.F.C./R.A.F. Sqns. Nos. 18, 25, 27, 49, 55 and 57; R.N.A.S. Sqns. Nos. 5, 6 and 11 (later Nos. 205, 206 and 211, R.A.F.).

Coastal patrol (based in France): R.N.A.S. Sqns. Nos. 2, 5 and 17 (later Nos. 202, 205 and 217, R.A.F.).

Coastal patrol (U.K.): R.N.A.S. stations Port Victoria and Redcar; R.A.F. Sqns. Nos. 212 (part) and 273 (part).

Home Defence: A few D.H.4s used *ad hoc* from various stations, e.g., Great Yarmouth, Martlesham Heath.

Mesopotamia: Two D.H.4s with No. 30 Sqn., R.F.C., January 1918; 'A' Flight of No. 72 Sqn.

Macedonia: One D.H.4 (from Mudros) attached to No. 17 Sqn., September 1918.

Aegean: 'C' Sqn., Imbros; 'D' Sqn., Stavros; R.N.A.S. Mudros; R.A.F. Sqns. Nos. 220, 221, 222 and 223.

Adriatic: Sqns. Nos. 224, 225, 226 and 227.

Russia: Eight D.H.4s (R.A.F.3a) with R.A.F. Contingent Archangel, May 1918; some Fiat-powered D.H.4s later used in northern Russia.

Belgian use: Six escadrilles (Nos. 7/III, 8/III, 9/III, 10/V, 11/V and 12/V).

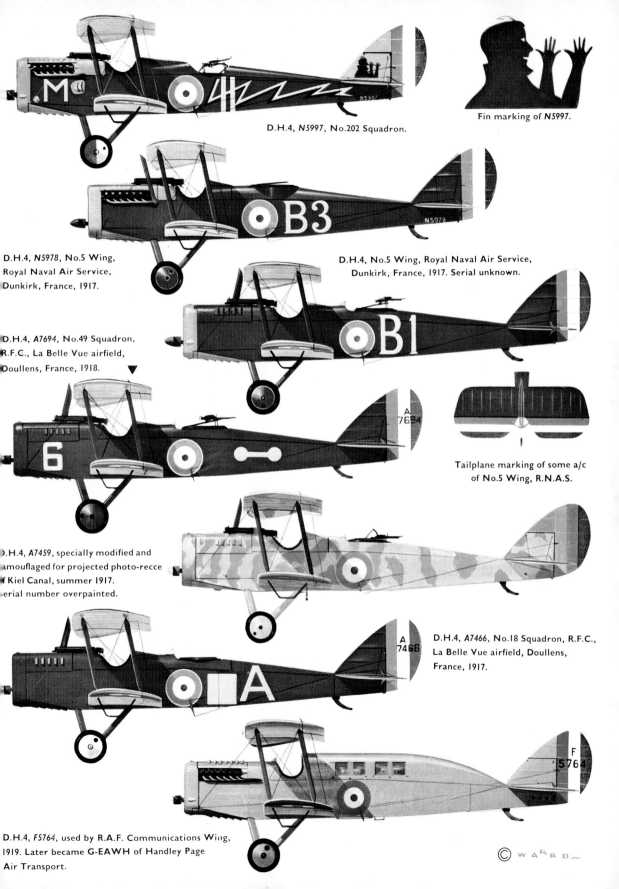

D.H.4, N5997, No.202 Squadron.

Fin marking of *N5997*.

D.H.4, *N5978*, No.5 Wing,
Royal Naval Air Service,
Dunkirk, France, 1917.

D.H.4, No.5 Wing, Royal Naval Air Service,
Dunkirk, France, 1917. Serial unknown.

D.H.4, *A7694*, No.49 Squadron,
R.F.C., La Belle Vue airfield,
Doullens, France, 1918.

Tailplane marking of some a/c
of No.5 Wing, R.N.A.S.

D.H.4, *A7459*, specially modified and
camouflaged for projected photo-recce
of Kiel Canal, summer 1917.
Serial number overpainted.

D.H.4, *A7466*, No.18 Squadron, R.F.C.,
La Belle Vue airfield, Doullens,
France, 1917.

D.H.4, *F5764*, used by R.A.F. Communications Wing,
1919. Later became **G-EAWH** of Handley Page
Air Transport.

© WARD

G-CYDK was originally F2711, one of the twelve D.H.4s presented to Canada. It was taken on strength by the Canadian Air Force on 19th April 1921 and was written off after a crash at Waldemar on 23rd April 1922. (Photo: via K. M. Molson)

Power: 200-h.p. B.H.P.; 230-h.p. Siddeley Puma; 230-h.p. Galloway Adriatic; 250-h.p. Rolls-Royce Mks III and IV (284-h.p. Eagles III and IV); 275-h.p. Rolls-Royce Mks II and III (322-h.p. Eagle VI and 325-h.p. Eagle VII); 375-h.p. Rolls-Royce Eagle VIII; 353-h.p. Rolls-Royce Experimental 'G'; 200-h.p. R.A.F.3a; 200-h.p. R.A.F.4d; 260-h.p. Fiat A-12; 300-h.p. Renault 12Fe; 400-h.p. Sunbeam Matabele.
Dimensions: Span 42 ft. 4⅝ in.; length (B.H.P. prototype) 31 ft. 1 in., (Puma and Adriatic) 30 ft. 8 in., (Eagle VI and VII) 30 ft. 2 3/16 in.; height (B.H.P. prototype and Eagle III) 10 ft., (Eagle VI and VII) 10 ft. 1¾ in., (Eagle VIII) 11 ft.; chord 5 ft. 6 in.; gap 6 ft.; stagger 12 in. Dihedral 3 deg.; incidence 3 deg. Span of tail 14 ft. Wheel track 6 ft.; tyres 750×125 mm. Airscrew diameter (B.H.P. prototype) 8 ft. 1 in., (Puma and Eagle III) 8 ft. 9 in., (R.A.F.3a) 10 ft., (Fiat) 8 ft. 11 in., (Eagle VIII) 10 ft. 2 in.
Areas: Wings 434 sq. ft.; ailerons each 20·5 sq. ft., total 82 sq. ft.; tailplane 38 sq. ft.; elevators 24 sq. ft.; fin 5·4 sq. ft.; rudder 13·7 sq. ft.
Production: According to official statistics, 1,449 British-built D.H.4s were produced, 848 in 1917, 601 in 1918; these totals apparently excluded prototypes. Serial numbers were allocated as follows:
Aircraft Manufacturing Co. Ltd., Hendon, London N.W.: 3696–

3697; A2125–A2174; A7401–A8089 and B1482; C4501–C4540; D8351–D8430; D9231–D9280.
F. W. Berwick & Co. Ltd., Park Royal, London N.W.10: B2051–B2150.
Glendower Aircraft Co. Ltd., Sussex Place, South Kensington, London S.W.3: F2633–F2732; H5290.
Palladium Autocars Ltd., Felsham Road, Putney, London S.W.15: F5699–F5798.
Vulcan Motor & Engineering Co. (1906) Ltd., Crossens, Southport: B5451–B5550.
Waring & Gillow Ltd., Cambridge Road, Hammersmith, London: H5894–H5943.
Westland Aircraft Works, Yeovil, Somerset: B3954–B3970 (probably renumbered from N-series D.H.4s transferred to R.F.C.); B9476–B9500; D1751–D1775; N5960–N6009; N6380–N6429.
Known A.R.D. rebuilds: B774, B7747, B7812, B7910, B7933, B7941, B7950, B7969, B7987, B7991, B9458, F5828, F5833, F5837, F6001, F6114, F6222, H7118, H7123, H7147.
It is also known that E4626, F1551 and F1552 were D.H.4s.
Production in Belgium: Société Anonyme Belge de Constructions Aeronautiques, 13 rue de Bréderode, Brussels: Fifteen D.H.4s for l'Aeronautique Militaire Belge.

WEIGHTS AND PERFORMANCE

Aircraft	Prototype		B9458	D1769 with flotation gear & hydrovane	D1769 with 2 Guardian Angel parachutes	A7671		A2129	A7446	A2168	A2148	A7532		A8083
Engine	B.H.P.		Siddeley Puma			Galloway Adriatic		Eagle III	Eagle VIII	R.A.F. 3a	Renault 12Fe	Fiat	R-R Exp'tal G	Matabele
Bomb load	Nil	One 262 lb.	Nil	Four 112 lb.	Nil	Nil	Nil	Four 112 lb.	Nil	Nil	Nil	Nil	Two 230 lb.	Nil	Nil
Weights (lb.)															
Empty	2,010	2,010	2,197	2,197	—	—	2,209	2,209	2,303	2,387	2,304	—	2,306	2,468	—
Military load	185	436	185	559	—	—	185	559	185	185	166	185	655	185	—
Crew	360	360	360	360	—	—	360	360	360	360	360	360	360	360	—
Fuel & oil	390	340	492	494	—	—	513	513	465	540	510	623	501	513	—
Loaded	2,945	3,146	3,234	3,610	3,495	3,430	3,267	3,641	3,313	3,472	3,340	—	3,822	3,526	—
Max. speed (m.p.h.)															
At 6,500 ft.	117	112	—	—	96	—	—	—	117	136·5	120	120·5	110	—	—
At 10,000 ft.	113	109	114	106	88	101·5	110	104·5	113	133·5	117·5	116	106·5	118	122
At 15,000 ft.	105	103	106·5	—	—	94	100·5	—	102·5	126	110·5	103	—	110	110·5
Climb to:	m. s.	m. s.	m. s.	m. s.	m. s.	m. s.	m. s.	m. s.	m. s.	m. s.	m. s.	m. s.	m. s.	m. s.	m. s.
6,500 ft.	9 30	11 00	11 00	15 30	10 30	6 00	9 30	13 10	8 55	5 9	8 00	7 40	14 00	7 30	—
10,000 ft.	16 20	19 00	18 55	24 36	19 10	21 40	16 55	24 55	16 25	9 00	14 15	13 5	26 40	12 55	8 35
15,000 ft.	29 00	—	37 55	—	44 20	48 50	34 55	—	36 40	16 30	29 20	25 45	—	23 35	16 00
Service ceiling (ft.)	—	—	17,500	13,500	15,000	15,000	17,000	13,500	16,000	22,000	17,500	—	14,000	18,000	21,000
Endurance (hours)	4½	4½	4½	—	—	—	—	3½	3¾	4	—	4½	—	—	—

PRINTED IN ENGLAND. © Profile Publications Ltd., P.O. Box 26, Leatherhead, Surrey, England, by George Falkner & Sons Ltd., for McCorquodale City Printing Division, London.

PROFILE
PUBLICATIONS

The
Boeing
F4B-4

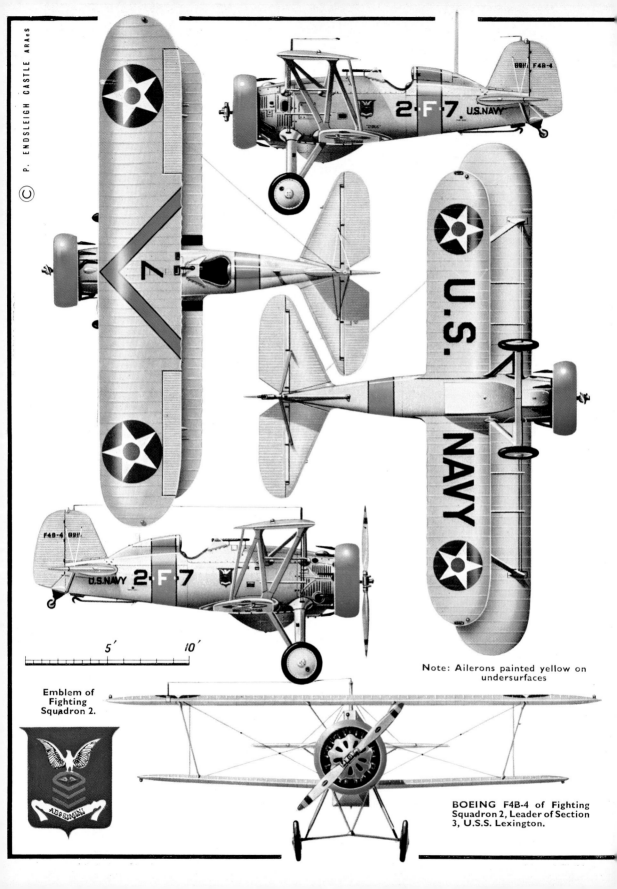

P. ENDSLEIGH CASTLE ARAeS

© C

BOH. F4B-4

2·F·7 U.S.NAVY

7

U.S. NAVY

F4B-4 B9H

U.S.NAVY 2·F·7

5′   10′

Note: Ailerons painted yellow on undersurfaces

Emblem of
Fighting
Squadron 2.

ADSRUM

BOEING F4B-4 of Fighting
Squadron 2, Leader of Section
3, U.S.S. Lexington.

The Boeing F4B-4

by Peter Bowers

An F4B-4, the third aircraft of Section 1, VF-3B, from U.S.S. Langley. *Though not painted here, the lower half of the Townend ring should have been red.*
(Photo: U.S. Navy)

The Boeing Airplane Company of Seattle, Washington, started out as the principal supplier of fighter aircraft to the U.S. Navy for the years 1925–33 as the result of Navy interest in fighters that Boeing had built for the U.S. Army. Boeing's experience in the manufacture of U.S. Naval aircraft dated back to 1917, nearly a year after the formation of the company as Pacific Aero Products in July 1916. Soon after U.S. entry into World War I in April 1917, the Navy ordered two examples of the Boeing Model C two-seat seaplane trainer for evaluation, the order being placed just before the name of the company was changed to Boeing Airplane Company in May 1917. Testing of the first Model Cs resulted in an order for 50 production versions which were delivered in 1918. Additional Navy production during World War I consisted of the manufacture of 25 Curtiss-designed HS-2L single-engine patrol flying boats.

In the early post-war years, Boeing's principal customer was the U.S. Army. Orders for new machines were scarce and the majority of the work consisted of rebuilding obsolescent D.H.4 "Liberty Planes", the notorious American-built version of the original British design of 1916. Following military policy of the period, the Army designed some of its own aircraft and then contracted with the industry to build them. Under this arrangement, Boeing built 10 examples of the ungainly Liberty-powered GA-1 twin-engine

attack triplane and two GA-2 single-engine attack biplanes with the experimental Army-designed 750-h.p. W-1 three-bank water-cooled engines.

Another peculiar practice of the period concerned aircraft design procurement by the Army. When the Army bought a prototype from a manufacturer, it also acquired the manufacturing rights. If production of the new model was considered desirable, the entire domestic aircraft industry was invited to bid on the order, with the result that a firm having better production facilities than the original designer frequently won the order. This proved to be the case with Boeing, and it entered the fighter business in 1920 by winning a production order for 200 MB-3As—improved versions of a single-seater designed by Thomas-Morse in 1918. The designing firm received an order for only 50 MB-3s after building four prototypes.

BOEING DEVELOPS NEW STRUCTURE

As a result of the MB-3 contract, Boeing became thoroughly familiar with the problems of fighter design, construction and operation. It also realised the shortcomings of established structures which had been developed early in World War I. The wire-braced wooden fuselage, with its mass of metal fittings, was not only a costly manufacturing headache but a major maintenance problem. Boeing engineers had been quick to appreciate the advantages of welded steel

Left: Boeing's first fighter, the MB-3A, 200 of which were built to Thomas-Morse design. *Right:* Boeing Model 15 as tested by U.S. Army before purchase as XPW-9.
(Photos: U.S.A.F.)

tube fuselage construction, having initially encountered it in war-prize German Fokker D-VIIs (see *Profile* No. 25) on hand in the U.S. Three had been sent to Boeing, two for destructive structural testing and one flyable two-seat conversion for use by Army personnel at the plant during production of the MB-3As. Further information on steel tube structures and thick-section cantilever wing design was obtained by Boeing engineers visiting the new Fokker factory in Holland during a fact-finding European tour.

New fighter designs were proposed to the military but were turned down because enough aircraft existed to meet current needs and no funds were available for development of new designs. In the face of such Government apathy, Boeing decided to gamble on the demonstration of a new privately developed design, superior to Army models then on hand or projected, creating a market for itself where "paper" designs could not. Consequently, the building of three prototypes of a new fighter, the Boeing Model 15, was authorised at company expense. Other than the thick-section tapered wings, which were new to American design practice, the outstanding feature of the new model was the steel tube fuselage, assembled by a Boeing-developed arc-welding process instead of the gas-welding system used by Fokker. The Army showed interest, but was still unable to support the project financially. It did, however, agree to loan three new 435-h.p. Curtiss D-12 engines, instruments and accessories, and to test the aircraft at the Air Test Centre at McCook Field, Dayton, Ohio, on a bailment contract.

The first Model 15 completed its company tests in September 1923 and was delivered by rail to McCook Field, where the Boeing gamble paid off almost immediately. The Army decided to buy the flying prototype and the two unfinished aircraft, and designated them PW-9 (i.e. Pursuit, Watercooled, Model 9). These became XPW-9 in 1924 when the X-prefix was added to standard designations to indicate prototype or other experimental status. A production order for 30 slightly improved PW-9s followed. The Army

FB-1, the first Boeing fighter, was similar to Army PW-9.
(Photo: U.S. Navy)

was so pleased with the tapered wing of the XPW-9 that it asked Curtiss to fit similar wings to its existing PW-8 model which was a straight-wing design; the resulting XPW-8B was so successful that it became the prototype of the long line of tapered-wing Curtiss "Hawk" fighters.

EARLY BOEING NAVY FIGHTERS

The Navy was also impressed by the new model and ordered 10 similar examples for the U.S. Marine Corps under the Navy designation FB-1* (Navy serial numbers A-6884 to A-6893). These were the direct Naval ancestors of the famous F4B-4 fighters. The FB-1s were intended to operate from land bases and were not equipped with aircraft carrier arrester gear; the Marines operated them for a while in China following their delivery in December 1925.

Two improved FB-2s (A-6894, A-6895) were developed for carrier operation and were essentially FB-1s with arrester hooks and re-designed landing gear. Three FB-3s (A6897, A-7089, A-7090) used similar airframes but were fitted with larger Packard 1A-1500 engines. The landing gear was again different and provision was made for the installation of twin wooden pontoons. A single FB-4 (A-6896) served as a test bed for a new Wright P-1 air-cooled radial

*Under the designation system adopted for Naval aircraft in 1922, the first letter identified the design as a fighter and the second the manufacturer, Boeing. The -1 indicated the first configuration of the new model. Minor variations were identified as FB-2 FB-3, etc.

Left: *Major production model of FB series was FB-5, Boeing Model 67, which could be operated as a landplane or a twin-float seaplane*. Right: *F2B-1, Boeing Model 69, was improved PW-9/FB-5 designed for P&W Wasp radial engine.*   (Photos: U.S. Navy)

Left: *XF3B-1, Boeing Model 74, resembled earlier F2B-1 and could operate as landplane or single-float seaplane. "American Flag" rudder stripes were developed by Boeing and adapted by U.S. Army in November 1926.* (Photo: U.S. Navy). Right: *Production F3B-1, Boeing Model 77, bore little resemblance to XF3B-1 prototype. It was fitted with engine drag ring several years after delivery.*
(Photo: P. M. Bowers)

engine of 450-h.p. This engine was unsuccessful and the Navy replaced it with the newer 450 h.p. Pratt & Whitney Wasp radial and redesignated the aircraft FB-6. The major production model of the Navy FB series was the FB-5, an improvement of the Packard-powered FB-3 in which the wings were heavily staggered in the manner of the Curtiss "Hawk". Twenty-seven were built with serials *A-7101* to *A-7127*. Several sets of Boeing-built wooden pontoons were delivered with the FB-5s and some of them were operated as twin-float seaplanes. Army PW-9 production eventually totalled 113 and 43 FBs were delivered to the Navy.

The success of the new Wasp engine in the FB-6 opened up a whole new field of Navy fighter development, and Boeing went to work on another design, the Model 69—essentially a refined PW-9/FB fitted with the new engine. One prototype XF2B-1 (*A-7385*) was delivered to the Navy in December 1926 and was followed by 32 production F2B-1s (*A-7424* to *A-7455*) starting in January 1928 (the number 2 preceding the B-for-Boeing in the designation indicated the second fighter model ordered from Boeing).

Even before the F2B-1s were in production, Boeing submitted an improved version to the Navy. This was the company-owned Model 74, a machine that resembled the F2B-1 but was tested by the Navy as XF3B-1; it did not win production orders in its original form. Extensively rebuilt as Model 77 and tested again in the spring of 1928, it won an order for 73 F3B-1s (*A-7675* to *A-7691* and *A-7708* to *A-7763*) that were delivered between August and December 1928. The company-owned prototype, brought up to production standard, was bought by the Navy and became an additional item on the contract (as *A-7674*). The F3B-1s had provisions for the installation of a single main pontoon and wing-tip floats, but the Navy lost interest in seaplane fighters at this time and flew the F3Bs on wheels only.

F4B DEVELOPMENT

Even as the modified XF3B-1 was being tested, Boeing saw opportunities for improvement; design of an

Three F4B-3s (8891, 8898, 8803) of VB-4M U.S. Marines, San Diego, California. (Photo: U.S. Navy)

entirely new model was laid down and the building of two company-financed prototypes was authorised. The two differed only in minor details of equipment but were given distinct Boeing model designations, 83 and 89; external differences between them were the use of cross-axle undercarriage and arrester hook on the 83, and tripod-type wheel gear and 500-lb. bomb-rack on the 89. The chief merit of the new design was the fact that there was nothing radical about it. Every feature had been developed and proven on previous models—including even the unique bolted aluminium fuselage frame which was made up of square-section aluminium tubing. The customary practice of installing a larger engine in a new model to increase the performance was not necessary as the performance

Left: *Boeing Model 89, the first XF4B-1 prototype, in company colours during early tests at Sand Point Naval Air Station, Seattle.* (Photo: Mike Pavone). Right: *Model 83 modified at the factory and brought up to F4B-1 standard. Was delivered on the production F4B-1 contract.*

Left: *Fourth production F4B-1 was converted to special unarmed executive model for Assistant Secretary of Navy for Sir Douglas Ingalls, under designation of F4B-1A.* (Photo: U.S. Navy). Right: *In their declining years F4B-1s were fitted with 4B-2 ring cowlings and 4B4 vertical tail surfaces.* (Photo: E. M. Sommerich)

Production F4B-1, Boeing Model 99, as delivered to Navy squadron VF-5. Engine cylinder streamline fairings of original installation deleted after short period of service.
(A. U. Schmidt Collection)

F4B-2, Boeing Model 223, was similar to Army P-12C and D Models. It differed from F4B-1 in aileron shape, undercarriage and use of engine cowling.

speed dashes and by the setting up of a new time-to-height record. Reversing the earlier PW-9/FB-1 situation, the Army borrowed the Model 89 from the Navy for evaluation and placed an order for 10 similar models under the Army designation P-12 (*Profile* No. 2). Army P-12 production eventually totalled 366.

An order for 27 F4B-1 fighter bombers (*A-8130* to *A-8156*) resulted from the Navy-testing of the two prototypes. Both XF4B-1s were re-worked to production F4B-1 standard (Boeing Model 99, which used the Model 89 undercarriage) and were purchased by the Navy as additional items on the F4B-1 contract (*A-8128* for the 89 and *A-8129* for the 83). The experimental prefix was deleted at this time and both machines were considered as standard F4B-1s although minor differences were noticeable.

The development of the new design continued along parallel lines for the U.S. Army and Navy. The next Navy order was for 46 F4B-2s (Boeing Model 223), generally similar to the Army P-12C and D Models, Navy serials *A-8613* to *A-8639* and *A-8791* to *A-8809*. External differences between the F4B-2 and the -1 were in the use of straight-chord Frise ailerons, balanced elevators, reversion to the cross-axle undercarriage of the Model 83, and use of a Townend anti-drag ring round the engine.

THE F4B-3/4 PROTOTYPE

With production orders for P-12s and F4Bs in hand, Boeing continued its practice of developing advanced models. Two monoplane fighters of 1930, the Model 202 tested by the Army as the XP-15 and the duplicate Model 205 eventually purchased by the Navy as the XF5B-1, were not notably successful. Both were essentially F4B/P-12 designs built as parasol monoplanes and as such were somewhat ahead of their time. Both, however, featured a new semi-monocoque sheet aluminium fuselage construction which had been introduced in the commercial Boeing Model 200 "monomail". The same construction was then tried in a more conventional Boeing biplane, the Model 218, which was virtually a P-12B with the new fuselage. Both the Army and Navy tested the Model 218 in 1930 and 1931 and placed production orders. Strangely, the major structural change, which was great enough to justify an entirely new model number, did not have this result. The following Navy models were the F4B-3 and -4, and the Army P-12E and F models. The Model 218 itself was sold to China and was destroyed when attacking superior numbers of Japanese aircraft over Shanghai in 1932.

In spite of minor structural improvements, notably the enlarged fin and higher load-factored wings on the F4B-4, both the F4B-3 and the F4B-4 used the same Boeing Model number of 235. The first 54 -4s were

advance of the new design was achieved mainly through aerodynamic refinement and decreased structural weight. A speed increase of 21·5 m.p.h. over the F3B-1 was obtained with an increased output of only 50 h.p. from the later model Wasp engine. Climb was 900 ft./min. greater than that of the F3B-1 and the absolute ceiling 7,300 feet higher. The Model 83 was 398 pounds lighter.

Both prototypes were tested by the Navy in the summer of 1928, one at various naval bases on the West Coast and the other at the naval test centres at Anacostia, Maryland, and Hampton Roads, Virginia, on the East Coast. Although both were still Boeing-owned aeroplanes with civil registrations *7133* and *7134*, they were designated XF4B-1 during Navy tests. In an unprecedented move, the Navy allowed public demonstration of one XF4B-1 (Model 83) at the 1928 National Air Races at Los Angeles. The potentialities of the new design were demonstrated by

Air shots of F4B-2s show how undercarriage wheels drop in flight. Right illustration is of 8638 (VF-6B) of Fighting Squadron 6, 3rd aircraft of 4th Section.
(Photo: F. C. Dickey, Jnr.)

additional items on the F4B-3 contract with continuing serial numbers, and were originally to have been -3s. The almost identical Army P-12E was Model 234 and the P-12F was Model 251. The 21 F4B-3s carried Navy serials *A-8891* to *A-8911*.

The 92 production F4B-4s were delivered under two contracts. The first for 75 aircraft, 21 of which were delivered as F4B-3, was signed on 23rd April 1931. Serials of the first 54 F4B-4s were *A-8912* to *A-8920* and *A-9009* to *A-9053*. The last 38 were *9226* to *9263*, the A-prefix having been discarded by the Navy after passing *A-9206* in 1932. One additional F4B-4, *9719*, was built from spare parts stored at the U.S. Marine Corps base at Quantico, Virginia In another unprecedented move, the Navy allowed 14 random machines from the first order to be diverted to Brazil—the first time that a first-line U S. military aircraft was released for export before deliveries began to U.S. forces. The Brazilian models were designated Model 256 by the Boeing Engineering Department but were referred to as "1932" by the Sales Department to identify them as the current export model. The Brazilian aircraft did not reduce the size of the Navy order as Boeing was allowed to build 14 replacement machines as part of the second F4B-4 contract, which was originally for 38 machines.

The first F4B-4 was delivered on 21st July 1932, and the last on 28th February 1933. Seventy-one were delivered to the U.S. Navy and 21 to the Marine Corps. The Brazilian 256s were all delivered between 14th September and 8th October 1932. A follow-on order for nine Model 267s, also for Brazil, was delivered in a block on 21st February 1933, a week before the final F4B-4 delivery. The 267 was a combination aircraft using P-12E wings on the F4B-3 fuselage, tail and undercarriage. In 1940, 23 obsolete P-12s of various series (but mostly P-12Es) were obtained from the Army and redesignated F4B-4A. Serials were *2489* to *2511* in the second Navy serial number range.

STRUCTURE

Except for the fuselage, which duplicated that of the Model 218, the structure of the F4B-3 and -4 was similar to that of the Model 83/89 prototypes. The one-piece upper wing used two full-span box spars with wing ribs cut from mahogany plywood and spruce cap strips and diagonal trusses nailed and glued in place; lightening holes were cut with a jig-saw. The wing-tip bows were laminated wood and the trailing edges were wire, which produced a scalloped effect—reminiscent of World War I days—when dope was applied to the fabric. The lower wing was similar in structural detail to the upper but was built in two separate pieces which were bolted together prior to assembly of the aircraft to form a single unit.

Metal ailerons, covered with corrugated sheet aluminium, were fitted to the upper wings only and were operated by push rods from actuating mechanism carried in the lower wing. Two flotation bags, inflated by bottled carbon dioxide, were carried in the upper wing just outboard of the centre-section struts. To allow their deployment from the under surface of the wing, the landing wires were lowered from their usual terminal points at the upper ends of the centre-section struts and attached to the upper longerons. This arrangement had been introduced on the F2B-1.

Construction of the tail surfaces was the same as that of the prototypes but had the revised vertical tail shape used on the P-12E and F4B-3 after modification

Boeing Model 205, essentially a monoplane version of P-12/F4B, was sold to Navy as XF5B-1. Its semi-monocoque fuselage construction re-appeared on Model 218 and on later production versions of P-12/F4B. (Photo: U.S. Navy)

With revised vertical tail shape, the modified Model 218 became prototype of Army P-12E and F, Navy F4B-3 and 4. (Photo: U.S.A.F.)

Twenty-one F4B-3s, Boeing Model 235, were delivered to fighter-bomber Squadron VF-3B, serving aboard carrier U.S.S. Saratoga in 1932–33. (A. U. Schmidt Collection)

Above: New vertical tail shape for still unbuilt F4B-4 was tested with this tube-and-fabric structure installed on a standard F4B-3. (Photo: U.S. Navy). *Below: F4B-4 of VF-2 Squadron with yellow tail. Blue band around fuselage of No. 7 a/c identified leader of third, three-plane element in squadron.*
(E. M. Sommerich Collection)

of the Model 218. The enlarged vertical fin of the F4B-4 provided relatively little improvement in directional stability over the F4B-3 but was considered so superior to earlier versions that the F4B-4 fin and rudder were ordered to be incorporated in F4B-1s and -2s then in service. Adjustment of longitudinal trim was effected by rotating the leading edge of the tailplane up and down by means of a jackscrew.

The forward portion of the fuselage was a composite structure, steel tube joining the tubular engine mounting to the stamped metal bulkheads and sheet aluminium covering skin. The cockpit cut-out was fairly large to permit pilot access in full flying gear, but draughtiness in flight was reduced by side curtains that could be drawn up to reduce the size of the opening. The 55-gallon fuel tank was located between the pilot and the engine, and the standard armament of two ·30-cal. machine guns or one ·30-cal. and one ·50-cal. gun were installed in deep channels forward of the pilot and above the tank. Ammunition was fed to the guns by belts folded into individual boxes below the guns. A telescopic gunsight passed through the windscreen.

Bombload consisted of a single 116-lb. bomb on a rack under each lower wing. Although the F4B-1s had on occasion been fitted with a single 500-lb. bomb under the fuselage, this position was generally used for the carriage of a 50-gallon auxiliary tank on Army P-12s and Navy F4Bs.

The spreader-bar undercarriage used solid-disc metal wheels with 30 × 5-in. tyres and the steerable tailwheel used a solid rubber type of 6-in. diameter. The standard deck-landing arrester hook was installed in the rear fuselage forward of the tailwheel.

The 52 F4B-4s on the second contract had more comprehensive radio, improved engine exhaust manifolds and additional night lighting. The earlier machines were later equipped to the same standard. The last 45 F4B-4s were built with removable engine mountings and enlarged headrests for storage of a pilot's life raft.

Some F4B-4s were assigned to bombing squadrons, as was this green-tailed member of Squadron VB-5. (Photo: P. M. Bowers)

F4B-4 without service markings. All metal parts light grey, fabric areas silver except upper wing surface.
(E. M. Sommerich Collection)

F4B-4 assigned to Naval Air Station Anacostia, with special polished Alclad finish used only at that station.
(Photo: P. M. Bowers)

Below: *Unusual shipboard stowage of green-tail F4B-4 of VF-3 aboard U.S.S. Ranger. Tails are run out along booms projecting overside to conserve deck space.* (Photo: U.S. Navy)

COLOUR SCHEMES

Standard U.S. Navy colour schemes underwent a slight change just at the time the F4B-3 appeared. Silver for fabric areas and chrome or orange-yellow for the upper wing surface remained the same, but the light grey previously used for metal components (seen on the F4B-2) was made even lighter, and the all-metal fuselage of the F4B-3s and -4s were practically an off-white shade. The F4B-1s were the last Boeing navy fighters to use the vertical red, white and blue tail stripes, and even then use was divided with the solid tail colour that identified aircraft of a particular squadron (station or aircraft carrier after 1936). All F4B-3s and -4s of the U.S. Marine Corps, however, continued to use the striped rudders with the exception of Squadron VF-9M at Quantico, Virginia, which used non-standard markings from 1933 until 1938, including solid-colour tails of red, white and blue for various flights within the Squadron.

The lettering U.S. NAVY, often but incorrectly assumed to appear below the lower wing of the F4B-4, was not in fact used on F4B-4s, and only briefly on F4B-3s, having been discontinued in May 1932. Marine Corps aircraft carried the lettering U.S. MARINES across the upper surface of the top wing until 1936. Prior to 1936, the Marines did not use the Navy system of a coloured band around the fuselage to identify section leaders' aircraft (six to a squadron), and distinguished their machines from equivalent Navy models until 1936 by painting a circle round the squadron designator letter on the fuselage (the F in 10-F-2). Since the Marine Corps emblem was carried on the fuselage where the Navy squadron insignia normally appeared, the squadron insignia of Marine aircraft, when used, was painted on the fin.

SERVICE RECORD

The F4B-4s entered service with the Navy and Marines in mid-1932 and served as first-line equipment with seven squadrons until replaced by Grumman F2F and F3F biplanes in 1937–38. A study of photographs showing squadron markings would tend

F4B-4 in non-standard markings used by Marine Squadron VF-9M from 1933 through 1938. (Photo: P. M. Bowers)

F4B-4, 9241, with markings of Marine Squadron VF-10M after deletion of standard Marine Corps vertical tail stripes. Coloured top half of cowling indicates No. 2 a/c in three-plane element. (Photo: U.S. Navy). *Below: Same a/c following transfer VF-9M in the non-standard markings peculiar to that squadron.* (E. M. Sommerich Collection)

White fuselage band identifies leader of second element. "Felix the Cat", with bomb, was insignia of VF-6 when it flew from U.S.S. Saratoga from 1932 through 1936. Squadron was re-organised in 1937 and flew from U.S.S. Enterprise with blue tails and Comet insignia. (Photo: Art Whitmer)

F4B-4, 9251, as modified for air show work after W.W.II.
(Photo: P. M. Bowers)

Above: *F4B-4s 9241 and 9251 were turned over to Bureau of Air Commerce in 1940 and given civil licences NC-14 and 13 respectively.* (Photos: P. M. Bowers)

exhibition pilot. He retained the latter, *9251*, and sold *9241*.

Both machines were given new civil registrations, *9241* (*NC-14*) becoming *NR-9329* (later *NX-9329*), and *9251* (*NC-13*) becoming *NR-9486*.

Mr. Bristow modified *NR-9846* for a new air show routine. The standard N-struts were modified to I-type, a different undercarriage was fitted and a late-series 600-h.p. P. & W. R-1340-AN-1 Wasp engine with

to indicate a higher total of ten squadrons, but this was explained by the redesignation of existing units.

While not the last biplane fighters in U.S. Naval service, the F4B-4s were the last with fixed landing gear and as such marked the end of an era. Following their withdrawal from the Fleet, the F4Bs of all marks were assigned to training schools, utility duties, general transport of VIPs, etc. The appearance of F4B-4s with standard U.S. Navy camouflage in the background of photographs of other naval aircraft indicates that a few regained fighter status for a short time early in 1942. With most first-line fighters at sea with the Fleet after Pearl Harbour, some obsolete models were impressed for home defence. The ultimate fate of the F4Bs on hand in 1941–2 was to be shot down as unmanned aerial targets, being flown under radio control from ground stations or director aircraft to provide gunnery practice for anti-aircraft batteries.

CIVILIAN F4B-4s

By chance two F4B-4s survived World War II in civilian status. In 1940 the Marine Corps turned two F4B-4s (*9241* and *9251*) over to the Bureau of Air Commerce, predecessor of the present Federal Aviation Agency (FAA). These were given the civil registrations *NC-14* and *-13* respectively, and were issued Category 2 type Certificate No. 2–555. After a short period of civil service use, both were declared surplus and sold to Mr. Jesse Bristow, a well-known American

F4B-4, 9241, as used for air show work just prior to W.W.II.
(Photo: C. Schuler)

F4B-4 SQUADRON ASSIGNMENTS, 1932–8

Squadron	Dates	Carrier or Station	Tail Colour
VB–5	Nov. 1934 to June 1935	U.S.S. Ranger	Willow Green
VB–5	Nov. 1935 to June 1937	U.S.S. Lexington	Willow Green
as VB–2	July 1937 to Nov. 1937	U.S.S. Lexington	Lemon Yellow
VF–2	Nov. 1934 to June 1935	U.S.S. Lexington	Lemon Yellow
VF–6	Oct. 1932 to June 1936	U.S.S. Saratoga	White
VF–3	Oct. 1932 to June 1934	U.S.S. Langley	Willow Green
VF–3	Nov. 1934 to June 1935	U.S.S. Ranger	Willow Green
VF–1	Apr. 1935 to June 1936	U.S.S. Langley	Royal Red
as VF–8	June 1937	U.S.S. Enterprise	True Blue
as VF–6	June 1937 to Nov. 1937	U.S.S. Enterprise	True Blue
VF–10M	July 1932 to 1933	San Diego, Calif.	USMC Tail Stripes
to VB–4M	1933 to 1935	San Diego, Calif.	USMC Tail Stripes
VF–9M	1932 to 1938	Quantico, Virginia	Stripes to 1934; Special solid colours to 1938

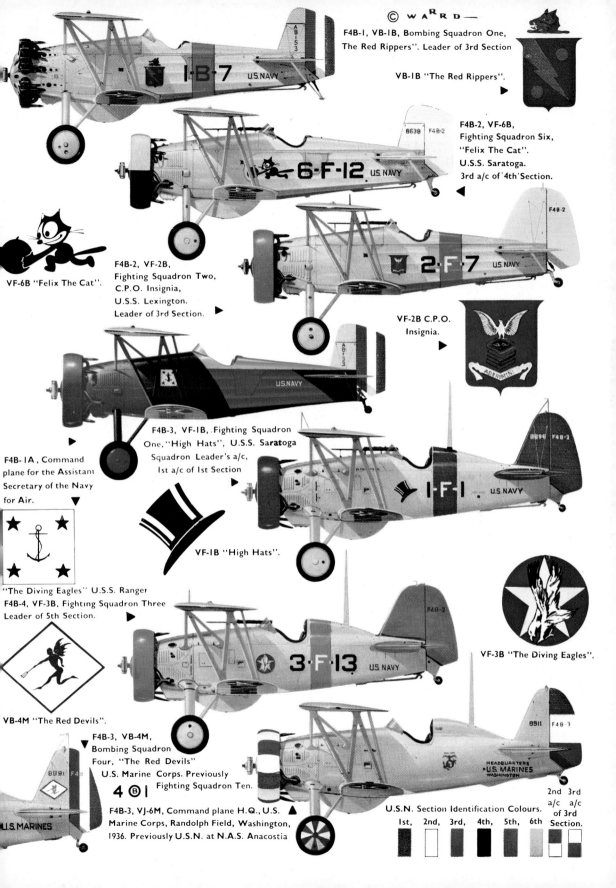

© WARRD —

F4B-1, VB-1B, Bombing Squadron One, The Red Rippers". Leader of 3rd Section

VB-1B "The Red Rippers". ▶

1-B-7 U.S. NAVY

F4B-2, VF-6B, Fighting Squadron Six, "Felix The Cat". U.S.S. Saratoga. 3rd a/c of '4th' Section. ◀

6-F-12 U.S. NAVY

VF-6B "Felix The Cat".

F4B-2, VF-2B, Fighting Squadron Two, C.P.O. Insignia, U.S.S. Lexington. Leader of 3rd Section. ▶

2-F-7 U.S. NAVY

VF-2B C.P.O. Insignia. ▶

ADFIMINT

F4B-1A, Command plane for the Assistant Secretary of the Navy for Air. ▼

F4B-3, VF-1B, Fighting Squadron One, "High Hats", U.S.S. Saratoga Squadron Leader's a/c, 1st a/c of 1st Section ▶

1-F-1 U.S. NAVY

VF-1B "High Hats".

"The Diving Eagles" U.S.S. Ranger F4B-4, VF-3B, Fighting Squadron Three Leader of 5th Section.

VF-3B "The Diving Eagles".

3-F-13 U.S. NAVY

VB-4M "The Red Devils".

F4B-3, VB-4M, Bombing Squadron Four, "The Red Devils" U.S. Marine Corps. Previously Fighting Squadron Ten.

4 B 1

U.S. MARINES

F4B-3, VJ-6M, Command plane H.Q., U.S. Marine Corps, Randolph Field, Washington, 1936. Previously U.S.N. at N.A.S. Anacostia ▲

HEADQUARTERS •U.S. MARINES WASHINGTON

U.S.N. Section Identification Colours.

1st, 2nd, 3rd, 4th, 5th, 6th

2nd 3rd a/c a/c of 3rd Section.

F4B4, 9241, *as restored by the former Naval Aircraft Factory in April 1961. This a/c served only with the Marine Corps and has since been repainted in the markings it carried in VF-9M.*
(Photo: Shipp)

controllable-pitch propeller was installed. A full NACA cowling was added to the engine and fittings were installed under the fuselage for two 300-lb. thrust JATO bottles. With the increased engine power and the rocket thrust, Mr. Bristow was able to make spectacular straight-up take-offs after a phenomenally short run. This unique exhibition variant was destroyed in 1948 soon after acquisition by a new owner.

The other civil F4B-4, registered *N-9329* after 1948, saw varied service for a few years (including crop dusting), and in 1960 was donated to the National Air Museum of the Smithsonian Institution by its final owner, Mr. Ray Hyland.

The Smithsonian prevailed upon the former U.S. Naval Aircraft factory in Philadelphia to restore it to a displayable, though non-flying, condition This work

was completed in time for the machine to be exhibited on Armed Forces day of 1961, the 50th anniversary year of U.S. Navy aviation. Unfortunately the markings selected for the restoration during the last-minute rush were copied from a proprietary plastic model kit and were of a combination that had never appeared on an F4B-4 but which had been seen on an F4B-3. Since its initial appearance as a restored fighter, this F4B-4 has been repainted in the actual colours and markings that it carried when assigned to Marine Corps Squadron VF-9M at Quantico, Virginia, from 1933 to 1938. Pending permanent installation in the new National Air Museum to be built in Washington, D.C., the last of the F4B-4s is on display in the National Aviation Museum at Pensacola, Florida.

© *Peter M. Bowers, 1965*

BOEING F4B SPECIFICATIONS

	F4B–1	F4B–2	F4B–3	F4B–4
Powerplant	450-h.p. P. & W. R-1340C rated at 6,000 ft. at 2,100 r.p.m.	500-h.p. P. & W. R-1340D rated at 6,000 ft. at 2,200 r.p.m.	500-h.p. P. & W. R-1340D rated at 6,000 ft. at 2,200 r.p.m.	500-h.p. P. & W. R-1340D rated at 6,000 ft. at 2,200 r.p.m.
Fuel Capacity*	57–107 U.S. gall.	55–110 U.S. gall.	55–110 U.S. gall.	55–110 U.S. gall.
Dimensions: Wing Span Length Height Wing Area	30 ft. 0 in. 20 ft. 1$\frac{3}{8}$ in. * 9 ft. 4$\frac{1}{2}$ in. * 227·5 sq. ft.	30 ft. 0 in. 20 ft. 0·69 in. * 9 ft. 1$\frac{1}{4}$ in. * 227·5 sq. ft.	30 ft. 0 in. 20 ft. 4·69 in. 9 ft. 9 in. * 227·5 sq. ft.	30 ft. 0 in. 20 ft. 4·69 in. 9 ft. 9 in. * 227·5 sq. ft.
Weights: Empty * Loaded as fighter * Loaded as bomber *	1,916 lb. 2,716 lb. 3,135 lb.	2,067 lb. 2,799 lb. 3,260 lb.	2,202 lb. 2,918 lb. 3,379 lb.	2,312 lb. 3,087 lb. 3,519 lb.
Performance: Max. Speed Cruising Speed Initial Climb Service Ceiling Range (normal) Range (max. economy) *	166·3 m.p.h. at sea level 150 m.p.h. at 60% power 2,110 ft./min. 26,400 feet * 500 miles 668 miles	186 m.p.h. at 6,000 ft. 158 m.p.h. at 60% power 5,000 ft. in 2·5 min. * 26,900 ft. 580 miles 738 miles	187 m.p.h. at 6,000 ft. 160 m.p.h. at 60% power 5,000 ft. in 2·9 min. * 27,500 ft. 585 miles 758 miles	184 m.p.h. at 6,000 ft. * 160 m.p.h. at 60% power — 24,800 feet * 585 miles 703 miles
Armament	Two ·30-cal. or one ·30-cal. and one ·50-cal. machine guns.			
Navy serials (all numbers inclusive)	A–8128 to A–8156 (29 aircraft)	A–8806, A–8613 to A–8638, A–8639, A–8791 to A–8809 (47 aircraft)	A–8891 to A–8911 (21 aircraft)	A–8912 to A–8920, A–9009 to A–9053, 9226 to 9263, 9719 (93 aircraft)
*U.S. Navy figures. (Remainder Boeing material)				

PRINTED IN ENGLAND. © Profile Publications Ltd., P.O. Box 26, Leatherhead, Surrey, England, by George Falkner & Sons Ltd., for McCorquodale City Printing Division, London.

PROFILE
PUBLICATIONS

The
Macchi
C.202

Number

MACCHI M.C. 202 Folgore of the 382
Squadriglia, 21° Gruppo, 51° Stormo,
Russia, Summer 1942.

0   5

The Macchi C.202
by Gianni Cattaneo

Macchi C.202 Folgore of 1° Stormo, 6° Gruppo, 79° Squadriglia, Libya, January 1942.   (Photo: G. Cattaneo)

One of the major obstacles facing Italian aircraft designers in the years immediately before W.W.II, was the lack of a suitable liquid-cooled, in-line engine of sufficient power to satisfy the growing aerodynamic needs of fighter aircraft. A strange situation when one considers the brilliant successes gained by the Italian Schneider Trophy racers powered with FIAT and Isotta-Fraschini in-line engines.

Abroad, the lessons of combining an in-line engine with a streamlined airframe were absorbed by aircraft designers, in particular Willy Messerschmitt and Reginald Mitchell. In England Mitchell refined the design theme initiated with the Supermarine Schneider Trophy machines, and perfected it until it culminated with the superlative Spitfire. Messerschmitt produced the angular, but functional, Bf 109 powered by the Daimler-Benz engine.

But the Italian aircraft industry ignored the in-line engine's potential and the more bulky radial gained pre-eminence. It was not until the opening months of 1940 that the Macchi Company imported a specimen of the Daimler-Benz DB 601 in-line engine from Germany, and around it the Macchi design team built the M.C.202 fighter.

The new fighter was a private venture by Macchi, and their Chief Designer, Mario Castoldi, took full advantage of previous experience of the in-line engine installation gained by the company with their series of racers—the M.39, M.52, M.67 and the M.C.72. The last named gained the World Air Speed Record in 1934 when clocking 441 m.p.h.

Based on the well-tried and proved M.C.200 airframe of 1938 vintage, the new fighter proved to be a thoroughbred, the prototype making its first flight on 10th August 1940, with Macchi's brilliant test pilot Com. Carestiato at the controls.

The first fights confirmed the calculated performance figures, and the new machine retained the control harmonisation and finger-tip manœuvrability of its predecessor. The 202 also enjoyed an exceptional climb rate, behaved well at altitude and was more than 60 m.p.h. faster than the 200. Thanks to a certain degree of inter-changeability of structural parts and tooling with the 200 (already well established in production) the 202 could be built in quantity in a short time.

The private venture of Macchi aroused the interest of the Italian *Ministero dell' Aeronautica*, and not only was the M.C.202 ordered into series production, but an important programme of licence production was organised with assembly lines at the Breda Company's plant near Milan in addition to the mother company's Varese factory and a wide network of sub-contractual work.

Supplies of the German Daimler-Benz engine in quantity were promised, at least on paper, direct from Germany to meet initial needs, and arrangements made for the licence production in Italy by the Alfa Romeo Company under the designation of R.A.100 R.C.41. Eight months after the contract was signed for the 202 the first production aircraft began to appear. In the intervening period the prototype was undergoing intensive testing at the Guidonia Experimental Centre to evaluate the potentialities of the new design.

With the M.C.202 the Italian fighter units had at last got an aircraft of international standard, with capabilities similar, and often superior to, the most modern types employed by the opposing forces engaged by the *Regia Aeronautica*. Also, the M.C.202 was without doubt the most effective fighter used in quantity by the Italian Air Force in W.W.II, and it maintained its service record up to the Armistice in September 1943, despite the introduction of more advanced Allied fighters late in 1942 which possessed superior speed and armament. In an effort to get on par with the new Allied machines a progressive development of the Folgore was the C.205V Veltro, virtually a 202 with a more powerful Daimler-Benz engine. Only a few were built and they arrived too late to alter the outcome of the war for Italy.

THE FOLGORE DESCRIBED

The M.C.202 was an interceptor fighter of all-metal construction and was initially armed with two 12·7 mm. (0·5-in.) calibre machine guns located in the engine cowling and synchronised to fire through the airscrew arc. This chronic armament deficiency, characteristic of Italian fighters, was improved on the Series VI* Folgore with the introduction of two 7·7 mm. machine guns (0·3-in.) in the wings.

Aerodynamically the Folgore (Lightning), as the new fighter was soon named, was of clean and well balanced proportions. Of robust construction it featured flush-riveting on all surfaces and careful attention had been paid to detail streamlining in an

Series of the M.C.202 were identified with Roman numerals from I to XI.   3

Top: *Macchi C.202 prototype (MM445) before application of camouflage scheme. Photo below shows same aircraft in camouflage scheme and national insignia. (Photos: G. Cattaneo and Aer Macchi).*

from the landing gear station to the wing tip. Flaps, of metallic structure, were of the split type and the metal-framed fabric-covered ailerons were statically and dynamically balanced.

Fixed tail surfaces were all-metal, whilst the movable surfaces were fabric covered. The stabiliser incidence was adjustable in flight. To compensate for propeller torque the port wing, while of the same profile and root chord as the starboard wing, was of slightly wider span and smaller tip chord. The landing gear was inwards folding with hydraulic action and equipped with oleo-pneumatic shock absorbers in the main wheel struts. The tailwheel, retractable only on the prototype, was fixed on production aircraft and partially enclosed by suitable fairings. Some aircraft lacked the rear fairing.

effort to reduce parasitic drag. The engine cowling had a well-balanced profile which ran in a smooth line from the propeller spinner to the cockpit canopy, the latter being faired into the rear fuselage.

Fuselage structure was a semi-monocoque shell consisting of four light alloy beams with ovoidal bulkheads and stringers forming a particularly robust unit. The engine bearers of steel tubing in the first series were soon replaced by two cleanly-designed forged elements of light alloy in later aircraft. The central section of the wing was built integral with the fuselage and carried the outer wing fittings and the main fuel tank. The pilot's seat was adjustable in height and length and was fitted with integral armour.

The shape of the head-fairing permitted a limited degree of rear vision, but provided excellent protection in the event of the Folgore nosing over on the ground. Immediately behind the cockpit was located the radio, the various systems and the auxiliary fuel tank.

The wing was a bi-longeron structure attached to the fuselage centre section by steel forgings; the leading edge was replaceable as a complete unit

Instrument array was adequate and the radio equipment included a direction finder. The gun sight was of the reflector type. Engine starting was electric or, alternatively, manual with an inertia system. The fuel system included the main fuselage tank of 60 Imp. gals. capacity, two tanks in the wing roots of 9 Imp. gals. each and a supplementary rear fuselage tank of 18 Imp. gals. capacity. All tanks were self-sealing.

The oil radiator was placed under the nose and the cooling liquid radiator under the fuselage, the latter equipped with a variable position flap with hydraulic action. The M.C.202 was equipped with an oxygen system, cabin ventilation and heating systems; armament and Pitot tube being heated electrically.

The aileron, elevator, flaps and rudder controls were actuated through push-pull rods and only the control of the adjustable stabiliser was via cables. The flaps control was connected to the hydraulic system of the landing gear.

The two fuselage guns carried 360 rounds each and

Macchi C.202 of 75° Squadriglia, Libya, March 1942.

Top: *Macchi C.202, Series 1 (MM-7762)*. Below: *Macchi C.202, Series IIIA.S. (MM7806)*. (Photos: G. Cattaneo)

the wing guns 500 rounds each. The armament installation was completed by a pneumatic re-arming system and round counter indicators in the cockpit.

From 1941 to 1943 about 1,500 M.C.202s were built, 392 by the parent company and the rest under licence by Breda, spread over eleven very similar series. The Folgore was changed little during production and only minor differences distinguished the sub-series. Among the most noticeable modifications the following can be recorded:

Two different types of tailwheel structures and relating fairings.

Two different models of gyro instruments with Venturi under or on the right side of the fuselage.

The wing guns installation.

Two types of radio set with different antenna mast.

Installation of dust-filters for use in the desert.

The last modification was soon introduced on the production line and the most conspicuous detail was the characteristic faired ram-air entry of the supercharger. As usual the aircraft modified for the desert war received the suffix A.S. (*Africa Settentrionale*) in the designation.

Only the last series were sometimes equipped with underwing strong points for jettisonable fuel tanks (22 Imp. gals. each and later 33 Imp. gals.) or for bombs (110 lb., 220 lb. and 330 lb.). As stated before the structure was quite strong, as were all fighters designed by Castoldi, and it was able to take heavy punishment and perform violent aerobatic manœuvres. Moreover, the exceptionally clean airframe permitted a high diving speed to be achieved quickly, and the M.C.202 encountered the effects of the then unknown compressibility factor.

But the 202 was a pilot's aeroplane and in the hands of an experienced airman was a dangerous adversary, even for a more heavily armed opponent.

SERVICE BEGINS

The first unit to receive the new fighter was the *1° Stormo C.T.*, its *6° Gruppo* and *17° Gruppo* transferring to Udine in the summer of 1941 for conversion training. By November of that year the complete *Stormo* was in Libya, participating in the last stages of the British campaign that led to the raising of the blockade around Tobruk, and to the retreat of German and Italian troops in Cyrenaica in late December.

It has sometimes been said that the late arrival of the *1° Stormo's* 202s in Cyrenaica was a contributing factor to the success of the British offensive. Loss of Axis air superiority enabled the R.A.F. to harass the German/Italian ground forces, and there is little doubt that the 202 might have helped stem the tide had it been available in quantity and in time. But it would have been hazardous to commit a semi-trained unit, equipped with a new aeroplane, into a major battle.

Folgores of 79° Squadriglia in company with Macchi C.200 Saettas.

(Photo: G. Apostolo)

Top: *Macchi C.202, 52° Stormo, 22° Gruppo, 369° Squadriglia.* (Photo: G. Apostolo). Bottom: *C.202 of 151° Squadriglia, 51° Stormo.*

The North African terrain was not conducive to easy serviceability, and the Folgore may have proved more of a liability than an asset.

Home-based Folgores, however, performed magnificently, and the inevitable period of ironing the bugs out of the new fighter was accomplished in comfort due to the availability of facilities. Every new aircraft type always presents its users with some problems during the early months of service and the 202 was no exception. But faults were rare, and after a short period of "running-in" the new machine was able to takes its place as the premier front-line fighter.

When the British offensive ground to a standstill in the first few days of January 1942, the Folgores of *1° Stormo* were deployed at Tamet (*17° Gruppo*) and Ara Fileni (*6° Gruppo*), and the most successful period for the Folgore was about to begin.

Other units were busily re-equipping with the new fighter—in November 1941 the *9° Gruppo* of the *4° Stormo C.T.*, in December the *10° Gruppo* of the same *Stormo*. Originally destined for Libya, the *4° Stormo* was transferred in April 1942 to Sicily to take part in the spring offensive against Malta. However, heavy demands on the Folgore for the North African Front resulted in the *4° Stormo* being transferred from Sicily to Libya in May 1942. During the same period a detached section of the photo-reconnaissance M.C.202 was formed in Sicily and based at Casteletrano.

The second offensive against Malta lasted from March until April 1942 and did not succeed in its objective—to neutralise the island and to force the Royal Navy to use Gibraltar as the main Mediterranean base. The Luftwaffe was responsible for the major portion of the offensive, but the Italian units using the 202 performed well against the defending Hurricanes and Spitfires, the latter arriving on the island via the carriers *Eagle* in March and *Wasp* the following month.

The opening of the great offensive that led the Italian and German forces under General Rommel's command to within sight of Alexandria began in January 1942. Benghazi was occupied on 29th January, thus removing the immediate Allied threat to Tripolitania.

Following a lull in February the offensive gained new momentum in March, and the Folgores of *1° Stormo* were in the forefront of the advance. The *3°, 8°* and *150° Gruppos* had the advantage of the Hurricanes and Tomahawks of the Desert Air Force for their 202s could turn inside both fighters, and only the Spitfire had a marginal advantage in climbing speed over 15,000 ft. In May the *1° Stormo* was joined by the *4° Stormo* from Sicily and both were deployed at Martuba. The third phase of the offensive started on 26th May, opening with the successful strafing of Gambut airfield by 59 Folgores. Results were very good. Accompanied by the Bf 109s of the *Afrika Korps* the Folgores were particularly active, escorting bombers against the fortress of Tobruk and on free interdiction missions along a rapidly fluctuating front line.

The Axis advance finally petered out at El Alamein on 30th June, one of the main reasons being problems of supply over long and exposed routes. The Axis advance had been rapid, and although the flying units were able to bring with them certain essential supplies, bulk deliveries had to come by road behind the advance. For this purpose two columns of vehicles followed the Axis ground forces to keep up with the progressive occupation of airfields, carrying supplies for five days fighting. At the eve of the battle of El Alamein Folgores were with the *4° Stormo* at Fuka, with *23° Gruppo* (*3° Stormo*) at Abug Aggag and with the *150° Gruppo* at Benghazi. The *1° Stormo* had been transferred back to Italy in June. The *4°*

Macchi C.202s, Series II, awaiting delivery at the Macchi factory in early 1942.   (Photo: via G. Cattaneo)

Folgores of 54° Stormo, 152° (7°) Gruppo "Asso Di Bastoni", 374° Squadriglia. (Photo: G. Apostolo)

Stormo, one of the most famous of Italian fighter units, distinguished itself particularly during the Axis advance and notched up its 500th victory from the time it began operations in 1940.

THE RETREAT IN AFRICA

The events of El Alamein in October 1942 and the progressive retreat of the Axis from Libya until final defeat are too well known to be retold here, but suffice it to say that the Folgore was always in the midst of the bitter fighting, trying unsuccessfully to stem the enormous flow of Allied armour, aircraft and men. The 202s suffered from lack of fuel, spares and replacements and by January 1943 only a handful remained, serving with the *3° Stormo* (this unit took over the surviving 202s of the *4° Stormo*) and a squadron of the *13° Gruppo C.T.*

From January to December 1942 the Italian fighter units performed a total of 23,555 sorties, about 30% of which must be attributed to the M.C.202. The average monthly efficiency of the Folgore on the Front varied from a minimum of 30 aircraft in January to a maximum of 74 aircraft in September.

The necessity of supplying the vital base of Malta and reinforcing the British Forces in Egypt resulted in a series of furious aero-naval battles in the summer of 1942 between the bombers of both the Italian and German Air Forces, the guns of the Allied convoys and the few Allied fighters based on Malta. M.C.202s and Re.2001s based in Sicily escorted the Ju 87s and the S.M.79s attacking the Allied ships. During one furious battle 202s of the *155° Gruppo* encountered the Sea Hurricanes and Fulmars of the escort carriers

and came away successful, and during other battles in August Folgores fought Spitfires and Beaufighters based on Malta.

SERVICE IN RUSSIA

In September 1942, to supplement the small Italian Air Force that operated in the Russian theatre from late summer 1941, a number of B.R.20s and M.C.202s were sent to the U.S.S.R. The heavy demands of the Mediterranean war permitted the despatch of only twelve M.C.202s, which were attached to the *21° Gruppo C.T.* (*256°, 382°* and *386° Sq.*), equipped mainly with M.C.200s transferred from Italy in Spring 1942. The precious Folgores were equally distributed among the squadrons of the groups. These units participated in the offensive of the *VIII Armata* towards the Don river and occupied successively the airfields at Voroscilovgrad, Millerovo and Kantemirovka. The Italian fighters encountered the Soviet Yaks and LaGGs and supported the troops with strafing actions. With the coming of winter '42–'43 the Russian counter-offensive developed with tremendous effectiveness and the M.C.200s and 202s were used in relieving actions against the spreading Russian columns. The Italian pilots, not numerous and with equipment unfit for the difficult conditions of the place, received on many occasions the acknowledgements of the German High Command; the last strafing sortie was performed on 17th January 1943 by 25 aircraft in the Millerovo area, helping some surrounded German troops. From August 1941 to January 1943 the fighters of the *22° Gruppo C.T.* (M.C.200) and later the *21° Gruppo C.T.* (M.C.200 and 202) accomplished a total of 6,361 escort, offensive sweep, ground support and strafing sorties. The Russian aircraft shot down were 88 and the Italian fighters lost in the battle and for various causes were 15.

With the development of the first great amphibious operation in the European theatre, Operation Torch, into the occupation of French North Africa and the expulsion of the Axis forces from Tunisia, some deployments were effected in order to bring as far westwards as possible the bases from which the German and Italian fighters contested the Allied advance. The *153° Gruppo* and the *17° Gruppo*, with 24 and 33 Folgores respectively, were transferred from Sicily to Sardinian airstrips. Offensive sorties by Re.2001 fighter-bombers over the harbours of Bone and Bougie were escorted by M.C.202s, and part of the *155° Gruppo* was transferred to El Alouina to help

Macchi C.202s, 4° Stormo, 10° Gruppo, 90° Squadriglia, Libya, Summer 1942. (Photo: G. Cattaneo)

cover the landing of last-minute reinforcements from Italy. By February 1943 the Folgore-equipped units in Tunisia comprised the *6° Gruppo* at Sfax, the *3° Stormo* at El Hamma, and the *16° Gruppo* on K34 and K41; total strength was 55 M.C.202s, far below the theoretical strength of a force of this size.

In this period occurred the first combats with American pilots of the USAAF 12th Air Force, the Folgores encountering on many occasions the P-38 Lightnings of the 1st and 14th Fighter Groups, the P-39 Airacobras of the 81st and 350th Fighter Groups, and Spitfires of the 31st and 52nd Fighter Groups. The M.C.202 enjoyed a certain superiority against the P-38 especially in turning radius and climb rate, while the Airacobras were no match for the Folgores at all and were soon relegated to ground attack duties. In all cases, however, the interior armament of the M.C.202 was apparent.

In March the *7° Gruppo C.T.* arrived in Tunisia, joining the *16° Gruppo* in the new *54° Stormo*. In May came the defeat of the Axis forces in Tunisia, which was itself only a prelude to the invasion of Sicily and the Italian mainland and the Armistice of September 1943. During these months the M.C.202 units, supplemented by the few available M.C.205s and Re.2005s, were heavily committed to interceptor duties against the mass formations of B-17s and B-24s

which systematically bombed important centres such as Palermo, Naples, Reggio Calabria and many other Italian cities, as well as Sicily and Sardinia. The M.C.202s scored numerous victories in these actions despite the heavy fighter escort forces; and their record is all the more creditable considering the great disparity between the opposing forces and the inevitability of defeat.

THE LAST MONTHS

In July 1943, prior to the invasion of Sicily, the M.C.202 equipped the following units: the first figure refers to assigned aircraft and the second to serviceable machines:

2° Stormo C.T.	Lonate Pozzolo	15	11
3° Stormo C.T.	Cerveteri	18	4
21° Gruppo C.T.	Firenze	11	7
22° Gruppo C.T.	Capodichino	16	9
51° Gruppo C.T.	Monserrato	23	21
24° Gruppo C.T.	Venafiorita	19	10
4° Stormo C.T.	Catania	38	12
161° Gruppo C.T.	Reggio Calabria	18	11
21° Gruppo C.T.	Chinisia	12	6
153° Gruppo C.T.	Palermo	7	3
154° Gruppo C.T.	Rhodes	9	6

Top of page: *Production Folgores Series IX, undergoing final checks before issue to squadrons. Note how the upper surface scheme comes to an end under the leading edge of wing.* (Photo: via G. Cattaneo)

Immediate right: *Instrument panel of Macchi C.202.* Far right: *Close-up of Folgore engine cowling reveals blister air intakes and gun troughs.* (Photos: via G. Cattaneo)

Engine installation of the C.202 reveals high quality of the bearer castings, typical of the workmanship in Macchi aircraft. (Photo: G. Cattaneo)

Close-up MM7768 showing the experimental chin radiator.

Hence a total of only 100 serviceable Folgores were dispersed over the whole of Italy. Most of the units in the South were annihilated during Operation Husky or later destroyed on the ground by Allied air attack. However, the Italian and German fighter forces flew 690 and 500 sorties respectively during the first ten days of July 1943 over the airfields of Sicily, and Allied losses were quite considerable. The Allies lost approximately 375 aircraft and the Axis approximately 270; but it was the operational swan song of the M.C.202.

The Italian industry made a great effort to make good the losses caused by the last actions in Italy; but by the Armistice only 122 Folgores were dispersed around the country from the South to the Alps, and of these machines only 53 were serviceable. Some reached the Allied-held sectors and were incorporated into the Co-Belligerent Air Force; in particular these were used by the *X° Gruppo* of the *4° Stormo* and by the new *5° Stormo*, soon re-equipped with Airacobras. Those aircraft which reached the Northern airfields

MM91974 was tested with underwing mounted 20-mm. Mauser M.G. 151 cannons.

The Macchi C.202 (MM7768) was fitted with a chin radiator, but increased drag lead to the rejection of the project. (Photo: Aer Macchi, via G. Cattaneo)

9

were taken on the strength of the R.S.I. Air Force, but due to a certain availability of M.C.205s and Fiat G.55s they were only used for training purposes. Two examples of the Folgore survived the war and were used at Lecce training school up to 1947, kept in condition by enthusiastic ground crew who "scrounged" spares from aircraft graveyards all over Southern Italy.

Ground crew re-loading the nose magazine of a Macchi C.202 —note personal insignia on cowling. (Photo: G. Cattaneo)

Unusual camouflage scheme displayed by a C.202, believed to be of 3° Stormo, Libya, Summer 1942. (Photo: G. Cattaneo)

Rare photographs of C.202s and a C.200 taken in the field in Sicily, Summer 1942. (Photos: via G. Cattaneo)

Above: *Folgore, believed 3° Stormo, Libya, Summer 1942.* (Photo: G. Cattaneo) Below: *Insignia of 51° Stormo.* (Photo: via Richard Ward)

1. AER. MACCHI C.202—PROTOTYPE M.M.545
Flight Test Data at Maximum Weight of 6,206 lbs.
a) Maximum speed at height of:
Sea level 305 m.p.h.; 3,280 ft. 319 m.p.h.; 6,560 ft. 334 m.p.h.; 9,840 ft. 349 m.p.h.; 13,120 ft. 362 m.p.h.; 16,405 ft. 372 m.p.h.; 19,685 ft. 362 m.p.h.
b) Absolute max. speed: 372·2 m.p.h. at 19,360 ft.
c) Minimum speed: 88·8 m.p.h. at sea level.
d) Climbing time to:
3,280 ft. 34 sec.; 6,560 ft. 1 min. 19 sec.; 9,840 ft. 2 min. 26 sec.; 13,120 ft. 3 min. 27 sec.; 16,405 ft. 4 min. 40 sec.; 19,685 ft. 6 min. 13 sec.
e) Take off run: 827 ft.
f) Landing run: 771 ft.

2. AER. MACCHI C.202
Typical Result of an Official Acceptance Test Series a/c M.M.9486.
Maximum weight: 6,475 lbs. Useful load: 1,279 lbs. Empty weight: 5,196 lbs.
a) Maximum speed and time to climb to:
Sea level 308 m.p.h.; 3,280 ft. 320 m.p.h. 52 sec.; 6,560 ft. 332 m.p.h. 1 min. 48 sec.; 9,840 ft. 343 m.p.h. 2 min. 47 sec.; 13,120 ft. 354 m.p.h. 3 min. 49 sec.; 16,405 ft. 363 m.p.h. 4 min. 57 sec.; 19,685 ft. 367 m.p.h. 6 min. 26 sec.
b) Service ceiling: 34,600 ft.
c) Range with 551 lbs. of fuel: 475 miles at 20,130 ft. at 267 m.p.h.
d) Max. dive speed (starting from 20,130 ft.): 475 m.p.h. at 8,330 ft.

3. AER. MACCHI C.202—OFFICIAL SPECIFICATION
(Data from Technical Manual C.A. 670/1— Series IV-VIII of "Ministero dell'Aeronautica".)
Powerplant: One Alfa Romeo R.A. 1000 R.C.411, twelve cylinder, inverted vee, rated at 1075 H.P. at 2,500 r.p.m. for take-off and 1040 H.P. at 2,400 r.p.m.—Piaggio P.1001 constant speed propeller, three blades, diameter 9·87 ft.
Dimension: Wing span 34·710 ft.; Wing area 180·834 sq. ft.; Root chord 21·097 ft.; Tip chord (left) 4·037 ft.; Tip chord (right) 4·268 ft.; Length 29·035 ft.; Height 11·450 ft.
Weight: Empty: 5,491 lbs. Useful load: 968 lbs. of which, Pilot 176 lbs.; Rounds 167 lbs.; Fuel 552 lbs.; Oil 73 lbs.
Total loaded 6,459 lbs.
Performance: (at maximum weight 6,459 lbs.)
Max. speed and time to climb to:
Sea level 309 m.p.h.; 3,280 ft. 324 m.p.h. 39 sec.; 6,560 ft. 338 m.p.h. 1 min. 28 sec.; 9,840 ft. 352 m.p.h. 2 min. 28 sec.; 13,120 ft. 364 m.p.h. 3 min. 32 sec.; 16,400 ft. 370 m.p.h. 4 min. 40 sec.; 19,685 ft. 365 m.p.h. 5 min. 55 sec.; 22,965 ft. 363 m.p.h.
Absolute max. speed: 373 m.p.h. at 18,370 ft. Service ceiling: 37,740 ft. Ultimate loading coefficient: 15·8.
Armament: Two 12·7 mm. cal. Safat machine guns with 360 rounds each. Provision for two 7·7 mm. cal. machine guns with 500 rounds each in wings.

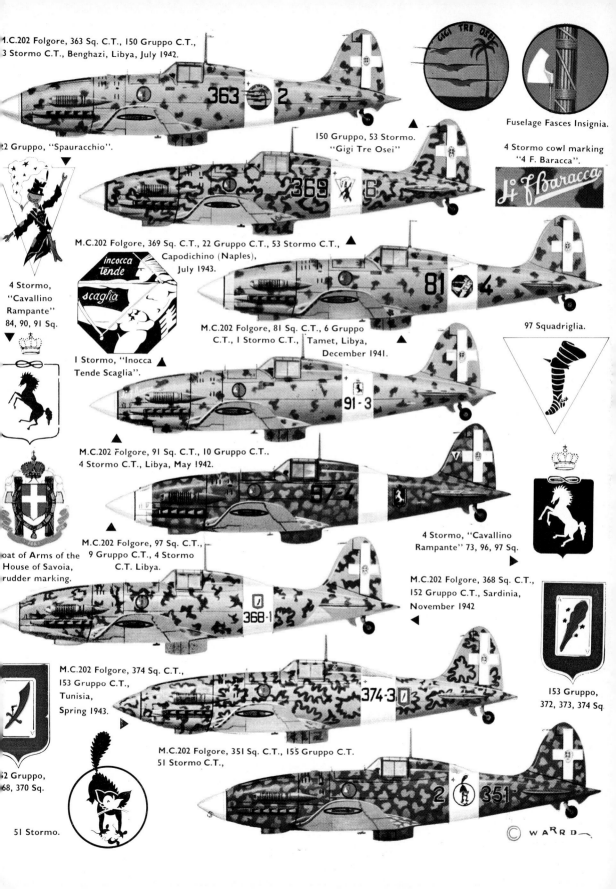

M.C.202 Folgore, 363 Sq. C.T., 150 Gruppo C.T., 53 Stormo C.T., Benghazi, Libya, July 1942.

Fuselage Fasces Insignia.

22 Gruppo, "Spauracchio".

150 Gruppo, 53 Stormo. "Gigi Tre Osei"

4 Stormo cowl marking "4 F. Baracca".

Lf Baracca

4 Stormo, "Cavallino Rampante" 84, 90, 91 Sq.

incocca tende scaglia

M.C.202 Folgore, 369 Sq. C.T., 22 Gruppo C.T., 53 Stormo C.T., Capodichino (Naples), July 1943.

1 Stormo, "Inocca Tende Scaglia".

M.C.202 Folgore, 81 Sq. C.T., 6 Gruppo C.T., 1 Stormo C.T., Tamet, Libya, December 1941.

97 Squadriglia.

M.C.202 Folgore, 91 Sq. C.T., 10 Gruppo C.T.. 4 Stormo C.T., Libya, May 1942.

Coat of Arms of the House of Savoia, rudder marking.

M.C.202 Folgore, 97 Sq. C.T., 9 Gruppo C.T., 4 Stormo C.T. Libya.

4 Stormo, "Cavallino Rampante" 73, 96, 97 Sq.

M.C.202 Folgore, 368 Sq. C.T., 152 Gruppo C.T., Sardinia, November 1942

M.C.202 Folgore, 374 Sq. C.T., 153 Gruppo C.T., Tunisia, Spring 1943.

153 Gruppo, 372, 373, 374 Sq.

52 Gruppo, 368, 370 Sq.

M.C.202 Folgore, 351 Sq. C.T., 155 Gruppo C.T. 51 Stormo C.T.,

51 Stormo.

© WARRD

Four guns were installed in MM7731, finished dark green upper surfaces with a yellow nose band. (Photo: G. Cattaneo)

As stated above, few modifications were introduced during the operational life of the M.C.202. Only two special prototypes are known; the first was the M.C.-202D (serial MM 7768) in which a new position for the radiator was tested under the engine. The increased drag cancelled the advantages of the simpler cooling pipe system and the installation was not repeated. The other experimental type was the airframe numbered MM 91974, with a trial installation of two 20 mm. Mauser cannon in pods under the wings.

The production of the M.C.202 was hampered throughout its life by the extreme scarcity of engines; the Italian industry was unable to provide more than 40 or 50 powerplants per month at best in the R.A. 1000 series and part of this output was reserved for the Re.2001. The German contribution can only be described as miserly. Despite this handicap, the sleek Folgore was one of the most interesting machines produced in quantity by the Italian aircraft industry; despite the inevitable distortion of facts by wartime propaganda, it was beloved by its pilots and highly respected by all its adversaries.

UNITS OF "REGIA AERONAUTICA" EQUIPPED WITH M.C.202 FIGHTER AIRCRAFT

Note: The Units very seldom reached the nominal strength in number of aircraft.

Gruppo	Stormo	Squadriglie	Date	Location
6°	1°	79°–81°–88°	Dec. 1941	Tamet (Libya)
			Jan. 1942	Ara Fileni (Libya)
			Feb. 1943	Sfax (Tunisia)
7° (152°)	54°	368°–370°–371°	March 1943	(Tunisia)
8°	2°	77°–78°–82°	July 1943	Sarzana (Italy)
9°	4°	73°–96°–97°	April 1942	(Sicily)
			May 1942	Martuba (Libya)
			July 1943	Catania (Italy)
10°	4°	84°–90°–91°	April 1942	(Sicily)
			May 1942	Martuba (Libya)
			July 1943	Catania (Italy)
13°	2°	92°–93°–94°	Sept. 1943	Venafiorita (Italy)
16°	54°		Feb. 1943	K34–K41 (Tunisia)
17°	1°	71°	Nov. 1941	Tamet (Libya)
			Nov. 1942	(Sardinia)
18°	3°	83°–85°–95°	Nov. 1942	Taourga (Libya)
			July 1943	Cerveteri (Italy)
20°	51°	351°–352°–353°	July 1943	Monserrato (Italy)
21°	51°	256°–382°–386°	Summer 1942	Voroscilovgrad(Russia)
			July 1943	Chinisia (Italy)
			Sept. 1943	Gioia del Colle (Italy)
22°	52°	359°–362°–369°	July 1943	Capodichino (Italy)
23°	3°	74°	June 1942	(Sicily)
			Aug. 1942	Abu-Aggag (Libya)
			July 1943	Ciampino (Italy)
24°	52°	354°–355°–370°	Sept. 1943	Metato (Italy)
150°	53°	363°–364°–365°	July 1942	Benghazi (Libya)
153°		372°–373°–374°	Sept. 1942	(Sicily)
			Nov. 1942	(Sardinia)
154°			July 1943	Rhodes (Aegean)
155°	51°	351°–360°–378°	May 1942	(Sicily)
			Nov. 1942	El Alouina (Tunisia)
161°		162°–163°–164°	July 1943	Reggio C. (Italy)

PRINTED IN ENGLAND. © Profile Publications Ltd., P.O. Box 26, Leatherhead, Surrey, England, by George Falkner & Sons Ltd., for McCorquodale City Printing Division, London.

PROFILE
PUBLICATIONS

The
Junkers
JU 88A

NUMBER 20

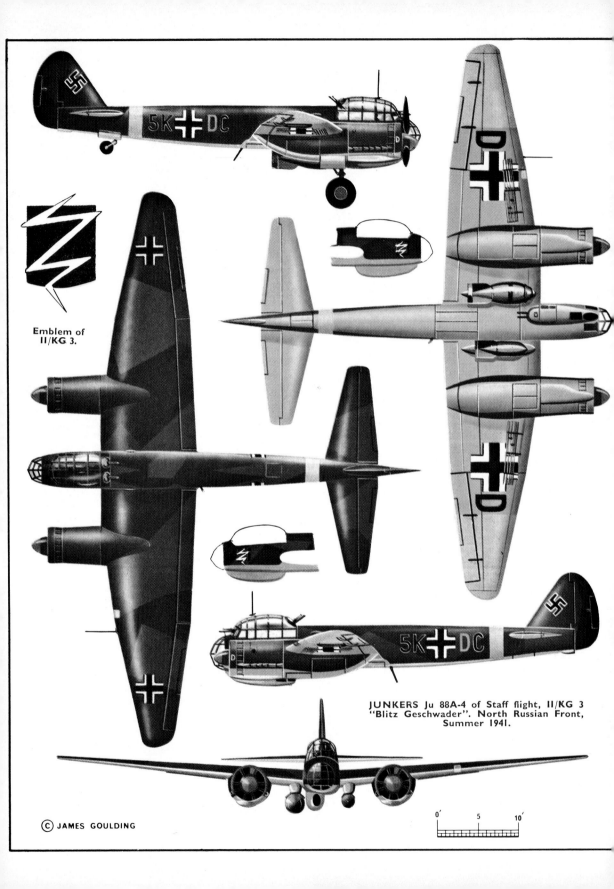

Emblem of
II/KG 3.

JUNKERS Ju 88A-4 of Staff flight, II/KG 3
"Blitz Geschwader". North Russian Front,
Summer 1941.

© JAMES GOULDING

0'   5   10'

The Junkers Ju 88A

by Martin C. Windrow

Junkers Ju 88As of 8/KG 1 "Hindenburg" run up their engines on a Russian airstrip.
(Photo: R. Ward Collection)

When on 21st December 1936 the first prototype Junkers Ju 88 lifted off the runway on its maiden flight, the watching officials of the *Junkers Flugzeug und Motorenwerke* could not know that they were watching the birth of an aircraft which was to become unique in the history of air warfare. They knew that they had produced a sleek, fast medium bomber which showed great promise—on paper. They had no way of foreseeing that by the time production of the Ju 88 series ceased in the spring of 1945 their "medium bomber" would have proved itself to be the nearest thing to a literally all-purpose aeroplane ever built. Flying and fighting on all fronts to which German forces were committed during the Second World War, the Ju 88 was to appear as a day fighter, night fighter, dive bomber, level bomber, torpedo bomber, mine-layer, reconnaissance aircraft, communications aircraft, close-support aircraft and flying bomb; and would fulfil many other specialised tasks, at home and in the field, whenever an aircraft of flexible performance was required. It was to be the most modifiable aircraft the world had known, and would prove itself the best by far of the rather indifferent selection of bombers which the *Luftwaffe* would operate during the war.

The requirement for a fast medium bomber to equip the *Luftwaffe*'s new *Kampfgeschwader* was announced to representatives of the German aircraft industry by *General-luftzeugmeister* Erhard Milch at an R.L.M. meeting held in the spring of 1935. Three designs were submitted in response by the firms of Messerschmitt, Focke-Wulf and Junkers. Messerschmitt's Bf 162 was eliminated when it was announced on a policy level that the company should in future concentrate solely upon fighter production. The Focke-Wulf Fw 57 project was abandoned following the loss of the first prototype; serious inconsistencies between the calculated and the actual weights had come to light. The Ju 88 thus won the competition by default of its rivals, but this implies no lack of positive merits.

The machine had been designed by W. H. Evers and the American Al Gassner, who was working in Europe during 1935-36. The period between the commencement of design work on 15th January 1936 and the maiden flight on 21st December of the same year was sensationally short by existing standards. The first prototype, the Ju 88V1, featured a low-silhouette streamlined canopy and was powered by DB 600 engines rated at 900 h.p. It was destroyed after only a part of the flight test programme had been completed. The Ju 88V2, which appeared in April 1937, achieved a speed of 289 m.p.h. and a range of over 1,200 miles.

It was in the Ju 88V3 and V4 that the features characteristic of later operational machines first

Left: *The third prototype, Ju 88V3, powered by Jumo 211A engines.* Right: *The Ju 88V5 "publicity prototype".*
(Photos: G. Heumann/Air Pictorial)

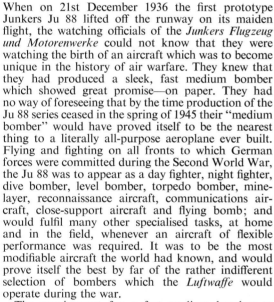

appeared. The V3 was powered by two twelve-cylinder liquid-cooled Junkers Jumo 211A engines. Rated at 950 h.p. and 1,000 h.p. at take-off and at 17,000 feet respectively, the 211A had direct fuel injection (a field in which German industry led the world), two stage supercharging, and the segmented radiators and circular cowlings which gave the Ju 88 the appearance of being a radial-engined aircraft.

With the V4, crew accommodation was raised to four and the characteristic nose of the Ju 88A series appeared for the first time. The tapered noses of the V1, V2 and V3 were replaced in this fourth prototype by a blunt, fully glazed unit with many braces. This nose was not "blown" but built up of twenty optically-flat glass panels arranged in a bulged "beetle's eye". Another important innovation was the ventral gondola offset under the starboard forward fuselage, to accommodate a prone gunner manning a rear-firing 7·9 mm. MG 15 machine gun. This addition had been foreshadowed by the small cupola which was fitted under the nose of the V3. The length of the V4 was, at 47 ft. 1 in., 1 ft. 8 in. greater than the preceding machines; the loaded weight was increased to 22,040 lb.

The Ju 88V5 was subjected to a rigorous "cleaning-up" programme, reverting to a tapered, unglazed nose unit. It was thought expedient that the Reich's new *schnellbomber* should be unveiled to the world in a suitably prestigious light, and the fifth prototype, powered by Jumo 211B-1 engines of 1,200 h.p., was adapted for record attempts. These efforts were handsomely rewarded when the V5 set up a record average speed of 321·25 m.p.h. over a closed circuit of 1,000 km. (621·3 miles) while carrying a 2,000 kg. (4,409 lb.) load. This record was established by Heintz and Siebert in March 1939; and in July of the same year the V5 achieved an average speed of 311 m.p.h. over 2,000 km. (1,242·7 miles) with the same payload.

PRODUCTION BEGINS

Quantity production of the Ju 88A was planned late in 1937 and plants began tooling up early in 1938. These tools and jigs were mainly produced at Junkers' Schoenebeck plant; wings, fuselage, and tail units were constructed at Halberstadt, Aschersleben and Leo-

Production prototype for the A series was the Ju 88V6, D-ASCY. (Photo: G. Heumann/Air Pictorial)

The eighth of ten pre-production Ju 88A-O machines. Aircraft of this batch were used by Kampfgeschwader 25 in the early weeks of W.W.II.

poldshall respectively, and final assembly lines and flight testing facilities were laid out at Bernburg. Henschel, Heinkel, Dornier, Arado and Volkswagen plants were all awarded contracts for the production of aircraft or component units.

The production prototype for the A series was the V6 (D-ASCY). Powered by Jumo 211 B-1s, the V6 was capable of 301 m.p.h. at a loaded weight of 22,590 lb., with a range of 1,522 miles and a service ceiling of 22,300 ft. The main undercarriage was redesigned and featured single hydraulic legs which retracted backwards into the nacelles, the wheels turning through a 90° arc to lie flat on the same plane as the wings.

The initial batch of ten pre-production Ju 88A-O machines were completed for service trials by *Erprobungskommando 88* in the spring of 1939. In accordance with the current German preference for aircraft with dive-bombing capabilities, slatted dive-brakes were hinged under the front spar outboard of the nacelles. The production Ju 88A-1, of which some sixty examples had been delivered by the close of 1939,

Nose emblem of a Junkers Ju 88A-1 of 1/KG 30 "Adler Geschwader". Note centre-hinged "quarter-light". (Photo: Imperial War Museum)

A machine of 4th Staffel, Long-Range Reconnaissance Gruppe 121 "on the bench". (Photo: Imperial War Museum)

also carried these brakes and was strictly limited in the scope of high-speed manœuvres permitted; the fuselage was already highly stressed and the operation of the brakes during maximum power flight involved a distinct danger of structural failure.

The A-1 was powered by Jumo 211B-1s and mounted a defensive armament of (initially) three 7·9 mm. machine guns; one in a fixed mounting on the starborad side of the canopy front, one slightly offset to port in the rear of the canopy and one in the ventral gondola. Experience in the Battle of Britain proved that this was an inadequate defensive battery and some machines were fitted with a second gun in the rear of the canopy. Normal warload was 3,968 lb.–5,510 lb., the bulk of which was carried on four external pylons. The pylons were installed, in pairs, under each wing between the fuselage and the nacelle. The four crew members were positioned close together in the nose; the pilot in a raised seat to port, the bombardier/air gunner to the pilot's right, and below him in the body of the fuselage; the engineer/air gunner occupied a prone position in the ventral gondola, facing to the rear. The wireless operator/air gunner sat behind the pilot facing to the rear. In four-gun aircraft the ventral gunner doubled as a second upper rear gunner.

DEVELOPMENT OF THE JU 88A SERIES

Further development of the Ju 88A series can be traced through the following variants:

Ju 88A-2 Bomber. *Engines:* 2×Jumo 211B-1 of 1,200 h.p. each. *Armament:* 4×7·9 mm. MG 15. *Bomb Load:* 3,968 lb. *Span:* 59 ft. $10\frac{3}{4}$ in. *Length:* 47 ft. 1 in. *Loaded Weight:* 25,353 lb. *Ceiling:* 22,300 ft. *Max. Speed:* 286 m.p.h. *Range:* 1,553 miles.

This variant was similar to the A-1 but carried assisted take-off equipment.

Ju 88A-3 Trainer. *Engines:* 2×Jumo 211B-1 of 1,200 h.p. each. *Armament:* 4×7·9 mm. MG 15. *Bomb Load:* None. *Span:* 59 ft. $10\frac{3}{4}$ in. *Length:* 47 ft. 1 in. *Loaded Weight:* 22,200 lb. *Ceiling:* 22,300 ft. *Max. Speed:* 286 m.p.h. *Range:* 1,553 miles.

The A-3 was a conversion training variant of the A-1 with dual controls and duplicated instrumentation.

Ju 88A-4 Bomber. *Engines:* 2×Jumo 211B-1 of 1,200 h.p. each. *Armament:* 2×13 mm. MG 131; 3/4×7·9 mm. MG 81. *Bomb Load:* 5,510 lb. *Span:* 65 ft. $10\frac{1}{2}$ in. *Length:* 47 ft. $1\frac{1}{2}$ in. *Loaded Weight:* 26,700 lb. *Ceiling:* 27,880 ft. *Max. Speed:* 293 m.p.h. *Range:* 1,900 miles.

The Ju 88A-4 was the most important variant of the series. Entering production late in 1940, it embodied modifications which the shortcomings of the A-1 during the first year of the war had shown to be essential. The wing span was increased by six feet, the undercarriage strengthened and considerable armour protection installed around the crew positions. The exact armament pattern varied, but usually consisted of one MG 131 and one MG 81 firing forward, one single or twin MG 81 firing aft from the ventral gondola, and two MG 81 or one MG 131 firing aft from the rear of the canopy. All gun mountings were armoured. The bomb load could be raised by A.T.O. measures to 6,614 lb., the underwing carriers accommodating various combinations of 550-lb., 1,100-lb., and 2,200-lb. bombs. The A-4/Trop was a tropicalised variant with suitable additions to the internal equipment but no structural changes.

Detail of "beetle's eye" nose panels.

Luftwaffe gunners in position at early-style double rear gun mountings. In later models armour-glass "lenses" were fitted on either side of the cockpit rear. (Photos: R. Ward Collection)

Ju 88A-4/R, as supplied to the Finnish Air Force.

Ju 88A-4/R Bomber. *Engines:* 2×Jumo 211J of 1,410 h.p. each. *Armament:* 5×7·9 mm. MG 81. *Bomb Load:* 6,614 lb. *Span:* 65 ft. 10½ in. *Length:* 47 ft. 1½ in. *Loaded Weight:* 31,000 lb. *Ceiling:* 27,880 ft. *Max. Speed:* 273 m.p.h. *Range:* 1,553 miles.

Twenty examples of the A-4/R variant were supplied to the Finnish Air Force for operations against Soviet forces.

Ju 88A-5 Bomber. *Engines:* 2×Jumo 211B-1 (or 211D) of 1,200 h.p. each. *Armament:* 2×13 mm. MG 131; 3×7·9 mm. MG 15. *Bomb Load:* 4,410 lb. *Span:* 65 ft. 10½ in. *Length:* 47 ft. 1½ in. *Loaded Weight:* 27,557 lb. *Ceiling:* 27,880 ft. *Max. Speed:* 280 m.p.h. *Range:* 1,398 miles.

Illogically, the A-5 variant preceded the A-4 into production by a few months late in 1940. It was basically an A-1 with the increased span and bomb load capacity, but lacked many of the other refinements which were built into the A-4. Balloon cable cutters could be fitted to the wing leading edges.

Ju 88A-6 Balloon destroyer. *Engines:* 2×Jumo 211G of 1,200 h.p. each. *Armament:* 4×7·9 mm. MG 15. *Bomb Load:* None. *Span:* 65 ft. 10½ in. *Length:* 47 ft. 1½ in. *Loaded Weight:* app. 27,900 lb. *Ceiling:* 23,620 ft. *Max. Speed:* 261 m.p.h. *Range:* 1,553 miles.

Basically similar to the A-5, the A-6 carried a balloon cable fender/cutter framework. This equipment, which extended as an angular frame from wingtip to wingtip along the leading edges and round the nose, was very unwieldy and made necessary the addition of a 130 lb. trimming weight in the tail section. The A-6 saw only limited service. (For a photograph of the fender gear as installed on the A-6, see page 6 of *Profile* No. 15, *The Heinkel He 111H*.)

Ju 88A-6/U Long-range reconnaissance aircraft. *Engines:* 2×Jumo 211H of 1,200 h.p. each. *Armament:* 3×7·9 mm. MG 81. *Bomb Load:* None. *Span:* 65 ft. 10½ in. *Length:* 47 ft. 1½ in. *Loaded Weight:* 24,250 lb. *Ceiling:* 23,620 ft. *Max. Speed:* 295 m.p.h. *Range:* 1,864 miles.

The A-6/U carried a three-man crew only. The ventral gondola was omitted and search radar equipment carried.

Ju 88A-7 Trainer. *Engines:* 2×Jumo 211B-1 of 1,200 h.p. each. *Armament:* 3/4×7·9 mm. MG 15. *Bomb Load:* None. *Span:* 65 ft. 10½ in. *Length:* 47 ft.

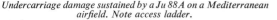

Left: *Luftwaffe aircrew await the order to "mount" their Ju-88A-4.* Right: *This captured Ju 88A-6U reconnaissance aircraft displays search radar antennae on the wing leading edge. The ventral gondola has been omitted and long-range fuel tanks are fitted under the wing roots.*

Undercarriage damage sustained by a Ju 88A on a Mediterranean airfield. Note access ladder.

Ju 88A-4s of 5/KG 3 "Blitz Geschwader" in tight formation; this Wing operated on the Russian Front throughout the campaign.

V 4 + K N, a Ju 88A-4 of 5/KG 1 "Hindenburg". The gondola, carrying twin MG 81 machine guns, is hanging open.
(Photo: Imperial War Museum)

$1\frac{1}{2}$ in. *Loaded Weight:* Unknown. *Ceiling:* 23,620 ft. *Max. Speed:* 295 m.p.h. *Range:* 1,550 miles.

A dual control training variant modified from early production A-4 airframes.

Ju 88A-8 Balloon destroyer. This version differed from the A-6 in being constructed around an A-4 airframe.

Ju 88A-9 Bomber. An alternative designation for tropicalised A-1 airframes.

Ju 88A-10 Bomber. An alternative designation for tropicalised A-5 airframes.

Ju 88A-11 Bomber. An alternative designation for tropicalised A-4 airframes.

Ju 88A-12 Trainer. *Engines:* $2 \times$ Jumo 211G of 1,200 h.p. each. *Armament:* None. *Bomb Load:* None. *Span:* 65 ft. $10\frac{1}{2}$ in. *Length:* 47 ft. $1\frac{1}{2}$ in. *Max. Speed:* 298 m.p.h. *Ceiling:* 23,620 ft.

A dual control trainer variant of the A-4 with ventral gondola removed and increased cockpit width.

Ju 88A-13 Close support aircraft. *Engines:* $2 \times$ Jumo 211H of 1,200 h.p. each. *Armament:* $10/16 \times 7\cdot9$ mm. MG 17; $4 \times 7\cdot9$ mm. MG 81. *Bomb Load:* 1,100 lb. *Span:* 65 ft. $10\frac{1}{2}$ in. *Length:* 47 ft. $1\frac{1}{2}$ in. *Loaded Weight:* 28,660 lb. *Ceiling:* 23,620 ft. *Max Speed:* 261 m.p.h. *Range:* Unknown.

The A-13 was a heavily armoured ground attack variant. Bomb load usually consisted of a *Schuett-kaesten* container of 72 small anti-personnel bombs under each wing. Many examples of this variant were fitted with automatic pull-out devices as the type was not equipped with dive brakes.

Ju 88A-14 Maritime attack bomber. *Engines:* $2 \times$ Jumo 211J of 1,410 h.p. each. *Armament:* $2 \times 7\cdot9$ mm. MG 15; 2×13 mm. MG 131. *Bomb Load:* 5,510 lb. *Span:* 65 ft. $10\frac{1}{2}$ in. *Length:* 47 ft. $1\frac{1}{2}$ in. *Loaded Weight:* 26,700 lb. *Ceiling:* 23,620 ft. *Max. Speed:* 273 m.p.h. *Range:* 1,550 miles.

The anti-shipping variant of the basic A-4 conception, the A-14 was fitted with electric balloon-cable cutters in the leading edges.

Ju 88A-15 Bomber. *Engines:* $2 \times$ Jumo 211G of 1,200 h.p. each. *Armament:* $2 \times 7\cdot9$ mm. MG 15; 2×13 mm. MG 131. *Bomb Load:* 6,614 lb. *Span:* 65 ft. $10\frac{1}{2}$ in. *Length:* 47 ft. $1\frac{1}{2}$ in. *Loaded Weight:* 28,247 lb. *Ceiling:* 23,620 ft. *Max. Speed:* 280 m.p.h. *Range:* 1,550 miles.

The A-15 variant was basically an A-4 airframe with a large bulged bomb bay. The 6,614-lb. bomb load was carried internally.

Ju 88A-16 Trainer. There was no essential difference between the A-12 and this improved version.

Ju 88A-17 Torpedo bomber. *Engines:* $2 \times$ Jumo 211J of 1,410 h.p. each. *Armament:* $3/5 \times 7\cdot9$ mm. MG 81. *Bomb Load:* Max. 6,614 lb. Usually, $2 \times 2,200$ lb. torpedoes. *Span:* 65 ft. $10\frac{1}{2}$ in. *Length:* 47 ft. $1\frac{1}{2}$ in. *Loaded Weight:* 25,350 lb. *Ceiling:* 28,215 ft. *Max. Speed:* 295 m.p.h. *Range:* 1,860 miles.

The Ju 88A-13 carried a battery of up to 16 MG 17 machine guns for close support missions. Containers of 72 anti-personnel bombs were carried under the wings.
(Photo: Imperial War Museum)

Snow-camouflaged Ju 88A during a pre-flight "warm-up" in Russia. (Photo: R. Ward Collection)

A torpedo-carrying conversion of the A-4 airframe. The two outboard bomb pylons were discarded; the two inboard pylons replaced by torpedo shackles, and a small instrument pod faired to the lower starboard side of the nose giving access to the torpedo steering gyros for in-flight adjustment.

THE JU 88A IN SERVICE

Pre-production Ju 88A-Os and the initial batch of A-1s served briefly with I/KG 25 in the summer of 1939. The unit had been formed by simply re-naming *Erprobungskommando 88* in August of that year. In September I/KG 25 became the first *Gruppe* of KG 30 "*Adler Geschwader*", the first and most famous of all operational Ju 88 units. KG 30 was occupied in the early months of the war on anti-shipping strikes in the North Sea and round the east coast of Scotland, and

participated in the major raid in March 1940 on the naval base of Scapa Flow. The unit was active during the invasion of Norway and operated from Denmark during the Battle of Britain. Other Ju 88-equipped units involved in that epic campaign included KG 51, KG 54, KG 76, KGr 806 and LG 1. In the reconnaissance rôle the Ju 88 served with *Aufklärungsgruppen* (F) 120, 121 and 123 on the establishment of *Luftflotte* III.

It would be impossible in a work of this size to give a complete breakdown of the Ju 88s unparalleled war service, but a brief summary of the main units which operated this aircraft follows. The symbols in brackets refer to unit codes; see paragraph on *Luftwaffe Units and Markings* below.

KG 1 "Hindenburg" (V4): The He 111Hs of III/KG 1 were replaced by Ju 88A-5s in the late summer of 1940. Complete re-equipment of I/KG 1, II/KG 1 and the *Geschwader* Staff with the Ju 88 was not achieved until October 1942. The unit was disbanded during the summer of 1944 after operations in Russia, Italy and the Middle East.

KG 2 "Holzhammer" (U5): This unit operated a single *Staffel* of Ju 88s on the Western Front for a short period.

KG 3 "Blitz" (5K): By June 1941 the *Geschwader* Staff, I/KG 3 and II/KG 3 had received the Ju 88A-5. The third *Gruppe* received the aircraft during operations in Russia, where the *Geschwader* operated throughout the war.

KG 4 "General Wever" (5J): The *Geschwader* Staff and III/KG 4 were equipped with the Ju 88 in the summer of 1940, but relinquished the aircraft for replacement by the He 111H before June 1941. It is unlikely that the unit ever used the Ju 88A on active service.

KG 6 (3E): Equipped with the Ju 88A for operations in the West upon its formation in May 1942. Saw limited service on all fronts, and relinquished the Ju 88 early in 1944.

KG 26 "Löwen Geschwader" (1H): III/KG 26 operated the Ju 88 briefly in July 1942. The A-14 variant was issued to the *Geschwader* in April/May 1944 for anti-shipping operations. The unit operated in Norway, the Baltic, and the Mediterranean theatre.

KG 30 "Adler Geschwader" (4D): As stated above, this unit was the first true *Kampfgeschwader* to receive the Ju 88A in 1939, and went on to operate the A-O, A-1, A-4, A-5 and later types in Scandinavia, the Balkans, Russia and Southern Europe throughout the

A Ju 88A of 7/KG 30 during that unit's service in the Balkans.

(Photo: R. Ward Collection)

Non-standard Ju 88A-4, with 20 mm. cannon mounted in the nose "glass-house".

Trial mounting of an MG FF cannon in the forward part of a Ju 88A-4 gondola. (Photo: G. Heumann/Air Pictorial)

whole duration of the European war. In the final stages of the hostilities KG 30 was equipped with a few examples of *Mistel* flying bombs, consisting of converted Ju 88A-4s containing a 7,726-lb. hollow charge warhead guided and controlled by a single-engined fighter mounted on a framework above it.

KG 40 (F8): Upon its formation in July 1940 the Staff element of this *Geschwader* was issued with the Ju 88A-1. II/KG 40 exchanged its He 177As for Ju 88s in September 1943 for operations in Italy.

KG 51 "Edelweis" (9K): The second *Geschwader* to receive the Ju 88(A-5), KG 51 participated in the Battle of Britain and in the first two years' operations on the Russian Front. The Ju 88 was withdrawn from this unit over a period of months beginning in April 1943.

KG 54 "Totenkopf" (B6): Fully equipped with the Ju 88 by August 1940, the three *Gruppen* of the

"Death's Head Wing" took part in the Battle of Britain. Operations in Russia in late 1941 were followed by service in the Mediterranean in the spring of 1942 and a limited participation in the night attacks on the United Kingdom during January 1944.

KG 60 (P1): A little-known unit which despite its *Geschwader* designation probably had an effective strength of only one *Gruppe*. Thought to have operated the Ju 88 in Scandinavia and the Mediterranean between October 1942 and the early spring of 1943.

KG 76 (F1): Flew the Ju 88A as part of *Luftflotte* II in the Battle of Britain. Saw service in Russia and Sicily, returning to France as part of the *Luftwaffe* build-up shortly after D-Day.

KG 77 (3Z): Equipped with the Ju 88A-5 in November/December 1940. Operated for a year in Russia until May/June 1942 when the unit was transferred to Sicily. Disbanded in Italy after the Axis defeats of mid-1943.

Lehregeschwader 1 (L1): Following there-organisation of this training *Geschwader* in the first winter of the war, LG 1 operated three *Gruppen* of Ju 88As. The unit saw service on all major fronts and remained an effective unit until 1945. It is best known for its operations in the North African campaign with the Ju 88A-4/Trop.

(The coastal strike units Ku.Fl.Gr.106 and Ku.Fl. Gr.506 were re-designated KGr 106 and KGr 506 in the spring of 1941. Coded M2 and S4 respectively, these units operated Ju 88A-4s and A-5s on mine-laying operations until the following summer, when they were disbanded. KGr 28, previously KGr 126, operated A-17s on torpedo strikes.)

KGr 806 (M7): Took part in the Battle of Britain with the Ju 88A-1, and later saw service in Russia and the Middle East with the Ju 88A-4.

Lehregeschwader 1 operated the Ju 88A-4/Trop during the Western Desert campaigns. This crash-landed machine served with the 1st Staffel of LG 1. (Photo: Imperial War Museum)

Russian Navy personnel examine a Ju 88A-4 of KG 30 brought down by naval gunfire on the shores of the Barents Sea. (Photo: Imperial War Museum)

Ju 88A REAR ARMAMENT

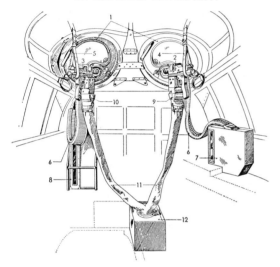

1. Armour-glass gun mountings LLK 81 VE.

2 & 3. Left and right 7·9 mm. MG 81 J machine guns.

4 & 5. Left and right strap rear mountings.

6. Flexible metal-link ammunition belts.

7 & 8. Ammunition belt storage lockers.

9 & 10. Left and right spent cartridge-case chutes.

11 & 12. Sleeve and box for collection of spent cartridge-cases.

LUFTWAFFE UNITS AND MARKINGS

The basic *Luftwaffe* tactical unit was the *Geschwader*. The bomber *Geschwader* (*Kampfgeschwader* or KG) consisted of three, four, or five *Gruppen*, each of which was in turn made up of three *Staffeln*. These sub-units were numbered independently; thus I/KG 76 (the first *Gruppe* of *Kampfgeschwader* 76) consisted of 1/KG 76 (the first *Staffel* of *Kampfgeschwader* 76), 2/KG 76 and 3/KG 76. Similarly, 7/KG 76, 8/KG 76 and 9/KG 76 made up the strength of III/KG 76.

The operational strengths of these formations varied greatly, but an average *Staffel* mustered between ten and sixteen aircraft, thus giving a *Geschwader* an establishment of some 110–150 machines.

Kampfgeschwader, Stuka Geschwader, Nachtjagdgeschwader, Zerstörergeschwader, Transportgeschwader, Aufklärungsgruppen (Reconnaissance Squadrons) and miscellaneous units used a four-symbol code on the fuselage sides of aircraft for identification purposes. A numerical/letter code appeared on the left-hand side of the national marking, identifying the *Geschwader*; e.g.,

A Ju 88A taxies out to take off with an external bomb load. (Photo: R. Ward Collection)

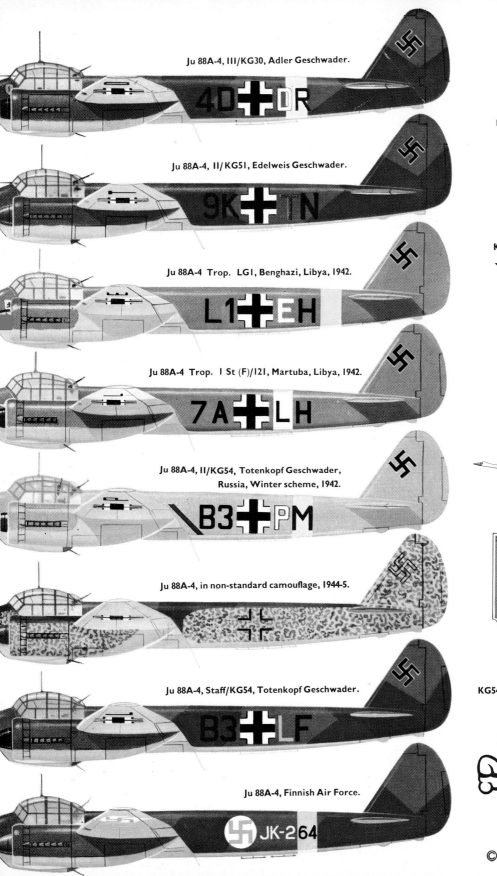

Ju 88A-4, III/KG30, Adler Geschwader.

4D+DR

Ju 88A-4, II/KG51, Edelweis Geschwader.

9K+TN

Ju 88A-4 Trop. LG1, Benghazi, Libya, 1942.

L1+EH

Ju 88A-4 Trop. 1 St (F)/121, Martuba, Libya, 1942.

7A+LH

Ju 88A-4, II/KG54, Totenkopf Geschwader, Russia, Winter scheme, 1942.

B3+PM

Ju 88A-4, in non-standard camouflage, 1944-5.

Ju 88A-4, Staff/KG54, Totenkopf Geschwader.

B3+LF

Ju 88A-4, Finnish Air Force.

JK-264

III/KG30, Adler Geschw.

KG51, Edelweis Geschw.

LG1.

1 St (F)/121.

II/KG54

KG54 Totenkopf Geschw.

© W ARRO

Converted Ju 88A-4s carried a 7,726-lb. hollow charge warhead as the lower component of the Great Beethoven/Mistel 2 composite weapon. The machine, illustrated here, was guided onto target by the Bf 109F mounted on the framework above the centre-section. Note the protruding detonators in the nose-probe.

4D=KG 30. From 1943 onwards this combination either appeared in very small characters or was omitted altogether. Sometimes it was reproduced in small characters on the vertical tail surfaces of bombers, and often temporary camouflage finishes were applied in such a way as to obscure it.

On the right of the national marking two letters appeared. The first, painted or outlined in the *Staffel* colour, or in green on staff aircraft, identified the individual aircraft. The second letter identified the *Staffel* within the *Geschwader*. Towards the end of the war, it increasingly became the practice for the individual marking only to be applied to the fuselage; and this was often repeated under the wingtips.

© *Martin C. Windrow, 1965.*

Ju 88A NOSE ARMAMENT

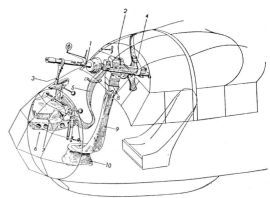

1. Lg 81 VE gun mounting.
2. MG 81 J machine gun (7·9 mm.).
3. Adjustable forward mount.
4. Strap rear mounting.
5. Flexible metal-link ammunition belt.
6 & 7. Ammunition belt storage locker.
8. Spent cartridge-case chute.
9 & 10. Spent cartridge-case collection bag.

Staff Aircraft Identification

These letters took the place of the fourth, or Staffel, symbol.

Geschwader Staff = A	III Gr.=D
I Gruppe = B	IV Gr.=E
II Gr. = C	V Gr.=F

STAFFEL IDENTIFICATION

Staffel Colour	I Gruppe	II Gruppe	III Gruppe	IV Gruppe	V Gruppe
White	1st Stfl. = H	4th Stfl. = M	7th Stfl. = R	10th Stfl. = U	13th Stfl. = X
Red	2nd Stfl. = K	5th Stfl. = N	8th Stfl. = S	11th Stfl. = V	14th Stfl. = Y
Yellow	3rd Stfl. = L	6th Stfl. = P	9th Stfl. = T	12th Stfl. = W	15th Stfl. = Z

Thus, machine B 3 + (White P) M was machine "P" of 4/KG 54.

PRINTED IN ENGLAND. © Profile Publications Ltd., P.O. Box 26, Leatherhead, Surrey, England, by George Falkner & Sons Ltd., for McCorquodale City Printing Division, London.

PROFILE
PUBLICATIONS

The
North
American
F-100
Super
Sabre

NUMBER 30

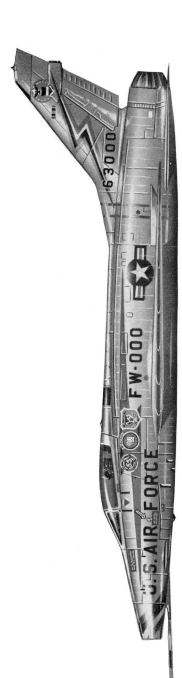

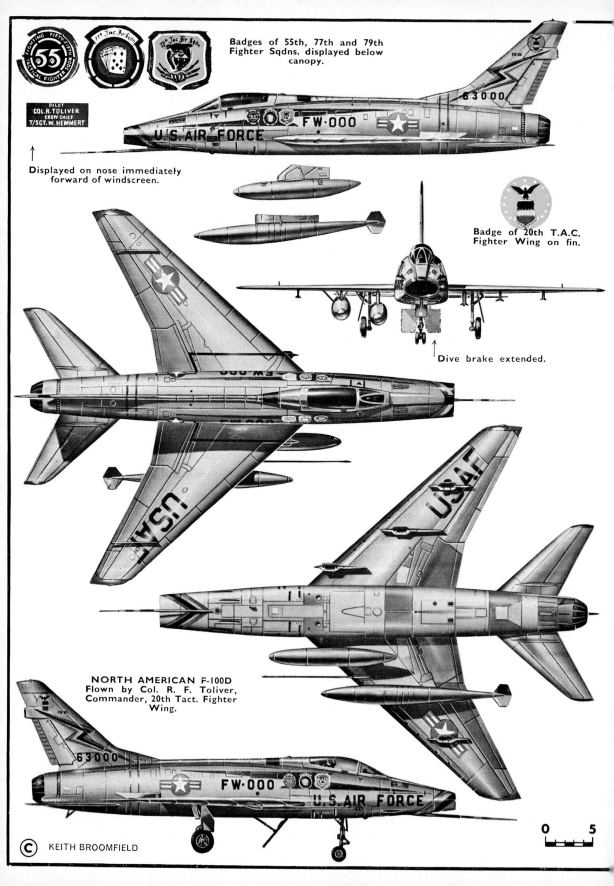

Badges of 55th, 77th and 79th Fighter Sqdns. displayed below canopy.

PILOT
COL. R. TOLIVER
CREW CHIEF
T/SGT. W. HEMMERT

Displayed on nose immediately forward of windscreen.

Badge of 20th T.A.C. Fighter Wing on fin.

Dive brake extended.

NORTH AMERICAN F-100D
Flown by Col. R. F. Toliver, Commander, 20th Tact. Fighter Wing.

0   5

The North American F-100 Super Sabre

by Ray Wagner

F-100C-10s of the Skyblazers in formation.   (Photo: U.S.A.F.)

As the first supersonic fighter in service in the Western world, the North American F-100 Super Sabre introduced the "Century Series" fighters with their greater complexity of construction, new dimensions of performance, and the sonic booms now common around military air bases.

The evolution of this design began in February 1949 with efforts to improve the F-86 Sabre by achieving supersonic speeds. By 14th September 1949, an advanced version of the F-86D interceptor was designed with 45 degree sweep on the wing and tail surfaces.

Demands for improved fighters increased after the appearance of the MiG-15 in the Korean war, and favourable Air Force reception of the "Sabre 45" prompted North American to initiate engineering work on their NA-180 design at Los Angeles on 19th January 1951.

An initial contract was awarded by the Air Force on 1st November 1951 for two YF-100A prototypes and a production version begun as the NA-192 (F-100A) on 20th November. Newly discovered aerodynamic refinements to improve speed were incorporated on the mockup, approved by the Air Force on 26th August 1952. Among these changes were the increase of the fuselage's fineness ratio, an extended clamshell canopy, and lowering the horizontal tail (as tested on a YF-86D).

The first YF-100A (*52-5754*) was completed on schedule, 24th April 1953, and was secretly moved from the Los Angeles factory to Edwards Air Force Base, California. There George Welch, the company's chief test pilot who had first flown the F-86, made the first flight of the YF-100A on 25th May. The speed of sound was exceeded on the first flight, and on a second one made that same day.

The source of the Super Sabre's speed was, in the first place, the powerplant, a Pratt & Whitney J57-P-7

two-stage turbojet rated at 9,700 lb. military thrust, and 14,800 lb. with afterburner. All the fuel was contained in the long fuselage, and air was fed in through the nose ram inlet.

The thin wing had 45-degree sweep, automatic leading edge slats, mid-span lateral control surfaces, and a span of 36 ft. 7 in. in its original form. Longitudinal control was achieved by movement of the entire one-piece horizontal tail, combining the functions of elevator and stabiliser in one surface set low enough to be almost directly behind the wing. The vertical fin was also swept back, with a thin rudder. The control system was hydraulically-powered and irreversible.

Other features of the F-100 included a hydraulically-operated speed brake underneath the fuselage, and a drag-chute to shorten ground roll. The cockpit had a one-piece clamshell canopy, ejection seat, and automatic air conditioning and pressurisation system. The main wheels retracted inwards into the fuselage, and twin nose wheels folded backwards.

Heat-resisting titanium was utilised from the initial design stage, for the first time in an aeroplane. North

The first Super Sabre prototype, the YF-100A, in flight.
(Photo: Peter M. Bowers)

The second F-100A-5 with original fin and rudder. (Photo: Peter M. Bowers)

American used 80 per cent of all the titanium produced in the United States until 1954. Empty weight on the YF-100A was 18,135 lb., and gross weight was 28,561 lb.; compared to 10,890 and 17,921 lb. for the F-86F being produced at the same time.

SPEED RECORD ATTEMPT

By 15th September 1953 the Air Force had completed the YF-100A Phase II test programme, making 39 flights of 19 hours and 42 minutes duration, and demonstrating performance superior to any U.S. fighter at that time. When the YF-100A was first shown to the public on 20th October 1953, the press reported that the sonic booms from its low-level supersonic dives shattered windows and "left on-lookers gasping and children crying". At that time, the world's speed record was 753·4 m.p.h., set by a Douglas A4D-1 Skyray. The first attempt by the YF-100A over a 3 km. course reached 757·75 m.p.h., but failed to beat the Skyray mark over the same course by the one per cent required in F.A.I. rules.

Another try was made over a 15 km. course, where the one per cent margin would not apply. On 29th October 1953, piloted by Lt.-Colonel F. K. (Pete) Everest, chief of flight test operations laboratory at Edwards Air Force Base, the YF-100A set a new record of 755·149 m.p.h. over a Salton Sea course. It was not then revealed that this speed, flown at only 100 feet from the ground, was about 100 m.p.h. under the plane's actual design speed in the thin air of 35,000 feet.

On the same day this record was set, George Welch made the first flight of a production F-100A, 52-5756. It was similar in appearance to the prototypes except for a shorter vertical tail, with a small rudder below a fuel vent tube. Armament consisted of four 20 mm. M-39 guns installed below the cockpit with 800 rounds of ammunition. This gun had been tested in Korea on modified F-86Fs as the T-160, and fired 1,500 rounds per minute at a muzzle velocity of 3,300 feet per second. A radar-ranging device was installed in the upper lip of the nose inlet.

The F-100A's mission was seen as "air superiority" fighting, of the kind the F-86 had done over Korea. It would take off with two 275-gallon tanks at a gross weight of 28,899 lb., fly out to a combat radius of over 350 miles, and drop its tanks for battle. At a combat weight (60 per cent fuel) of 24,996 lb., top speed ranged from 760 m.p.h. (Mach 1) at sea level to 852 m.p.h. (Mach 1·285) at 35,000 feet. At take-off weight, service ceiling (where climb is 100 ft./min.) was 44,900 feet, while at combat weight, the combat ceiling (500 ft./min. climb) reached 51,000 feet. These were the characteristics of the final service configura-

tion, and were far ahead of its contemporaries, but the Super Sabre was a highly sophisticated aircraft that would take a lot of experience to become fully operational.

INTO SQUADRON SERVICE

The first Air Force operational unit to receive the F-100A was the Tactical Air Command 479th Fighter Day Wing, which received its Super Sabres at George Air Foce Base, California, in September 1954. At that time the U.S.A.F. had 12 F-84F, 13 F-86F, and three F-86H wings available for day fighting, plus 28 all-weather defence wings. Operational service of the first supersonic type, however, was delayed by an order issued 11th November, suddenly grounding the F-100.

As the pioneer of supersonic flying, the Super Sabre had run into a stability problem that had caused a series of accidents, one causing the death of George Welch. On 12th October 1954, the veteran test pilot had taken 52-5764 for the most rugged structural test yet made; a supersonic dive with a pullout at 23,700 feet. The F-100A came apart in the dive, causing a hunt for clues that did succeed in recovering some of the test instruments.

It was realised that the danger came from violent

Sixtieth production F-100A-10. (Photo: Peter M. Bowers)

Above: *Thirtieth production F-100A-11 (ex-F-100A-10)*. Below: *F-100A-1 of the Connecticut Air Guard.*
(Photo: R. W. Harrison)

The first F-100C-1 with original short fin and rudder.
(Photo: North American Aviation)

and wild gyrations of the aircraft which the pilot was unable to control. Normally, aircraft pitch and yaw is restrained by the tail. If these forces exceed the power of the vertical tail to restrain the aircraft, it may go violently out of control.

Modifications were made in the F-100 to solve this problem, and after three months the Super Sabre could be restored to flying status. These modifications were made on planes still on the assembly line, as well as about 70 F-100As already built. The vertical tail was made higher, increasing area about 27 per cent. Another foot was added to each wing tip, increasing wing area from 376 to 385 sq. ft. These additions, along with minor changes in lateral and longitudinal control systems to improve pilot feel, made it possible to perform unco-ordinated rolls without trouble.

With the aircraft safety well in hand, the biggest problem facing U.S.A.F. units became the training of ground crews to keep the new type flying. Here the problem was that the U.S.A.F. was reaching its peak size at the time large numbers of mechanics enlisted during the Korean build-up were returning to civilian life. Operation Toolbox was a programme carried out

The 36th production F-100C-1 with production fin and rudder.
(Photo: Peter M. Bowers)

The second F-100D-1. Below: F-100F-10..
(Photos: Peter M. Bowers)

to provide the technical personnel needed to keep the Tactical Air Force types flying.

The various safety features of the Super Sabre stood up well in service. The pilot's ejection seat, for example, saved the life of company test pilot George F. Smith on 26th February 1955, in a low-altitude supersonic bailout. Smith was in F-100A-10 *53-1659* when a hydraulic lock caused an uncontrollable dive. He ejected at Mach 1·05 (777 m.p.h.) and was severely injured, but recovered to fly again.

Recognition of the Super Sabre's success came with the presentation of the Collier Trophy, the United States' outstanding aviation award, to North American's Board Chairman, J. H. Kindelberger, by President Dwight Eisenhower on 17th December 1954.

Production of the F-100A was completed in April 1955 with 203 aircraft. Those from number 167 on had the J57-P-39, of the same power as the P-7.

THE F-100 C

Meanwhile, new models of the Super Sabre were planned. An all-weather F-100B version was designed which developed into the NA-212 project begun 20th October 1953. The design eventually emerged as the F-107 fighter-bomber with a 23,500 lb. thrust Pratt & Whitney J75, and the air intake above and behind the cockpit.

A fighter-bomber version was planned in the F-100C, designated by the Air Force 30th December 1953, with the company designation NA-214. A production contract was placed in February 1954, the first strengthened wing was tested on F-100A-1, *52-5759*, in July, and the first F-100C was completed in October. Al White made the first flight on 17th January 1955 in 53-1709. It had the original F-100A tail then, but got a new fin later.

Bomb-carrying capability of the F-100A had been limited to a pair of 1,000 lb. bombs. The F-100C had six underwing stations for 750 lb. bombs or other stores up to a maximum of 5,000 lb. The largest store that could be carried was a MK-7 nuclear weapon, which was released by an MA-2 low altitude bombing system (LABS). This system permitted "toss" or loft-bombing, in which the aircraft escapes an explosion much larger than that at Hiroshima by releasing the weapon near the top of a loop, throwing it away from the flight path.

For air-to-air combat, the F-101C had the usual four 20 mm. M-39 guns, and could add 42 2·75 in. rockets in two packs. Internal fuel capacity was increased from 744 gallons in the F-100A to 1,702 gallons, and an in-flight refuelling system was added. These features increased the Super Sabre's capability

from local air superiority to long-range penetration for fighter-bomber or escort missions.

A Pratt & Whitney J57-P-21 giving 10,200 lb. military thrust and 16,000 lb. with afterburner increased the F-100C's top speed, despite nearly 2,600 lb. of added combat weight. This was demonstrated by a new world's speed record set 20th August 1955. New telescopic cameras were used to time runs made at 40,000 feet over the Mojave Desert, Palmdale, California, by Colonel Horace A. Haines, and recorded a speed of 870·627 m.p.h. in one direction and 733·644 m.p.h. in the other, for an average of 822·135 m.p.h. Even this record, however, was a modest exhibit of F-100C speed, actually listed by official records at 924 m.p.h. at 35,000 feet and 904 m.p.h. at 39,500 feet.

Other improvements in the C model included single-point refuelling and a modified vertical tail. Despite its similarity to the older model, the F-100C required more than 287,000 engineering man-hours and 6,934 engineering drawings to produce, in addition to the two million engineering man-hours expended on the F-100A.

The F-100C was delivered to the 322nd Fighter Day Group at Foster Air Base, Texas, on 14th July 1955. It soon joined other Tactical Air Command units in the U.S. and abroad, and was the colourful mount of the U.S.A.F. Skyblazers aerobatic team. A total of 451 F-100Cs were built in Los Angeles by April 1956.

North American's Columbus, Ohio, plant was designated as a second source for Super Sabre production on 11th October 1954. The company project number for the first Columbus F-100C was NA-222, while the Air Force designation was F-100C-10-NH, the NH suffix distinguishing this factory's products from the F-100C-5-NA, and other ships of the Los Angeles (NA) home plant. The first of 25 F-100C-10-NHs, *55-2709*, was flown 8th September 1955.

THE 'D' VARIANT

An improved version of the Super Sabre was designated F-100D by the Air Force on 27th September 1954, and NA-223 by the company, and manufacturing began in July 1955, with the first aircraft, *54-2121*, finished in November.

First flown by test pilot Dan Darnell on 24th January 1956, the F-100D had a higher tail fin and a wider wing root chord increasing wing area to 400·18

Above is a F-100D Super Sabre of the 405th Fighter Squadron, Bangkok, Thailand. The Cobra motif was adopted by the squadron when stationed in Thailand in 1962.

F-100C two seat trainer of the 405th Fighter Squadron featured the 'Speedbird' motif on the fin, but lacked the Thai Cobra.

Above: *FW-263, starboard side, with Cobra facing forward.*

Below: *FW-280 displays flight refuelling probe. Note various markings on nosewheel doors.*   (Photos: via Richard Ward)

'Triple Zilch', an F-100D-65-NA of the 55th Tactical Fighter Squadron, 20th Tactical Fighter Wing, with the blue lightning fuselage streak applied when it was allocated to the 55th.
(Photo: Official U.S.A.F., via G. Letzer)

Left: 'Triple Zilch' with lightning streak removed and new air intake colour scheme. Right: F-100D-25-NA in the colour scheme it bore when representing the U.S.A.F., Europe, (20th T.F.W.) at an Annual Gunnery Meet.
(Photos: Official U.S.A.F., via G. Letzer)

sq. ft. A Minneapolis-Honeywell MB-3 automatic pilot, the first developed expressly for a supersonic jet, was intended to allow the pilot to concentrate on navigation or tactics while the F-100D flew itself to the target.

Improved electronic LABS equipment was fitted to deliver a MK-7, MK-38, or MK-43 nuclear store. For plane-to-plane "buddy tanker" refuelling, a pair of 450-gallon air-refuelling tanks could be carried. Conventional war loads might include six 750-lb. or four 1,000-lb. bombs, or two GAM-83A Bulldog air-to-surface missiles. For air-to-air combat, four GAR-8 Sidewinder heat-seeking missiles could be handled by the F-100D-60-NA (NA-235), and provision for launching these were added to some earlier aircraft.

North American made 940 F-100Ds in Los Angeles and 334 in Columbus, the latter beginning with the F-100D-35-NH (NA-224), 55-2734, first flown 12th June 1956.

TWO-SEAT F-100s

The last version of the Super Sabre built was a two-seater, intended for use as a combat proficiency trainer without loss of tactical capability. The front cockpit contained all controls for the armament, which is reduced to two 20 mm. guns, although external loads remained the same.

The first such two-seater was the TF-100C (NA-230), converted from F-100C-20, 54-1966. The first production F-100F-1 (no F-100E was made) was first flown by Alvin S. White on 3rd August 1956. Production of the F-100F continued until October 1959,

The final colour scheme of 'Triple Zilch', with fuselage flash and nose scheme removed.
(Photo: Official U.S.A.F., via G. Letzer)

Above: *F-100D-25-'000-HA'- of the 416th T.F.S.* (Photo: Mr. Menard)

Below: *F-100D of the 79th T.F.S., 20th T.F.W., Alconbury AFB, Hunts, U.K.* (Photo: via G. Letzer)

with 339 built, all in Los Angeles. Super Sabre production finally totalled 2,294, including 359 at Columbus.

The manufacture of the F-100 Super Sabre required new manufacturing techniques and processes, as well as the refinement of old methods.

A greater percentage of parts are machine milled for the F-100 than for any other aeroplane in North American's history. In addition, these parts are more complex. F-100 tooling has to be heavy and strong to hold parts milled from heavy gauge material.

The integrally stiffened wings are produced by sculpturing longerons and ribs out of aluminium plate up to one and three-quarters inch thick and then milling the plate to tapered thickness. These operations are performed on large horizontal milling machines which operate in tandem.

The trend towards large integrally stiffened parts

offers some offsetting advantages in reduced assembly time. For example, the F-86 wing structural box was made up of 462 pieces and put together with 16,084 fasteners. In contrast, the F-100A wing box requires 36 pieces and 264 fasteners.

The use of Keller type drilling is approximately 180 per cent greater for the F-100A than for the F-86 types.

The tolerances required on the F-100 are so small that normal temperature changes in the plant in the course of a day cause tool and material dimensions to change to such an extent that tolerances could not be held without special handling.

Only one F-100 wing, the 479th, was operational in June 1955, but six wings were ready the following year, and 16 by June 1957. After the U.S.A.F. passed the peak of its expansion, the F-100A and F-100C were passed down to Air National Guard units and some were sent to allied powers.

In 1964, ten F-100D wings were in operation, along

F-100D, Wright-Patterson AFB. (Photo: G. Letzer)

F-100D-20. (Photo: R. Beseker)

An F-100 D-15 with speed brake open. (Photo: North American Aviation)

The first F-100 F-1 undergoing flight tests. (Photo: North American Aviation)

Test TF-100C which was modified from an F-100C-20. Below: *F-100D-20s on a 'Buddy' flight refuelling sortie.*
(Photos: North American Aviation)

9

with eleven F-100A and F-100C squadrons in the Air National Guard.

Tactical Air Force wings with the F-100D, their associated squadrons, and headquarters were:

In the U.S.:

3 TFW (90, 416, 510, and 531) England AFB, La.

27 TFW (478, 522, 523, and 524) Cannon AFB, N.M.

31 TFW (306, 307, 308, and 309) Homestead AFB, Fla.

354 TFW (352, 353, 355, and 356) Myrtle Beach AFB, S.C.

401 TFW (612, 613, 614, and 615) England AFB, La.

474 TFW (428, 429, 430, and 481) Cannon AFB, N.M.
Overseas:

20 TFW (55, 77, and 79) Wethersfield, U.K.

48 TFW (492, 493, and 494) Lakenheath, U.K.

50 TFW (10, 81, and 417) Hahn, Germany.

405 TFW (511 [509 has F-102]) Clark AFB, Philippines.

Air National Guard squadrons:

152 FIS Tucson, Ariz.

188 TFS Albuquerque, N.M.

110 TFS St. Louis, Mo.

118 FIS Hartford, Conn.

119 TFS Atlantic City, N.J.

120 TFS Denver, Colo.

121 TFS District of Colombia.

127 TFS Wichita, Kansas.

136 TFS Niagara Falls, N.Y.

166 TFS Lcokbourne, Ohio.

174 TFS Sioux City, Iowa.

The first Super Sabres to go to foreign air forces were 80 F-100As modernised to D standards, sent to

One of the last F-100F-15s in service with the Danish Air Force.
(Photo- R. Beseker)

F-100F-15 of the French Air Force.   (Photo: R. Beseker)

F-100D-55.   (Photo: U.S.A.F. official)

Left: *Line-up of the Skyblazers F-100C-10s.* Right: *The Thunderbird's F-100C-25s.*   Below: *F-100C two-seater of the Skyblazers*
(Photos: G. Beseker and R. W. Harrison)

Stbd. side "Butcher Boy II" FW-263.

405th Fighter Squadron.

Thai. Cobra adopted by 405th.

F-100D Super Sabre, 405th Fighter Squadron, Bangkok, Thailand, 1962.

Outstanding Unit Award Ribbon.

Thunderbird insignia.

Marking detail of FW-235.

118 F. Sqdn. (the background colour varied).

100C, Thunderbirds Aerobatic Team. ▲

F-100C, 118 F. Sqdn. Connecticut Air National Guard.

55th T.F.S.

77th T.F.S.

79th Tactical Fighter Sqdn.

20th Tactical Fighter Wing.

100D-65-NA, "Triple Zilch", 20th Tactical Fighter Wing, R.A.F. Wethersfield, U.K., 1960.

F-100D-65-NA, 55th Tactical Fighter Squadron, 20th T.F.W., R.A.F. Wethersfield, U.K., 1957.

F-100D-65-NA, 79th Tactical Fighter Squadron, 20th T.F.W., R.A.F. Wethersfield, U.K., 1957.

© WARRD

F-100C at Wright-Patterson Air Force Base. Note the various modifications—under nose strake, afterburner and store on wing pylon.
(Photo: R. Beseker)

Nationalist China in 1960. Turkey received 260 F.100Cs for four fighter-bomber wings. The Royal Danish Air Force used the F-100D for its 725, 727, and 730 squadrons, while France's Armee de l'Air had Super Sabres for the 3rd and 11th Escadres de Chasse. All of these nations also used F-100Fs for pilot proficiency practice.

© *Ray Wagner, 1965.*

F-100 Serial Numbers

U.S.A.F. Type	N.A.A.	U.S.A.F. Serials	No. A/c
YF–100A–NA	NA–180	52–5754 thru 5755	2
F–100A–1–NA	–192	52–5756 thru 5765	107
F–100A–5–NA	,,	52–5766 thru 5778	13
F–100A–10–NA	,,	53–1529 thru 1568	40
F–100A–15–NA	,,	53–1569 thru 1608	40
F–100A–20–NA	,,	53–1609 thru 1708	100
F–100C–1–NA	–214	53–1709 thru 1778	70
F–100C–1–NA	–217	54–1740 thru 1769	30
F–100C–5–NA	,,	54–1770 thru 1814	45
F–100C–15–NA	,,	54–1815 thru 1859	45
F–100C–20–NA	,,	54–1860 thru 1970	111
F–100C–25–NA	,,	54–1971 thru 2120	150
F–100C–10–NH	–222	55–2709 thru 2733	25
F–100D–1–NA	–223	54–2121 thru 2132	12
F–100D–5–NA	,,	54–2133 thru 2151	19
F–100D–10–NA	,,	54–2152 thru 2221	70
F–100D–15–NA	,,	54–2222 thru 2303	82
F–100D–20–NA	,,	55–3502 thru 3601	100
F–100D–25–NA	,,	55–3602 thru 3701	100
F–100D–30–NA	,,	55–3702 thru 3814	113
F–100D–35–NH	–224	55–2734 thru 2743	10
F–100D–40–NH	,,	55–2744 thru 2783	40
F–100D–45–NH	,,	55–2784 thru 2863	80
F–100D–50–NH	,,	55–2864 thru 2908	45
F–100D–55–NH	,,	55–2909 thru 2954	46
F–100D–60–NA	–235	56–2903 thru 2962	60
F–100D–65–NA	,,	56–2963 thru 3022	60
F–100D–70–NA	,,	56–3023 thru 3142	120
F–100D–75–NA	,,	56–3143 thru 3198	56
F–100D–80–NH	–245	56–3351 thru 3378	28
F–100D–85–NH	,,	56–3379 thru 3463	85
F–100D–90–NA	–235	56–3199 thru 3346	148
F–100F–1–NA	–243	56–3725 thru 3739	15
F–100F–5–NA	,,	56–3740 thru 3769	30
F–100F–10–NA	,,	56–3770 thru 3919	150
F–100F–15–NA	,,	56–3920 thru 4019	100
F–100F–15–NA	–261	58–6975 thru 6983	9
F–100F–15–NA	–262	59–2558 thru 2563	6
F–100F–20–NA	–255	58–1205 thru 1233	29
		Total	2,294

SPECIFICATION

	F-100A	F-100C	F-100D
Span	38 ft. 9¾ in.	38 ft. 9⅞ in.	38 ft. 9¾ in.
Length	47 ft. 1¼ in.	47 ft. 1¼ in.	49 ft. 4 in.
Height	15 ft. 6 in.	15 ft. 6 in.	16 ft. 2 in.
Wing Area	385 sq. ft.	385 sq. ft.	400 sq. ft.
Engine	J57–P–7	J57–P–21	J57–P–21, or 21A
Thrust (Military)	9,700 lb.	10,200 lb.	10,200 lb.
Thrust (Afterburner)	14,800 lb.	16,000 lb.	16,000 lb.
Weight, Empty	18,185 lb.	19,270 lb.	20,638 lb.
Weight, Takeoff	28,899 lb.	32,615 lb.	34,050 lb.
Weight, Maximum Ferry	—	35,696 lb.	37,124 lb.
Weight, Combat	24,996 lb.	27,585 lb.	28,847 lb.
Fuel, Internal	744 gal.	1,702 gal.	1,739 gal.
Fuel, Maximum	1,294 gal.	2,139 gal.	2,139 gal.
Speed, Top (at 35,000 ft.)	852 m.p.h. (740 kts.)	925 m.p.h. (803 kts.)	910 m.p.h. (790 kts.)
Speed, Av. Cruising	589 m.p.h. (512 kts.)	593 m.p.h. (515 kts.)	590 m.p.h. (512 kts.)
Speed, Stalling	159 m.p.h. (138 kts.)	178 m.p.h. (146 kts.)	169 m.p.h. (147 kts.)
Service Ceiling	44,900 ft.	38,700 ft.	66,100 ft.
Combat Ceiling	51,000 ft.	49,100 ft.	47,700 ft.
Climb	23,800 ft./1 min.	21,600 ft./1 min. 35,000 ft./2·3 min.	19,000 ft./1 min. 35,000 ft./2·2min.
Combat Radius	358 miles (311 kts.)	572 miles (497 kts.)	534 miles (464 kts.)
Ferry Range	1,294 miles (1,124 kts.)	1,954 miles (1,697 kts.)	1,995 miles (1,750 kts.)

This data is from the official Standard Aircraft Characteristics charts dated January 1961 (F-100A), and September 1963 (F-100C and F-100D).

PRINTED IN ENGLAND. © Profile Publications Ltd., P.O. Box 26, Leatherhead, Surrey, England, by George Falkner & Sons Ltd., for McCorquodale City Printing Division, London.

PROFILE
PUBLICATIONS

The
Sopwith
Camel
F.1

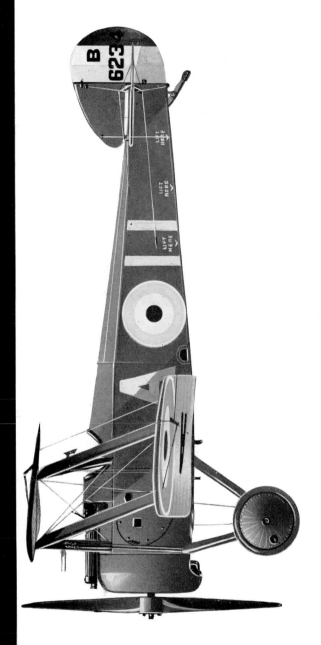

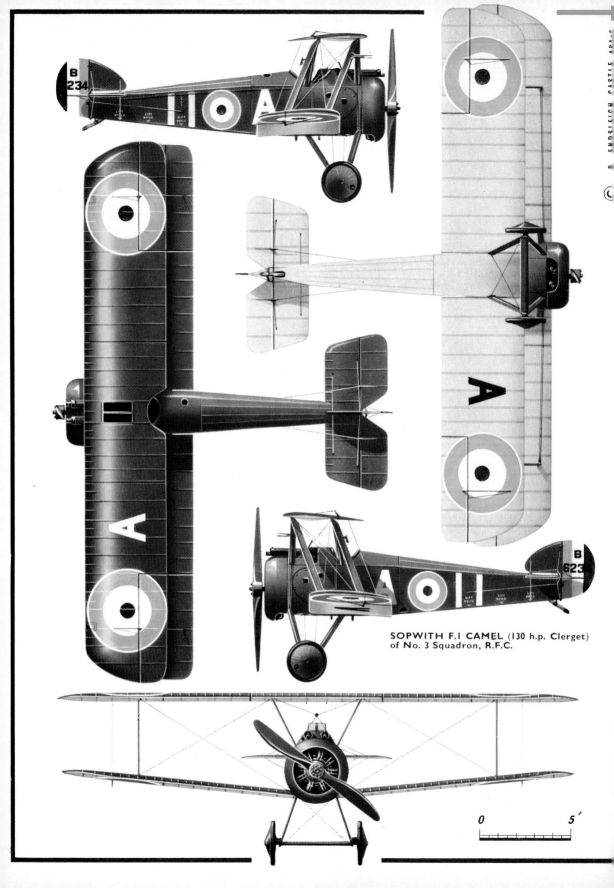

SOPWITH F.I CAMEL (130 h.p. Clerget)
of No. 3 Squadron, R.F.C.

0   5′

The Sopwith Camel F.I
by J. M. Bruce

Some of the Camels of No. 28 Squadron, operating in Italy, were given striking paint schemes. Captain Wilson stands beside "C", which bore its individual letter to the left of the cut-out, above the upper wing, with the squadron marking (a white square) to starboard.
(Photo: K. M. Molson)

In war's relentless school of experience the flying services quickly learned that, in aerial combat, victory most frequently went to the aircraft in which speed, climb, manœuvrability, strength, armament and a good view for the pilot were combined in the best proportions. In 1916 the slow but sturdy D.H.2 and F.E.2b had proved to be effective enough to combat the Fokker monoplanes, but the introduction in mid-September 1916 of the twin-gun Albatros D I, closely followed by the D II, placed aerial supremacy within the grasp of German fighter pilots.

The unequalled tractability of the Sopwith Pup and triplane enabled them to hold their own for several months, but it was obvious that a faster and more heavily armed single-seater would soon be needed to match the developments of the Albatros fighters. Herbert Smith's successor to his elegant little Pup and triplane was an unprepossessing little biplane the first example of which, powered by a 110-h.p. Clerget 9Z rotary engine, was passed by the Sopwith company's experimental department on 22nd December, 1916.

This aicraft, designated Sopwith F.1, was clearly descended from the Pup but had a deeper fuselage with a pair of Vickers guns partly faired over by a humped top decking immediately behind the engine cowling. The entire wooden airframe was conventional in structure, being typical of the period and, in

particular, of Herbert Smith's design. The F.1 was originally intended to have equal dihedral on upper and lower wings, but Fred Sigrist decided that the upper wing should be flat so that it could be made in one piece and thus speed production. As a rough rule-of-thumb compensation the dihedral of the lower wing was doubled. In the event, production aircraft had the upper wing made in three parts, but no attempt to restore equal dihedral was made. Ailerons were fitted to upper and lower mainplanes.

The number and relationship of the F.1 prototypes is not at present clear, but the following facts are known. The unnumbered prototype F.1/3 was built under Licence No. 6: this suggests that the Sopwith F.1 was conceived and the building of at least four prototypes undertaken as a private venture. Two prototypes, *N517* and *N518*, were ordered (separately, it seems, from the others) by the Admiralty at a very early stage: *N517* was tested at Brooklands on 26th February 1917. Two official reports describe the taper-wing prototype as the F.1/1 (apparently it did not acquire an official serial number), suggesting that it had followed the 110-h.p. F.1 in the Sopwith shops. A recorded reference to an F.1/2 has yet to be found, but an aircraft that might have qualified for that designation existed. It displayed several minor differences from the first F.1. The one-piece upper wing was

Left: The first Sopwith F.1 at Brooklands, winter 1916–17, with one-piece upper wing and short-span ailerons. There was no central cut-out, and the humped fairing over the guns sloped upwards to the cockpit in lieu of a windscreen. (Photo: Imperial War Museum).
Right: The Sopwith F.1/1 at Brooklands, spring 1917.

3

retained but had a central cut-out between the spars to improve the pilot's upward view; the shape of the top decking immediately behind the guns was modified and a small windscreen was fitted.

A further prototype, known to be F.1/3, was tested at Martlesham Heath in March 1917, powered originally by a 130-h.p. Clerget 9B No. 2730. The official report states:

> "Of the series of F.1 experimental machines the above No. F.1/3 was the type upon which the standard F.1 is based. The dimensions and tank capacities of the latter vary slightly from the above."

It seems that the F.1/3 prototype, like the F.1/1, did not receive an official serial number. In May 1917 it was tested with a 110-h.p. Le Rhône 9J engine (No. 100508/W.D.7917); in July it was being flown at Martlesham with a 130-h.p. long-stroke Clerget. The latter engine was probably the 140-h.p. Clerget 9Bf, which had a stroke of 172 mm.; the stroke of the 130-h.p. Clerget 9B was 160 mm. The diameter of both was 1,020 mm.; the compression ratio of the 9B was 4·56 to 1, that of the 9Bf either 5·29 or 5·14 to 1.

The second Admiralty prototype, N518, was tested in May 1917 with the first example of the 150-h.p. A.R.1 (Admiralty Rotary). This was a nine-cylinder rotary of the same bore (120 mm.) as the Clerget 9B and 9Bf; its stroke was 170 mm. Although in appearance somewhat similar to the Clerget, the A.R.1 was a little larger (diameter 1,064 mm.) and differed considerably: it has a place in aero-engine history as the first production engine to embody aluminium as an air-cooled cylinder material. This engine was designed by Lt. W. O. Bentley and was later renamed B.R.1 (Bentley Rotary).

F.1/1 version of the design was also subjected to official tests at Martlesham in May 1917 but its performance with the 130-h.p. Clerget was no better than that of the constant-chord type. Its landing speed was higher and it would have been more complicated to manufacture because wing ribs of varying sizes had to be made; it is therefore not surprising that it was abandoned. The chord of the centre section was 5 ft. on the F.1/1; at the outboard end of the straight portion of the leading edge it was 3 ft. 6 in. (chord of the standard F.1 was 4 ft. 6 in.). The spars of the tapered panels were 2 ft. 6 in. apart at the roots but converged sufficiently to enable single plank-type interplane struts to be fitted; these were attached by sheet-steel fittings similar to those used on the Sopwith triplane.

On the production aircraft the top wing was made in three parts, presumably to facilitate assembly and maintenance; the ailerons were longer than those of

The precise identity of this aircraft is uncertain. It might have been the F.1/3 modified to production standard with three-piece upper wing and lengthened ailerons; alternatively it might have been a later prototype or an early production aircraft.
(Photo: Imperial War Museum)

The second Admiralty prototype, N518, at the Isle of Grain.

the early prototypes. The 130-h.p. Clerget 9B and 150-h.p. B.R.1 were the standard engines, and the aluminium panels behind the engine were of the modified shape that first appeared on the F.1/3.

The flying services were quite as quick to find a name for the F.1 as they had been in the case of the Pup. The humped fairing over the gun breeches was somewhat accentuated by the downward slope of the upper longerons behind the cockpit and by the sharp

The third production Camel, N6332, which was transferred to the Royal Flying Corps.

Below: A famous Bentley Camel of No. 209 Squadron, R.A.F. Captain Roy Brown stands beside B7270, the Camel he was flying during the combat in which Rittmeister Manfred, Freiherr von Richthofen, was killed on 21st April 1918. In common with many of No. 209's Camels, the fuselage roundel on B7270 was obliterated, and it is possible that the serial numbers were also painted over.
(Photo: R.C.A.F., via K. M. Molson)

Clerget Camel B6290, with rack for four Cooper bombs under the fuselage. (Photo: Peter M. Bowers)

B3811 with 100-h.p. Gnôme Monosoupape engine.
(Photo: "Aeromodeller")

dihedral of the lower wing. Given the characteristic sense of humour of the flying men of the time, the choice of the name Camel was inevitable, and it swiftly gained universal currency. It was never an official designation.

By the time *N518* had reached Martlesham for its official trials production of the B.R.1 was under way, and this engine was installed in some of the first production Camels of the Sopwith-built batch *N6330–N6379*, deliveries from which began on 7th May 1917. Bentley Camels of No. 4 Naval Squadron were in action on 4th July 1917, when five attacked sixteen Gothas about thirty miles north-west of Ostend. Flight Commander A. M. Shook claimed to have shot down one Gotha in flames and Flight Sub-Lieut.

S. E. Ellis claimed to have driven down another apparently out of control.

By the end of July 1917 the Camel equipped Naval Squadrons No. 3, 4 and 6; No. 9 Naval Squadron received its first Camel on 13th July and was fully re-equipped with the type by 4th August. The triplanes of Naval Eight were replaced by the stubby little biplane between July and September, and No. 10 Naval Squadron likewise relinquished its beloved triplanes in August.

The first production contract (A.S. 1809) for the War Office was given to Ruston Proctor & Co. on 22nd May 1917 and was initially for 250 Camels numbered *B2301–B2550*; the 130-h.p. Clerget was specified. Later, *B5551–B5650*, *B7281–B7480*, *C8201–C8300* and *D1776–D1975* were all delivered under that same contract. From Portholme Aerodrome *B4601–B4650* were ordered under Contract No. 87/A/1836 on 2nd June 1917 (*B7131–B7180* were later ordered under the same contract); and a week later the Sopwith company undertook to supply *B3751–B3950* under Contract No. A.S. 6175, an order that was subsequently augmented by *B6201–B6450*.

For the aircraft ordered from the Portholme Aerodrome, Hooper & Co., and March, Jones & Cribb, the 110-h.p. Le Rhône 9J was specified; it was also quoted as an alternative to the Clerget 9B in the Sopwith contract. In reality not all of the Camels for which the Le Rhône was specified had that engine exclusively: either in production or in service the Clerget was substituted. Many Camels of the Sopwith batches *B3751–B3950* and *B6201–B6400* went to Naval squadrons and were fitted with B.R.1 engines.

An engine change apparently entailed a change of gun-synchronising gear. The standard mechanism of the Clerget-powered Camel was the Sopwith-Kauper No. 3, a mechanical interrupter gear; the Le Rhône version had the superior Constantinesco hydraulic gear.

As noted above, the first installation of a Le Rhône was made in the F.1/3 prototype. The airscrew used on the Martlesham tests in May 1917 was the same Lang type (L.P.2850) that had been used on F.1/3 when it was tested with the Clerget. With the Le Rhône engine the aircraft was a little slower in level flight, but its climbing performance was better.

Pilots who had been accustomed to the docile tractability of the Pup and triplane or to the stable 1½-Strutter found the Camel dangerously different. "Here was a buzzing hornet," wrote Wing Commander Norman Macmillan in *Into the Blue*, "a wild thing, burning the air like raw spirit fires the throat."

Camel in U.S. Air Service markings, fitted with 150-h.p. Gnôme Monosoupape engine, at Martlesham Heath, October 1917.

F6394 *with 170-h.p. Le Rhône 9R engine, at Martlesham Heath, February 1919. An enlarged rudder was fitted.*
(Photo: Imperial War Museum)

The Camel's response to the controls was remarkably swift; its elevators were especially powerful. The strong torque reaction of the rotary engine had a pronounced effect on the aircraft's handling characteristics. The Camel could turn very tightly because the main masses of engine, fuel, armament and pilot were grouped close together, but the engine torque caused the nose to rise in a left-hand turn and drop in a right-hand turn. Fairly coarse rudder was required to correct these tendencies, and so sensitive was the Camel that the turn needed to be tightened very little before the aircraft would spin, quickly and without warning.

Those who mastered the Camel's idiosyncrasies found in it an ideal fighting aeroplane. Although it was not the stable gun platform that the S.E.5a was, its extraordinary manœuvrability enabled it to hold its own as a combat aircraft until the end of the war. Its best fighting altitude was about 12,000 ft. At that height a skilled Camel pilot could dictate fighting terms to any enemy fighter. The Camel was flown by such distinguished pilots as Lt.-Col. R. Collishaw, D.S.O., D.S.C., D.F.C. (60 victories), Major D. R. MacLaren, D.S.O., M.C., D.F.C. (54 victories), Major W. G. Barker, V.C., D.S.O., M.C. (53 victories), and Captain H. W. Woollett, D.S.O., M.C., whose total victory score of 35 included six shot down in one day, 12th April 1918.

The first R.F.C. unit to be fully equipped with F.1 Camels was No. 70 Squadron, which had replaced its 1½-Strutters by the end of July 1917. In that same month No. 45 Squadron began to re-equip with Camels, and many other fighter squadrons flew the little Sopwith in the months that were to follow.

Production gathered momentum as 1917 advanced. By the end of March 135 Camels had been delivered; 471 passed inspection in the next three months, followed by a further 719 in the last quarter of the year. The year's total of 1,325 must have consisted almost entirely of F.1 Camels, as deliveries in quantity of the 2F.1 ship-board variant did not start until early 1918. In 1917 a total of 1,546 Clerget and 540 Le Rhône engines passed inspection for the British flying services, and 879 Clergets and 1,314 Le Rhônes of French manufacture were delivered. Output of the 150-h.p. B.R.1 totalled 269 by the end of 1917.

Left: C42, *painted white all over and bearing the name "The White Feather", was used at Central Flying School* (Photo: Air Ministry).
Right: *Another famous training-unit Camel was the immaculate B5584, the mauve Camel of the School of Special Flying, Gosport. Its stable-mate, the white Camel, was B5157, formerly "M" of No. 210 Squadron. Sitting on the wheel of B5584 is Captain S. Milner-Deighton, Commander of "A" Flight at Gosport; standing, Lt. F. Dudley Hobbs.* (Photo: C. A. Nepean Bishop)

Standard Le Rhône Camels equipped for night flying with flare brackets and navigation lights. These aircraft are said to have belonged to No. 44 (Home Defence) Squadron, but it is equally possible that they may have belonged to No. 78. (Photo: K. M. Molson)

On 29th December 1917 Contract No. A.S. 34277 (for *D8101–D8250*) was given to Ruston Proctor & Co., and A.S. 37028 (for *D9381–D9580*) to Boulton & Paul Ltd.; these brought the total of F.1 Camels ordered during 1917 to 3,450. Hundreds more were going to be needed and it must have seemed unlikely that engine deliveries could possibly match the output of airframes, for the rotaries that powered the Camel were in considerable demand for several other types of aircraft.

It may have been in anticipation of this situation that *B3811* was tested in August 1917 with a 100-h.p. Gnôme Monosoupape engine (No. 30748/W.D.1182). The aircraft was flown with an 8 ft. 7 in. airscrew of the type usually fitted to the D.H.5 (Aircraft Manufacturing Co. drawing No. T.1708), and its performance did not compare unfavourably with that of the Clerget and Le Rhône Camels. It is almost certain that operational use of the Monosoupape Camel was envisaged, for it was fully armed and was tested with an oxygen cylinder in various positions. Confirmation that any 100-h.p. Monosoupape Camel went to an operational unit has yet to be found. The variant has been linked with training units because its engine was regarded as being easier to control than the Clerget or Le Rhône. It is likely that some did in fact see service with training squadrons, but references to this version of the Camel are scanty; indeed it seems unlikely that many aircraft had the engine.

In July 1917, as noted above, F.1/3 was tested at Martlesham with a Clerget 9Bf engine at both compression ratios. The higher ratio (5·29 to 1) gave the

Night-fighter version of the F.1 Camel, almost certainly of No. 78 Squadron, in post-Armistice colour scheme.
(Photo: National Aviation Museum of Canada)

better performance. As Clergets of this type became available they were fitted to production Camels.

During that same month the B.R.1 engine of *B3835* was subjected to a series of modifications. W. O. Bentley, designer of the engine, had discovered that it could be persuaded to give 11 h.p. more if a 2-mm. hole was bored in the top casting of each induction pipe. *B3835* was tested with its engine in five different conditions, viz.:

(1) compression ratio 5·2 to 1, standard induction pipes with 2-mm. holes;
(2) compression ratio 5·5 to 1, standard induction pipes with 2-mm. holes;
(3) compression ratio 5·2 to 1, large induction pipes without holes;
(4) compression ratio 5·5 to 1, large induction pipes with 2-mm. holes;
(5) compression ratio 5·7 to 1, large induction pipes with 2-mm. holes.

The Sopwith TF.1, with two downward-firing Lewis guns between the undercarriage legs and a third Lewis gun above the centre section. The underside of the fuselage was armoured back to the rear of the cockpit.

The best results were obtained with the engine in the fifth condition.

On all fronts the Camel was used until the Armistice. On 31st October 1918 the Royal Air Force had on charge 385 B.R.1 Camels, 1,342 Clerget Camels, and 821 with the Le Rhône or Monosoupape engine. With the exception of the Home Defence version described below, these Camels were not materially different from those that had gone into service eighteen months earlier, and the redoubtable little Sopwith had earned a warlike reputation wherever it had fought. In service, pilots made their own minor modifications: some liked to have the windscreen forward of the gun breeches to facilitate jam clearing; the cut-out in the centre section was frequently enlarged. For ground-attack work (of which the Camel did a great deal in the Battles of Ypres and Cambrai) a rack for four 20-lb. Cooper bombs was fitted under the fuselage just behind the rear undercarriage legs.

In December 1917 Martlesham tested a Camel with a 150-h.p. Gnôme Monosoupape engine. This rotary power unit was of the same diameter (980 mm.) as the earlier 100-h.p. Monosoupape, but its bore and stroke were respectively 115 mm. and 170 mm.; those of the 100-h.p. engine were 110 mm. and 150 mm. The 150-h.p. engine had a compression ratio of 5·2 to 1 (4·85 to 1 on the 100-h.p. type); and dual ignition, with two plugs per cylinder, was fitted. The most unusual feature of the 150-h.p. Monosoupape was a multi-position ignition switch that enabled the engine to run on 9, 7, 5, 3 or 1 cylinders. "It was an amusing experience," wrote the late S. D. Heron,[*] "to watch a fighter aircraft flying close to the ground on one cylinder and then suddenly cut in all nine with a terrific blast of flame from the engine cowl."

That first test of a Camel with the 150-h.p. Monosoupape produced performance figures that compared well with those of the B.R.1 Camel, but the engine was not adopted for British use. British Camels known to have been fitted with it were B2541 and B6329.

The Camel was flown by four squadrons of the United States Air Service in 1918; in June of that year 143 Clerget Camels were bought from the British Government for the equipment of these units. The U.S.A. had also bought a number of 150-h.p. Gnôme Monosoupape engines, and the Air Service wanted these installed in Camels. The job of fitting the engines to camels on a production basis was entrusted to Boulton & Paul Ltd., major contractors for the type. Of this combination Captain Frank Courtney

wrote:[†]

"The history of the Mono Camel was brief but highly eventful. B. & P. built wonderful Camels, but they could not control the mixed marriage with the Monos, and this was one more problem which was removed by the ending of the war."

An unnumbered Camel with the 150-h.p. Monosoupape, in American markings, was tested at Martlesham in October 1918. This aircraft was 82 lb. heavier than the Camel that had been tested in December 1917, and its performance was somewhat poorer.

The last experimental engine installation to be made in a Camel was of a 170-h.p. Le Rhône 9R. Its bore (115 mm.) was 3 mm. greater than that of the earlier 110-h.p. Le Rhône 9J; the compression ratios of the 170-h.p. and 110-h.p. engines were respectively 5·6 to 1 and 4·83 to 1. There is little doubt that an earlier installation of the 170-h.p. Le Rhône was made in France in B3891, which had been transferred to the French government (and may also have had a 150-h.p. Gnôme Monosoupape at one time).

Subject of the later British installation was F6394, on which the engine mounting and cowling had to be modified to accommodate the engine. The Le Rhône was reported to throttle down well and to have good slow-running qualities. Martlesham did not test this Camel until February 1919, but it might not have seen service even if the war had continued: its performance was no better than that of the B.R.1 Camel, and the engine had several small air scoops on the crankcase of which the official report said:

"These might prove disadvantageous on a dusty aerodrome when the machine was left standing with the wooden plugs in or when running up on the ground."

Above and left: *Experiments in dazzle-painting, using a night-fighter Camel as subject. The object was apparently to lead enemy pilots to fire at a false aiming point.*
(Photos:
Imperial War Museum)
(Top left depicts the upper surface of the top wing; bottom left, its undersurface).

     [*]History of the Aircraft Piston Engine (*Ethy Corporation, Detroit, 1961*), page 8.   [†]Flight, *8th July 1955, page 50.*

This aircraft had an enlarged rudder of the type fitted to a few Camels late in 1918.

The Camel was introduced to Home Defence duties in August 1917, and on 3rd September Captain C. J. Q. Brand and Lt. C. C. Banks of No. 44 Squadron, R.F.C., proved that, tricky though it was, it could be flown at night. Early night combats showed that pilots were momentarily blinded by the flash of their guns, and it was considered that there was danger in firing explosive and incendiary ammunition through the airscrew.

To overcome these difficulties a special version of the Camel was evolved for night fighting; this was done primarily by modifying existing airframes. Twin Lewis guns on a double Foster mounting were carried above the centre section, and the cockpit was moved aft of the upper wing to enable the pilot to operate the guns effectively. In the standard Camel the main fuel tank was behind the pilot's seat, but in the night fighter a standard B.E.2e petrol tank was installed between the centre-section struts within the fuselage. One of the upper horizontal spacers of the fuselage had to be removed because the cockpit was moved aft, and the upper longerons had to be reinforced. The strengthening pieces were glued and bound to the inboard sides of the longerons, making the cockpit somewhat more cramped than that of the standard Camel. The flying controls were modified, a B.E.2e rudder bar replacing the standard Sopwith component; navigation lights and flare brackets were fitted. The 110-h.p. Le Rhône was the standard engine of this variant, which apparently shared with the single-seat Home Defence version of the 1½-Strutter the nickname "Sopwith Comic".

In service the armament of the modified Camel varied. Some pilots kept one of the Lewis guns at a 45-degree upward angle; others preferred to retain one Vickers gun, despite its disadvantages. One or two of the night-fighter Camels acquired colourful paint schemes, doubtless after the Armistice: in wartime service dark green dope was used and the national markings were either obliterated altogether or had the white painted out. The fuselage and wings of one of the night fighters were used in experiments in dazzle painting.

Losses of Camels on ground-attack duties were high. In February 1918 an armoured trench-strafing development, armed with two downward-firing Lewis guns and a third on the centre section, appeared with the new Sopwith type number TF.1. Its engine was a

E9968 *was a Camel two-seater of the South-East Area Flying Instructors' School, hence the word* SEAFIS *on the fin.*
(Photo: C. A. Nepean Bishop)

110-h.p. Le Rhône, and the TF.1 was a straightforward modification of the F.1 Camel *B9278*. The TF.1 did not go into production, but it provided information that helped in the design of the more advanced TF.2, the Salamander.

Inevitably, many accidents involving Camels occurred at training aerodromes. Many were caused by pupils' inability to alter quickly enough the fine-adjustment fuel control of the engine after take-off; their reactions to sudden loss of power were not swift enough to forestall the Camel's ruthless spin. A two-seat version of the Camel was therefore made, with the second cockpit in the same position as that of the night fighter. Flying controls, instruments, air-speed indicator pressure heads, and landing wires were all duplicated. The fuel system was revised, a smaller main tank being fitted, and the armament was removed.

Several F.1 Camels participated in experiments in launching fighter aircraft from lighters towed at high speed by destroyers. The significant achievements in this activity belong to the 2F.1 version of the Camel, but at least one F.1 that was used in the tests had a jettisonable steel-tube undercarriage and was armed in the 2F.1 manner with one Vickers gun and a Lewis gun on an Admiralty Top Plane Mounting.

These and other oversea duties led to an interest in the ditching of Camels: in early 1918 the end of a mission at sea usually left a pilot no choice but to come down on the water. Experiments began in July 1918 with a Camel numbered *6341* (prefix *B*, *F* or *N* not determined); in the following month *B3878* was tested with a hydrovane on its undercarriage; and later in August a third Camel, possibly *B6229*, was

Left: *The 9-inch (chord) hydrovane fitted in front of the undercarriage of* B3878, *August 1918.* Right: *The tail-skid of* B3878 *was fitted with a small hydrovane. This was intended to prevent the aircraft from nosing over after alighting.*

flown by the Slavo-British Aviation Group. Some of the twenty Camels given to Poland in 1920 also went into action again in August of that year, flown by the *Eskadra Kosciuszkowska* at Lwòw against the Russians.

After the war the U.S. Navy had at least six Camels, two of which were allocated to the U.S.S. *Texas*, another to U.S.S. *Arkansas*. These were flown from shipboard platforms and were fitted with jettisonable wheels and Grain flotation gear. A small number also went to Canada; these included *F1337, F6310, F6473* and *F6481*, of which the first survived at least until July 1928.

Camels were used for various experimental purposes at the R.A.E. Farnborough. In spinning experiments a Camel had an enlarged rudder and elevators; *B2312* and *H7363* were fitted with Imber self-sealing tanks in February 1920; and *D1965* and *F6456* were extensively used in inverted-flight tests and experiments. The two last-named Camels were almost certainly the last in British official service. Had the war gone on longer than it did, the Camel would have been replaced everywhere by the Snipe, and in peacetime the Snipe remained the R.A.F.'s standard single-seat fighter for some years.

© *J. M. Bruce, 1965.*

tested with a narrower hydrovane and small (450 × 60 mm.) wheels. Finally jettisonable wheels were fitted. All these Camels had flotation gear consisting of airbags in the fuselage.

In addition to its use by the U.S. Air Service the Camel was used by four escadrilles of l'Aviation Militaire Belge. As many as 36 Camels may have been sent to Belgium, but this total is unconfirmed. Known serial numbers include *B5710, B5711, B5745, B5747* (Belgian number Sc-11), *B5748* and *B7235–B7237*. A few Camels remained in Belgian use until 1922, and *B5747* is preserved in Brussels. During the war some pilots of the Royal Hellenic Naval Air Service flew Camels.

Some Camels had gone to Russia in 1918, and the type remained in operational use there until 1920 with R.A.F. Squadrons Nos. 47 and 221. Camels were also

PRODUCTION DETAILS

Production: Known serial numbers for production F.1 Camels total 5,695 aircraft, but at least 100 of these were cancelled, others may not have been delivered. The known batches are as follows.

Sopwith Aviation Co. Ltd., Canbury Park Road, Kingston-on-Thames—N517–N518, N6330–N6379, B3751–B3950, B6201–B6450.

Boulton & Paul Ltd., Rose Lane Works, Norwich—B5151–B5250, B9131–B9330, C1601–C1700, C3281–C3380, D6401–D6700, D9381–D9530, F1301–F1550, F1883–F1957, F6301–F6500, F8646–F8695, H2646–H2745.

British Caudron Co. Ltd., Broadway, Cricklewood, London, N.W.2—C6701–C6800, H3996–H4045 (cancelled).

Clayton & Shuttleworth Ltd., Lincoln—B5651–B5750, B7181–B7280, D3326–D3425, D9581–D9680, E4374–E4423, F3096–F3145, F4974–F5073.

Hooper & Co. Ltd., St. James's Street, London, S.W.1—B5401–B5450, C1551–C1600, F2083–F2182, H734–H833, H7343–H7412.

March, Jones & Cribb Ltd., Leeds—C8301–C8400, F5174–F5248.

Nieuport & General Aircraft Co. Ltd., Langton Road, Cricklewood, London, N.W.2—C1–C200, F3196–F3245, F3918–F3967.

Portholme Aerodrome Ltd., St. John's Street, Huntingdon—B4601–B4650, B7131–B7180, D9531–D9580, E5129–E5178, F1958–F2007.

Ruston, Proctor & Co. Ltd., Lincoln—B2301–B2550, B5551–B5650, B7281–B7480, C8201–C8300, D1776–D1975, D8101–D8250, E1401–E1600, E7137–E7336, F2008–F2082, F3968–F4067. The serial numbers F8496–F8595 were also allotted for Camels, but the manufacturer is unknown.

Known A.R.D. rebuilds—B778, B7745, B7756, B7860, B7869, B7896, B8025, B8155, E9968, E9973, E9975, F2209, F4178, F4187, F4193, F4194, F4199–F4201, F4204, F5914, F5918, F5938, F5939, F5941, F5943, F5946, F5951, F5958, F5967, F5968, F5972, F5981, F5990, F5991, F5993, F6022, F6024, F6030, F6032, F6034, F6037, F6063, F6084, F6089, F6102, F6110, F6117, F6135, F6138, F6176, F6180, F6185, F6191, F6192, F6194, F6201, F6210, F6211, F6221, F6223, F6240, F6249, F6250, F6254, F6257, F6258, F6295, F9579, H6847, H6997, H7003, H7007, H7012, H7092, H7098, H7272, H7281.

Service use: *Western Front, Clerget Camel*—R.F.C. Squadrons Nos. 28, 43, 45, 54, 65, 70, 71 (Australian; later No. 4 Sqn., Australian Flying Corps) and 73. R.N.A.S. Sqns. Nos. 6, 8, 9 and 12. United States Air Service 41st, 148th and 185th Aero Sqns. Aviation Militaire Belge, Iere, 4me, 6me and 11me escadrilles. *Western Front, Le Rhône Camel*—R.F.C. Sqns. Nos. 3, 46, 54, 71 (Australian), 73 and 80; night-fighting duties, Nos. 151 and 152. U.S. Air Service, No. 17th Aero Sqn.

B.R.1 Camel—R.N.A.S. Sqns. Nos. 1, 3, 4, 8, 9 and 10 (later Nos. 201, 203, 204, 208, 209 and 210, R.A.F.).

R.A.F. Fifth Group—No. 213 Sqn. (previously No. 13 Sqn., R.N.A.S.; originally R.N.A.S. Seaplane Defence Squadron, St. Pol); No. 471 Flight.

Italy—R.F.C. Sqns., Nos. 28, 45 and 66; Maj. W. G. Barker's Camel with No. 139 Sqn.

Adriatic Group—Sqns. Nos. 224, 225, 226 and 227.

Aegean Group—"C" Sqn., R.N.A.S., Gliki; "D" Sqn., R.N.A.S., Stavros; "F" Sqn., R.N.A.S., Thermi Mudros; R.A.F. Sqns. Nos. 220, 222 and 223; Royal Hellenic Naval Air Service.

Macedonia—R.F.C./R.A.F. Sqns. Nos. 17, 47, 150, 221.

Mesopotamia—No. 72 Sqn.

Russia—R.A.F. Sqns. Nos. 47 and 221; R.A.F. Contingent, Archangel; Slavo-British Aviation Group.

Home Defence—Sqns. Nos. 37, 44, 50, 61, 78, 112, 143, 212, 273; R.N.A.S. Stations Dover, Isle of Grain, Manston, Felixstowe, Great Yarmouth.

Grand Fleet and Northern Patrol—A few F.1 Camels were flown as shipboard fighters; some were used during experiments with towed lighters.

U.S. Navy—F.1 Camels allocated to U.S.S. *Texas* and *Arkansas*.

Examples of F.1 Camels used by operational squadrons:
No. 3 Sqn., R.F.C.—B6442 (Aircraft "A"), C8374 ("G"), D6477 ("Y"), E1402, F2153 ("7"), H801. No. 28 Sqn., R.F.C.—B2461, B6344 ("G"), D1911, D8239 ("R"), E1581, F1921 ("C"). No. 43 Sqn., R.F.C.—B2431, B2510 ("A"), C8247, C8281, D1848, E1467. No. 44 Sqn., R.F.C.—B5402 ("2"), B9175, No. 45 Sqn., France—B2323, B4609, B6235, B6236, B6285, B6372. No. 45 Sqn., Italy—B2340, B2430, B3872, B6238, B6412 ("D"), B7381 ("H"). No. 46 Sqn., R.F.C.—B4618, B9149, C1559, C6722, D5585, H802. No. 47 Sqn., R.A.F., Russia—F6396 (flown by Collishaw). No. 54 Sqn., R.F.C.—B5243, B9315, C8336, D1946, D6569, F5968. No. 65 Sqn.,

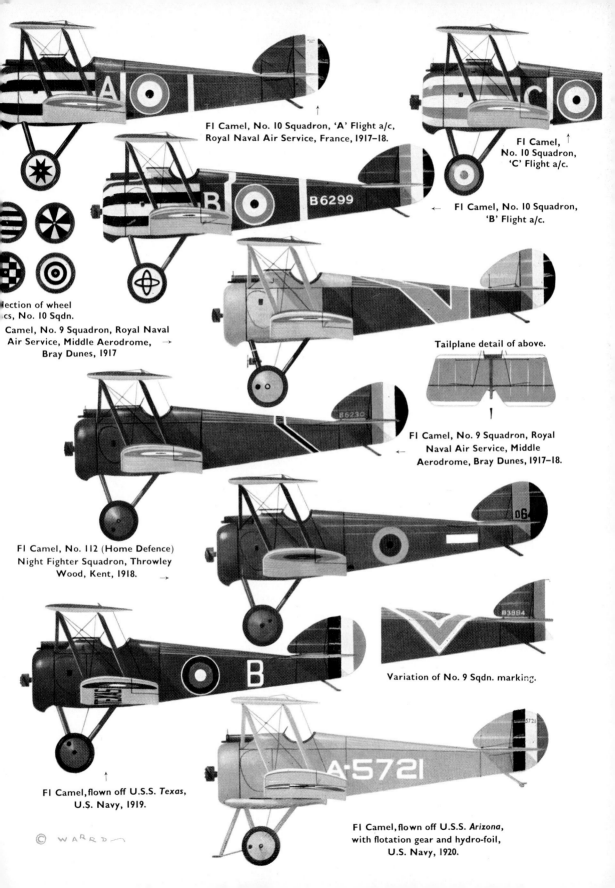

FI Camel, No. 10 Squadron, 'A' Flight a/c,
Royal Naval Air Service, France, 1917–18.

FI Camel,
No. 10 Squadron,
'C' Flight a/c.

FI Camel, No. 10 Squadron,
'B' Flight a/c.

B6299

Selection of wheel
discs, No. 10 Sqdn.

Camel, No. 9 Squadron, Royal Naval
Air Service, Middle Aerodrome, →
Bray Dunes, 1917

Tailplane detail of above.

FI Camel, No. 9 Squadron, Royal
Naval Air Service, Middle
Aerodrome, Bray Dunes, 1917–18.

FI Camel, No. 112 (Home Defence)
Night Fighter Squadron, Throwley
Wood, Kent, 1918.   →

Variation of No. 9 Sqdn. marking.

FI Camel, flown off U.S.S. Texas,
U.S. Navy, 1919.

A·5721

FI Camel, flown off U.S.S. Arizona,
with flotation gear and hydro-foil,
U.S. Navy, 1920.

© WARRD

R.F.C.—B6289, C8264, D1903, E7217, F6355, H7007. No. 66 Sqn., R.F.C.—B2514, B5190, D1913, D8101, D9390, E7209. No. 70 Sqn., R.F.C.—B2449, B5598, C1670, D6564, D8214, E7176. No. 71 Sqn., (No. 4 Sqn., A.F.C.)—B2520, B7180, C8261, D8231, D9468, E7187. No. 73 Sqn., R.F.C.—B5590, C3312, D1841, D6476, E1553, F6063. No. 80 Sqn., R.F.C.—B9132, B9170, B9325, C1647, D9429, F6110. No. 112 Sqn., R.F.C.—D6403, D6405, D6415, D6473, D6664. No. 139 Sqn., R.A.F.—B6313 (Maj. Barker's Camel; also with Nos. 28 and 66 Sqns.). No. 151 Sqn., R.A.F.—B5412, C6725, D6660, E5142, F6084, H826. No. 1 Sqn., R.N.A.S. (No. 201, R.A.F.)—B3884, B7248, C191, D3393, E4411, F5989. No. 3 Sqn., R.N.A.S. (No. 203, R.A.F.)—B2442, B3936, B7187, C3363, D9594, N6364. No. 4 Sqn., R.N.A.S. (No. 204, R.A.F.)—B7234, C76, D8188, E4418, F3929, N6361. No. 6 Sqn., R.N.A.S. (No. 206, R.A.F.)—B3821, B6311, D1873, E7165, F5188, N6355. No. 8 Sqn., R.N.A.S. (No. 208 R.A.F.)—B3819, B6349, B7192, D1867, D3352, N6342. No. 9 Sqn., R.N.A.S. (No. 209, R.A.F.)—B3896, C58, D3327, E4389, H6997, N6370. No. 10 Sqn., R.N.A.S. (No. 201, R.A.F.)—B6276, C144, D9616, E4407, F5914, N6347. No. 12 Sqn., R.N.A.S.—B3759, B3905, B6259, B6297, N6357, N6372. Seaplane Defence Sqn. and No. 13 Sqn., R.N.A.S. (No. 213, R.A.F.)—B3774, B6407, D3409, F3239, N6348, N6363. No. 227 Sqn., R.A.F.—C43, C53, C133. C' Sqn., R.N.A.S., Gliki—B6254. D Sqn., R.N.A.S., Stavros—B3769, N6367. F Sqn., R.N.A.S., Thermi and Mudros—B6254, B6255, N6353. 17th Aero Sqn., U.S.A.S.—B7407, C8337, D3396, F2146, F6034, H7272, 148th Aero Sqn., U.S.A.S.—B7869, C3302, D6574, D8171, E1471, F5191.

SPECIFICATION

Power: 110-h.p. Clerget 9Z (first prototype only); 130-h.p. Clerget 9B; 140-h.p. Clerget 9Bf; 110-h.p. Le Rhône 9 J; 100-h.p. Gnôme Monosoupape; 150-h.p. B.R.I; 150-h.p. Gnôme Monosoupape; 170-h.p. Le Rhône 9R.

Dimensions: Span 28 ft.; length (Clerget) 18 ft. 9 in., (110-h.p. Le Rhône) 18 ft. 8 in., (B.R.I and 150-h.p. Monosoupape) 18 ft. 6 in., (100-h.p. Monosoupape and 170-h.p. Le Rhône) 19 ft.; height 8 ft. 6 in.; chord 4 ft. 6 in.; gap at fuselage 5 ft.; stagger at fuselage 18 in., at struts $18\frac{5}{16}$ in.; dihedral, upper nil, lower 5 deg.; incidence 2 deg.; span of tail 8 ft.; wheel track 4 ft. 6 in.; tyres, Palmer 700 × 75 mm.; airscrew diameter 8 ft. 6 in.

Areas: Wings 231 sq. ft.; ailerons, each 9 sq. ft., total 36 sq. ft.; tailplane 14 sq. ft.; elevators 10·5 sq. ft.; fin 3 sq. ft.; rudder 4·9 sq. ft.

Armament: Two fixed 0·303-in. Vickers machine guns with Constantinesco C.C. synchronising mechanism for 110-h.p. Le Rhône engine, Kauper No. 3 interrupter gear for 130-h.p. Clerget; Hyland Type A loading handles and Feroto jam clearers; Aldis and ring-and-bead sights. Four 20-lb. Cooper bombs in racks under the fuselage. The night-fighter Camel usually had two 0·303-in. Lewis guns on a double Foster mounting with Hutton or Neame illuminated sights, but various combinations of Vickers and Lewis guns were tried.

WEIGHTS AND PERFORMANCE

Aircraft	F.1/1	F.1/3	B2312	F.1/3	F.1/3	B3829	N518
Engine	130-h.p. Clerget	130-h.p. Clerget No. 2730	130-h.p. Clerget No. 1498/ W.D.11647	140-h.p. Clerget 9Bf (1)	110-h.p. Le Rhône No. 100508/ W.D.7917	110-h.p. Le Rhône No. 35554/ W.D.9303	150-h.p. B.R.I No. 1
Weights (lb.)							
Empty	950	929	962	—	889	—	977
Military load	100	101	101	101	101	101	101
Crew	180	180	180	180	180	180	180
Fuel and oil	252	243	239	—	238	—	250
Loaded	1,482	1,453	1,482	1,452	1,408	1,422	1,508
Max. speed (m.p.h.)							
At 6,500 ft.	—		108				116·5
At 10,000 ft.	112·5	113	104·5	—	108·5	—	111
At 15,000 ft.	106	106·5	97·5	113·5	103	111·5	103
Climb to	m. s.	m. s.	m. s.	m. s.	m. s.	m. s.	m. s.
6,500 ft.	6 00	6 00	6 40	5 00	5 15	5 10	5 30
10,000 ft.	10 35	10 35	11 45	8 30	9 00	9 10	9 50
15,000 ft.	21 5	20 40	23 15	15 45	17 20	16 50	20 00
Service ceiling (ft.)	19,000	19,000	18,500	24,000	21,000	24,000	18,000
Endurance (hours)	$2\frac{3}{4}$	$2\frac{1}{2}$	—		$2\frac{3}{4}$	—	$2\frac{1}{2}$

Aircraft		B3835		B3811	U.S.A.S. Camel	F6394	Two-seater
Engine	150-h.p. B.R.I (2)	150-h.p. B.R.I (3)	150-h.p. B.R.I (4)	100-h.p. Mono-soupape No. 30748/ W.D.1182	150-h.p. Mono-soupape	170-h.p. Le Rhône	110-h.p. Le Rhône
Weights (lb.)							
Empty	—	—	—	882	993	1,048	889
Military load	101	101	101	101	101	101	Nil
Crew	180	180	180	180	180	180	360
Fuel and oil	—	—	—	224	249	238	159
Loaded	1,470	1,470	1,470	1,387	1,523	1,567	1,408
Max. speed (m.p.h.)							
At 6,500 ft.	—	—	—			—	
At 10,000 ft.	—	111·5	121	110·5	117·5	113	103
At 15,000 ft.	110	107·5	114·5	102·5	107	108·5	—
Climb to	m. s.	m. s.	m. s.	m. s.	m. s.	m. s.	m. s.
6,500 ft.	5 30	5 00	4 35	6 50	5 50	5 30	10 35
10,000 ft.	9 25	8 50	8 20	11 50	10 20	9 35	18 55
15,000 ft.	18 00	17 10	15 55	23 15	19 40	17 30	41 30
Service ceiling (ft.)	20,000	19,500	22,000	18,500	21,500	21,500	
Endurance (hours)	—	—	$2\frac{1}{2}$	$2\frac{3}{4}$	$2\frac{1}{4}$	—	—

(1) Compression ratio 5·29 to 1. (2) Standard induction pipes with 2-mm. holes, compression ratio 5·2 to 1. (3) Large induction pipes without holes, compression ratio 5·2 to 1. (4) Large induction pipes with 2-mm. holes, compression ratio 5·7 to 1.

PRINTED IN ENGLAND. © Profile Publications Ltd., P.O. Box 26, Leatherhead, Surrey, England, by George Falkner & Sons Ltd., for McCorquodale City Printing Division, London.

PROFILE
PUBLICATIONS

The
Westland
Wapiti

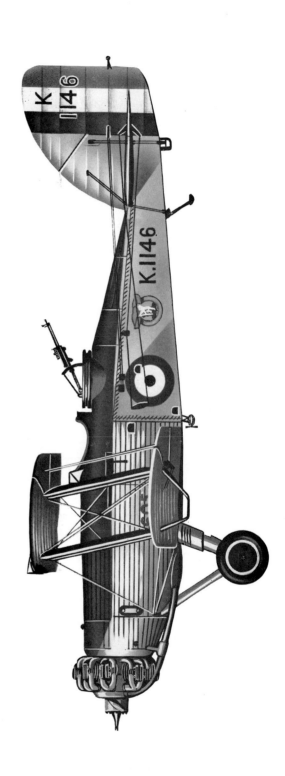

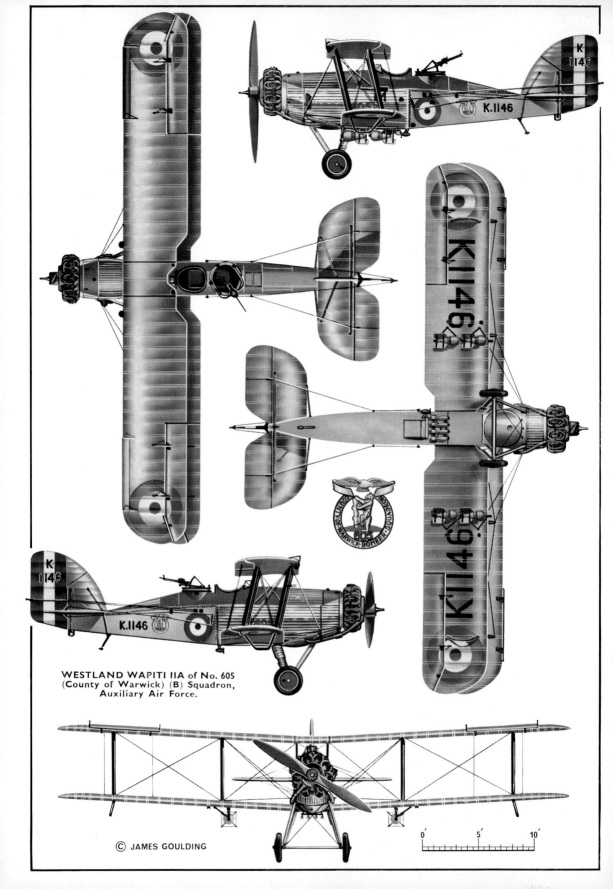

WESTLAND WAPITI IIA of No. 605
(County of Warwick) (B) Squadron,
Auxiliary Air Force.

© JAMES GOULDING

The Westland Wapiti

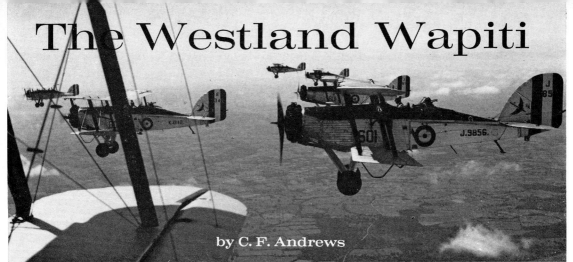

by C. F. Andrews

Wapitis of No. 601 (County of London) Squadron.

The general purpose military aeroplane grew out of the practice in W.W.I of utilising the same type of aircraft for different tactical duties. It was not uncommon for the same machine to be used for light bombing sorties, artillery observation patrols and other reconnaissance flights involving the use of wireless and photographic apparatus; for message carrying by direct ground signals or purely between airfield and airfield, or for individual personnel-carrying duties, including ambulance patients. After the war, these diverse requirements tended to be channelled into two distinct classes, the Army co-operation aeroplane, exemplified by the Bristol Fighter, and the general purpose type, the first of which was the D.H.9A.

Both these aircraft, known popularly and respectively as the "Brisfit" and "Nine-Ack", soldiered on bravely in the years following the war at a time when the Royal Air Force was reduced to a mere skeleton for want of Government funds. The time arrived at length when replacements became inevitable, despite the reluctance of the authorities to sanction financial outlay for new types on the one hand and of the R.A.F. to surrender their beloved "old timers" on the other. In the case of the D.H.9A this came in 1927 when a long-drawn-out competition was held at the Aircraft and Armament Experimental Establishment at Martlesham Heath to decide on a replacement. Eventually the contract was awarded to the Westland Wapiti, for reasons now stated.*

One of the requirements issued by the Air Ministry for the D.H.9A replacement was that it should be able to use as many parts of that aeroplane as possible. The parent firm for the D.H.9A had been the Westland Aircraft Works of Yeovil, Somerset, and it was quite natural, therefore, that this Company should enter an aeroplane for the competition closely resembling the D.H.9A, with so many components on hand from which to re-design and re-engineer a prototype.

The Westland Aircraft Works were founded in 1915 by Percy and Ernest Petter as a branch of Petters Limited, the West Country oil engine manufacturers, principally to construct aircraft for the Admiralty. The first contract was for Short seaplanes. Later contracts included the D.H.4 day bomber and its successor, the D.H.9. The job of converting the D.H.9 to take the more powerful and reliable Liberty engine in place of the Siddeley Puma was given to Westlands and the airframe was re-designed to larger dimensions. Westland drawings were then used by all other sub-contractors.

SPECIFICATION 26/27

From the requirement for a general purpose aeroplane in 1927 the specification 26/27 was drawn up and no fewer than eight entries emerged, not all of which were to official tender, for some entered as private ventures. They were the Armstrong Whitworth Atlas G.P., Bristol Beaver, Gloster Goral, de Havilland Stag, Fairey IIIF, Vickers Valiant, Vickers Vixen VI (Condor) and the Westland Wapiti. Supplementary preferences were expressed for all-metal airframes, then not mandatory but desirable, and for the Napier Lion liquid-cooled engine, large stocks of which were held in stores. None of the Lion-powered entries showed up very well in the competition.

One of the most favoured entries was the Vickers Valiant with an all-metal airframe and the same engine as the Wapiti, the 420 h.p. Bristol Jupiter VI air-cooled radial. However, the facility of the Wapiti in absorbing D.H.9A spares carried the day as large stocks of components for "Nine-Acks" were held on R.A.F. stations, particularly overseas. The financial saving in accepting the Wapiti was, therefore, attractive to the Air Ministry on its limited budget, and the all-round performance of the aeroplane clinched the deal.

Most of the early Westland designs were attributable to Robert Bruce, who had been closely connected with Admiralty aircraft design and had joined the Westland Aircraft Works as manager soon after its establishment. With him was Arthur Davenport who at that time was responsible as chief draughtsman for component and detail design and who later became chief designer. After the D.H.9A, Westlands undertook a second re-design of the original D.H.9 for a fleet-spotting type with pilot, gunner and a prone observer. This machine, known as the Westland Walrus, was of much greater span than the "Nine-Ack" and its ungainly appearance was symptomatic of the times, that of "make-do and mend". Bruce and Davenport thus had some experience of utilising 9A design techniques when the Wapiti came along, which was in effect the third re-design of the D.H.9, itself intended as a development of the D.H.4.

*The name Wapiti appears to have been adopted from the project design stage and conformed to Air Ministry nomenclature for the general purpose class as that of a mammal. It is another name for the North American elk.

3

The prototype Wapiti *J8495*, had wings, tail surfaces, ailerons and interplane struts which were all D.H.9A components. The fuselage entailed considerable re-design to meet Service requirements and was a little wider and a foot deeper than that of the D.H.9A. The undercarriage was of an improved type originally schemed for that aeroplane by Westlands. A curious error only showed up on the first test flight of the Wapiti prototype, made early in 1927 by Major L. P. Openshaw. He reported that the rudder was ineffective. On investigation it was found that in the detail design of the fuselage a bay of a foot and a half had been omitted from the fuselage structure as compared with the length of the wind tunnel model, on which calculations of stability and control had been based. In addition, the increased side area of the new fuselage must have affected the problem to a certain extent.

The prototype Wapiti with D.H.9A-type wings and tail.

FIN/RUDDER GROWTH

As the drawings were completed and production of the first 25 aircraft already planned no attempt was made to rectify the omission, so the fin and rudder of the Wapiti grew and grew as flight trials proceeded until from the original D.H.9A configuration emerged the familiar large shape so characteristic of all Wapitis. Not until a fourth re-design of the basic D.H. configuration was undertaken in the Wapiti Mark V was the correct tail moment arm incorporated by restoring the missing bay, so increasing the overall length.

The prototype Wapiti appeared in the R.A.F. Display of 1927 with a larger rudder, but the final form of the vertical surfaces was decided later when the production line was established. The first 25 aircraft were of wooden construction with the

Engine installation of the prototype.

exception of the front fuselage which was a structure of square section duralumin tubes. Westlands were developing all-metal airframes at that time, like most other constructors, in response to the official edict that after a certain period no new aircraft orders would

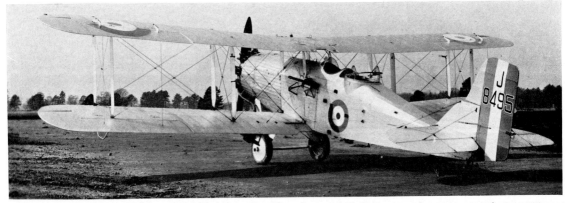

Above: *Prototype Wapiti, J8495, with modified fin and rudder, photographed during general purpose aircraft competition at Martlesham Heath* (Photo: Air Ministry). Below: *J8495 with large fin and rudder and fin fillet, as perpared at Yeovil for the R.A.F. Display, Hendon 1927.*

be placed unless they conformed to that requirement. As stated later this was achieved in the Wapiti when the Marks II and IIA arrived. Handley Page slots were fitted from the Mark IA onwards as standard and the Wapiti was in fact the first production aeroplane so equipped, at least as far as new Service aircraft were concerned.

The Wapiti was officially adopted in 1928 as the standard R.A.F. general purpose type. In its subsequent career many variants appeared, to satisfy varying requirements and duties and while the basic configuration of the aeroplane remained static, its internal construction and equipment underwent changes.

THE WAPITI MARK BY MARK

Wapiti I

This first production version of the Wapiti had a front fuselage of square-section duralumin tubes, wooden rear fuselage, wooden wings and centre-section, and a wooden tail unit—except the rudder, which was metal. The major portion of the front fuselage was covered with aluminium and there were differences in ailerons and undercarriage from the prototype. The large fin-and-rudder assembly finally used was characteristic of all later Wapitis.

Wapiti IA

This designation related to the Wapiti I as fitted with a geared Jupiter VIII engine in place of the direct-drive Jupiter VI and having increased wing stagger. The type was supplied to the Royal Australian Air Force.

Wapiti II

This was a development, to specification 16/31, of the composite construction Mark I. In this later Mark II airframe, the rear fuselage members were of duralumin tube similar to those in the front fuselage and the wings

were metallised but closely corresponding in general detail to the wooden members of the D.H.9A. The Wapiti Mark II, powered with the geared Jupiter VIII, may be regarded as an interim sub-type preceding the standard Mark IIA and according to Air Ministry records, only ten were made.

Wapiti IIA

The all-metal version of the Wapiti, first fitted with a geared Jupiter VIII engine and widely used in the R.A.F. by Regular and Auxiliary Squadrons. Front and rear fuselage were of square-section duralumin tube, and the mainplanes were designed and manufactured by the Steel Wing Company, a subsidiary of Gloster Aircraft Ltd. Towards the end of the Wapiti contracts the metal wings and interplane struts were being made by Westland, to the Steel Wing Company's designs. The ailerons, centre-section, tailplane, elevator, fin and rudder were mainly of duralumin, the ribs being dural pressings.

Extensively used by the R.A.F. overseas, the Wapiti IIA was employed both as a general purpose aircraft and—to a lesser extent—on Army co-operation duties. As used by the R.A.F. it had a Jupiter VIII, VIIIF, IXF or XFA, but a Jupiter XIF was installed experimentally. With the Jupiter VIII, and flying at the normal gross weight of 4,900 lb. the maximum speed was 140 m.p.h. at 5,000 ft. Normal range was 530 miles, but this could be increased to 560 miles by fitting an auxiliary tank beneath the fuselage. Landing speed was 58 m.p.h. and stalling speed (engine on) a

Wapiti IA for the Royal Australian Air Force with Jupiter VIII and "split axle" undercarriage.

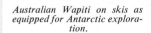

It was used by the South African Civil Air Board as an executive transport and was powered with a Jupiter IXF.

Wapiti IV

A further improved Wapiti was projected by restoring the missing fuselage bay referred to in connection with the prototype. This Mark was a submission for Spain and was to be powered with the 650-h.p. Hispano-Suiza 12N*bis* engine. It had a rakish nose with a Fairey-Reed metal propeller and spinner. As far as can be ascertained it was not completed in this form (see Mark VIII) but from the project the Mark V was developed.

Wapiti V

In one form the Wapiti V had an Armstrong Siddeley Panther engine, a long fuselage as on the Mark IV and a strengthened cross-axle undercarriage, with brakes. Early in 1931 as G-AAWA it was demonstrated by Mr. H. J. Penrose, Westland's chief test pilot, in Argentina and Uruguay in connection with the British Empire Exhibition at Buenos Aires. The same designation was applied to the long-fuselage Wapiti supplied to the Air Ministry and adapted for general purpose and Army co-operation duties. The lengthened fuselage gave the necessary wide c.g. travel to meet varying conditions of loading and conferred a greater measure of fore-and-aft control near the ground. Other innovations were a rudder of deeper chord, a strengthened undercarriage, with wheel brakes, and a tailwheel. This Wapiti was exhibited in the "New and Experimental" park at the R.A.F. Display of 1930, and for a period was fitted with the Bristol Draco direct-injection engine and an experimental four-blade magnesium-alloy airscrew. The Mark V was built in small numbers.

Wapiti VI

In 1932 a dual control trainer to specification 17/31 was built in for the Air Ministry. It was powered with the Jupiter IXF and carried no armament.

Wapiti IIA fitted with long-range underwing tanks and Jupiter IXF with distinctive exhaust collector ring. The latter was standardised on R.A.F. Wapitis of later vintage.

mere 42 m.p.h. Armament, as on earlier Marks, was a synchronised Vickers gun, mounted outside the fuselage to port, and a Lewis gun on a Scarff ring. Provision was made under the wings for bomb loads up to 590 lb. A special undercarriage, known as the Army co-operation type, floats or skis could be fitted in place of the normal cross-axle undercarriage, as standardised on R.A.F. production machines. Goodyear "airwheels" were fitted to a number of Wapiti IIAs in R.A.F. service overseas.

Wapiti III

This Mark number was applied to the South African Wapitis, four of which were built at Yeovil in 1932 with the Jupiter IXF engine and 27 by the S.A.A.F. workshops at Roberts Heights, Pretoria, with the Jaguar VI engine. One of the S.A.A.F. Wapitis was equipped with an enclosed cabin and carried the abbreviated civil registration "615" (PFA-*J615* in full).

Wapiti VI trainer as used by the Royal Air Force.

Uncovered Wapiti IIA disclosing all-metal construction.

Wapiti VII
This was the original designation of the P.V.6, or Wallace, later described.

Wapiti VIII
In 1931, the last variant of the Wapiti appeared as the Mark VIII. The completed Mark IV, fitted with a Jaguar VI, was demonstrated to the Central Chinese Government, who subsequently bought four of the improved type, powered with the Armstrong Siddeley Panther IIA and equipped with the split-axle undercarriage. These were designated as Mark VIII Wapitis.

SPECIAL WAPITIS

Wapiti (Bristol Phoenix)
A Wapiti I airframe, first adapted as a flying test bed for the Bristol Phoenix I compressed-ignition air-cooled engine, was later fitted with a moderately supercharged Phoenix II. With this engine, and piloted by Harald Penrose, it attained a height of 28,000 ft.—a record for a diesel-engined aircraft. At ceiling, Mr. Penrose reported, there was little sign of failure to burn the fuel properly. Special precautions had to be taken to avoid excessive cooling of the oil and the tank was covered with felt. Mr. Penrose himself used oxygen gear with electric heating to prevent moisture in the oxygen from freezing at the reducing valve.

Wapiti (Bristol Pegasus)
The records of the engine division of the Bristol Aeroplane Company show that Wapiti prototype *J8495* was used as a test-bed for the Pegasus I.

Wapiti (for H.R.H. The Prince of Wales)
A Jupiter VI-engined Wapiti I, resembling in appearance the Wapiti VI (T), was used by the then Prince of Wales as his personal aircraft. A similar machine was built to act as escort.

Wapiti (Flight Refuelling)
A standard Wapiti IIA, *K1142*, was equipped for the early experiments with flight refuelling, as a receiver

The first Wapiti V, with civil registration and A-S Panther engine, as demonstrated by Mr. Harald Penrose for the Westland Aircraft Company in South America in 1931.

aircraft, in official trials with that system of extending the range, the tanker aircraft were the Virginia, and similar types. It operated mainly from the R.A.E.

Wapiti VII Conversion (P.V.6)
Early in 1932 Westland were able to annouce a new, private-venture, general purpose aircraft, developed from the Wapiti and known at the time as the P.V.6 but later named the Wallace. It was a conversion of the original Panther-engined Wapiti V which Mr. Penrose had demonstrated in South America during 1931, and the engine was one of the earliest of the Bristol Pegasus moderately supercharged series. Later this same aeroplane was converted for the Houston Mount Everest expedition of 1932–33.

THE WAPITI IN SERVICE

In service with the R.A.F. and other air forces, the Wapiti faithfully followed the pattern pioneered by

The sleek Wapiti VIII as supplied to the Central Chinese Government in 1931 with Panther IIA engine. Note tailwheel and exhaust collector ring.

its famous forebear, the "Nine-Ack" and earned as undying a tradition, very largely as an Empire "policeman". There was no operational duty that was beyond it and whether over the desert wastes of Iraq, in the mountains of the North-West Frontier of India or the burning sands of Arabia, over the outback of Australia or the sub-tropical bush of South Africa, the Wapiti served with distinction, decorated at times with all sorts of official and unofficial excrescensies (including a spare wheel) as an all-purpose transport, looking like the proverbial airborne Christmas tree thus following D.H.9A tradition.

Many variants of the Wapiti and its development, the Wallace, were produced, as would be expected of a general purpose aeroplane that was in active service from 1928 to at least the outbreak of W.W.II in 1939, when No. 27 Squadron of the R.A.F. in India received Bristol Blenheims as replacements. Previously the Middle East Squadrons had been re-equipped with Vickers Vincents in place of Wapitis. There was for example an Army co-operation version, a seaplane version with floats by Short Bros. of Rochester, an Arctic Wapiti with a ski undercarriage, a long-range version for desert operation, the target-towing variant and the two-seat trainer.

The first R.A.F. Squadron to receive the Wapiti was No. 84 at Shaibah, Iraq in 1928, and re-equipping of Nos. 30 and 55 there followed. In India it was used by Nos. 5, 11, 20, 27, 28, 31 and 60 Squadrons. It entered service with the Auxiliary Air Force at home with No. 600 Squadron at Hendon in October 1929 and later equipped A.A.F. Squadrons Nos. 501 (Filton), 502 (Aldergrove), 601 (Hendon), 602 (Renfrew and Abbotsinch), 603 (Turnhouse), 604 (Hendon), 605 (Castle Bromwich), 607 (Usworth) and 608 (Thornaby). Impressive demonstrations of air drill were given by Wapitis of the Auxiliary Air Force in the R.A.F. Displays at Hendon in 1931, 1932 and 1933.

During the historic air evacuation of civilians from Kabul, Afghanistan at the end of 1929, a Wapiti made the first flight from Peshawar on the North-West Frontier to Kabul through the hazardous Khyber Pass and Wapitis of No. 20 Squadron escorted Vickers Victoria transports of No. 70 Squadron in the same operation. In January 1933 four Wapitis of No. 28 Squadron flew 6,200 miles from Ambala in the Punjab to Singapore and return.

A Wapiti of No. 30 Squadron flying over the desert in Iraq.

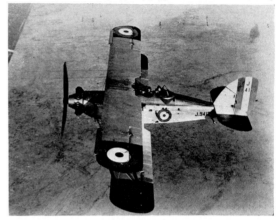

Sister aircraft with red wing and tailplane tips. Paint was aid to locate aircraft grounded in desert in the event of a forced landing. This practice was first introduced on D.H.9As, which the Wapiti replaced. (R.A.F. official photos)

In 1935 the Royal Canadian Air Force purchased 24 Wapitis from the R.A.F. and equipped No. 3 Squadron, R.C.A.F. at Trenton in 1937. In 1938 the Squadron flew its Wapitis from Ottawa to Calgary and later in 1939, to Halifax. Re-designated No. 10 (Bomber Reconnaissance) this Squadron used its Wapitis as an air strike force and as trainers until April 1940 when they were replaced by Digbys. In July, 1940 the remaining Wapitis were sent to the Technical Training School at St. Thomas. Although the "payload" of the Wapiti was supposed to be 1,000 lb. the most that No. 10 R.C.A.F. could carry on its aging Wapitis was 500 lb. without an excessively long take-off run. The

The last Wapiti of No. 84 Squadron flying between Shaibah and Hinaidi. Long-range tanks were fitted and picketing gear installed under the centre fuselage. (R.A.F. official photo)

The special Wapiti IA for the Prince of Wales (now Duke of Windsor) with V.I.P. rear cockpit, metal rear fuselage panels and Fairey-Reed metal propeller.

first of the Wapitis for the Royal Australian Air Force was delivered in February, 1929 but the 27 South African Air Force Wapitis were built in Australia under licence. In 1931 the Hedjaz created an air force of four Wapitis while the Central Government of China also acquired four about the same time.

Westlands built 565 Wapitis in all the variants including some completed as Wallaces. Many Wapitis were also converted to Wallace standard at a later date. So the basic de Havilland conception for a single-engined day bomber, the D.H.4 of 1916, survived through its re-designs up to and including at least part of W.W.II largely through the ingenuity of the Westland designers and engineers in the successive stages of development outlined in this *Profile*.

SPECIFICATION OF WAPITI MARK IIA (with Bristol Jupiter VIIIF and XFA and Armstrong Siddeley Jaguar and Panther geared engines)

Type: Two-seat general purpose landplane or seaplane.

Wings: Equal-wing, staggered, two-bay biplane. Top centre-section carried above fuselage on four cross-braced struts. Two pairs of steel interplane struts on either side of fuselage. Wing structure of metal, covered with fabric. "Frise" type ailerons fitted to all four planes. Handley Page automatic slots fitted as standard.

Fuselage: Rectangular section, with domed top. Of all-metal construction. Fuselage in three sections, the front section including the engine-plate and first bay, the central section running from the first bay to aft of the pilot's cockpit, and the rear section from the pilot's cockpit to the rudder-post. These sections were built of square tube, either of duralumin or steel, steel being used in the most highly stressed positions. The first two sections were covered with aluminium cowling, with longitudinal corrugations to give stiffness, and the rear section covered with fabric.

Tail Unit: Monoplane type. Metal-framed, covered with fabric. Balanced rudder. Adjustable tailplane.

Undercarriage: Straight or split-axle type. Rear legs incorporate Westland patent oleo-pneumatic shock-absorbing units. Twin, long, single-step, duralumin floats, or skis may be substituted for the wheel undercarriage. Army co-operation aircraft fitted with swivelling and self-centring tailwheel.

Powerplant: One Bristol "Jupiter" VIII.F, IX.F or X.FA, Armstrong Siddeley "Jaguar S" or "Panther II" partially or fully supercharged radial air-cooled engine. Fuel contained in two tanks, the main tank holding 68 gallons (308 litres) and gravity tank 40 gallons (182 litres), both tanks being in the fuselage. An auxiliary tank of 23 gallons (104.5 litres) capacity may be installed for long-distance flying, and 15 gallons (68.25 litres) of oil can be carried for long-range work, all in the fuselage.

Wapiti V with Bristol Draco direct injection engine and Bristol magnesium four-blade propeller. The engine down-draught air intake is located behind top cylinders.

Wapiti with Bristol Phoenix diesel engine and Townend drag-reducing cowling ring as used for high altitude research.

Accommodation: Pilot's cockpit behind the trailing-edge of top plane, with observer's cockpit immediately behind. Pilot's cockpit fitted with a special rudder bias-gear taking torque load off pilot's feet on rudder-bar. Armament consists of one Vickers gun, on left side of fuselage, firing forward through airscrew, and one Lewis gun, on Scarff mounting, on rear cockpit. Prone bombing position for observer, complete with instruments. Bomb loading up to 580 lb. can be carried. Photographic camera in bay behind rear cockpit. Wireless apparatus in deck fairing, behind observer. Oxygen equipment for crew of two carried. Additional equipment, including extra petrol tank, spare wheel and tail-skid, fitter's tool box, engine spares, normal and emergency rations, water, bedding, personal equipment, etc., may be stowed inside the machine.

Dimensions: Span 46 ft. 5 in. (14·1 m.). Length (landplane—short fuselage) 32 ft. 6 in. (9·9 m.). Length (landplane—long fuselage) 34 ft. 2 in. (10·42 m.). Length (seaplane—short fuselage) 33 ft 10¾ in. (10·3 m.). Length (seaplane—long fuselage) 35 ft. 8¾ in. (10·9 m.). Height (landplane) 11 ft. 10 in. (3·6 m.). Wing area 488 sq. ft. (45·4 sq. m.).

LANDPLANE

Weights: ("Jupiter" VIII.F geared engine).—Weight empty 3,810 lb. (1,440 kg.). Disposable load 2,220 lb. (1,010 kg.). Weight loaded 5,400 lb. (2,450 kg.).

Weights: ("Jupiter" X.FA geared and supercharged engine).— Weight empty 3,320 lb. (1,507 kg.). Disposable load 2,080 lb. (943 kg.). Weight loaded 5,400 lb. (2,450 kg.).

Weights: ("Jaguar" geared engine).—Weight empty 3,160 lb. (1,433 kg.). Disposable load 2,240 lb. (1,017 kg.). Weight loaded 5,400 lb. (2,450 kg.).

Weights: ("Panther" geared and supercharged engine).— Weight empty 3,200 lb. (1,450 kg.). Disposable load 2,200 lb. (1,000 kg.). Weight loaded 5,400 lb. (2,450 kg.).

Weights: ("Panther" geared and supercharged engine).— Weight empty 3,340 lb. (1,515 kg.). Disposable load 2,060 lb. (935 kg.). Weight loaded 5,400 lb. (2,450 kg.).

SEAPLANE

Weights: ("Jupiter" VIII.F geared engine). Weight empty 3,630 lb. (1,645 kg.). Disposable load 1,770 lb. (805 kg.). Weight loaded 5,400 lb. (2,450 kg.).

Weights: ("Jupiter" X.FA and "Panther" geared and supercharged engines).—Weight empty 3,720 lb. (1,685 kg.). Disposable load 2,130 lb. (965 kg.). Weight loaded 5,850 lb. (2,720 kg.).

Weights: ("Jaguar" geared engine).—Weight empty 3,610 lb. (1,635 kg.). Disposable load 1,790 lb. (815 kg.). Weight loaded 5,400 lb. (2,450 kg.).

Weights: ("Panther" geared engine).—Weight empty 3,650 lb. (1,655 kg.). Disposable load 1,750 lb. (795 kg.). Weight loaded 5,400 lb. (2,450 kg.).

LANDPLANE

Performance: (460/480 h.p. "Jupiter" VIII.F geared engine).— Speed at 5,000 ft. (1,525 m.) 140 m.p.h. (225 km.h.). Speed at 10,000 ft. (3,050 m.) 136 m.p.h. (218 km.h.). Speed at 15,000 ft. (4,575 m.) 129 m.p.h. (207 km.h.). Stalling speed (engine off) 56 m.p.h. (90 km.h.). Climb to 5,000 ft. (1,525 m.) 4·3 mins. Climb to 10,000 ft. (3,050 m.) 9·5 mins. Climb to 15,000 ft. (4,575 m.) 17·5 mins. Service ceiling 20,600 ft. (6,300 m.). Range (normal) 530 miles. Range (with extra tank) 660 miles (1,060 m.).

Performance: (510/573 h.p. "Jupiter" X.FA. geared and supercharged engine).—Speed at 12,000 ft. (3,650 m.) 160 m.p.h. (258 km.h.). Speed at 15,000 ft. (4,575 m.) 159 m.p.h. (256 km.h.). Speed at 20,000 ft. (6,100 m.) 155 m.p.h. (248 km.h.). Landing speed 58 m.p.h. (93 km.h.). Initial rate of climb 1,210 ft./min. (370 m./min.). Climb to 10,000 ft. (3,050 m.) 8·2 mins. Climb to 15,000 ft. (4,575 m.) 12·6 mins. Climb to 20,000 ft. (6,100 m.) 19·3 mins. Service ceiling 27,000 ft. (8,250 m.). Range at cruising speed (normal) 310 miles (500 km.). Range (with extra tank) 560 miles (900 km.).

Performance: (486/512 h.p. "Jaguar" geared engine).—Speed at ground level 136 m.p.h. (218 km.h.). Speed at 5,000 ft. (1,525 m.)

No. 605 (County of Warwick) Auxiliary Squadron in "Vee" formation.

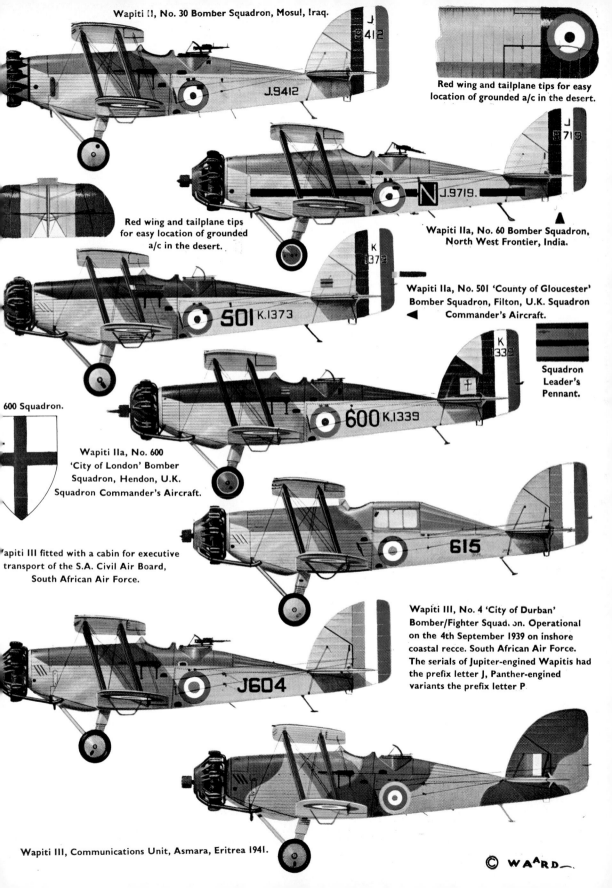

Wapiti II, No. 30 Bomber Squadron, Mosul, Iraq.

J.9412

Red wing and tailplane tips for easy location of grounded a/c in the desert.

Red wing and tailplane tips for easy location of grounded a/c in the desert.

J.9719.

Wapiti IIa, No. 60 Bomber Squadron, North West Frontier, India.

Wapiti IIa, No. 501 'County of Gloucester' Bomber Squadron, Filton, U.K. Squadron Commander's Aircraft.

501 K.1373

Squadron Leader's Pennant.

600 Squadron.

Wapiti IIa, No. 600 'City of London' Bomber Squadron, Hendon, U.K. Squadron Commander's Aircraft.

600 K.1339

Wapiti III fitted with a cabin for executive transport of the S.A. Civil Air Board, South African Air Force.

615

Wapiti III, No. 4 'City of Durban' Bomber/Fighter Squadron. Operational on the 4th September 1939 on inshore coastal recce. South African Air Force. The serials of Jupiter-engined Wapitis had the prefix letter J, Panther-engined variants the prefix letter P.

J604

Wapiti III, Communications Unit, Asmara, Eritrea 1941.

© WAARD

Wapitis of No. 600 Squadron. Note Squadron Leader's tail pennant.

132 m.p.h. (212 km.h.). Speed at 10,000 ft. (3,050 m.) 126 m.p.h. (203 km.h.). Speed at 15,000 ft. (4,575 m.) 116 m.p.h. (187 km.h.). Stalling speed (engine off) 56 m.p.h. (90 km.h.). Climb to 5,000 ft. (1,525 m.) 5·2 mins. Climb to 10,000 ft. (3,050 m.) 12·7 mins. Climb to 15,000 ft. (4,575 m.) 25·4 mins. Service ceiling 18,200 ft. (5,550 m.). Range (normal) 530 miles (852 km.). Range (with extra tank) 650 miles (1,045 km.).

Performance: (527/570 h.p. "Panther" geared engined).—Speed at 5,000 ft. (1,525 m.) 139 m.p.h. (224 km.h.). Speed at 10,000 ft. (3,050 m.) 134 m.p.h. (215 km.h.). Speed at 15,000 ft. 125 m.p.h. (201 km.h.). Stalling speed (engine off) 56 m.p.h. (90 km.h.). Climb to 5,000 ft. (1,525 m.) 4·3 mins. Climb to 10,000 ft. (3,050 m.) 10 mins. Climb to 15,000 ft. (4,575 m.) 18·5 mins. Service ceiling 20, 600 ft. (6.300 m.). Range (normal) 500 miles (804 km.). Range (with extra tank) 610 miles (980 km.).

Performance: (499/546 h.p. "Panther" geared and supercharged engine).—Speed at 11,500 ft. (3,500 m.) 155 m.p.h. (250 km.h.). Speed at 15,000 ft. (4,575 m.) 152 m.p.h. (245 km.h.). Speed at 20,000 ft. (6,100 m.) 144 m.p.h. (232 km.h.). Landing speed 58 m.p.h. (93 km.h.). Initial rate of climb 910 ft./min. (277 m./min.). Climb to 10,000 ft. (3,050 m.) 10·5 mins. Climb to 15,000 ft. (4,575 m.) 16·3 mins. Climb to 20,000 ft. (6,100 m.) 16·3 mins. Service ceiling 26,000 ft. (7,920 m.). Range at cruising speed (normal) 310 miles (500 km.). Range (extra tank) 560 miles (900 km.).

SEAPLANE

Performance: (460/480 h.p. "Jupiter" VIII.F geared engine).— Speed at 5,000 ft. (1,525 m.) 134 m.p.h. (215 km.h.). Speed at 10,000 ft. (3,050 m.) 129 m.p.h. (207 km.h.). Speed at 15,000 ft. (4,575 m.) 121 m.p.h. (195 km.h.). Climb to 5,000 ft. (1,525 m.) 5·5 mins. Climb to 10,000 ft. (3,050 m.) 12·3 mins. Climb to 15,000 ft. (4,575 m.) 24 mins. Service ceiling 18,100 ft. (5,510 m.). Range (normal 490 miles (788 km.). Range (with extra tank) 610 miles (980 km.).

Performance: (510/573 h.p. "Jupiter" X.FA geared and super- charged engine).—Speed at 12,000 ft. (3,940 m.) 155 m.p.h. (250 km.h.). Speed at 15,000 ft. (4,575 m.) 153·5 m.p.h. (247 km.h.). Speed at 20,000 ft. (6,100 m.) 147 m.p.h. (236 km.h.). Initial rate of climb 970 ft./min. (295 m./min.). Climb to 10,000 ft. (3,050 m.) 10 mins. Climb to 15,000 ft. (4,575 m.) 15·5 mins. Climb to 20,000 ft. (6,100 m.) 24·5 mins. Service ceiling 24,300 ft. (7,400 m.). Range at cruising speed (normal) 290 miles (470 km.). Range (with extra tank) 520 miles (840 km.).

Performance: (486/512 h.p. "Jaguar" geared engine).—Speed at sea level 131 m.p.h. (210 km.h.). Speed at 5,000 ft. (1,525 m.) 127 m.p.h. (204 km.h.). Speed at 10,000 ft. (3,050 m.) 118 m.p.h. (190 km.h.). Climb to 5,000 ft. (1,525 m.) 7 mins. Climb to 10,000 ft. (3,050 m.) 18 mins. Climb to 15,000 ft. (4,575 m.) 45 mins. Service ceiling 15,500 ft. (4,730 m.). Range (normal) 490 miles (790 km.). Range (with extra tank) 600 miles (965 km.).

Performance: (527/570 h.p. "Panther" geared engine).—Speed at 5,000 ft. (1,525 m.) 134 m.p.h. (215 km.h.). Speed at 10,000 ft. (3,050 m.) 128 m.p.h. (205 km.h.). Speed at 15,000 ft. (4,575 m.) 118 m.p.h. (190 km.h.). Climb to 5,000 ft. (1,525 m.) 5·3 mins. Climb to 10,000 ft. (3,050 m.) 12 mins. Climb to 15,000 ft. (4,575 m.) 24·5 mins. Service ceiling 18,000 ft. (5,500 m.). Range (normal) 450 miles (724 km.). Range (with extra tank) 560 miles (900 km.).

Performance: (499/546 h.p. "Panther" geared and super- charged engine).—Speed at 11,500 ft. (3,500 m.) 142 m.p.h. (229 km.h.). Speed at 15,000 ft. (4,575 m.) 138 m.p.h. (222

km.h.). Speed at 20,000 ft. (6,100 m.) 127 m.p.h. (204 km.h.). initial rate of climb 740 ft./min. (225 m./min.). Climb to 10,000 ft. (3,050 m.) 13·2 mins. Climb to 15,000 ft. (4,575 m.) 20·8 mins. Climb to 20,000 ft. (6,100 m.) 34 mins. Service ceiling 22,300 ft. (6,800 m.). Range at cruising speed (normal) 290 miles (470 km.). Range (with extra tank) 520 miles (840 km.).

(*Note: All the above performances are based on results obtained by the Company and also by official Air Ministry tests under standard atmospheric conditions.*)

© *C. F. Andrews, 1965.*

WAPITI PRODUCTION FOR A.M.

Prototype
J8495

MARK I
J9078–J9102 (25)

MARK II
J9237–J9246 (10)

MARK IIA
J9247 (proto.), J9380–J9414 (35), J9481–J9514 (34), J9592– J9636 (45), J9708–J9724 (17), J9835–J9871 (37), K1122– K1157 (36), K1254–K1309 (56), K1316–K1415 (100), K2252–K2320 (69).

MARK V
J9725–J9759 (35)

T. MARK VI
K2236–K2251 (16)
TOTAL : 517

INDIVIDUAL SERIALS AND CONVERSIONS

J9084 was floatplane; J9082 and J9083 had dual control; J9380–J9414 Mk.IIAs composite wood/metal structure for overseas (see ref. to 9A spares in text); J9497 and J9498 were floatplanes; batch J9481–J9514 went to India; J9605 and J9864 converted to Wallaces K3677 and K3676; K2306–K2320 converted to Wallaces K4337–K4348 and K5071, K5072, K5073; K2289–K2305 went to India; batch K1254–K1309 was for Army co-op. in India.

R.A.F. WAPITIS TRANSFERRED TO R.C.A.F.

J9612, J9617, J9868–J9871, K1139, K1143, K1146, K1148, K1149, K1152, K1318, K1322, K1324–K1330, K1336, K1342, K1366, K1378.

R.A.A.F. SERIALS
A5-1 – A5-28 (28)

S.A.A.F. SERIALS
P601–P604 (4)

Export
P605–P631 (27)
S.A. Production

PRINTED IN ENGLAND. © Profile Publications Ltd., P.O. Box 26, Leatherhead, Surrey, England, by George Falkner & Sons Ltd., for McCorquodale City Printing Division, London.

PROFILE
PUBLICATIONS

the
Gloster
Gamecock

NUMBER 43

No. 17 (F)
Squadron
Emblem.

GLOSTER GAMECOCK I
Aircraft of H.Q. Flight, No. 17 (Fighter) Squadron,
Upavon, 1928, flown by Squadron Commander
(As far as is known, this aircraft was never flown with
Command pennants.)

0   5'

The Gloster Gamecock

by Francis K. Mason

Gamecock of No. 23 (Fighter) Squadron taking off at Northolt during the Sassoon Cup competition in May 1929. Most squadron Gamecocks had by this time acquired the extra Vee-interplane struts. (Photo: "Flight")

The aftermath of the two world wars displayed a number of strikingly similar facets with regard to the apathetic attitudes towards Britain's armed forces. In the years following W.W.II, while America sought to exploit the tremendous momentum achieved by her gargantuan aircraft industry and maintained a smooth flow of advanced aircraft year by year (a policy which enabled the North American F-86A to uphold American ascendancy over Korea), Britian virtually accepted the wartime-designed Gloster Meteor and de Havilland Vampire as being adequate for metropolitan defence for almost ten years after VJ-Day. The result of this was a singularly pathetic technical contribution to the United Nations' responsibility in Korea. A similar technical apathy had been evident after the Armistice in 1918, and counterparts for the Gloster Meteor 4 and 8 may be recognised in the Gloster Grebe and Gamecock of twenty years earlier for, although the latter were designed some years after the war, they still employed outdated design features with little regard for advances in technology. Such aircraft as the Boeing P-12 (see *Profile* No. 2) were contemporaries of the Gamecock and, exploiting the painful disabilities of wood structures, adopted metal construction—while the British aircraft did not.

The truth lay in Britain's attitudes of mind, both political and economic. Eagerly sought and administered, the Ten-Year Rule dictated an attitude that Britain could "co-exist" with the world without fear of domestic interference, and so she set about pruning her non-essential forces to the point of near-disarmament. For several years no new fighters were produced for the R.A.F., with the result that the defence of metropolitan Britain rested upon a single squadron of Sopwith Snipes. At the same time the jealous and partisan attitudes of the Admiralty and War Office contributed nothing at all to the suvival of Britain as an air power. Indeed, only such difficult commitments as the Turkish and Iraqi operations, successfully concluded by the R.A.F., lent support to Trenchard's

demands in Whitehall for survival of the flying service.

The apathy towards the Air Force and the continuing lack of support for the aircraft industry brought ruin to many British companies with the result that little or no justification for the expenditure on research was forthcoming. Any technical improvement to be seen in successive aircraft design thus lay in the individual abilities and instincts of the aircraft designers. Allied to this were the benefits from air-racing—fast gaining its old popularity of pre-war years.

As already remarked, the successful Snipe survived long after the war, but its parent company was less fortunate, Sopwiths going into liquidation in 1920. The Air Ministry issued a number of fighter specifications in 1921 and 1922, and from these stemmed designs for a Snipe replacement. The Siddeley Siskin, with the temperamental Dragonfly radial engine, suffered political birthpangs and eventually materialised as the Armstrong Siddeley Siskin III in limited R.A.F. service during 1924. The Siskin III shared the replacement honours with the Gloster Grebe which first entered service with No. 111 (Fighter) Squadron at Northolt in the autumn of 1923. Whereas the Siskin made token gesture to technical advance in adoption of mixed metal and wood construction, the Grebe still used an all-wood structure.

The Grebe, designed by H. P. Folland of the Gloucestershire Aircraft Company, owed its origins to the S.E.5 and was evolved through the multitude of fighters built for export and in prototype form (such as the Mars and Grouse) of the early 'twenties. Hallmark of the design evolved was Folland's development of a high-lift upper wing and a lower wing of "high-speed" section and moderate lift—these features contributing a characteristic manœuvrability combined with a marked increase in top speed. (Compared with the Snipe's top speed of about 120 m.p.h., the Grebe achieved 152 m.p.h.)

It was, however, in the powerplant where deficiencies lay. The 14-cylinder Jaguar engine in the Siskin and

Gloster Grebes of No. 25 (Fighter) Squadron lined up at the manufacturer's Brockworth airfield. Powered by a Jaguar engine, the Grebe represented the design transition from the wartime fighting scout concept to the pure interceptor.

(Photo: Francis Mason collection)

Grebe was a heavy and complex engine for its output; lubrication problems often led to fire in the air, and short engine life served to reduce the "on line" strength of a squadron to but one-fifth of its Unit Establishment. Thus the promising development of the Bristol Jupiter IV encouraged the Air Ministry to issue Specification 37/23 for a development of the Grebe to be powered by the lighter and simpler engine.

Ordered in August 1924 as a Grebe II, the prototype of the new design, J7497, was tested at Martlesham Heath in February 1925 with a Jupiter IV engine and unbalanced S.E.5A/Grebe-type rudder, but the latter was changed to horn-balancing in the following months. Two further Jupiter-powered Grebes were ordered in late 1924, J7756 with Mk.IV engine, and J7757 with Jupiter VI.

GAMECOCK PRODUCTION AND SERVICE

Following the initial trials on J7497, accomplished pilots at Martlesham Heath waxed enthusiastic with the new design. It is interesting, however, to note that with all their experience of shortcomings in the Grebe —notably lack of remedial stability in the spin and with wing and tail flutter—they made no mention of such failings in the new prototype; and there is no

The Gamecock prototype and company demonstrator. Differences lay in the exhaust manifold and spinner. The close-up view (above) shows the demonstrator G-EBNT. Photos taken in March 1926.

(Photos: "Flight")

The demonstrator G-EBNT in flight. (Photo: "Flight")

doubt that these failings existed. Such may be an early reflection on the disadvantage of placing sole reliance for assessment of new aircraft in the hands of highly experienced service evaluation pilots. (It certainly brought about the introduction of service-trained pilots to the aircraft industry.)

Prompted by this optimistic appraisal, the Air Ministry placed an order with the Gloster Aircraft Company in September 1925 for thirty Gamecock Is (*J7891–J7920*) to be powered by Bristol Jupiter VIs as fitted in the third prototype. Most of these aircraft were delivered to No. 23 (Fighter) Squadron at Henlow in May 1926, this squadron retaining Gamecocks until July 1931 when it received Bulldogs—long after other Gamecock squadrons had been re-equipped. It was at the Hendon Air Pageant of 1931 that two No. 23 Squadron Gamecocks gave a memorable display of integrated solo aerobatics—flown by Flight Lieutenant M. M. Day and a certain Pilot Officer Douglas R. S. Bader.

In July 1926, forty-two further Gamecock Is were ordered (*J8033–J8047* and *J8069–J8095*) and were followed in November that year by eighteen more (*J8405–J8422*). The sixty aircraft were issued to No. 32 Squadron at Kenley (to which airfield No. 23 Squadron also moved) and No. 43 Squadron at Tangmere. Unit Establishment of these squadrons during the nineteen-twenties was twenty-one aircraft—six aircraft in A, B and C Flights and up to three in H.Q. Flight. Replacement level in 1927 was just adequate to maintain the three squadrons at U.E.*

Nevertheless the accident rate on Gamecock Is was extremely high having regard to the numbers in service, four crashing in 1926 and eighteen in 1927. Contemporary records show that seven pilots lost their lives as the result of spinning and landing accidents, and another appears to have died after his Gamecock broke up in the air. Certainly wing flutter gave cause for Air Ministry consternation and in late 1927 additional struts were mounted outboard of the interplane struts, an innovation which, added to the aileron tie rods, gave rise to the soubriquet, Folland's "Cock's Cradle".

Notwithstanding these criticisms, for pilots long exasperated with war-weary Snipes the Gamecock was immensely popular. With careful and sensible handling it was a delightful aerobatic mount, essentially simple to maintain and a moderately steady gun platform. That great Gloster pilot, Captain Howard Saint, performed a 275-m.p.h. terminal velocity dive and retained possession of his mainplanes throughout the recovery, and several pilots survived 22-turn left-handed spins. For reasons of engine torque and slipstream blanking, however, intentional right-hand spins were dangerous owing to immediate flattening, and were forbidden. One Gamecock I, *J7910*, was experimentally fitted with narrow-chord ailerons for anti-flutter trials.

In 1928 two further R.A.F. squadrons were equipped with Gamecocks, this time with limited modification as specialist night fighters. These were the two night interceptor Squadrons, Nos. 3 and 17, at Upavon, which gave up their Hawker Woodcock IIs. Service with these units was shortlived and in May the following year No. 3 was re-equipped with Bulldogs.

G-EBNT with minor modifications to exhaust manifolds. (Photo: Imperial War Museum)

*Repaired aircraft amounted to one in 1926 and ten in 1927.

FURTHER DEVELOPMENT

Perhaps the most characteristic of Glosters' development procedures between the wars was their ability to apply successive improvements to single prototypes over relatively long periods. The Gloster S.S. 18/19 was a first-class example of this (see the Gloster Gauntlet, *Profile* No. 10) and the Gamecock I, *J8047*, was another.

J8047 had been delivered, new and to R.A.F. standard, to the Central Flying School at Wittering in October 1926. Thence it went to the Royal Aircraft Establishment at Farnborough in April 1927 for spinning trials; recommendations following these led to the wings being repositioned a few inches aft, and further trials commenced.

Later in 1927, *J8047* returned to Glosters who virtually rebuilt the airframe with extended fuselage, revised rudder, narrow-chord ailerons and wide-track undercarriage. Unofficially termed by Glosters the Gamecock III, *J8047* was not flown by Saint until August 1928, and in November it was re-delivered to Farnborough. Here it was found to be considerably nose-heavy and was flown with ballast in the W/T tray in the aft fuselage.

By March 1929 it was back at Brockworth having the Jupiter VI replaced by a Jupiter VII (in sympathy with recent R.A.F. acceptance of this engine in the Bulldog). Thereafter and until late 1930, *J8047* was used for trials with the Hele-Shaw-Beecham variable-pitch propeller, a heavy but ingenious excrescence that demanded considerable additions to the tail ballasting, which created almost insuperable difficulties in measuring any real improvements in performance anyway!

In 1932 a Jupiter VI re-appeared in *J8047* and further spinning was undertaken for academic purposes. When the Gamecock was declared obsolete in 1933, *J8047* had completed 202 flying hours and was offered for sale; its fuselage became part of *G-ADIN*, a Gamecock rebuilt by J. W. Tomkins in 1934 with a Jupiter VIIFP.

Captain Howard Saint, Chief Test Pilot of the Gloster Aircraft Company and responsible for Gamecock development flying. Photo taken in late 1926. (Photo: Hawker Siddeley Aviation)

THE GAMECOCK II

Intended as a replacement for the Gamecock I (but overtaken by the Bulldog), the Gamecock II was a company-sponsored project but one which gained official sanction in the purchase of a prototype, *J8804*, in January 1928. This was the outcome of the various 1927 trials, and included slightly larger rudder

Below and on facing page: Fitted with narrow-chord ailerons, Gamecock J7910 was used in some of the many "anti-flutter" trials of 1927 both at Brockworth and Farnborough. (Photo: "Flight")

Judging by A. & A.E.E. reports on *J8804*, the Gamecock II displayed a great improvement over the Mark I—especially in handling—few of the earlier vices remaining. However, R.A.F. service was not for the Gamecock II, and Glosters faced something of a crisis with the end of Mark I production. A delegation from Finland had visited Britain during 1927, had seen the Gamecock I and seemed impressed by what it had seen. No order had been placed, but when *J8804* performed a number of demonstration flights in 1928 fresh interest was generated. Two pattern aircraft were ordered from Brockworth and these were delivered by sea to Helsinki in November that year; within six months,

and narrow-chord ailerons. One other aircraft, previously *J8075* from the Gamecock I production, was used in the flight trials of the Bristol Mercury IIA engine and was eventually brought up to Gamecock II standard.

Gamecocks of No. 43 (Fighter) Squadron at the Birmingham Air Pageant of June 1928. Note additional interplane struts and also Flight Commander's pennants, coloured wheel discs and fins.
(Photo: "Flight")

Two views of the experimental Gamecock III J8047 at an early stage in its career (August 1928) showing parallel-chord ailerons, lengthened fuselage and enlarged fin. (Photos: "Flight")

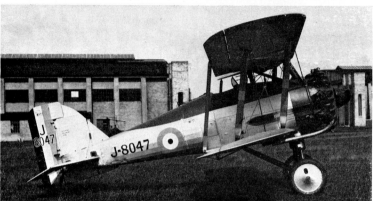

via the Bulldog. And so in July 1931, No. 23 Squadron gave up the last operational Gamecocks to receive Bulldogs, and in March 1933 the Gamecock was declared obsolete for all R.A.F. purposes, at the same time as that other great aeroplane of the nineteen-twenties, the Fairey Fox light bomber.

FLYING THE GAMECOCK

Immensely popular in the air, the Gamecock presented fewer pitfalls than the Grebe, but the wary pilot was nevertheless mindful of legion warnings and in-flight limitations. Due to the high cockpit position, pilot vision on the ground was good but when lined up for take-off, as in the air, the upper wing constituted a severe handicap; for downward view, the lower wing could scarcely have been located worse! Take-off was sprightly, the elevators becoming effective at about 20 m.p.h. despite the short fuselage, As speed increased to 90–100 m.p.h. lateral control improved, but care was needed when raising the nose as speed decreased very quickly, and if a wing dropped lateral control was quite inadequate to avert a spin.

licence-built Gamecock IIs (with interchangeable wheel and ski landing gear) were being produced in Finland. At home, the entry into R.A.F. service of the 174-m.p.h. metal Bulldog spelt the end of the 152-m.p.h. all-wooden Gamecock—and also the end of an era. Not even the technically-starved Royal Air Force of 1930 could long endure the ridiculous anomaly of supporting the maintenance spectrum whose responsibility ranged from the Gamecock to the Fury,

Owing to the large mass of the propeller, right-hand spins were more easily entered than left and were tricky to handle. The conventional "stick-forward-full-opposite-rudder" remedy was seldom entirely

Below and on facing page: *Another experimental Gamecock was J8075, used in 1929 for flight trials of the Hele-Shaw variable-pitch propeller. Louvres on the spinner were for cooling of bearings.*

Finnish Gamecock II in "pre-delivery" colour scheme. Anti-glare panel extended aft to the fin. Aircraft were dismantled after flight test for delivery by sea.
(Photos: "Flight")

successful owing to the blanking-off by the deep fuselage and it was averred that if pushing the stick forward did not unstall the aeroplane, abandoning the aircraft forthwith (before the spin went flat and utterly uncontrollable) was the immediate recourse.

In the upper speed range (100–150 m.p.h.) all controls were highly sensitive and effective, and it has been said that the Gamecock was the first fighter to do a 360-degree upward roll vertically, and still be pushed over the top. Rolls and loops (the "flick" loop in particular) were spectacular, and popular so long as the pilot did not apply coarse aileron too quickly above speeds of about 130 m.p.h. This would result almost invariably in alarming wing flutter for which the only remedy was to cut the throttle, centralise the controls and then slowly raise the nose. Too often, however, the onset of flutter was manifest during a roll or in the course of a diving turn and the effects were so destructive that the tip flutter would be accompanied by the loss of one or two ailerons and the possibly disastrous fracture of an interplane strut.

As with so many aircraft of those years, prolonged inverted flying was impossible and even in rolls and loops ignition usually failed momentarily until gravity restored the fuel supply. Low level rolls were therefore discouraged as insufficient height existed to air-start the engine-

In the landing phase a tail-down attitude was important due to the lack of propeller clearance, and this entailed some degree of yawing to maintain forward visibility. Touchdown at 42 m.p.h. could be effected by use of plenty of throttle, but coarse throttle movement in the approach was accompanied by sympathetic rolling. The inexperienced pilot was advised to touchdown at rather higher speeds as instinctive corrections to rolling on the approach often led to wing-dropping (one-wing stall) and disastrous results.

No wheelbrakes were fitted, but on grass landing surfaces the tailskid contributed—by ploughing a furrow—to pull the aeroplane up in well under 100 yards.

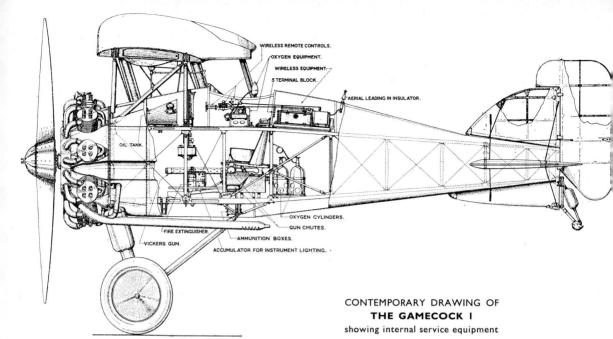

WIRELESS REMOTE CONTROLS.
OXYGEN EQUIPMENT.
WIRELESS EQUIPMENT.
5 TERMINAL BLOCK.
AERIAL LEADING IN INSULATOR.
OIL TANK.
OXYGEN CYLINDERS.
GUN CHUTES.
FIRE EXTINGUISHER.
AMMUNITION BOXES.
VICKERS GUN.
ACCUMULATOR FOR INSTRUMENT LIGHTING.

CONTEMPORARY DRAWING OF
THE GAMECOCK I
showing internal service equipment

THE GAMECOCK DESCRIBED

Structure of the Gamecock was almost entirely of wood. The fuselage was a built-up structure using ash longerons with ash, spruce or laminated ply supports and distancing struts, the whole box structure being tensioned by rigging wires with turnbuckles attached to bolts passed through fishplates on the longerons.

There were four single-piece bulkheads: the front bulkhead, of mild steel plate, carried the engine attached by nine radial bolts. No. 2 bulkhead was a fireproof screen consisting of an $\frac{1}{8}$-in. sheet of asbestos sandwiched between sheets of aluminium. No. 3 bulkhead carried the instrument panel and fire extinguisher, and the rear bulkhead accommodated

Ski-equipped Gamecock (GA-38) of the Finnish Air Force. Note swastika on the airscrew blade. (Photo: Finnish Air Force)

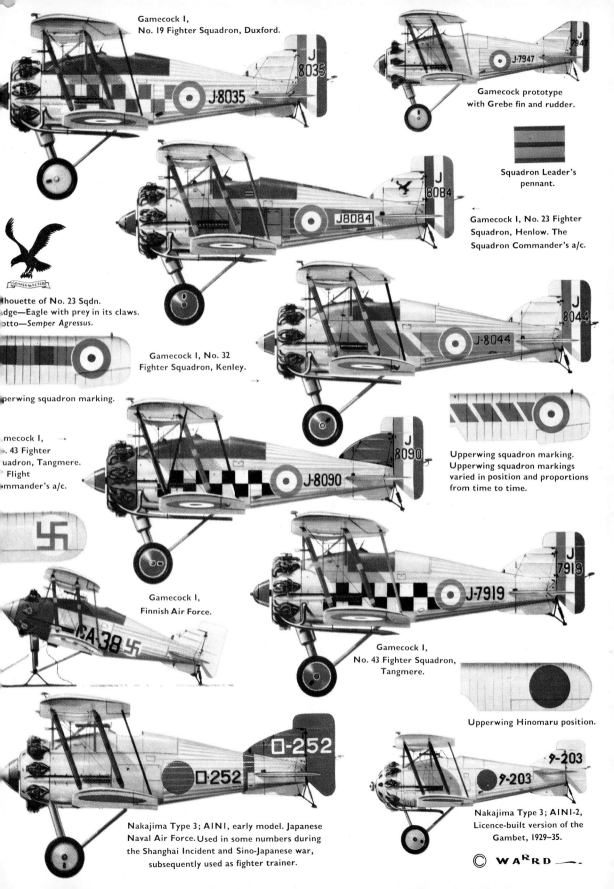

Gamecock I,
No. 19 Fighter Squadron, Duxford.

J·8035

Gamecock prototype
with Grebe fin and rudder.

J·7947

Squadron Leader's
pennant.

Gamecock I, No. 23 Fighter
Squadron, Henlow. The
Squadron Commander's a/c.

J8084

...houette of No. 23 Sqdn.
...dge—Eagle with prey in its claws.
...otto—Semper Agressus.

SEMPER AGRESSU

Gamecock I, No. 32
Fighter Squadron, Kenley.

J·8044

...perwing squadron marking.

...mecock I, →
. 43 Fighter
...uadron, Tangmere.
...Flight
...mmander's a/c.

J·8090

Upperwing squadron marking.
Upperwing squadron markings
varied in position and proportions
from time to time.

Gamecock I,
Finnish Air Force.

GA·38

J·7919

Gamecock I,
No. 43 Fighter Squadron,
Tangmere.

Upperwing Hinomaru position.

O·252

9·203

Nakajima Type 3; A1N1, early model. Japanese
Naval Air Force. Used in some numbers during
the Shanghai Incident and Sino-Japanese war,
subsequently used as fighter trainer.

Nakajima Type 3; A1N1-2,
Licence-built version of the
Gambet, 1929–35.

© WARRD

No. 23 (Fighter) Squadron Gamecocks J7914 and J8409 at Northolt for the 1929 Sassoon Cup. Fuselage and wing dicing were alternate red and blue squares; fuselage roundel size differed between aircraft.
(Photo: "Flight")

mountings for the pilot's seat and brackets for the machine guns on each side of the fuselage. Three more strut-fabricated bulkheads provided rear fuselage strength aft of the cockpit, and aft of these structure bays were three sets of side struts culminating in a sternpost to which were attached rudder hinges and tailskid. The underfin was a relic of the S.E.5 design. All joints in this wooden structure were faced with plywood, wrapped with tape and reinforced with fishplates.

The upper wing was built up in two halves, meeting at a butt joint on the aircraft centreline. The two main spars were made of spruce and there were two alternative designs; one in which the spars were produced from one piece of timber, and the other in which laminated strips of timber were used. The laminated spar was more commonly used owing to the difficulty of obtaining sound timber of the length required for the whole spar. Ailerons were fitted in both upper and lower wings, control runs passing through the lower wing and movement being transmitted to the upper ailerons through tie-rods. Wings, tail surfaces and rear fuselage were fabric covered.

The uncowled nine-cylinder Bristol Jupiter VI engine drove a wooden fixed-pitch two-blade propeller. Sixty gallons of fuel were carried in two top wing gravity tanks, gravity feed being employed and controlled by a manual stopcock on the port side of the cockpit, and by cocks on the feed pipes under the top wing. A six-gallon oil tank was situated immediately forward of the instrument panel.

Armament consisted of two 0·303-in. Vickers Mk.I machine guns mounted on trays on the sides of the fuselage and synchronised to fire through the airscrew. Six hundred rounds of Mark VII ammunition were fed to each gun from magazine boxes mounted between Nos. 4 and 5 bulkheads. Both Aldis and ring-and-bead gunsights were included, the former on the aircraft centreline and the latter offset to starboard. Four 20-lb. bomb racks were attachable to the underfuselage; bomb release was by toggle and Bowden cable.

© *Francis K. Mason, 1965.*

SPECIFICATION OF GAMECOCK I

Powerplant: 425-h.p. Bristol Jupiter VI nine-cylinder air-cooled radial engine driving 2-blade fixed-pitch wooden propeller.
Dimensions: Wing span, upper wing 29 ft. 9½ in.; lower wing 25 ft. 11 in. Chord, upper wing 5 ft. 3 in.; lower wing 5 ft. 2½ in. Incidence, upper wing 3 degrees; lower wing 2 degrees. Dihedral 4 degrees. Stagger 20 in. Total area 264 sq. ft. Wing loading 10·85 lb./sq. ft. Tailplane span 9 ft. Overall length 19 ft. 8 in. Overall height (aircraft centreline horizontal) 9 ft. 8 in. Undercarriage 750 × 125 mm. Palmer No. 77 wheels, 5 ft. track.
Fuel and Oil: Total fuel capacity 60 Imp. gal. Oil capacity 6 Imp. gal.
Radio and Equipment: R.31 receiver, T.25 transmitter; two 500 litre oxygen cylinders; fire extinguisher.
Weights: Empty 1,930 lb. Loaded 2,863 lb. Overload 2,980 lb.
Performance: Maximum speeds, 155 m.p.h. at 5,000 ft.; 145 m.p.h. at 10,000 ft. Time to height 7 min. 40 sec. to 10,000 ft.; 20 min. to 20,000 ft. Service ceiling 22,100 ft. Absolute ceiling 22,900 ft. Range at best range speed 365 statute miles.
Armament: Two 0·303-in. Vickers Mk.I machine guns with 600 rounds per gun allowing approximately 25 seconds duration of fire.

PRODUCTION

Three prototypes (ordered as Grebe IIs) J7497, J7756, J7757.
First production batch, 30 aircraft, ordered in 9/25, J7891–J7920.
Second production batch, 42 aircraft, ordered in 7/26, J8033–J8047, J8069–8095.
Third production batch, 18 aircraft, ordered in 11/26, J8405–J8422.
Gamecock II: One aircraft, J8804, newly built; one other, J8075, previously a Mark I modified to Mark II state. Two pattern aircraft built for Finland; further licence production of Mark II in Finland.

SERVICE ALLOCATION

Representative aircraft in R.A.F. service
No. 3 (Fighter) Squadron, Upavon: J8407, J8410, J8411.
No. 17 (Fighter) Squadron, Upavon: J8405, J8408, J8414.
No. 23 (Fighter) Squadron, Henlow and Kenley: J7894, J7895, J7898, J7903, J7907, J7914. J7915, J8040, J8041, J8082, J8406, J8420, J8421.
No. 32 (Fighter) Squadron, Kenley: J7907, J7909, J8420.
No. 43 (Fighter) Squadron, Tangmere: J7905, J7906, J7908, J8037, J8090, J8415, J8418, J8421.
Central Flying School, Wittering: J8046, J8047, J8089.
Armament & Gunnery School, Eastchurch: J8033, J8034.

PRINTED IN ENGLAND. © Profile Publications Ltd., P.O. Box 26, Leatherhead, Surrey, England,
by George Falkner & Sons Ltd., for McCorquodale City Printing Division, London.

PROFILE
PUBLICATIONS

The
Fairey
Battle

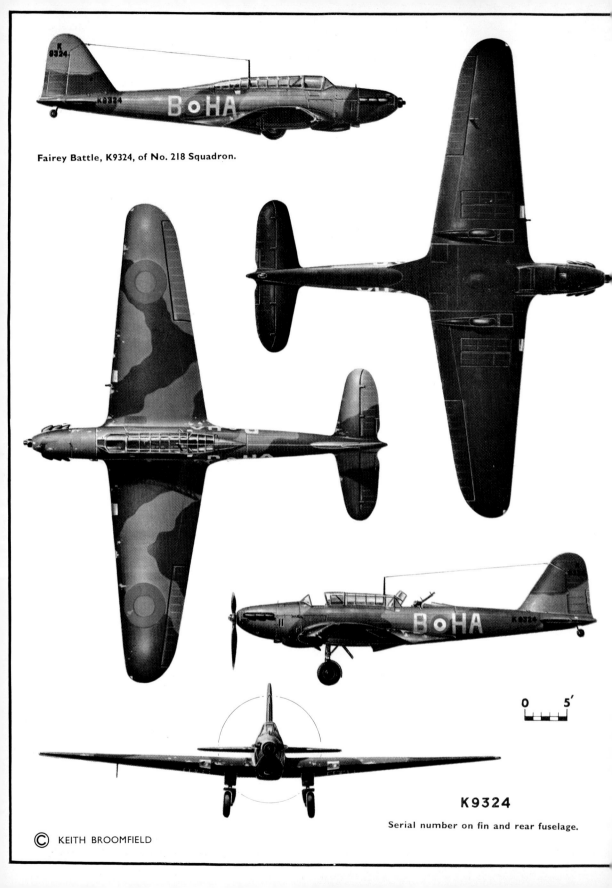

Fairey Battle, K9324, of No. 218 Squadron.

K9324

Serial number on fin and rear fuselage.

0 ___ 5′

© KEITH BROOMFIELD

The Fairey Battle

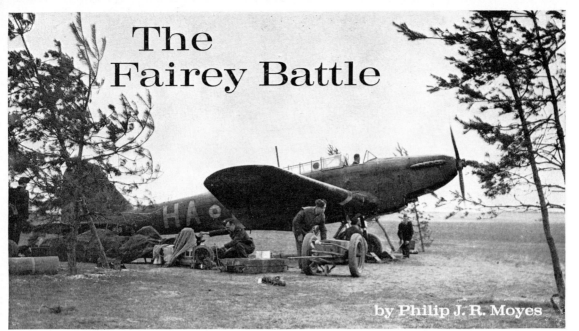

by Philip J. R. Moyes

A Battle of No. 218 Squadron at Auberives-sur-Suippes, France, during the "phoney" war. The roundels on fuselage and under wing appear to have been washed over with a darkish paint. (Photo: Imperial War Museum)

First flown in March 1936, the Fairey Battle was operationally obsolete by 1939 when it was in service as a front-line bomber. Following a gallant and hopeless career in France and, afterwards, a more fortunate spell of operations from Britain, it was relegated (except in a few isolated cases) to training duties in which it contributed more to the war effort that it ever did as an operational machine.

The Battle originated in Air Ministry Specification P.27/32 which was issued in April 1933, and called for a 2-seat single-engined monoplane day bomber which could carry 1,000 lb. of bombs for 1,000 miles at 200 m.p.h. and which would replace the Hawker Hart. Four companies submitted design proposals to meet the specification, Armstrong Whitworth, Bristol, Fairey and Hawker, and from these the A.W.29 and the Fairey entry were ordered in prototype form.

The Fairey day bomber was designed by Marcel Lobelle. The prototype (K4303) was built at Hayes and flew for the first time on 10th March 1936 at Northolt, with a 1,030-h.p. Rolls-Royce Merlin I engine driving a three-bladed de Havilland variable-pitch airscrew. Lobelle chose the Merlin on account of its power and compact frontal area and was thus able to design an aircraft which combined exceptionally clean lines with a good speed performance. Service trials at Martlesham Heath showed that the new Fairey bomber offered a performance far in advance of any contemporary day bomber and a maximum speed of 257 m.p.h. was reached.

Meanwhile some (if not all) of the Air Staff had reached the conclusion that the light bomber was outmoded on the score of insufficient range and bomb load to attack the obvious enemy, Germany. However, the pressure for immediate expansion of the R.A.F.'s first-line strength so as to maintain at least numerical parity with the *Luftwaffe* had become irresistible and provision was made for large scale production of the Fairey bomber which later became

known as the Battle. The initial production contract for 155 Battles to Specification P.23/35 was placed with Fairey in 1935—before the prototype flew—and a production line was subsequently established at the new factory at Heaton Chapel (Stockport). The first production Battle (K7558) made its maiden flight in June 1937, and it was with this aircraft that official handling and performance trials were conducted.

In the performance trials K7558 did 243 m.p.h. at 16,200 ft. and had a range of 1,050 miles with its maximum bomb load. The powerplant of the first 136 Fairey-built Battles remained the Merlin I and it is interesting to note, incidentally, that the initial order for 200 Merlins for the Battle was the first to be received by Rolls-Royce and it was for this order that the Merlin I was put into production.

THE BATTLE DESCRIBED

The Battle was Fairey's first venture into light alloy stressed-skin construction and it was also the company's first low-wing monoplane. The slim, oval section fuselage was built in two portions. The section

Battle prototype K4303 in original form.

3

Battle prototype K4303 with original cockpit canopy.

forward of the pilot's cockpit—the engine mounting in fact—was largely made up of steel tubes, bolted and riveted together, while the rear portion was a metal monocoque comprising hoop frames, stamped out in one piece, and Z-section stringers; the rear portion was built up on core jigs. The wings were of two-spar construction, the centre section—partly of steel struts—being built integral with the fuselage. The spars were girder-like at the roots and changed in section to flanged beams as they neared the wing-tips. Inspection panels ran spanwise along the undersides of the wings. The ailerons—like the elevators and rudder—were metal framed with fabric covering while the split trailing-edge flaps were constructed entirely of metal.

Provision was made in the production Battle for a crew of three, a radio operator/air gunner being added to the pilot and the observer specified by P.27/32. The bombs were carried on hydraulic jacks which retracted into wing cells. When released the bombs fell through specially designed trap-doors except in the case of dive-bombing, when the jacks and their load were lowered below the wing surfaces. Normal bomb load was 1,000 lb. (usually comprising four 250-lb. G.P. bombs) but allowance was made for an overload of 500 lb., the extra bombs being carried on external racks. The observer-cum-bomb-aimer's cabin was situated immediately below the pilot's seat. Bomb aiming was done from the prone position, the target being exposed to view through a large screened aperture which was covered by a sliding panel when not in use. Defensive armament consisted of a fixed 0·303 in. Browning gun in the starboard wing, outside the airscrew arc. Provision was also made for a single Vickers 'K' gun of similar calibre on a Fairey high-speed mounting in the rear cockpit; this mounting allowed the gun to be stowed within the fairing of the fuselage when not in use, but was not in fact installed until the twenty-eighth aircraft (K7585).

The Battle was an extremely robust aircraft and has been described as "just too easy" to fly, even for someone who had previously done only an hour's solo in any single-engined type of similar size and complexity. The pilot was seated in a roomy, comfortable cockpit and forward visibility was reasonably good; rear vision, however, was poor. The rear gunner's cockpit, about six feet farther back, featured a tilting hood which was intended, when raised, to screen the gunner from the slipstream. Unfortunately it only did half the job; for although it successfully screened the gunner's back from the slipstream, it allowed the backdraught to curl in and slap him full in the face. Mr. H. A. Taylor, a test pilot who flew a wide variety of aircraft during the war, and afterwards wrote of his experiences in *Flight* under the pseudonym

Battle prototype K4303 at the 1936 R.A.F. Display with revised cockpit canopy adopted on production a/c.

Cabin (looking aft).

Cabin (looking forward).

"Indicator", said of the Battle:

"Undoubtedly my most lasting impression . . . was of the intense heat which could sometimes fill the driving compartment and, in cases where there was an open flare chute, of the cloud of dust which, combined with the overheating, produced quaintly Saharan conditions. Otherwise this aircraft, even to the complete newcomer, handled like a large tin Swallow."

(The B.A. Swallow was a lightly-loaded two-seater, based on the German Klemm, and was a familiar feature of club aerodromes in the 1930s.)

The flap and undercarriage selector levers sprouted from the floor on the pilot's left and, since the undercarriage lever had a not-too-easily-found safety catch,

Above: *Gunner in an R.C.A.F. Battle Trainer.*
(Photo: R.C.A.F.)

retraction after take-off could be quite a contortionist performance. According to "Indicator", one of the mildly disturbing features of the Battle's take-off was the fact that the change of pitch of the two-position airscrew reduced the recorded revs of the Merlin on the climb to something which had very much the appearance of complete engine failure.

"However, one soon became accustomed to this, and to the extraordinary arrangement of the undercarriage lights which, in a very real sense, shouted 'wheels' at the driver in unmistakable terms."

INTO SERVICE

Further orders for the Battle were placed with Fairey in 1936 to Specification P.14/36 and when the Shadow Factory Scheme came into operation, the resources of Austin Motors at Longbridge (Birmingham) were added to the Battle production programme, the firm receiving an initial order for 863 aircraft to Specification P.32/36.

As mentioned earlier, the first production Battle flew early in 1937. By the end of that year 85 Battles had been completed by the parent company and several R.A.F. squadrons had been re-equipped, or were in process of re-equipping, with the type. The first of these was No. 63 Squadron which had reformed at Andover in February 1937, flown Hinds,

Below: *Rows of Battles nearing completion in The Austin Motor Company's Longbridge (Birmingham) factory before the war. This photograph vividly depicts the production capacity of a "shadow factory": some seventy Battles can be seen in various stages of construction.*
(Photo: "The Aeroplane")

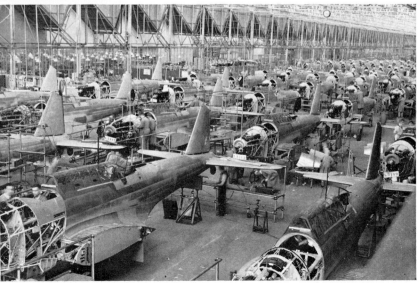

Battle K7650 of No. 63 Squadron in pre-Munich markings.

Battle varied constantly, the majority receiving Merlins II and III but some getting the Mks. IV and V; the last-named mark of Merlin operated at higher boost pressures and produced increased power at altitude. In order to differentiate between the types of Merlin installed, the Battles were retrospectively designated Mks. II, III, IV and V according to the powerplant.

By May 1939 a total of 17 Battle squadrons was in being, and these are enumerated below:

No. 1 Group (An all-Battle Group)

Nos. 15 and 40 Sqdns.	Abingdon
Nos. 103 and 150 Sqdns.	Benson
Nos. 12 and 142 Sqdns.	Bicester
Nos. 88 and 218 Sqdns.	Boscombe Down
Nos. 105 and 226 Sqdns.	Harwell

No. 2 Group

Nos. 35 and 207 Sqdns.	Cottesmore
Nos. 52 and 63 Sqdns.	Upwood
No. 98 Sqdn.	Hucknall

No. 5 Group

Nos. 106 and 185 Sqdns.	Thornaby

The No. 2 Group Battle squadrons assumed a non-mobilising training rôle and in September 1939 they were transferred to No. 6 (Training) Group of Bomber Command and made into Group pool squadrons or, in the case of No. 98 Squadron, a reserve squadron. It was from the No. 6 Group pool squadrons that some of the Operational Training Units were formed in the spring of 1940.

then Audaxes and had, since March, been based at Upwood. It received its first Battle (*K7559*) on 20th May 1937, got three more in June and by the year's end had 15 on charge. Between 2nd July and 21st March 1938, No. 63 conducted Battle development trials using *K7562, 7563* and *7566*. Other squadrons which received Battles in 1937 were Nos. 105, 226, 52 and 88 in that order. No. 105 Squadron's link with the Battle is commemorated in the unit's badge—a battle axe, with the motto "Valiant in Battles".

The first Austin Motors-built Battle (*L4935* with Merlin II engine) flew on—or else shortly before—22nd July 1938 (*not* on 25th August 1938 as sometimes stated) and before the year was out 29 aircraft had been completed at Longbridge. By now the Battle was indubitable obsolescent but because of the need to maintain existing labour forces intact and difficulties in getting other types into production at Heaton Chapel and Longbridge to take its place, the type was kept in production. As a result of stop-gap orders, the steady flow of Battles continued from the two factories until late 1940, by which time a grand total of 2,185 aircraft had been manufactured. Not all of these were bomber aircraft (some being built as dual-control trainers or target-tugs, as will be mentioned later) nor were they all powered by the Merlin I. The type of Merlin available for installation in the

WAR OPERATIONS WITH R.A.F.

The ten mobilising squadrons of No. 1 Group formed the first echelon of the Advanced Air Striking Force, flying on 2nd September 1939 to previously-selected airfields and landing grounds in the heart of the champagne country to await the arrival, some days later, of the ground crews. One Battle (from No. 40 Squadron) failed to arrive; it came down in the Channel owing to engine failure but the crew were rescued. The Battles were quickly dispersed about their landing grounds and hidden among trees or under

Battle L4958 of No. 63 Squadron in pre-war but post-Munich markings. Photo shows that codes were "ON" and not "NE" as thought by air historians hitherto.

(Photo: S/L F. E. Dymond)

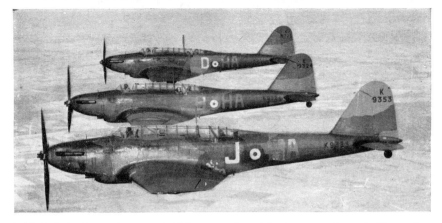

camouflage nets. The idea behind their despatch to France was that, should the Germans begin bombing, these light bombers could retaliate on Ruhr targets at closer range than from Britain. As things turned out, both the Allies and the Germans refrained from starting any unrestricted bombing offensive and this phase became known as the "phoney" war. The Battles were employed on armed daylight reconnaissance over the Siegfried Line, albeit not without suffering losses. On 20th September three Battles from No. 88 Squadron (Mourmelon-le-Grand) were intercepted by enemy fighters during a patrol and two of them shot down. However, the score was partly levelled: for Sgt. F. Letchford, rear gunner in the other Battle (*K9243*) destroyed a Messerschmitt Bf. 109; this was the R.A.F.'s first air combat "kill" of W.W.II. Ten days later, on 30th September, five Battles of No. 150 Squadron (Écury-sur-Coole) on their way to reconnoitre a strongly-defended position in the Saar, were "jumped" by 15 Bf. 109s and in the long running-fight that ensued three Battles were shot down and the other two were so badly damaged that they eventually force-landed (one of them force-landed in France but somersaulted and was destroyed by fire). This incident underlined forcibly the necessity for bombers to be escorted by fighters when over enemy territory during daylight.

Following No. 150 Squadron's tragic encounter, efforts were made to mount a "free" gun underneath the Battle to eliminate a dangerous blind spot, but though various mountings were tried none proved entirely satisfactory, so the Battle remained extremely vulnerable to fighter attack from below. During the winter of 1939–40 the activities of the Battle force

(which was reduced by two squadrons in December when Nos. 15 and 40 Squadrons returned to the U.K. to re-arm with Blenheims) were largely confined to training and exercises. About the middle of March 1940 it was given the task of making several short-range leaflet raids over Rhineland towns but otherwise it saw little activity until the German offensive against France and the Low Countries.

The German assault came at dawn on 10th May 1940, and at midday (and when the already long-overdue permission of the French Generalissimo to start bombing the enemy was still not forthcoming) the R.A.F. C.-in-C. British Air Forces in France, ordered the first wave of Battles into action against German troops advancing through Luxembourg. As it was impossible to provide the Battles with a close fighter escort, the bombers were briefed to make a very low approach to the target and to attack from 250 feet, using bombs fused for eleven seconds' delay. The orders were carried out, but a storm of machine gun and small arms fire rose from the German columns and three of the Battles were shot down. A similar fate overtook the second wave of bombers which attacked during the afternoon. Of the 32 Battles despatched that day, 13 were lost and all the rest damaged. On the following day, of eight Battles despatched (by Nos. 88 and 218 Squadrons) only one returned. On 12th May an attempt was made to check the German advance towards Brussels by bombing two road bridges over the Albert Canal. Five volunteer crews of No. 12 Squadron—the "Dirty Dozen"

Above and left: *Battle (T) R7365 of R.A.F. The first dual-control trainer Battle flew in 1939 and production began with P6616.* Below: *Battle Target-tug 1699 of R.C.A.F. The prototype (L5598) was built in February 1940 and some T.T.s were converted from Battle bombers. Battle T.T.s also served with the R.A.F., Royal Navy, and R.A.A.F.*

(Photos: Imperial War Museum)

as it was now known in the Service—were despatched and all attacked the bridges through withering flak and small arms fire. All were shot down but one of the bridges, that at Veldwezelt, was seriously damaged, and the action resulted in the posthumous award of the Victoria Cross to F/O D. E. Garland and his observer, Sgt. T. Gray, who led the formation attacking the Veldwezelt bridge. They were the first R.A.F. V.C.s of W.W.II.

In the early morning of 14th May ten Battles of Nos. 103 and 150 Squadrons attacked German pontoon bridges in the Sedan area and, furthermore, did so without loss—for no enemy fighters were encountered and the tactical low approach had now been abandoned. In the afternoon the entire available force of these aircraft in France was despatched against bridges and troop columns at Sedan. This time, however, things were very different: the Bf. 109s were now on guard. No. 12 Squadron lost four aircraft out of five; No. 142 Squadron, four out of eight; No. 226 Squadron, three out of six; No. 105 Squadron, six out of eleven; No. 150 Squadron, four out of four; No. 88 Squadron, one out of ten; No. 103 Squadron, three out of eight; and No. 218 Squadron, ten out of eleven. In all, from the 63 Battles which took off, 35 did not return. To these losses were added five out of eight Blenheims of Nos. 114 and 139 Squadrons which had also figured in the attack. This brought the total losses in the raid to 40 bombers out of 71. No higher rate of loss in an operation of comparable size has ever been experienced by the R.A.F.

Despite their appalling losses and frequent transfer of bases as the enemy advanced, the Battle squadrons struggled on valiantly until mid-June when, with the war situation in France now hopeless, the few remaining serviceable aircraft were flown back to England and No. 1 Group was re-formed. It was once again equipped with Battles and for several months its squadrons (which eventually included some Polish units) operated by night from Newton (Notts.) and northern airfields against Dutch and French ports in which Hitler was massing his invasion craft for Operation *Sea Lion*—the projected invasion of Britain. The last operational sorties by No. 1 Group's Battles were flown on 15/16th October 1940, when No. 301 (Polish) Squadron bombed Boulogne and Nos. 12 and 142 Squadrons bombed Calais. During late 1940 No. 1 Group's Battle squadrons converted to Wellington aircraft.

When Nos. 88 and 226 Squadrons had remustered following the French collapse they took their new Battles to Sydenham (Belfast) and were engaged until 1941 in flying regular dawn and dusk patrols along the entire coast of Northern Ireland as a precaution against possible landings by enemy agents. In July 1940, No. 98 (Battle) Squadron which had also flown Battles in France—though not in an operational rôle—was posted to Iceland where it subsequently saw eleven and a half months' active service with No. 15 Group, Coastal Command.

EXPORTS AND TRAINING ROLES

The South African Air Force purchased a few Battles (beginning with *L5374* for evaluation tests, two others being *R3938* and *R3945*) and operated them in the Western Desert and also in East Africa; one of its squadrons (No. 11) is known to have used Battles until early 1942. Four Battles were reserved for Turkey and actually painted in Turkish markings before their delivery was halted by the British Government. Others sold to Turkey in mid-1939 were *N2111*–

Right: *Battle 1640 of No. 1 Bombing and Gunnery School near Jarvis, Ontario.*

Below: *Another R.C.A.F. Battle bombing and gunnery trainer—No. 1737.*
(Photo: R.C.A.F.)

2117, N2120–2123, N2130–2131, N2149, N2153–2155, N2211–2218 and N2220–2222 (29 a/c.). The Battle was popular with the Turkish Air Force crews, particularly on account of its manœuvrability and much time was spent in low flying—a pastime which reportedly wrote-off most of the aircraft! One Battle (N2219) was consigned by sea to Poland in September 1939, but is believed to have been diverted to the Middle East. Nine aircraft earmarked for the Greek Air Force (P6607–6615) were retained for R.A.F. use.

In addition to being used for operational duties, the Battle was used for a variety of training rôles. It served as a dual-control trainer (with two separate cockpit covers in place of the long canopy), a bombing and gunnery trainer (sometimes fitted with a Bristol

Type I turret) and also as a target-tug; and it not only flew with the R.A.F. in the training rôle but also with the R.C.A.F., the R.A.A.F. and the S.A.A.F.

The R.C.A.F. received its first Battles in August 1939, when eight were allocated to Camp Borden. More followed from England and a total of 802 eventually served with the R.C.A.F. They were used as dual-control trainers, target-tugs and gunnery trainers in the Bombing and Gunnery Schools of the British Commonwealth Air Training Plan. With the introduction of Bolingbrokes and Harvards, the number of Battles in service declined, but they continued in service until the end of hostilities. Battles were also flown by Nos. 111 and 122 Squadrons of the R.C.A.F.

One of the many Battles shipped to Canada (R7439) was re-engined by Fairchild at Quebec with an 840-h.p. Wright Cyclone GR–1820–G3B, which would have been installed in more Battles had supplies of the Merlin failed. In the event, this did not happen and only R7439, complete with a Bristol turret, was converted.

In Australia the R.A.A.F. prefix A22 was allocated to the Battle, but the aircraft (unlike those shipped to Canada) retained their R.A.F. serial numbers. The

Right and below: *The Wright-Cyclone Battle R7439.*

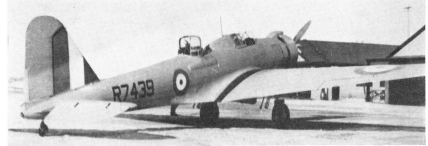

first four Battles (*P2167*, *P2169*, *P5239* and *P5247*) were delivered to No. 1 Aircraft Park at Geelong on 30th April 1940 and the first assembled aircraft, *P5239*, was test flown on 29th June 1940. Thereafter, Battle deliveries steadily increased until the 366th and last Battle, *V1202*, was received at No. 2 A.P. on 7th December, 1943. In addition to the bomber version, a number of Battle target-tugs and Battle dual-control trainers were imported. Battles served mainly at Bombing and Gunnery Schools until 1945, and were finally phased out after service in 1949. In 1940 P/O R. Givens of No. 88 Squadron, R.A.F., flew Battle *K9297* in operations over France with the R.A.F. and in 1941 he flew the same aircraft, *K9297*, in Australia as a F/Lt. instructor on exchange duty with the R.A.A.F.

Of the many Battles used at home by the R.A.F. for training, one eventually found its way to Eire. This was *V1222* of No. 4 Air Observers' School, West Freugh, which was interned on 24th April 1941 after landing in Waterford due to a navigational error made by its Polish pilot. Impressed into the Irish Air Corps as '92', it was used for some years as a target-tug, being eventually struck off charge on 3rd May 1946.

ENGINE TEST-BEDS

Several Battles were adapted as engine test-beds and the most noteworthy of these special variants are set out below:

K9370. Test-bed for 2,000 h.p. experimental Fairey P.24 Prince 24-cylinder, double-banked engine,

driving two three-blade co-axial airscrews independently. Had a very large ventral radiator and double-row exhausts. First flew with P.24 on 30th June 1939 and after 86 hrs. 50 mins. test flying in Britain up until 5th December 1941 was shipped to U.S.A. where it was air tested at Wright Field. In all, the Prince F.T.B. is believed to have accomplished some 250 hours in flight.

K9222. Test-bed for 1,200-h.p. Rolls-Royce Exe 24-cylinder 'X'-type engine which was a pressure-air-cooled variant of the Vulture. *K9222* was converted before the war and testing continued at Hicknall for a long time. A stubby intake was situated under the spinner and two small nostril intakes over the cowling; the intake, however, proved inefficient and the square-cut entry was re-shaped to more pleasing lines with an auxiliary intake underneath. The Exe was considered for a Fairey Spearfish project, but no production was forthcoming and it is believed that *K9222* was used for the R.-R. Griffon.

K9270 and *L5286*. Test-beds for Napier Sabre. Both a/c fitted with a fixed undercarriage, large ventral radiator and auxiliary intake. *K9270* (Sabre) first flew at Northolt on 31st May 1939 and subsequently logged 375 flying hours from Luton before retirement in June 1942. *L5286* (Sabre) was completed at Luton in March 1941 and after logging 33 hours' flying from that airfield it was handed over to the R.A.E. for further tests. In all the Sabre Battles logged about 700 hours.

K9240. Test-bed for 955-h.p. Napier Dagger VIII. Supplied to Napier in 1938 and tested both at Northolt and R.A.E. Experiments conducted with super-charging, cooling and water injection, the latter providing very useful data for the water injection system on the Sabre later in the war.

K9331. Test-bed for 1,010-h.p. Bristol Taurus T.E.1M. Began flight trials in June 1938 and subsequently fitted with Taurus III, trials with latter starting in February, 1939. Fixed undercarriage.

N2042 and *N2184*. Test-beds for 1,300-h.p. Bristol Hercules II. Trials began February 1939. *N2042* later fitted with a fan-cooled Hercules XI and flown with this at R.A.E. in 1942, being eventually scrapped at Filton in Feburary 1945. Both aircraft had fixed undercarriages.

K2234. Test-bed for 1,280-h.p. Rolls-Royce Merlin XII. Chin radiator installed.

Two views of the Fairey P.24 Prince Battle, K9370. In the nose close-up one half of the engine is not running and its airscrew is static.

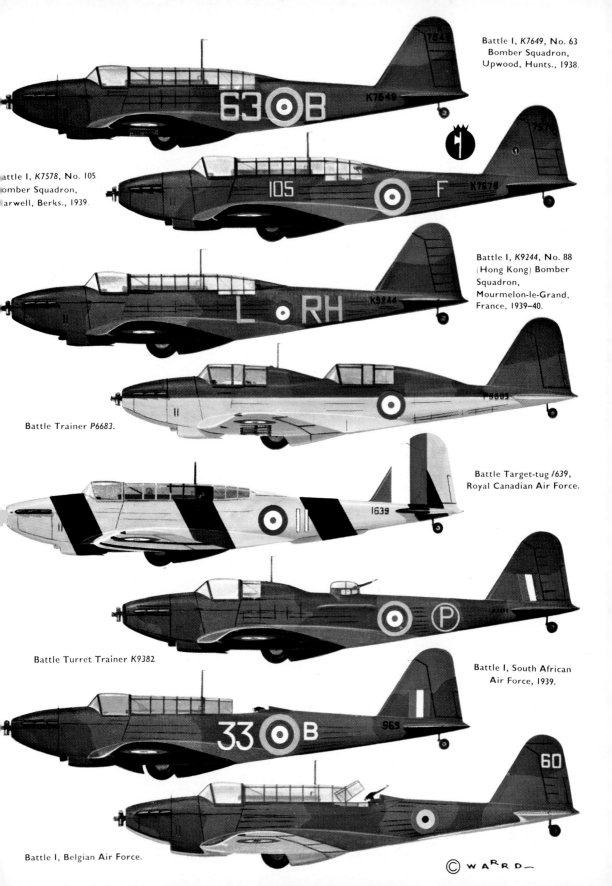

Battle I, K7649, No. 63 Bomber Squadron, Upwood, Hunts., 1938.

attle I, K7578, No. 105 omber Squadron, larwell, Berks., 1939.

Battle I, K9244, No. 88 (Hong Kong) Bomber Squadron, Mourmelon-le-Grand, France, 1939–40.

Battle Trainer P6683.

Battle Target-tug I639, Royal Canadian Air Force.

Battle Turret Trainer K9382

Battle I, South African Air Force, 1939.

Battle I, Belgian Air Force.

© WARD

The Exe Battle K9222.

One of the two Sabre Battles.

Above: *The Taurus Battle, K9331.*
Below: *One of the Hercules Battles (N2042).*

BELGIAN-BUILT BATTLES

In addition to the 2,185 Battles built in the U.K., eighteen were constructed by Avions Fairey at Gosselies for the Belgian Air Force. These aircraft were delivered early in 1938 and orginally equipped Nos. 5 and 7 Squadrons of the 3rd Group, based at Evère. The Belgian Battles, incidentally, had a longer radiator cowling and a smoother camouflage finish

Belgian Battles Nos. 63 and 71.

than the British aircraft, both of which refinements contributed to a slightly improved performance They were powered by Merlin III engines. On 11th May 1940 nine of the Battles made a gallant attempt to destroy the Albert Canal bridges and in the process six of them were lost.

© *Philip J. R. Moyes, 1965.*

PRODUCTION

A total of 2,185 Battles was built in Britain (1,156 by Fairey and 1,029 by Austin Motors) out of 2,419 ordered. Figure of 2,185 included 226 Battle T.T.Is and 100 Battle(T)s. Several aircraft built as bombers were subsequently converted to target-tugs or trainers.

1 prototype	K4303
155	K7558–7712. (First 136 a/c built with Merlin I. Remainder had Merlin II. K7587 delivered to Austin as pattern m/c.)
311	K9176–9486. (Merlin II standard powerplant. K9181 and 9188 delivered to Austin as pattern m/c's).
863 (Austin)	L4935–5797. (L4935–4937 non-standard. L4935–4993, Merlin II; L4994 *et seq.*, Merlin III. L5598–5797 (200 a/c) produced as T.T.Is).
189	N2020–2066, N2082–2131, N2147–2190, N2211–2258. (Several conversions to trainers. N2219 consigned to Poland and others to Turkey—see pp. 8 & 9).
150	P2155–2204, P2233–2278, P2300–2336, P2353–2369.
50	P5228–5252, P5270–5294.
200	P6480–6509, P6523–6572, P6596–6645, P6663–6692, P6718–6737, P6750–6769 (P6616–6769 (100 a/c) built as trainers, i.e. Battle (T)s).
100 (Austin)	R3922–3971, R3990–4019, R3035–3054 (mostly for Empire Air Training Scheme).
100	R7356–7385, R7399–7448, R7461–7480 (mostly delivered direct to Canada).
66 (Austin	V1201–1250, V1265–1280 (T.T.Is).

An additional 18 Battles were built by Avions Fairey in Belgium.

SPECIFICATION

Powerplant (Battle Mk.III): One Rolls-Royce Merlin III 12-cylinder 60° Vee, liquid-cooled, supercharged engine developing 880 h.p. for take-off and 1,440 h.p. at 5,500 ft.
Dimensions: Span 54 ft.; length 52 ft. 1¾ in.; height 15 ft. 6 in.; chord at root 11 ft. 4 in.; chord at tip 5 ft.; wing area 422 sq. ft.; track 9 ft. 9 in.
Weights: Weight empty 6,647 lb.; crew and parachutes 400 lb.; fixed military equipment 573 lb.; removable military equipment 1,432 lb.; fuel and oil 1,740 lb.; weight loaded 10,792 lb.
Loadings: Wing loading 25·6 lb./sq. ft.; power loading 10·4 lb./h.p.
Performance: Max. level speed at sea level 210 m.p.h.; at 10,000 ft. 240 m.p.h.; at 15,000 ft. 257 m.p.h.; at 20,000 ft. 250 m.p.h. Landing speed 60 m.p.h. Time to 5,000 ft. 4·1 min.; to 10,000 ft. 8·4 min.; to 15,000 ft. 13·6 min.; to 20,000 ft. 21·4 min. Service ceiling 25,000 ft. Range at 16,000 ft. at 200 m.p.h. 1,000 mls.; at 16,000 ft. at 257 m.p.h. 640 miles.

PRINTED IN ENGLAND. © Profile Publications Ltd., P.O. Box 26, Leatherhead, Surrey, England, by George Falkner & Sons Ltd., for McCorquodale City Printing Division, London.

PROFILE
PUBLICATIONS

The
Curtiss
P-40
(Tomahawk)

SEPTEMBER 93

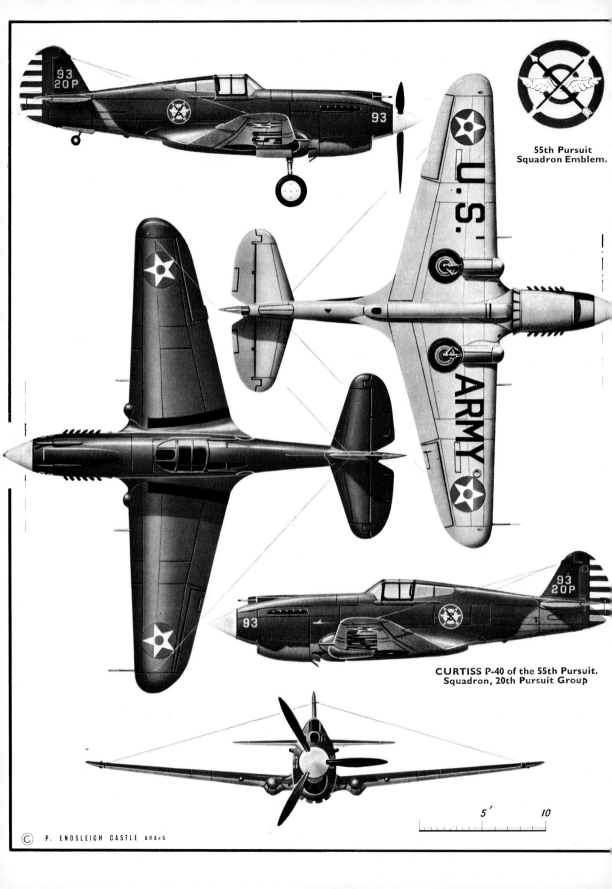

93
20P

93

93
20P

93

U.S.

ARMY

55th Pursuit
Squadron Emblem.

CURTISS P-40 of the 55th Pursuit.
Squadron, 20th Pursuit Group

5'   10

The Curtiss P-40 Tomahawk

by Ray Wagner

Tomahawk IIBs of No. 112 Squadron, R.A.F., at Sidi Heneish in the Western Desert, November, 1941.
(Photo: Imperial War Museum)

When the United States entered World War Two, its most important fighter was the Curtiss P-40, for more had been constructed than all other Army fighters put together. In December 1941 the P-40 was fighting the Axis Powers from Egypt and Moscow to China and the Philippines, and it was either praised fervently or damned vigorously for the part it played in the great struggle.

The P-40 went into full-scale production during the summer of 1939 and from then until December 1944, when the P-40N-40 was withdrawn from production, it had been the subject of continuous development; had served with the Allies in practically every war theatre, and had worn the insignia of twenty-eight Allied and friendly nations. On 22nd November 1944 the Curtiss Aviation Division delivered its 15,000th fighter—this was a P-40N Warhawk.

Some indication of the enormous P-40 production programme undertaken by Curtiss can be assessed by its claim upon floor space and manpower. During 1941 the Curtiss Airplane Division expanded its manufacturing area by approximately 400 per cent and it totalled 4,268,410 square feet. The total work force was 45,000. This expansion included construction of a second factory at Buffalo, known as Plant Two and totalling some 1,200,000 sq. ft. of working area and, a newly-created plant at Columbus, Ohio, with a floor area of 1,156,000 sq. ft. The original St. Louis facility was expanded to 1,210,450 sq. ft. Production at St. Louis was in excess of eight aircraft per working day, and production of the whole Air plane Division eventually reached sixty aircraft. P-40s produced at St. Louis (No. 1 Plant) carried the suffix CS, while those built at Buffalo and Columbus were designated CU.

How did this fighter which was recognised as being inferior in performance and firepower to contemporary types, ever reach such large scale production?

The Curtiss P-40 was an immediate development of the Curtiss P-36. Aircraft illustrated served with the 95th Pursuit Squadron, U.S.A.A.F.
(Photo: R. Ward Collection)

Above: *The original XP-40 prototype with belly radiator scoop.* Below: *The XP-40 as modified with chin radiator, modified exhaust stacks and revised undercarriage.*

To discover the answer to this question we must examine the history of the P-40, beginning with the Curtiss 75 Hawk, an all-metal, low-wing monoplane designed for the Army Air Corps in November 1934. After several revisions, and overcoming the Seversky P-35S competition, the Curtiss single-seater won a contract for 210 aircraft on 30th July 1937. Most of them were delivered as the P-36A and powered by a single Pratt & Whitney R-1830-13 radial, air-cooled engine.

Operationally the P-36A had a short career, and was considered to be obsolete when Japan attacked America at Pearl Harbour in December 1941. Apart from a brief brush with Japanese fighters it was soon relegated to the advanced training rôle. Export P-36s, or Hawk 75As, saw action with the French on the Western Front, claiming several victories over the much vaunted Messerschmitt Bf 109. After the French collapse a number of Hawks served with the Vichy Air Force. It is a little-known fact that a number of Hawks, captured by the Germans, were refurbished and sold to Finland.

During 1937 the in-line, liquid-cooled Allison engine became available, and Curtiss decided to install one in a P-36 airframe. In March 1937 design work was started and the tenth P-36A aircraft—serial number *38–010*—was selected to mount the new power-plant in. With the new engine the aircraft was designated XP-40.

THE XP-40 IS ORDERED

The XP-40 was ordered by the Air Force in July 1937 and when first flown in October 1938 was similar to the P-36A with the exception of the Allison V-1710-19 (C-13) engine, developing 1,160 h.p. at take-off, and 1,000 h.p. at 10,000 feet. The carburettor air intake was on top of the engine cowling between a ·50 calibre and a ·30 calibre machine gun, standard armament of United States fighters between the wars. A small oil cooler was located beneath the pencil-point nose, with the ventral radiator in a scoop behind the wing.

Maximum speed of the XP-40 was 342 m.p.h. at 12,200 feet, at a gross weight of 6,260 lb. This exceeded that of the Hawker Hurricane, but was inferior to the Supermarine Spitfire and Messerschmitt Bf 109E. Range with 100 gallons of fuel was 460 miles at 299 m.p.h., and with 159 gallons at 200 m.p.h. 1,180 miles was claimed.

Conventional in appearance the XP-40 had a wing span of 37 ft. 4 in. and an area of 236 sq. ft., dimensions that remained the same throughout its history. Fuselage length was 31 ft. 1 in., height 12 ft. 4 in. The XP-40 tipped the scales at 5,417 lb. when empty and 6,870 lb. fully loaded.

The Army Air Corps was planning to expand in the late 1930s and aircraft manufacturers were invited to submit bids for pursuit aircraft on 25th January 1930. The minimum and maximum performance requirements specified indicated that the Army still thought in terms of low-altitude, short-range fighters. Minimum top speed was 310 m.p.h. at 15,000 feet and climb to that altitude in 4·5 to 6 minutes, plus an endurance of two hours at 280 to 355 m.p.h. Maximum speed demanded was 370 m.p.h. at 15,000 feet. Actual wartime air battles, however, were to be fought at altitudes and ranges far greater than those of the specification, and the fighters following the P-40, such as the Mustang and Thunderbolt, were to fight at altitudes of between 30,000 and 35,000 feet, whilst range was in the region of 2,200 miles with auxiliary fuel tanks.

Among the many designs submitted to the specification was the sophisticated Lockheed XP-38 (Lightning) with two turbo-supercharged engines; the Bell XP-39 with its unique arrangement of engine located behind the cockpit; the Seversky XP-41 and AP-4 and Curtiss' own H-75R, P-37 and XP-42.

While not matching the performance, especially at altitudes, of the turbo-supercharged types, the P-40 was less expensive and could reach quantity production a year ahead of the other machines. It was based on an airframe already proven in U.S. service and was in large scale production in the Curtiss plant which had been expanded to fill French orders for the H-75A, the export P-36.

Neither Bell nor Lockheed could go into quantity production for two years, and although the Republic P-43 was based on the P-35 airframe, production facilities were restricted and a large-scale programme could not be attempted until the factory was expanded. Also, the Lockheed fighter was a very advanced concept and it was four years before it was able to take a decisive part in the war in the air.

This, then was the situation facing the Army and one that had to be resolved quickly if the Air Corps was to get a modern fighter. On 27th April 1939 the

An early P-40 showing production pattern landing gear and radiator scoop.

Pilot's view of the P-40 (Tomahawk IIB) cowling. Ring and bead sight can be clearly seen. (Photo: R. Ward Collection)

War Department announced a contract, approved the day before, for 524 P-40 pursuit aircraft at $12,872,898. This was the largest warplane contract ever placed since 1918 and it dwarfed the service test orders placed for the more radical YP-38 and YP-39 designs. The contracts for the Lockheed and Bell fighters were placed on the same day and 13 of each type were ordered. Two weeks later the Army authorised a contract for 13 Republic YP-43s.

PRODUCTION COMMENCES

Work was put in hand immediately the contract was signed and the Curtiss engineers carried out an extensive modification programme on the prototype

Head-on view of R.A.F. Tomahawk IIB reveals radiator air intake, cooling gills and two-tone under-surface colour scheme of blue and black. (Photo: Imperial War Museum)

Tomahawk IIA, AH973, of the R.A.F. Wing guns are installed. (Photo: Curtiss Aircraft Corp.

to improve performance. First the coolant radiator was moved from its original position aft of the wing trailing edge to under the nose, and the exhaust manifolds altered. Later, the aircraft was brought nearer to production standard by adding above the engine cowling the long intake for the single-speed supercharger that became characteristic of early models, as well as individual exhaust stacks, and a modified landing gear. The wheel still rotated through 90 degrees as it folded back to fit flat into the wing, but the fairing plates inherited from the P-36 were deleted and two small doors closed over the wheel strut. The radiator intake was redesigned to include an oil cooler and two coolers for the ethylene/glycol engine coolant.

In May 1940 delivery began on the first production P-40s, which had the Allison V-1710-33 (C15) engine rated at 1,040 h.p. at 15,000 feet, and use of flush riveting to reduce drag. Armament included two ·50 calibre machine guns mounted above the engine cowling and firing through the airscrew disc, and provision for a single ·30 calibre machine gun in each wing. Flight tests of the first machine, 39–156, demonstrated a top speed of 357 m.p.h. at 15,000 feet, a service ceiling of 32,750 feet and a climb rate of 3,080 feet in the first minute and 15,000 feet in 5·3 minutes. Cruising speed was 277 m.p.h. and landing speed 80 m.p.h. The first three P-40s off the production line were utilised for service trials, for the Air Force contract made no provision for the standard practice of supplying YP models.

The production P-40's length of 31 feet 8¾ inches became standard for all early models, but the weight. 5,376 lb. empty, 6,787 lb. gross and 7,215 lb, maximum loaded, was to increase sharply. Two hundred P-40s were delivered to the Army by September 1940 and they had only two synchronised guns. The remaining 324 of the first contract had delivery deferred to enable Curtiss to expedite the 140 H-81A (export P-40s) ordered by France. These aircraft never reached the French Air Force for France collapsed and surrendered to Germany in September 1940. The contract was taken over by the Royal Air Force, and such was the urgency of delivery that many of the 140 machines reached the United Kingdom with French instruments and cockpit lettering. On reaching Britain the P-40s had four ·303 Browning machine guns installed in the wings. They lacked armour plate for the pilot's protection, a bullet-proof windscreen and self-sealing fuel tanks. However, they were re-

placed much later by ships incorporating these refinements, plus more firepower. When the final 324 aircraft for the U.S. Army Air Corps were delivered in September 1940, they, too, were to this standard.

The first H81-A-1 export models reached England in September 1940 and were designated the Tomahawk Mark I, but because of their lack of defence and fire power were relegated to the training rôle. The first Tomahawk bore the serial number AH741 and the following 139 aircraft had serials running from this through to AH880. As more aircraft became available they were issued to Nos. 2, 13, 16, 26, 94, 112, 168, 171, 208, 231, 239, 241, 250, 260, 268, 349, 400, 403, 414, 430 and 613 Squadrons as the Tomahawk Marks I, IA and IB. No. 2 Squadron was the first to operate the Tomahawk. Overseas, the first Desert Air Force squadron to be fully equipped with Tomahawks was No. 112, which exchanged its Gloster Gladiators for the Curtiss fighter. No. 112 became famous for its "Shark's Tooth" insignia on the engine cowling, and this scheme was later adopted by the American Volunteer Group in China.

THE P-40B VARIANT

More warlike was the H81-A-2, or Tomahawk IIA, which carried two ·303 in. machine guns in the wings

Above: *Early production P-40 with pre-war U.S.A.F. insignia and wing guns.* Below: *P-40 of the 35th Pursuit Squadron, 8th Pursuit Group. It lacks wing guns; squadron insignia (black cougar) has been painted out.*

Above: *P-40 of the 35th Fighter Squadron.* (Photo: F. C. Dickey, Jnr.)   Below: *P-40 of the 55th Pursuit Squadron, 20th Pursuit Group*

Above: *P-40 of the 79th Pursuit Squadron, 20th Pursuit Group.*   Below: *Squadron Leader's aircraft, 33rd Pursuit Squadron.*

7

Above: *P-40C of the 77th Pursuit Squadron, 20th Pursuit Group.*   Below: *P-40C, 77th Pursuit Squadron.*

in addition to other refinements, and 110 were delivered to the Royal Air Force. Serials of this batch started at *AH881* and ran through to *AH990*. In September 1940 the U.S. Army adopted this model as the P-40B, the P-40A designation having been dropped, and 131 were procured to replace the deferred P-40s. They began reaching U.S. squadrons in February 1941 and most were eventually deployed to Hawaii and the Philippines. The colourful rudder stripes of the P-40 and earlier Army pursuit aircraft were abandoned for the drab olive camouflage finish. The Hawaii-based

aircraft, sixty-two "B"s and eleven "C"s were caught on the ground when the Japanese attacked Pearl Harbour on 7th December 1941 and the majority destroyed.

The P-40B retained the same dimensions of earlier models, but weight was increased to 5,590 empty, 7,326 lb. gross and 7,600 maximum loaded. The "B" had an inferior performance to that of the original P-40, for top speed was depressed to 352 m.p.h., service ceiling to 32,400 feet and climb rate to 2,860 feet per minute. The fuel capacity of between 120 to

P-40s of the 33rd Pursuit Squadron at Reykjavik, Iceland, 1941.   (Photo: Imperial War Museum)

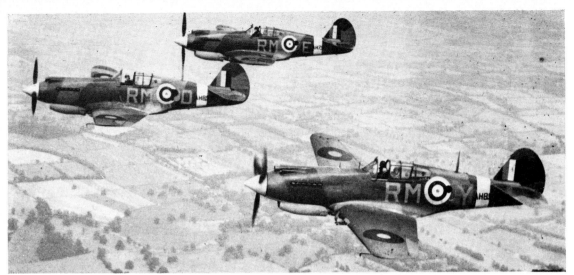

Tomahawk Mk. I and two Mk. IIAs of No. 26 Squadron, England, 1941. (Photo: Imperial War Museum)

160 gallons provided a normal range of 730 miles, and a maximum range of 1,230 miles at the minimum cruise setting.

THE P-40C, TOMAHAWK IIB.

A new fuel system, with 134 gallons in new tanks with improved self-sealing, plus fittings for a 52-gallon drop tank below the fuselage, was employed on the H81A-3, which also incorporated two additional wing mounted ·30 calibre machine guns. bringing the total to six and including the two nose mounted ·50s.

Curtiss built 930 similar aircraft for the R.A.F., in whose service they were known as the Tomahawk IIB, and 193 for the U.S. Army as the P-40C (commencing with *41–13328*). The P-40C, in addition to its extra guns and other internal equipment, had a SCR-247N radio instead of the SCR-283, and it weighed 5,812 lb. empty, 7,459 lb. gross and 8,058 lb. maximum loaded. Maximum speed was 345 m.p.h. at 15,000 feet, service ceiling 29,500 feet and climb rate 2,650 feet per minute. The R.A.F. aircraft had ·303 Browning machine guns instead of the American armament.

P-40B of the A.V.G., Rangoon, 1942.

Serial batches of R.A.F. Tomahawk IIBs ran as follows: *AH991* to *AH999*, nine aircraft with four wing guns and sundry changes. *AK100* to *AK570*, 471 aircraft. Thirty-six of this batch were shipped to China and were selected at random with no particular sequence. *AM370* to *AM519*, 150 aircraft. Sixty-four shipped to China, selected at random. *AN218* to *AN517*, 300 aircraft. One hundred and ninety-five were shipped to Russia, some from America, the remainder from the United Kingdom. Tomahawk IIBs were issued to Nos. 73, 136, 231 and 414 Squadrons.

INTO BATTLE

The exported Tomahawks became the first of the P-40s to see action. Several hundred were kept in England as a reserve force against the expected German invasion of the summer of 1941, and they were issued to army co-operation squadrons for low-level tactical support. In August 1941 they replaced the Westland Lysander two-seaters in Nos. 2, 13 and 26 Squadrons. Sixteen home-based British and Canadian

(Photo: Imperial War Museum)

Study in shark's teeth. Left: *No. 112 Squadron.* Right: *Unit unknown, possibly training unit.* (Photo: Imperial War Museum)

squadrons practised with the type. One unauthorised strafing sortie took place on 28th August by a Tomahawk I from No. 410 Squadron R.C.A.F., and it was the only British-based machine to see action.

Many other Tomahawks were shipped to Takoradi, West Africa, and then ferried to Egypt and the Middle East, where they first went into action in June 1941. Ironically, some of their first victims were the Martin Maryland twin-engined bombers, flown by Syrian-based Vichy French forces. In this area five R.A.F. squadrons as well as Nos. 2 and 4 Squadrons of the South African Air Force, and No. 3 Squadron of the R.A.A.F. used the Tomahawk, strafing Rommel's troops and supply lines. A total of 1,080 Tomahawks of three types were ordered by the R.A.F. Other Tomahawks included two stragglers, namely *AX900* and *BK852*.

After the German invasion of Soviet Russia 146 Tomahawk IIBs were re-shipped there, selected from the reserve force based in the United Kingdom. The last 49 aircraft were sent directly from the U.S.A. They went into action on the Moscow and Leningrad fronts in October 1941, and were the first U.S. planes to be used in the new battle areas.

Another batch of Tomahawks went to bolster Turkish neutrality in November 1941, but the most famous of all Tomahawks were the 100 diverted from the British contracts for shipment to the American Volunteer Group (the A.V.G.) of the Chinese Air Force.

Painted with the shark's teeth inspired by the markings of the Desert Air Force's No. 112 Squadron, the "Flying Tigers" came into existence in August 1941 under the command of Major Claire Lee Chenault. Newly promoted to Brigadier General in the Chinese Army fighting the Japanese. Chenault went to the States in November 1940 to recruit pilots. Of the 100 aircraft sent to China only 90 reached Kyedaw, and these, together with eighty American pilots began operating out of Kumming and Mingaladon in December 1941. They first fought and defeated the Japanese when shooting down six out of a force of ten bombers attacking the town of Kumming on 20th December 1941. The Mingaladon-based squadron did not do so well for they began their operational life with the loss of two pilots when intercepting Japanese bombers three days later.

The A.V.G. was credited with 286 victories over Burma and Southern China before it became the 23rd Fighter Group of the U.S.A.F. The "Flying Tigers" developed tactics whereby the superior climb and manœuvrability of the Japanese fighters could be balanced by the P-40's superior speed and rugged construction. They worked their aircraft hard and

without replacement losses rose rapidly. Some were destroyed on the ground by strafing Japanese fighters, and cannibalisation provided spares for those that could be kept airworthy. By March 1942 only twenty P-40Bs were available, but the U.S. Government furnished a small number of the improved P-40E, thirty being ferried to the A.V.G.

P-40 VARIANTS

A small number of P-40s were converted to RP-40 reconnaissance fighters in 1941, and one aircraft was modified to accept installation of the 1,200-h.p. Pratt & Whitney R-1830 Twin Wasp, radial, air-cooled engine. This was housed in a close fitting cowling and, ironically, was found to give the P-40 a better performance than the standard Allison-powered model. The circle of radial-engine, in-line, radial had been completed.

THE TOMAHAWK DESCRIBED

Low-wing cantilever monoplane with N.A.C.A. aerofoil 2215 at root and 2209 at tip. Structurally it consisted of two wing panels joined at the fuselage centre-line, with longitudinal stringers, shear beams and bulkhead of aluminium alloy covered with a flush-riveted smooth Alclad skin. Ailerons were of aluminium alloy frames covered with fabric. Hydraulically-operated split trailing-edge flaps extended between the ailerons and fuselage. The fuselage was an aluminium alloy semi-monocoque structure built up of Alclad bulkheads, aluminium alloy stringers and a flush-riveted, stressed Alclad skin.

Tail unit was a cantilever monoplane with all-metal framework, the fixed surfaces having a smooth metal covering, whilst moving surfaces were covered with

Tomahawk IIB of No. 26 Squadron, R.A.F.
(Photo: Imperial War Museum)

P-40, 35th Pursuit Squadron.

© WARRD.—

58 8P

35th Pursuit Sqdn.

P-40, 36th Pursuit Squadron.

80 8P

36th Pursuit Sqdn.

-40B,
3rd Pursuit Squadron, Reykjavik,
celand, Aug. 1941.

36

-40B,
4th Pursuit Wing, Wheeler Field,
Hawaii, Dec. 1941.

333

7 7 A 7 7

▲ 77th Pursuit Sqdn. 48
20th Pursuit Group 20P

Tomahawk Mk.IIB, No. 112 Squadron, No. 262 Wing, LG 75,
idi Haneish, Egypt, Sept. 1941.

A AK461

Tomahawk Mk.I, No. 26 Squadron.

RM E AH79

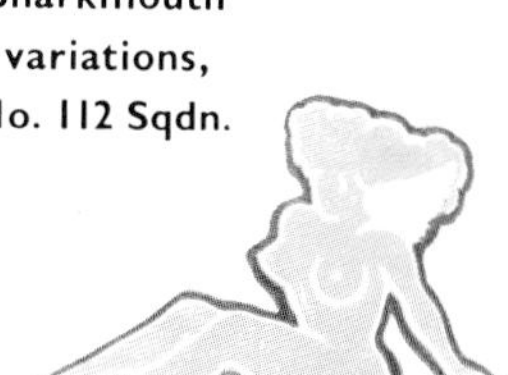

"Sharkmouth"
variations,
No. 112 Sqdn.

-40B, AVG, Mingaladon, Rangoon,
Burma, Jan./Feb. 1942.

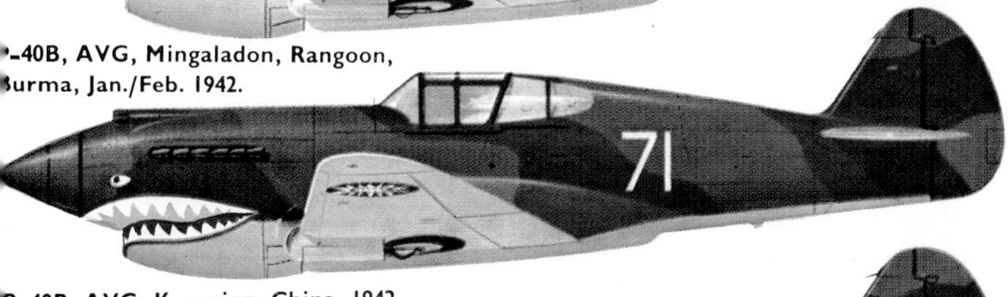

71

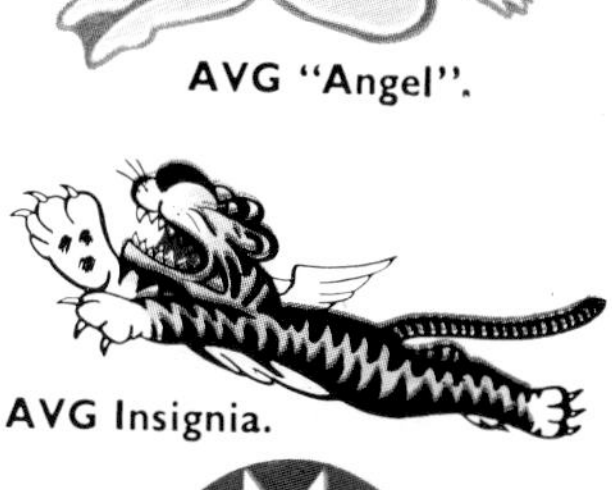

AVG "Angel".

P-40B, AVG, Kunming, China, 1942.

66

AVG Insignia.

AVG wing marking.
▶

Interesting and unusual colour scheme is carried by this P-40 in the Western Desert. Thought to be early camouflage pattern.

fabric. Adjustable trim tabs were fitted to the elevators and rudder.

Undercarriage consisted of two Curtiss oleo-pneumatic, shock absorber legs with wheels retracting backwards and rotating through 90 degrees to lie flush within the wing. Struts were enclosed in hinged fairings beneath the wing. Tail wheel was retractable and steerable, and when in the up position was enclosed by two doors.

Powerplant was a single Allison V–1710–33, twelve cylinder, liquid-cooled Vee engine developing 1,150 h.p. at take-off. It had a single speed, internal blower (supercharger) and integral reduction gears driving a three-blade, fully-feathering variable-pitch Curtiss electric propeller. Twin radiators were installed in a scoop under the engine cowling, and they cooled the ethylene/glycol coolant, 3·7 gallons of which was stored in a tank on the engine bulkhead. The oil cooler was also installed in this scoop. The Allison operated most efficiently at 12,000 feet, but power fell off at 15,000 feet and over.

Fuel, 148 gallons, was contained in three main tanks—front wing 35 gallons; main wing 50·5 gallons and fuselage 62·5 gallons. Normal fuel consumption of 50 to 60 gallons per hour provided 2½ hours flying. A belly tank, varying between 52 and 150 gallons could be installed.

Armament consisted of two to four free-firing ·30 calibre (·303 Brownings in the British P-40s) in the wings, and two ·50 calibre on the engine cowling. Each gun was charged manually on the ground and carried 235 rounds of ammunition, enough for approximately 10 seconds continuous firing.

© *Ray Wagner, 1965.*

U.S.A.F. PRODUCTION				
Quantity	Model	Contract	Date approved	Serial Nos.
1	XP–40	AC–10136	30 July 1937 (ord.)	38–010
65	P–40	AC–12414	26 April 1939	38–156 to 220
68	P–40	AC–12414	26 April 1939	39–222 ro 289
(390 P–40s to this contract cancelled)				39–290 to 679
66	P–40	AC–12414	26 April 1939	40–292 to 357
100	P–40B	AC–15802	13 Sept. 1940	41–5205 to 5304
31	P–40B	AC–15802	13 Sept. 1940	41–13297 to 13327
193	P–40C	AC–15802	13 Sept. 1940	41–13328 to 13520

SPECIFICATION				
	P-40 Tomahawk I, IA, IB	P-40B Tomahawk IIA	P-40C Tomahawk IIB	
Dimensions				
Wing Span	37 ft. 4 in.	37 ft. 4 in.	37 ft. 4 in.	
Wing Area—Sq. ft.	236	236	236	
Length	31 ft. 8¾ in.	31 ft. 8¾ in.	31 ft. 8¾ in.	
Height	10 ft. 7 in.	10 ft. 7 in.	10 ft. 7 in.	
Weight—lbs.				
Empty	5,376	5,590	5,812	
Normal loaded	6,787	7,326	7,459	
Maximum loaded	7,215	7,600	8,058	
Performance				
Max. Speed at 15,000 ft.	357	352	345	
Cruising—m.p.h.	277	273	270	
Landing	80	80	85	
Normal Range—miles	650	730	730	
Maximum Range	1,400*	1,230	1,230	*160 U.S. Gallons of
Service Ceiling—ft.	32,750	32,400	29,500	fuel.
Climb Rate—f.p.m.	3,080	2,860	2,650	
Armament				
·30 M/gns.	2	4**	4	**British ·303 M/gns.
·50 M/gns.	2	2	2	
Fuel—Gallons	100–168	120–160	134–186	
Engine	Allison V–1710–33	Allison V–1710–33	Allison V–1710–33	
H.P.	1,040	1,040	1,040	

PRINTED IN ENGLAND. © Profile Publications Ltd., P.O. Box 26, Leatherhead, Surrey, England,
by George Falkner & Sons Ltd., for McCorquodale City Printing Division, London.

PROFILE
PUBLICATIONS

THE
SAAB
J29

NUMBER 99

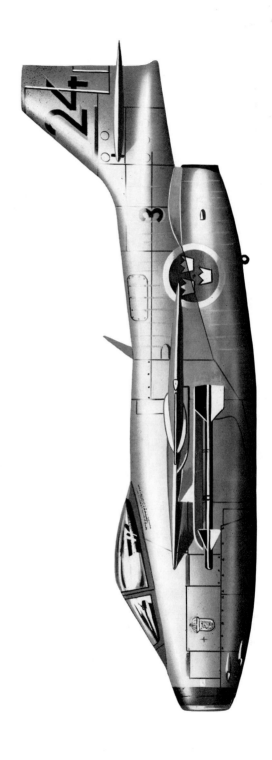

The crowns of the Swedish national insignia are edged in black.

29606

Emblem of
Flygflottilj 3.

SAAB J 29F (29606) of Flygflottilj 3, 2nd Division,
Malmen, Linkoping, Sweden.

© JAMES GOULDING

0'   5'   10'

The SAAB J 29
by Bo Widfeldt

An S 29C photo-reconnaissance aircraft of the F 11 Wing. Serialled 29930 it had a light grey fin with a yellow "K", and the F 11 Wing badge was displayed on the nose.

During W.W.II Sweden experienced a degree of technical isolation, for all aeronautical engineering progress achieved abroad was carefully shrouded in so far as it possessed any military value. Towards the end of the war many of the engineers employed at Svenska Aeroplan A.B. (SAAB) were aware that they had fallen behind in aeronautical progress, particularly in the field of jet propulsion, in which both the British and Germans had carried out secret development on a large scale. The results of this work were disclosed suddenly at the end of the war with the appearance of several types of jet aircraft, which were superior to all contemporary propeller-driven types.

SAAB made strenuous efforts to catch the leaders in the jet propulsion race, and they achieved a great deal despite the lack of suitable research facilities. Certain resources were available and a number of prominent Swedish engineers were working on design studies although no actual development work had taken place. The view held then was that the practical application of the system belonged to the future.

On the initiative of the Swedish Air Force, however, the design of jet engines was undertaken by a number of Swedish companies, and in the spring of 1945, SAAB was commissioned to investigate the most suitable configuration for a jet propelled fighter.

PRELIMINARY STUDIES

The first design drawn up during this period was the RX 1. It featured twin tail booms, similar to those of the SAAB 21A and de Havilland Vampire, and was to be powered by an engine delivering some 13,300 lb. thrust. Maximum speed was estimated at (740 km/hr.). The Swedish companies concerned with the design of jet engines at this period were Svenska Flyg-motor AB (SFA), AB Lundströms Ångturbin (ALA/AB) and Svenska Turbinfabrike AB Ljungström (STAL). Another SAAB design of the period was a development of the RX 1 designated the RX 2 "Merry Widow".

In the autumn of 1945 the first SAAB design on more detailed lines was revealed and was known as the R 101. Its appearance could be likened to the well-known Lockheed F-80 Shooting Star, of which SAAB had no knowledge at that time. When the design

reached the stage when more detailed development was to be proceeded with, illustrations and a description was published of the Shooting Star, which was in series production. It was obvious that the entire SAAB design was bordering on obsolescence and there was little prospect of overtaking the lead gained by other manufacturers. As a result the R 101 was abandoned with reluctance, for SAAB were anxious to obtain experience in the design and construction of a jet fighter.

SWEDEN'S FIRST JET

During autumn 1945 it was decided that a jet propelled version of the SAAB 21A (J 21A) should be produced. At that time the de Havilland Goblin jet engine was released for export and some examples were purchased, one being installed in a conversion of the 21A designation SAAB 21R (J 21R). The prototype 21R flew for the first time on 10th March 1947 and a total of sixty were later delivered to the Swedish Air Force. Having established and produced a stop-gap jet fighter, SAAB were now able to give full attention to designing a jet fighter of advanced configuration.

The first prototype SAAB 29 "Tunnan" (serial 29001) flew for the first time on 1st September 1948.

Second prototype J 29 (29002) bearing Swedish national markings.

First production J 29A (29101) in flight. (Photo: SAAB)

A J 29F of the F 4 Wing, Yellow F on fin.

A J 29B of the F 22 Wing with drop tanks and underwing pylons.

"BARREL" DEVELOPMENT

The first scheme for a new type of jet aircraft was drawn up at the end of October 1945, and the power-plant specified was the de Havilland Goblin engine with a thrust of approximately 3,100 lb. (1400 kp.) mounted immediately behind the centre of the fuselage. The pilot was seated above a single, straight air duct, producing a deep fuselage, and in order to keep the high speed profile wing free from cut-outs the retract-able landing gear was located in the fuselage sides, thus imparting a circular cross-section to the fuselage.

For reasons of stability the tail boom supporting the empennage was lengthened beyond the lower, shortened section of the fuselage in which the engine exhaust was located. This enabled the full landing angle to be obtained with the low-positioned under-carriage.

Notwithstanding certain aesthetic imperfections, the many obvious advantages of the aircraft aroused the interest of the Swedish Air Force and work on the design was proceeded with experimentally. But certain events took place which were to result in a revised pro-gramme by the SAAB team. First, technical informa-tion from de Havillands in England was obtained relating to a larger engine—the Ghost—which was undergoing development, and which was estimated to produce a thrust of 5,000 lb. (2270 kp.). It was obvious that such a powerful engine would enable SAAB to design and produce a far more advanced fighter, and after negotiations between de Havillands and the Swedish Air Force SAAB was able to in-corporate the engine in the new design. It was dis-covered that the relatively large diameter of the engine (approximately 4·5 ft. (1·35 m.)) was ideal for the fuselage dimensions, these being desirable for many reasons. The fact that the engine could also be fed via a central, circular air intake rendered it eminently suitable for the design.

Secondly, the SAAB engineers were able to obtain first-hand access to an immense quantity of experi-mental material devoted to high speed flight accumu-lated by German scientists during the war. This related primarily to the phenomena of drag and lift approach-ing sonic speed, and the possibilities of improving the performance of an aircraft in the higher speed range by the use of swept wings. This information led SAAB designers to select a wing with a moderate sweep back of 25 degrees combined with a thin profile. From the experimental material it was also possible to calculate how slender the fuselage should be in order that its critical Mach number should not reduce the advan-tages gained with the wing. The first "final" design sketches drawn during January 1946 incorporated all the new information, and the resultant aeroplane was of advance configuration.

Attack version of the J 29 was designated the A 29B. This aircraft served with the F 6 Wing at Karlsborg. Serial number 29439; *letter "I" on fin in yellow.*

PROJECT WORK—R 1001

With the new design it now seemed that SAAB was able to produce a fighter of such advanced performance that it would remain in service for a considerable period. SAAB estimated that a speed of "considerably exceeding 620 m.p.h. (1,000 km./hr.)" could be attained. The main outline was thus clear by February 1946, and the Swedish Air Force now requested that actual work be put in hand on the aircraft R 1001, as this type had been designated. Ten senior engineers and teams were seconded to the design programme and they were to be fully occupied for a total of six months in finding solutions to all the essential construction problems and verifying the preliminary particulars concerning weights and performance with the help of wind tunnel tests and exhaustive calculations.

The wind tunnel tests were started at the Royal University of Technology and the Aeronautical Research Institute, both in the low and high speed tunnels, a number of modified models being subsequently tested and the aircraft shape subjected to final modifications.

In order to give the new fighter the best conceivable lateral stability at take-off and touch-down, automatic slots were introduced on the outer wing section. These were to be interconnected with the flaps so that they were extended with the latter in the take-off and landing positions, but were automatically locked closed with the flaps retracted for high speed flight. To test the new system "Aircraft 201" was constructed; this was a converted SAAB 91A Safir fitted with a half-scale wing of the R 1001.

In the autumn of 1946 all main questions of principle had been solved and a complete specification of the aircraft drawn up. On the basis of this the Air Force placed orders for completing the design and manufacture of three prototypes (serials *29 001* to *29 003*). When this significant step had been taken the type received its definite designation—the J 29.

Two J 29Fs of the F 3 Wing with Sidewinder missiles. Serial of nearest aircraft is 29606, code 24.

One of the first Wings to take delivery of the J 29A was F 9 at Göteborg. This aircraft (serial 29185) lacks code on fin.

A J 29F of the F 10 Wing. Serialled 29549 it bore a blue "N" on the fin, and a black "N" on the blue stripe around the nose air intake.

FINAL DESIGN

An experimental mock-up of the front portion of the SAAB 29 was constructed in order to test various sealing materials for the pressurised cabin, and after various attempts leakage was reduced to an acceptable maximum.

A new innovation for SAAB was the introduction of servo-controlled ailerons. During the summer of 1948 the complete aileron system was tested in a special rig, and as these tests appeared to be satisfactory it was expected that the first prototype J 29 (*29 001*) would fly before 1st August that year. But the servo system developed serious faults, and it was several weeks before these faults were traced and corrected; it was not until the end of August that the prototype was ready for initial taxiing tests.

J 29F, 29506, of the F 10 Wing carrying air exercise "friend or foe" identification markings.

An S 29C photo-reconnaissance aircraft of the F 11 Wing.

Test pilot, Squadron Leader Robert Moore, was in charge of the flying end of the test programme, and in the accepted sequence of events he made several short hops during the taxiing tests. All systems then underwent a final inspection and on 1st September a first flight of 30 minutes was made. On this occasion speed was kept to a minimum for the automatic slots were locked in the extended position and the landing gear doors only partially closed. The flying programme was so arranged that level speed runs were increased in stages with careful control of the many intermediate steps, but the J 29 soon reached and even exceeded the maximum permissible Mach-number for which it was designed. Manœuvrability was excellent and performance figures were in excess of those calculated.

The two first prototypes lacked armament but

A J 29A of the F 13 Wing as used for missile tests, etc. Note fairing for observation camera under tailplane and the wing pylon.

carried heavy test equipment, while the third prototype carried four 20-mm. automatic guns. The fourth, and final, prototype (*29 004*) was flown in 1950.

THE J-29 VARIANTS

J 29A
First version of the SAAB 29 to be built in quantity was the J 29A. The first sixteen (*29 101* to *29 116*) had trim tabs and wing dive brakes. Aircraft *29 117* to *29 132* also featured trim tabs and wing dive brakes, but subsequent aircraft had the dive brakes mounted in the fuselage sides forward of the landing gear doors. A total of 224 J 29As were built and delivered to the Swedish Air Force during the period May 1951 to June 1954.

During June 1946 the F 13 Wing at Norrköping began converting to the J 28A (Vampire FB Mk.1), the Swedish Air Force's first jet fighter. The J 28A was replaced by the J 29A as from May 1951, but the new fighter was not approved by the Air Force until January 1952. By that time it had survived intensive service tests in different climatic environments. In 1960 the F 13 Wing received the J 35A "Draken", but the last J 29A served until 1962.

Deliveries of the J 29A continued and in 1952 the

A J 29A of the F 12 Wing. Red letter "I" on fin; serial 29290.

A J 29F of the F 20 Wing. Serialled 29649, it carried a red "O" outlined in white on the fin, and a white "O" in a red band round the nose air intake.

F 9 Wing at Göteborg converted from the J 28B (Vampire FB Mk.50) to the new fighter. Some of the J 29As served with the Wing until 1962. In 1956 the F 9 Wing also received the up-rated F conversion.

The F 12 Wing, stationed near Kalmar, converted from the J 21A to the 29A in 1952, and the last of the 29As were replaced by the J 32B Lansen in 1960. The F 16 and F 20 Wings took delivery of a quantity of J 29s in 1952 and these were phased out of service in 1963.

The F 3 Wing converted from J 28As to J 29As in 1953, and the latter served with the Wing for ten years. F 10 Wing at Ängelholm converted from the J 21R to the 29A in 1953 and the Wing operated the "Flying Barrel" for ten years.

A number of J 29As equipped the F 8 Wing at Barkarby from 1954, and the last remaining A conversion was still flying with F 8 in 1965.

J 29B

The B conversion differed little from the A, the main modification being extra fuel tanks installed in the wing, increasing the 1,400 litre (310 Imp. gal.) to 2100 litre (460 Imp. gal.) (internal). The J 28B was used as an attack aircraft and for this purpose could be equipped with rockets and napalm bombs. The first B prototype was flown on March 11th 1953 and

during 1954 the B model set up a world air speed record of an average of 607·05 m.p.h. over a 310-mile closed circuit. A total of 332 J 29Bs (or A 29 (A-attack) as it was designated) were built and delivered during the period May 1953 to December 1955. Two hundred and eighty-nine J 29Bs were converted to the J 29F configuration. During 1953 the F6 Wing at Karlsborg converted from the A 21A to the A 29B, the latter serving until 1957 when the A 32A entered service.

The F 8 Wing at Barkarby received the 29B in 1953, and from 1955 it served parallel with the J 34 (Hunter F.4) until 1964.

Another Attack Wing to receive the A 29B was the F 7 Wing at Såtenäs. The Wing's A 21Rs were replaced by the 29B in 1954, the latter serving for two years before being replaced themselves by the A 32A.

S 29C

On 3rd June 1953 the first prototype (*29 901*) of a new photo-reconnaissance plane made its first flight. This was the SAAB 29C which was given the designation S 29C by the Swedish Air Force. During the period May 1954 to May 1956 a total of 76 29Cs were built and delivered, and the type was basically similar to its immediate predecessor with the exception of the fuselage nose section, which was modified to accept the installation of seven cameras. A new international

An S 29C of the F 21 Wing, Lulea. Red "E" on fin outlined in white; serial 29920. Note radar antenna under tailplane.

The first SAAB 29 to be converted to D-standard was 29325. This aircraft, an experimental variant, never saw service in this guise with the Flygvapnet.

speed record over a 621-mile closed circuit was established by a flight of two S 29Cs in 1955.

The F 11 Wing at Nyköping took delivery of the first 29Cs during August 1953 as replacements for their S 31S (Spitfire Mk.19s), but the SAAB machine did not receive Air Force approval until the following May. The 29C was still serving alongside the S 32C Lansen in 1965 until replaced by the S 35E Draken.

The F 21 Wing at Luleå converted from the S 26 (photo-reconnaissance version of the Mustang fighter) in 1954, and in late 1965 the 29C was still serving in parallel with the J 32B.

Originally the S 29C had the same wing as the J 29A and B, but this was modified to E/F standards ("Dog tooth" leading edge). An external antenna for backwards-looking radar was originally installed in the tail cone, but this was later re-located in the fuselage.

SAAB 29D

Parallel with the licence-production of the de Havilland Ghost engine, Svenska Flyg-motor AB (SFA) developed an afterburner which was installed in a standard J 29B (*29 325*) airframe. After a period of flight and other tests, during which it was designated the SAAB 29D, the aircraft was converted to J 29F standard and delivered to the Air Force.

J 29E

During the same period when tests on the SAAB 29D were taking place work was also proceeding on a modified wing shape intended to raise the critical Mach number of the J 29. The first aircraft to be fitted with the new wing was designated the 29E and it flew for the first time on 3rd December 1953. The wing incorporated the "dog tooth" leading edge and a total of 29 J 29Es were built and delivered during the period March to December 1955. All served with the F4 Wing at Östersund for one year when the 19 remaining aircraft of the original batch were converted to F standard.

J 29F

The J 29F was the last variant of the Flying Barrel design and it differed from previous versions in many respects. The most noticeable modification was the introduction of the afterburner developed by the Royal Swedish Air Board in co-operation with SFA and flight tested in the SAAB 29D. The afterburner increased thrust of the Swedish-built Ghost engine by a considerable margin, and it is interesting to note that the SFA afterburner was the first to be successfully used with a British jet engine. The 29F prototype

flew for the first time on 20th March 1954 and was fitted with the modified wing as standardised on the 29E. A total of 210 J 29B/Es were modified by SAAB to F standard and delivered between February 1955 and May 1958. A further 98 aircraft were modified to F standard by the Central Workshop of the Swedish Air Force at Västerås (CVV) during May 1957 to December 1958.

The first unit to re-equip with the new 29F was the F 3 Wing at Malmslätt and it served with this Wing until 1965, when replaced by the J 35 Draken. The F 4 Wing received the J 29F in 1956 and the aircraft was still front-line equipment in 1965.

During 1956 both the F 9 and F 10 Wings were equipped with the J 29F. The former Wing operated their machines until 1963 when they converted to the J 34 (the aircraft being transferred from the F 8 and F 18 Wings). A number of J 29Fs were still serving alongside J 35Ds with F 10 in 1965.

The F 15 Wing at Söderham converted from the

SAAB J 29E of the F 4 Wing. Serial 29357.

One of the first of 15 J 29Fs delivered to Austria. Serial 29457.

SAAB 29 PRODUCTION AND DELIVERIES

Type	Number	Sw AF serials	Delivery periods	Notes
J 29A	224	29101–29324	May 10, 1951–June 8, 1954	
J 29B	332	29328, 29329, 29334, 29335, 29338, 29341, 29344, 29354, 29358, 29363–29366, 29370, 29371, 29374, 29375, 29378, 29385, 29386, 29391, 29393, 29298, 29414, 29418, 29430, 29438, 29440, 29445, 29465, 29473, 29475, 29478, 29481, 29494, 29521, 29523, 29533, 29544, 29546, 29580, 29584, 29645	May 26, 1953–Dec. 2, 1955	The serials are from those 43 a/c which never were converted to J 29F standard.
S 29C	76	29901–29976	May 3, 1954–May 3, 1956	
SAAB 29D	1	29325	—	Experimental: not delivered to the Flygvapnet.
J 29E	29	29345, 29460, 29477, 29532, 29556, 29574, 29600, 29615, 29623, 29639	March 15, 1955–Dec. 29, 1955	Serials only given for those 10 a/c which were never fully converted to J 29F standard.
J 29F	308	29325–29327, 29330–29333, 29336, 29337, 29339, 29340, 29342, 29343, 29346–29353, 29355–29357, 29359–29362, 29367–29369, 29372, 29373, 29376, 29377, 29379–29384, 29387–29390, 29392, 29394–29397, 29399–29413, 29415–29417, 29419–29429, 29431–29437, 29439, 29441–29444, 29446–29459, 29461–29464, 29466–29472, 29474, 29476, 29479, 29480, 29482–29493, 29495–29520, 29522, 29524–29531, 29534–29543, 29545, 29547–29555, 29557–29573, 29575–29579, 29581–29583, 29585–29599, 29601–29614, 29616–29622, 29624–29638, 29640–29644, 29646–29685	Feb. 11, 1955–Dec. 15, 1958	Serials for those 289 J 29B + 19 J 29E which were converted to J 29F standard.

J 28B to the J 29F during 1957, and the latter served with this Wing until 1961 when it re-equipped with the A 32A and became an attack unit.

The F 16 and F 20 Wings at Uppsala successively equipped with the J 29F and a number of them were still serving with these units in 1965. From the end of 1963 all 29Fs in front-line service were equipped with the American Sidewinder infra-red seeking missile (Rb 24), one under each wing.

A total of 661 SAAB 29s were constructed and delivered from May 1951 to May 1956, and of these 308 (29B and Es) were converted to J 29F standards. In 1965 two Air Force Units were still equipped with the 29F as front-line types, and two reconnaissance units, F 11 and F 21, were still operating the S 29C.

FOREIGN SERVICE

In 1961, following an appeal by the United Nations, the Swedish Government sent five J 29Bs to the Congo to provide support and cover for the UNO ground forces. The Swedish UN unit was called the F 22 Voluntary Air Component and the 29Bs carried the legend "UN" in black on a large, white, square

J 29F (29517), the final variant of the "Tunnan". Afterburner alters the aircraft's configuration aft of the wing.

background. The 29Bs were equipped with eight 140-mm. rockets and could also carry two jettisonable fuel tanks under the wings. The J 29Bs were the only combat aircraft at UNO's disposal in the Congo following the withdrawal of Indian Canberras and Ethiopian Sabres and in October 1926 two S 29C reconnaissance fighters joined the original detachment.

The story of F 22 began on 24th September 1961 when the Swedish Government placed the J 29 fighter bombers at UNO's disposal, and the aircraft and personnel arrived at Leopoldville on 4th October. The

The five J 29Bs in Sweden before shipment to the Congo in 1961.

unit's first temporary base was Luluaborg, but they moved on to Kamina where they stayed until their return to Sweden in 1963. The two 29Cs followed the original 29Bs, and in late 1962 a further four 29Bs reached the Congo. Four of the eleven aircraft returned to Sweden in 1963, the other seven being destroyed in August/September 1963. A detailed list of F 22's J 29s and their eventual fate is as follows:—

Type	Serial	Coded	From Sweden	Notes
J 29B	29374	White D	28.9.1961 (F 8)	Crashed after fall out of engine 23.3.63 at Kamina. Blown up.
J 29B	29393	White E	28.9.1961 (F 8)	Blown up at Kamina 1963.
J 29B	29398	White F	28.9.1961 (F 8)	Returned to Sweden 27.4.63 and placed at F 3 for museum.
J 29B	29440	White G	28.9.1961 (F 8)	Crashed at Kamina 16.3.62. Blown up.
J 29B	29475	White J	28.9.1961 (F 8)	Seriously war damaged, blown up at Kamina 1963.
J 29B	29364	White G	7.12.1962 (Arlanda)	Blown up at Kamina 1963.
J 29B	29445	White H	10.12.1962 (Arlanda)	Blown up at Kamina 1963.
J 29B	29371	White C	13.12.1962 (Arlanda)	Returned to Sweden 27.4.1963 and scrapped.
J 29B	29365	White I	16.12.1962 (Arlanda)	Blown up at Kamina 1963.
S 29C	29944	White A	22.10.1962 (Arlanda)	Returned to Sweden 27.4.1963 and put in Air Force service.
S 29C	29906	White B	18.10.1962 (Arlanda)	Returned to Sweden 27.4.1963 and put in Air Force service.

FOREIGN DELIVERIES

On 27th January 1961 the Swedish Government granted the Air Board permission to sell 15 J 29Fs to SAAB for delivery to Austria. The amount was 8 050 000 Sw crowns (£536,500). The 15 aircraft were restored at SAAB and delivered to the Austrian Air Force, forming the first Jagdbomber-Staffel.

In 1962 the Air Board received Swedish Government permission to sell a further 15 J 29Fs to Austria. The amount was 7 700 000 Sw Crowns (£513,300). These aircraft were restored and specially converted by AB Svenska Flygverkstäderna in Malmö. Instead of the two guns in the port side of the nose three cameras could be mounted in a special capsule. The cameras

(Continued on page 12)

SAAB 29 SERVICE WITH THE SWEDISH AIR FORCE

Wing	Type	Period	Notice
F 3 (Malmslätt)	J 29A	1953-1963	
	J 29F	1955-current	First-line service.
F 4 (Östersund)	J 29E	1955-1956	
	J 29F	1958-current	First-line service.
F 6 (Karlsborg)	A 29B	1953-1957	
F 7 (Såtenäs)	A 29B	1954-1965	
F 8 (Bakarby)	J 29B	1953-1964	
	J 29A	1954-current	The last J 29A at the F 8 Wing in 1965.
F 9 (Säve)	J 29A	1952-1962	
	J 29F	1956-1963	
F 10 (Ängelholm)	J 29A	1953-1963	
	J 29F	1956-1965	
F 11 (Nyköping)	S 29C	1954-current	First-line service.
F 12 (Kalmar)	J 29A	1952-1960	
F 13 (Norrköping)	J 29A	1951-1962	
F 15 (Söderhamn)	J 29F	1957-1961	
F 16/20 (Uppsala)	J 29A	1952-1963	
	J 29F	1961-current	At F 20.
F 21 (Luleå)	S 29C	1954-current	First-line service.
F 22 (UNO forces in Congo)	J 29B	1961-1963	
	S 29C	1962-1963	

The Flottilj emblems illustrated on the opposite page were nearly always applied to the a/c with rounded base surmounted by a crown. There were exceptions as shown by the emblem of F 13 which was applied to the a/c in the shape and colours illustrated (green ground, white and red).

Plan view detail showing air exercise "enemy" and "friendly" markings. The markings varied somewhat in position and area covered but were exactly similar above and below.

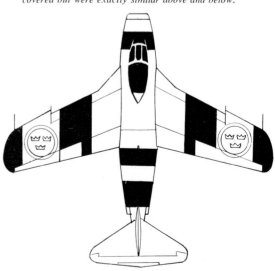

1st Wing, F 9.

J 29F, F 9, 1st Wing, Haglind-Group aerobatic team.

S 29C, F 11, Skavsta, Nyköping.

S 29C, F 21, Kallax, Luleå.

A 29B, F 7, Såtenäs, Tun.

29C, United Nations Force, Kamina, Congo.

J 29E, F 4, Frösön, Östersund.

29F, 2nd Jagdbomber Staffel, Austrian Air Force.

© WARRD

F 3 Malmen, Linköping.   F 6 Karlsborg.

F 7 Såtenäs, Tun.   ▲   F 8 Barkarby, Stockholm.

F 21 Kallax, Luleå.   F 10 Barkåkra, Ängelholm.

F 11 Skavsta, Nyköping.   ▶

F 4 Frösön, Östersund.

F 12 Kalmar.   ▶

F 13 variation.   F 13 Norrköping.

F 15 Söderham.   F 14 Halmstad.

The two S 29C photo-reconnaissance aircraft allocated for the Congo are seen here in the revised colour scheme. Aircraft "A" was serialled 29944 and "B" 29906.
(Photo: Air Britain)

were movable in different directions from the cockpit during flight. The exchange of equipment took about 30 minutes.

The second batch of 15 J 29Fs equipped the second Jagdbomber-Staffel of the Austrian Air Force.

© *Bo Widfeldt, 1965.*

SAAB 29 SPECIFICATION

Designation	J 29A	J 29B (A 29B)	S 29C	J 29E	J 29F
Powerplant:					
Original designation	De Havilland Ghost DGT3	De Havilland Ghost DGT3	De Havilland Ghost DGT3	De Havilland Ghost DGT3	De Havilland Ghost DGT3 + afterburner
Built by	SFA	SFA	SFA	SFA	SFA
Military designation	RM2	RM2	RM2	RM2	RM2B
Thrust (lb.)	4,750	4,750	4,750	4,750	4,750+
Weight (lb.)	1,900	1,900	1,900	1,900	1,930
Dimensions:					
Span (ft./in.)	36 ft. 1 in.	36 ft. 1 in.	36 ft. 1 in.	36 ft. 1 in.	36 ft. 1 in.
Length (ft./in.)	33 ft. 2 in.	33 ft. 2 in.	33 ft. 2 in.	33 ft. 2 in.	33 ft. 2 in.
Height (ft./in.)	12 ft. 3 in.	12 ft. 3 in.	12 ft. 3 in.	12 ft. 3 in.	12 ft. 3 in.
Wing area (sq. ft.)	258 sq. ft.	258 sq. ft.	300 sq. ft.	300 sq. ft.	300 sq. ft.
Fuel Capacities:					
Internal in the fuselage (l)	875	875	875	875	875
Internal in the wing (l)	—	430	430	430	430
Drop tanks (l)	2×250	2×310	2×310	2×310	2×310
Weights:					
Empty (lb.)	9,500	9,500	9,700	9,500	9,900
Normal flight (kg)	12,000	13,200	13,360	13,200	13,700
Maximum overload (lb.)	14,200	15,600	15,900	15,600	16,000
Performance:					
Maximum speed (m.p.h.)	636	636	636	636	658
Cruising speed (m.p.h.)	500	500	500	500	500
Landing speed (m.p.h.)	90	90	90	90	90
Rate of climb (ft./s)	7,500	7,500	7,500	7,500	7,500
Ceiling (ft.)	45,000	45,000	45,000	45,000	50,800
Take-off runway to 15 m. (m.)	984	984	984	984	900
Landing run from 15 m. (m.)	1,000	1,000	1,000	1,000	1,020
Cameras:	— — — —	— — — —	Ska 5, Ska 10, Ska 15, Ska 16 — Maximum seven at the same time. Alternative mountings.	— — — —	— — — —
Armament:					
Guns	Four 20 mm.	Four 20 mm.	—	Four 20 mm.	Four 20 mm.
Rockets and bombs	14×105 mm. rockets or 4 heavy rockets	14×105 mm. rockets or 4 heavy rockets	—	8 × 140 mm. rockets or 4 heavy rockets	24 × 75 mm. rockets or 8 × 140 mm. rockets + 2 firebombs.
Missiles	—	—	—	—	2 Sidewinder R6 24.

PRINTED IN ENGLAND. © Profile Publications Ltd., P.O. Box 26, Leatherhead, Surrey, England,
by George Falkner & Sons Ltd., for McCorquodale City Printing Division, London

PROFILE
PUBLICATIONS

The
Curtiss
JN-4

NUMBER 37

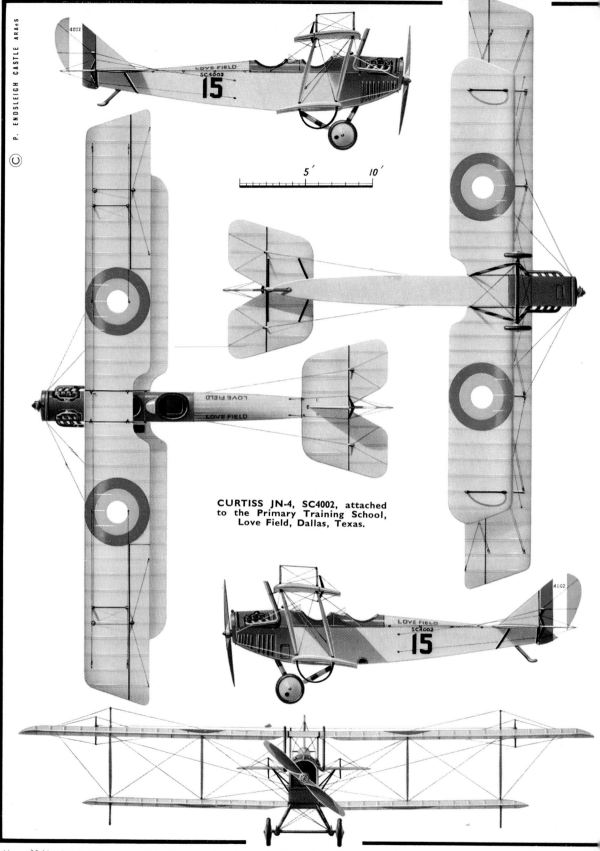

5' 10'

CURTISS JN-4, SC4002, attached to the Primary Training School, Love Field, Dallas, Texas.

Name of field and combination of small serial and large aircraft number were peculiar to primary training aircraft. National markings and colouring are standard for 1918 peri

The Curtiss JN-4

by Peter M. Bowers

JN-4D with clear-doped surfaces and the star-in-circle wing marking that was adopted in May 1917.

The Curtiss "Jenny", to apply the name to the entire JN-4/JN-6 production series, was one of those ordinary designs that attained immortality through the fortunate coincidences of timing and circumstance. As an aeroplane, it was little better than its contemporaries, and its fame was all out of proportion to its capabilities. Although it was developed and used under wartime conditions, it did not win fame as a combat machine. The major production models were primary trainers and most never left the United States. While the career of a 1914 design should logically have ended at the end of the war in 1918, a whole new career opened up after the Armistice that was destined to add to the fame of the now venerable bird. Thousands of war-surplus JN-4s came on the market and were available to civilian owners at fractions of the price of factory-new machines. Practically every civilian flying school used the Jenny as standard equipment during the early post-war years, and owners by the hundreds took their surplus machines into the countryside on barnstorming tours, flying exhibitions at county fairs, hopping passengers, carrying advertising, etc.

Progress finally caught up with the Jenny. Increasingly stringent regulations pertaining to airworthiness finally drove it from the skies in 1928, but that was not the end of the legend. A few survived on experimental licences to work in motion pictures, and in the years since W.W.II, a surprising number have been unearthed from various hiding places and are now being restored and flown as part of the very active antique airplane boom now taking place in America.

ORIGIN OF THE DESIGN

The requirement for a tractor-type training plane for the U.S. Army originated in 1914. Army officials had become greatly concerned over the poor safety record of the service flying schools, notably that at North Island, San Diego. The crashes and fatalities were laid to the inefficiency of the open pusher aircraft designs then in use. With an eye toward contemporary European designs, which were recognised as being more advanced, the Army encouraged American manufacturers to adopt the tractor configuration and the enclosed fuselage.

The Curtiss Aeroplane Company of Hammondsport, New York, was a principal supplier of training machines to the Army. Recognising that the days of the pusher were numbered, the company had set about developing a tractor model on its own before the ban on pushers took effect. The new design, a side-by-side two-seater designated Model G, was not notably successful even though the Army did buy both of the examples that were built. The company was short in tractor design and operating experience, so to save on the necessary development time, Curtiss decided to buy experience rather than develop it. After the decision was made to obtain an experienced designer, Mr. Glenn Curtiss hired B. Douglas Thomas, who had been a designer for Avro in England and was at the time a designer for Sopwith.

Mr. Thomas began the design of the new Curtiss tractor, to be designated the Model "J", while still in England, and completed it at Hammondsport. Powered with the 90-h.p. water-cooled OX engine built by the Curtiss Motor Company, the "J" drew heavily on Thomas's experience with Sopwith tractor designs, even to the shape of the one-piece vertical tail. The airfoil was the proven French Eiffel No. 36. A purely Curtiss feature, however, was the control system. Forward and aft motion of the control column operated the elevators and the wheel worked the rudder. Aileron control was by means of a yoke fitted to the pilot's shoulders, and he leaned in the direction he wanted to bank the machine.

While the "J" was a successful design from the start, it was recognised as being only a beginning, and improved models followed it closely. The "N" was a very similar design, but with ailerons located between the wings as on earlier Curtiss models while the "O" was essentially the "N" modified to side-by-side seating. The best features of the "J" and the "N" were combined into a new model, the "JN". Development of the basic Model "J" ended at this point, but the "JN" and the "N" models continued to be developed separately. A slightly improved JN-1 model brought small orders from both the Army and the Navy, while significant production for the period was achieved

* All the photographs appearing in this profile are part of the Peter M. Bowers' Collection.

The Curtiss Model "J" in completed form. Its initial flights had been made without fabric covering on the fuselage.

Curtiss Model "N", similar to the "J" except for minor details and between-wings ailerons.

with an order for ten JN-2s placed by the Army in 1915. Outwardly, these resembled the original Model "J" except for having a revised undercarriage, equal-span wings, and ailerons on both upper and lower wings. The second JN-2, however, U.S. Army Serial Number 42, had an overhanging upper wing, as on the JN, with ailerons on the upper wing only. It was this machine that effectively crystallised the "Jenny" configuration with its nose, undercarriage, and wing details.

The name "Jenny" was itself another product of coincidence. As with boats, airplanes seemed to develop personalities of their own, and were regarded by their crews as having feminine characteristics. The appearance of the new "JN" model from the marriage of the "J" and the "N" naturally resulted in the corruption of the new model designation into the feminine name "Jenny". Somehow, this particular name was perfectly suited to the personality of the airplane—much more so than some other, such as "Betty" or "Ann". So firmly did the name become associated with the particular airplane that the whole barnstorming era of 1920–26 is generally referred to by latter-day historians as "The Jenny Era" even though there were nearly as many contemporary and similar-looking Standard Model J trainers being used for the same purpose at the same time.

INITIAL JN-4 PRODUCTION

While initial orders from the U.S. military services were slow, the war then raging in Europe provided a large market for the new trainer and for other Curtiss models then in production. An improved JN-3 model, strongly resembling the second JN-2 but fitted with a fixed vertical fin, and the more conventional "Deperdussin" control system, in which the wheel operated the ailerons and a rudder bar operated the rudder, was sold in large numbers to both the Royal Flying Corps and the Royal Naval Air Service. A Canadian subsidiary of the Curtiss Company was established in Toronto, and some of the British production was undertaken in this plant. There were certain features of the JN-3 that the British didn't care for, however, and changes were requested. These were undertaken by a separate firm, Canadian Aeroplanes Ltd., also of Toronto, under the direction of Mr. F. G. Ericson.

The major change was replacement of the Deperdussin control, with the "Stick" type preferred by the R.F.C. In the interest of improved control, ailerons were fitted to both wings and were inter-connected by struts. Wing, fuselage, undercarriage, engine installation, and horizontal tail surface construction remained essentially the same, but the vertical tail construction

The "JN", created by combining the better features of the "J" and "N" models.

Ten JN-2s were built with this long-wing pattern. The second machine had a shorter lower wing on the pattern of the JN.

Model JN-3, which was built in quantity for the R.F.C. and the R.N.A.S.

and shape were both revised. Even though the improvements were not developed through Curtiss engineering channels, the new 1917 model was given the designation of JN-4, since it was a direct development of the JN-3. The fact that the American firm had produced a JN-4 model of its own was not considered. When Canadian-built JN-4s were acquired later by the U.S. Army for its expanded training programme, and when Canadian aircraft and crews were sent to U.S. bases in Texas for winter training, distinction between the U.S. and Canadian models became necessary. The official designation given to the Canadian model was JN-4Can, to designate its Canadian manufacture, but it was universally referred to as the "Canuck", a slang term used for Canadians and anything Canadian. The American models, in spite of a number of separate model designations, were still "Jennies". Canadian

The Canadian J-4, introduced early in 1917, was developed from the JN-3 quite independently of the American production series. This was the first aeroplane in Canada to use skiis.

Late production Canadian JN-4 with 1918 U.S. military markings. Compare wingtip and tail surface shapes with JN-4D on page 3.

Prototype American Curtiss JN-4. Tail is virtually identical to JN-3, but was modified on production versions.

Aeroplanes Ltd. also produced a number of American-designed JN-4As along with the "Canucks", but since these had the features of the other late American models, they did not pick up the Canadian nickname.

JN-4 DEVELOPMENT

Only the one version of the JN-4 was developed by Canadian Aeroplanes Ltd., but the Curtiss firm, now reorganised as the Curtiss Aeroplane and Motor Company, and re-located in new plants at Buffalo, New York, continued to develop the basic "JN" and "N" designs and assigned different designations to indicate their improved status. The American JN-4 model appeared in July 1916, and was virtually indistinguishable from the JN-3. The "Dep" control was retained, as was the tail skid pivoted to the bottom of the rudder post, which terminated a considerable distance below the fuselage. A new twin-engine design appeared at the same time as the JN-4. It was tentatively designated "JN-5", but the name was never adopted. This design, using JN-4 outer wing panels and engines, was referred to by Curtiss and its military customers alike as "Twin JN".

The JN-4 was followed within four months by the greatly improved JN-4A model, which incorporated several noticeable external changes. The greatest change was in the tail surfaces, both the horizontal and vertical surfaces receiving new and enlarged shapes that were to stay with the design through the rest of its development. The wings, which incorporated only one degree of dihedral on the earlier models, were rigged with four degrees, and ailerons were added to the lower wing, the rear of the wing tip was pointed in duplication of the upper wing shape. Models without lower wing ailerons, from the second JN-2 onward, had nicely rounded lower wing tips. The final distinguishing feature of the JN-4A was the pronounced downthrust of the 90-h.p. Curtiss OX-5 motor. JN-4s were produced both for the U.S. Army and the R.N.A.S. by Curtiss and by Canadian Aeroplanes Ltd.

The JN-4B was very similar to the JN-4A and was distinguishable from it only in the return to low-dihedral wings, ailerons on the upper wing only, and no downthrust for the engine. There was an American-built JN-4C, but only one was built as an experimental variant of the JN-4B, using the R.A.F. 6 airfoil of the "N" series in place of the Eiffel 36 section.

Twin JN used JN-4 wing panels and engines on a modified fuselage. Starboard engine modified to turn opposite to port engine to neutralise propeller torque in flight.

The major production model in the JN-4 series was the JN-4D, the prototype of which appeared in June 1917. The major change was replacement of the Deperdussin wheel control with the stick type previously adopted on the "Canuck". The engine had the downthrust of the JN-4A. The wings of the prototype were identical to those of the JN-4A except for a centre-section cut short at the rear spar and trailing edge cut-outs on the inboard end of each wing panel to improve visibility from the rear cockpit. The production JN-4Ds deleted the lower wing ailerons and reverted to the rounded lower wing tips. A total of 3,354 Ds were built by Curtiss and six other American firms for the American war effort. Manufacture of JN-4Ds is sometimes credited to Canadian Aeroplanes Ltd., but these were actually JN-4Can's and possibly JN-4As procured at the same time the D orders were being placed.

Curtiss built one prototype of an improved model, the JN-4D-2 (Serial No. *34191*) which was outwardly identical to the JN-4D. Production was scheduled for several of the sub-contracting plants, but these were cancelled at the end of the war and only the 100 ordered from the Liberty Iron Works of Sacramento, California, were delivered. The Liberty products differed from the Curtiss prototypes in not having the downthrust for the engine.

Up to the end of 1917, the Curtiss JN-4 models to D were regarded as primary trainers. When aircraft of increased horse-power and performance were needed for advanced training, new designs were sought and developed, notably the Vought VE-7. However, in the interests of economy both in design and tooling time, the government decided to put the larger 150-h.p. Hispano-Suiza engine in the existing Curtiss JN-4D design. This engine, a water-cooled V-8 quite similar in size to the Curtiss OX-5, was of Spanish origin, and produced by the famous motor-car concern located in Paris, France. It appeared late in 1915 and achieved an immediate reputation for performance and reliability after the Spad VII fighter was designated specifically to use it. Even before the United States entered the war in April 1917, manufacturing rights had been obtained by the Simplex Automobile Company, a subsidiary of the Wright-Martin Company. This latter company was itself the result of a 1916 merger of The Wright Company, the original Wright Brothers firm, and the Glenn L. Martin Company, formerly of California. Simplex had been a subsidiary of Wright, and remained a part of the new company. Orders were in hand to manufacture the 150-h.p. Hispano-Suiza engine for the French Government, and the facilities were expanded to permit production for the U.S. services as well. The engine was soon nicknamed "The Hisso", and the modified JN-4 airplane in which it was installed became the JN-4H. The latter did not signify the normal sequence of model evolution, as JN-4, JN-4A, JN-4B, etc., but identified the particular installation with "H-for-Hisso".

The changes made in the aeroplanes to accommodate the new engine were relatively minor. Since the larger engine required additional cooling surface for the radiator, the original radiator was enlarged by adding a rounded area at the bottom. The downthrust was deleted, and the fuel capacity was increased. At first, it was intended that the JN-4H be used in one configuration for a number of advanced training duties, but all the necessary equipment proved to be a weight and performance handicap. In May 1918, a

JN-4A was distinguished by new vertical tail shape and increased dihedral angle of wings.

JN-4B was produced as a civil model just before U.S. entry into W.W.I, and very few were acquired by the military.

Prototype JN-4D had ailerons on both wings as the JN-4A and introduced the centre-section cutouts that were a feature of all subsequent JN models.

JN-4D on its nose, showing to advantage the 1918 markings, khaki-brown metal cowling, clear-doped fabric, and a comparison of upper and lower wingtip shapes.

decision was reached by the government to divide JN-4H production into specialised aircraft functions, with appropriate designations for the airplanes. Gunnery trainers became JN-4HG-1 and -2 for one- and two-gun machines, the bomber trainers became JN-4HB, observation trainers JN-4HO, and pursuit trainers JN-4HP.

Curtiss did not build a JN-5 as such. Seeking to improve the JN-4H, the Army modified one JN-4H (Serial No. *41358*) by adding minor equipment and the larger tail surfaces of the Curtiss Model R-4, a somewhat similar but more powerful biplane. The prototype retained the upper-wings-only ailerons of the JN-4H, but the production versions had ailerons on both wings. Early production JN-6Hs had the R-4 type tail surfaces, but the majority reverted to the JN-4 type. The same special-purpose designation letters assigned to the JN-4Hs were used on the -6s.

JN-4Ds with special colouring and markings of an Army Ambulance plane. Section behind rear cockpit lifts off to permit insertion of patient on a stretcher.

One of 100 JN-4D-2s built by Liberty Iron Works, identical to Curtiss-built prototype except for elimination of the engine downthrust.

The single JN-4D-2 prototype built by Curtiss had the engine downthrust of the standard JN-4D model. Khaki-brown colouring adopted for trainers late in 1918.

MODEL "N" DEVELOPMENT

While not true "Jennies", the later "N" models deserve a place in this study. There is no record of any

models between the original "N" and the N-8, and it must be assumed that the intervening numbers were assigned to paper studies. The N-8, used on active service by the Army in the Mexican expedition of 1915–16, was virtually identical to the JN-3 except for the old shoulder aileron control and the use of the R.A.F. -6 airfoil in place of the Eiffel. By far the most famous "N", however, was the N-9 developed for the Navy late in 1916. This was essentially a JN-4B fitted with the 100-h.p. Curtiss OX-6 engine and with the wingspan increased by 10 feet in order to carry the additional weight of a large centre pontoon and two wing tip pontoons. The extra span was obtained by using a wider upper centre-section and fitting in extra lower panels inboard of the standard size outer panels. As with the JN-4H, the Hispano-powered version of the N-9 became the N-9H. Five hundred and sixty N-9s were built for the U.S. Navy to war's end, but only 100 were by Curtiss. The remainder were built by the Burgess Co. of Marblehead, Massachusetts, under licence. An additional 50 were created in post-war years by assembling spare parts at the Pensacola Naval Air Station. One N-10 (Serial No. 2573), was created at Burgess by shortening the wingspan of a standard N-9, but the design was not adopted for production.

POST-WAR MILITARY SERVICE

After the Armistice, most of the JN-4 models to D were declared surplus. Before sales were opened to the public, the Curtiss Company bought hundreds, not only of its own JN-4D model, but of the very similar Standard Model J. These were reworked slightly to suit them to civilian operation and were placed on the market. This phase of Curtiss' business was soon ended, and at a considerable financial loss, when remaining military stocks of the primary trainers were made available directly to the public at practically give-away prices.

Most of the Hisso-powered models, both JN-4H and JN-6H, were retained by the military following the decision that 90 h.p. was inadequate power even for a primary training machine at that period. The JNs, along with their naval equivalent, the N-9 seaplane, remained the principal primary trainers of both the U.S. Army and Navy for the first five post-war years. Because of post-war economy moves, replacements of new design did not begin to appear until about 1923. With both JN-4 and JN-6 models on hand, the Army sought a degree of standardisation, and rebuilt many of the machines on hand as JNS,

JN-4H airframe was identical to the JN-4D except for revised nose contours and radiator shape necessary to accommodate the 150 Wright-Hispano engine.

meaning JN—standardised. This work was carried on as late as 1925. There were some differences in powerplant, and these were reflected in the designation JNS-A and I (not to be confused with the figure 1) for the 150-h.p. Hispano-Suiza "A" and "I" models, and JNS-E for the model with the improved 180-h.p. "E" engine. In spite of the fact that these engines were officially called "Wright", after their American manufacturer, they were still universally referred to as "Hissos" by their users.

The military life of both the JNs and the N-9s continued until 1927. The last few in the Army, assigned to National Guard and reserve units, were scrapped in September 1927.

BARNSTORMING

The second career of the "Jenny" was unplanned. It just happened because the Jenny was available in quantity at low war-surplus prices at a time when thousands of former military pilots as well as those trained just after the war wanted a plane of their own in which to fly. Before the war, civilian flying had been a rich man's sport and the relatively few machines turned out were virtually custom models. They were neither docile nor reliable. The rapid advances made in aircraft design during the war years brought the machines to the point where they could be handled easily by relatively unskilled pilots. Actually, the State-of-the-Art had moved well past the Jenny by war's end, but the new machines could not be built and put on the market at a price that could begin to compete with the surplus prices of the Jennies, the Standards, and the Canucks. Consequently, it was not until about 1925, when the war-surplus trainers began to wear out, that the new production types were able to assume a significant rôle in U.S. commercial aviation. So thoroughly did the Jenny and its contemporaries dominate the early post-war years that they became known as "The Jenny Era".

The most famous rôle of the Jenny in this period was that of barnstorming, a term borrowed from travelling theatrical troupes that performed in barns. A pilot with a single airplane and his mechanic-helper

Rear cockpit of the JN-4D. Full complement of instruments includes water temperature gauge, altimeter, oil pressure gauge, and tachometer.

would travel from town to town, stopping in suitable pastures from which they would fly passengers for as long as they came forward. For a great many Americans, especially among the rural population, the Jenny was the first airplane they ever saw or took a ride in. Other pilots banded together into "Flying Circuses", performing all manner of now-illegal operations on the county-fair circuit. Some of these shows included such fantastic feats as a car-to-airplane transfer accomplished within the confines of a county fair race track, wing walking, and plane-to-plane changes at altitudes low enough for the grandstand customers to see.

There was no government regulation of aviation in the United States until 1927, consequently, there was no supervision of maintenance, modification, or piloting proficiency. In some of the flying schools, the student that soloed first became the instructor for the others. The standards of maintenance in some of the better schools was quite satisfactory, but on the part of most individual owners and the barnstormers, it

Left: *U.S. Navy JN-4H in postwar colouring with reduced-size wing markings. Note that this machine is being flown without the side engine cowling.* Right: *Early JN-6HB with the larger Curtiss Model "R" vertical tail. Note bomb racks mounted aft of undercarriage.*

Left: *The single JN-5 was a JN-4H modified by the Army to serve as a prototype for the JN-6.* Right: *JN-4H's and JN-6H's rebuilt after W.W.I in U.S. Army depots were redesignated JNS for "JN Standardised".*

Production version of JN-6H with original JN-4A type vertical tail. Fuel capacity increased by building a tank into the upper wing centre section.

Curtiss N-8 of 1916 was outwardly similar to the JN-3 but retained the shoulder-yoke aileron control of earlier models.

was atrocious. Fence wire seemed to be the essential ingredient in almost any Jenny repair. Individual modifications were a wonder to behold, too. Many different engine installations other than the Curtiss OX-5 and the Wright-Hispano were tried, even rotaries. Since the attrition rate for lower wing panels was quite high in cow pasture operations, spares for these items were sometimes in short supply. It was not uncommon to see a Jenny flying with two sets of upper wing panels on it—a set of upper panels with the strut fittings reversed for the bottom installation and an extra set of outer struts to brace the overhang area in compression.

The Jenny, along with the Standard J-1 and the Canuck, was probably the best stage in the world for the wing-walker's art. Not only did it have a handy maze of struts and wires between the wings and a good old-fashioned straight axle between the wheels, but it had king-posts and bracing wire above the wings and stout wing tip skids underneath. These made it possible for the aerialist to climb over and under as well as through the wings. Performances on top of the wings would have been impossible without

the presence of the king-posts. This type of performance passed from the American scene with the effective passing of the Jenny in 1927–28. When it was desired to revive the old act for post-W.W.II air shows, it was necessary to find and refurbish a Jenny to allow real wing-walking.

BASIC COLOURING

The original colouring of the military JNs—Army and Navy alike—was clear-doped fabric that resulted in an off-white appearance. Sometimes a coat or two of clear varnish was applied over the dope and imparted a burnt umber or amber colour. The JN-3s and -4s supplied to Britain were painted to established specifications, with khaki brown top and side surfaces and clear-doped undersurfaces. By the time of the large U.S. war contracts of 1917, basic colouring was still clear dope, but with the metal engine and cockpit cowling sheet metal painted khaki brown. Late in 1918, trainer planes were given the same overall khaki brown colouring that has recently been adopted for combat types. This remained standard until well into 1927, at which time Army aircraft, in the interest of increased visibility as a safety factor in peacetime years, adopted orange-yellow wing and tail surfaces but retained the khaki brown (now olive drab) fuselage. A few of the military Jennies survived long enough to carry this colouring.

Late in 1917, overall light grey became standard Navy colouring, but most wartime Navy Jennies were clear-doped. By 1921, grey was abandoned in favour of all-silver with orange-yellow on the top surface of the upper wing and the top of the horizontal tail. The

N-9, essentially a JN-4B with longer wings, was the standard U.S. Navy seaplane trainer of 1917–18 and the early post-war years. Note unique vertical radiator design.

Left: *The famous Lt. Ormer Locklear doing a handstand on a war-surplus JN-4D, a feat impossible to accomplish without the aid of the Jenny's upper wing king-posts.* Right: *Typical of the stunts performed in the barnstorming era—a "Canuck" picks up a man from a speeding car on a racetrack. To revive the old wing-walking act for a post-W.W.II air show, it was necessary to restore a suitable aeroplane—the Jenny. Wings and horizontal tail of this JN-4D (Above) are original, but a new steel-tube fuselage carries a W.W.II surplus 200-h.p. Ranger engine.*

early Navy N-9s were clear-doped, were re-done in grey, and the post-war survivors carried the silver and yellow until their retirement in 1927.

NATIONAL MARKINGS

Being trainers, the Jennies did not carry the colourful insignia and striping used by the combat squadrons. Other than the standardised national marking, they carried only their military serial number or a training plane number for a particular base on the fuselage.

There was no standardised U.S. National marking prior to 17th May 1917, more than a month after U.S. entry into W.W.I. During the Mexican punitive expedition of 1916, U.S. Army JN-4s and N-8s were marked with a five-pointed red star on fuselage and rudder. Navy planes carried a blue anchor on the rudder and sometimes under the wings. The marking adopted in 1917 used the three national colours of red, white and blue in the British and French pattern of three vertical rudder stripes, with the red at the trailing edge. The wing marking was a white five-pointed star superimposed on a circle of blue with a smaller red circle tangent to the inner projections of the star points.

After this wing marking was applied to some U.S. trainers in France, it was pointed out that the white star could be mistaken for a white-bordered German cross in the heat of combat. Consequently, the U.S. was asked to adopt a tricolour circle similar to those used by the other Allies. In January 1918, the former Imperial Russian marking was adopted, consisting of a red outer ring, blue middle ring, and a white centre. At the same time, the order of tail stripes was reversed to put the blue at the trailing edge. This arrangement of stripes and circle remained standard until August 1919, at which time the 1917 arrangement was re-adopted. Meanwhile, not all of the 1917 machines were repainted with 1918 markings, and the use of spare parts with one marking on an airplane with the other was not at all uncommon.

As originally adopted, the wing marking was full-chord of the wing and located immediately inboard of the aileron. This was standard for all wartime Jennies. In the post-war years, the readopted star, still full-chord, was moved to the wing tip. By 1925, the size was reduced to fit in between the leading edge and the aileron spar. One final marking change that applied to

A private owner attempted to improve the performance of this JN-4D by installing a 160-h.p. Gnome rotary engine, clipping the upper wingtip, and adding alance area to the ailerons.

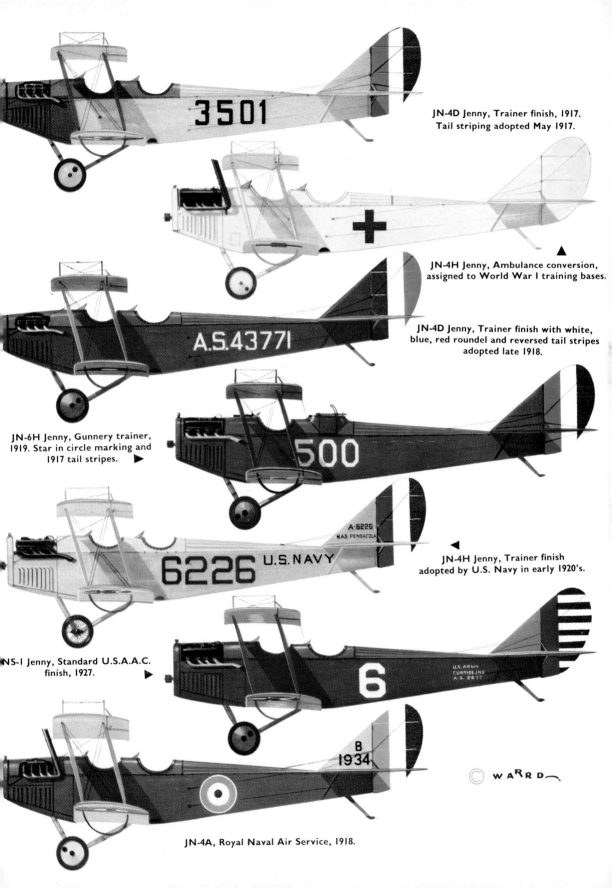

JN-4D Jenny, Trainer finish, 1917.
Tail striping adopted May 1917.

JN-4H Jenny, Ambulance conversion,
assigned to World War I training bases.

JN-4D Jenny, Trainer finish with white,
blue, red roundel and reversed tail stripes
adopted late 1918.

JN-6H Jenny, Gunnery trainer,
1919. Star in circle marking and
1917 tail stripes.

JN-4H Jenny, Trainer finish
adopted by U.S. Navy in early 1920's.

NS-1 Jenny, Standard U.S.A.A.C.
finish, 1927.

JN-4A, Royal Naval Air Service, 1918.

A.S.43771

500

6226 U.S. NAVY
A-6226
NAS PENSACOLA

6

B
1934

U.S. ARMY
CURTISS JN6
A.S. 2637

© WARD

A JN-4D fitted with a monoplane wing built by Sikorsky. Several small firms developed improved wing designs for the war-surplus Jennies and Canucks.

very few military Jennies was the adoption, in November 1926, of a new tail stripe arrangement for U.S. Army planes. This retained the original vertical blue stripe but substituted thirteen alternating red and white horizontal stripes for the verticals, in the manner of the U.S. flag.

PRODUCTION FIGURES

Exact production figures for the JN and N series are unavailable, and existing records are contradictory. The following list has been assembled from compilations made independently by the author, James C. Fahey of "Ships and Aircraft", and Mr. K. M. Molson, curator of the Canadian National Aviation Museum.

© *Peter M. Bowers, 1965*

SPECIFICATION CURTISS JN-4

	JN-4D	JN-4H
Wing Span	43 ft. 7⅛ in.	43 ft. 7⅛ in.
Length	27 ft. 4 in.	27 ft. 0½ in.
Height	9 ft. 10⅝ in.	9 ft. 10⅝ in.
Wing Area	352.5 sq. ft.	352.5 sq. ft.
Powerplant	Curtiss OX-5	Wright-Hispano "A"
Rating	90-h.p. at 1,400 r.p.m.	150-h.p. at 1,600 r.p.m.
Empty Weight	1,580 lb.	1,595 lb.
Gross Weight	2,130 lb.	2,145 lb.
Maximum Speed	75 m.p.h.	93 m.p.h.
Minimum Speed	45 m.p.h.	41 m.p.h.
Climb	2,000 ft. in 10 min.	6,500 ft. in 10 min.
Service Ceiling	11,000 ft.	18,000 ft.
Endurance at Full Throttle	2 hrs. 18 min.	2 hrs. 30 min.

Manufacturer	J	JN	JN-1	JN-2	JN-3	JN-4	JN-4A	JN-4B	JN-4C	JN-4CAN	JN-4D	JN-4D-2	JN-4H	JN-6H	Twin JN	Z	N-8	N-9
Curtiss (U.S.A.)	1	1	1+	10+	86+	701	781	5+	1	—	1404	1	929	1035	9	1	4	100
Curtiss (Canada)	—	—	—	—	18	—	—	—	—	—	—	—	—	—	—	—	—	—
Canadian Aeroplanes	—	—	—	—	—	—	—	—	—	1260	—	—	—	—	—	—	—	—
The Burgess Co.	—	—	—	—	—	—	—	—	—	—	—	—	—	—	—	—	—	460
Howell & Lesser	—	—	—	—	—	—	—	—	—	75	—	—	—	—	—	—	—	—
Liberty Iron Works	—	—	—	—	—	—	—	—	—	100	100	—	—	—	—	—	—	—
Springfield Aircraft Corp.	—	—	—	—	—	—	—	—	—	585	—	—	—	—	—	—	—	—
St. Louis Aircraft Corp.	—	—	—	—	—	—	—	—	—	450	—	—	—	—	—	—	—	—
U.S. Aircraft Corp.	—	—	—	—	—	—	—	—	—	50	—	—	—	—	—	—	—	—
Totals	1	1	1+	10+	104+	701	781	5+	1	1260	2664	101	929	1035	9	1	4	560

PRINTED IN ENGLAND. © Profile Publications Ltd., P.O. Box 26, Leatherhead, Surrey, England, by George Falkner & Sons Ltd., for McCorquodale City Printing Division, London.

PROFILE
PUBLICATIONS

The
Fokker
Monoplanes

NUMBER

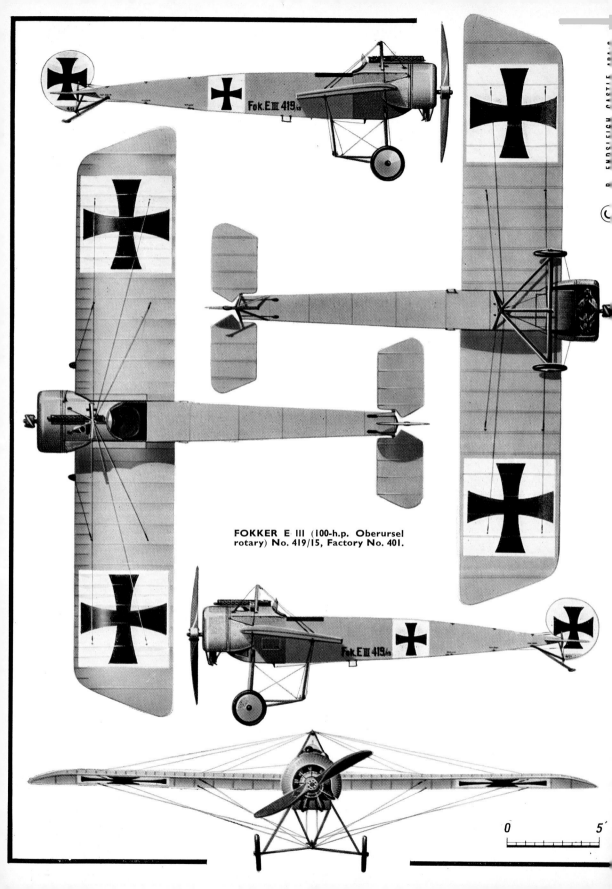

FOKKER E III (100-h.p. Oberursel rotary) No. 419/15, Factory No. 401.

0   5'

The Fokker Monoplanes

by J. M. Bruce

The Fok. E III that was fitted experimentally with a full circular cowling and oil recovery system.

It would not be too great an exaggeration to say of the series of monoplane fighters that emerged from the Fokker factory during the 1914–18 war that their aerodynamics were French.

From the primitive Fokker Spider of 1910 an earlier series of crude monoplanes had descended, some incorporating refinements such as fairings about the seats, but all known as Spiders and all basically similar in construction to the first of the series.

The Royal Prussian War Ministry ordered a 100-h.p. (Argus) Spider in June 1912, followed by two more early in 1913, one with the Argus engine, the other with a 95-h.p. Mercedes. The latter two aircraft were designated Fokker M.1, the M signifying *Militär* (military, as a noun). These aircraft were not popular with their pilots. Their immediate successors, the M.2, M.3, M.3A and M.4, were all different and owed virtually nothing to the Spider design; they were, if anything, less successful than the M.1.

When the M.4 had been condemned by Leutnant A. Muehlig-Hofmann late in 1913, Fokker dismissed Palm, the designer of the aircraft. Palm's successor was his former assistant, Martin Kreutzer.

With the M.1 type obsolete and unpopular, and its successor's failures, Fokker had to produce a successful new design if his firm was to survive. He had seen a Morane-Saulnier Type H monoplane at Johannisthal in 1913, and, so it is said, had had sketches made of its design details. The Morane-Saulnier achieved a number of considerable successes that year, and Fokker determined to copy it. He was not the first to do this: Bruno Hanuschke had built a copy of the Morane-Saulnier in the autumn of 1913.

For this purpose Fokker bought, cheaply, a damaged Type H and had it rebuilt at Schwerin. It was flown by Fokker and a few of his closest associates: all were enormously impressed by its performance. Drawings were prepared for a Chinese copy of the Morane-Saulnier, but the copying was of the principal shapes only: the structure was original and generally stronger than that of the French type. Whereas the original Morane-Saulnier fuselage was a wire-braced wooden box-girder, the Fokker monoplane's fuselage was a welded structure made of steel tubing; a welder named Reinhold Platz, who was later to be Fokker's chief designer for many years, had a hand in its design. The wing spars were larger in section, and compression struts replaced the Morane's compression

ribs. The larger spars produced a slightly different aerofoil section, and the Fokker wing not only had more ribs than the French original but also had riblets to preserve the nose contour of the aerofoil. The rudder was that of the unsuccessful M.4; the elevator was a balanced cantilever surface like that of the Morane-Saulnier. The undercarriage was completely original and of appreciably greater track than that of the Type H.

The new Fokker was given the type number M.5 and Fokker had such confidence in it that a small batch was put in hand. He had ordered some 80-h.p. Oberursel-built Gnôme engines for the aircraft, but these had not been delivered by the time when the first M.5 was ready. It was therefore fitted with the 50-h.p. Gnôme taken from there built Morane-Saulnier Type H; the engine had an overhung mounting and its cowling was a copy of the French original.

The M.5's performance on its early flights was somewhat poor and the M.4 rudder was not large enough. An enlarged rudder was designed and fitted to the second M.5, which was completed soon after

The Fokker M.5K prototype in its original form with the rudder of the unsuccessful Fokker M.4.

The prototype M.5L.

3

This M.5K may have been one of the Fokkers used as flying dispatch riders in the early stages of the war. It was unarmed.
(Photo: P. L. Gray)

An M.5L in Austro-Hungarian service.
(Photo: Imperial War Museum)

the first machine's maiden flight. This revised rudder was of the balanced "comma" shape that was to characterise Fokker aircraft until the Fok. D VII appeared in 1918.

A longer wing of greater area was fitted to the second M.5, which came to be known as the M.5L, the other prototype being distinguished as the M.5K. The suffix letters denoted the type of wing that was fitted: L signified *lang* (long-span); K, *kurz* (short-span). Both versions could, if need be, carry a passenger, who had to straddle a rearward extension of the pilot's seat. The first M.5L was fitted with a second-hand 70-h.p. Gnôme while awaiting its 80-h.p. Oberursel-built engine.

Both prototypes were fitted with the 80-h.p. engines as soon as they were delivered, and direct comparison of the two aircraft could be made. The M.5L proved to be slightly the slower of the two but was more responsive to the controls. After military pilots had flown both types an official order was placed for a small batch of M.5Ls in the summer of 1914; deliveries began late in June. It seems that, possibly at a later stage, a few M.5Ks were also ordered.

In the opening weeks of the war the M.5Ls saw considerable operational service, but their usefulness became limited after the unreliability of their Oberursel engines had led to several forced landings behind the Allied lines. The type was also used in small numbers by the Austro-Hungarian *Luftfahrttruppen*.

The few M.5Ks that were in operational use were employed as a means of fast communication; others were with training units. The military designations Fok. A I and Fok. A III have been connected with the M.5L and M.5K respectively, but the former was properly the official designation of the Fokker M.8 two-seater.

Long before the war the possibility of mounting a machine-gun on an aeroplane had been considered. Franz Schneider of the L.V.G. designed a synchroni-

sing mechanism that was the subject of the German patent D.R.P. 276,396 dated 15th July 1913. Early in 1914 he applied to the German military authorities for the loan of a machine-gun in order to put his invention to the test. His request was either ignored or overlooked, for he never received a gun. It has been said that the device appearing in Schneider's patent specification was unworkable. However that may be, it is interesting to speculate about what might have happened if a man of Schneider's ability had been given the means of testing and developing his idea.

In France, during the winter of 1913, Raymond Saulnier conceived a form of synchronising mechanism that by April 1914 had been developed under the direction of Louis Peyret to the point where it could be submitted to the French Ministry of War. It was subjected to firing tests at the Hotchkiss establishment near the Eiffel Tower. The tests were made on a test rig, using an 80-h.p. Gnôme engine and a Hotchkiss machine-gun, under the direction of Colonel de Boigne.

The Saulnier mechanism worked but was not adopted or developed because the ammunition that was used did not have a precisely uniform period of ignition; hand-fire rounds occurred unpredictably and some of them struck the airscrew. To avoid the delay of further research and experimentation, Saulnier dispensed with the mechanism and fitted steel deflector plates to the airscrew in line with the gun; three types of deflector plates were tested. On the outbreak of war Saulnier's Hotchkiss gun was reclaimed by the authorities and his experiments ceased.

The Fokker M.5K/MG (Werke Nr 216) with Parabellum gun, which still had its shoulder stock and pistol grip.

The M.5K/MG with Parabellum gun and head-rest fitted behind the cockpit.

In December 1914 Lieutenant Roland Garros, the celebrated pre-war pilot who had flown Morane-Saulnier monoplanes, notably the Type H, with such distinction, visited Raymond Saulnier. He told Saulnier that he had obtained permission from Commandant (later Colonel) Barès, head of the Air Service at French General Headquarters, to test the Saulnier deflector-plate device. With an aircraft, engine and armoured airscrew lent by the Morane-Saulnier company and a machine-gun entrusted to him by the French War Ministry, Garros made what were probably the first airborne firing tests of any kind of device for firing through the revolving blades of a tractor airscrew.

Flying a Morane-Saulnier Type L parasol monoplane armed with the Saulnier device, Garros opened the era of true fighter aircraft on 1st April 1915, when he shot down an Albatros two-seater. This victory came exactly a month to the day after the formation of the first fighter squadron, *Escadrille de Chasse* MS 12, equipped with the Type L; some of MS 12's aircraft had a machine-gun firing forward over the wing and airscrew. Garros was a member of MS 23.

On 19th April 1915 Garros' Type L* was hit by ground fire from the neighbourhood of Courtrai and he was obliged to land in enemy territory near Ingelmunster. His attempts to set fire to his Morane were only partially successful and the half-burnt parasol monoplane with its gun and armoured airscrew were taken to Iseghem. The secret was out.

Having obtained an undamaged example of the

Installation of LMG·08 machine-gun in Werke Nr 258. *This aircraft also had a head-positioning rest for the pilot.*

* German reports, contrary to a long-held belief that Garros was flying a Morane-Saulnier Type N, leave no doubt that on 19th April he was flying a Type L parasol monoplane with an 80-h.p. Le Rhône engine.

device that had enabled Garros to shoot down five enemy aircraft in less than three weeks, the Germans naturally decided to copy it. The first attempt, by Simon Brunnhuber, was unsuccessful. Hauptmann Helmuth Foerster, the *Feldflugchef's* adjutant, then sent for Fokker, who left Doeberitz with the armoured airscrew of Garros' Morane-Saulnier, a brand-new Parabellum machine-gun and a supply of ammunition.

It is unlikely that any of Fokker's staff at Schwerin had any knowledge of the Russian synchronising gears (Poplavko and Smyslov-Dybovski) that were then in existence, but someone may have known something about Schneider's 1913 patent. The likelihood that Fokker personally had anything to do with the design of the mechanical interrupter gear that was evolved at Schwerin can be dismissed, and there is little doubt that the mechanism that Fokker proudly took back to Doeberitz less than a week after he had been summoned there was designed by Heinrich Luebbe, Fritz Heber and Leimberger.

A Fokker M.5K (*Werke Nr 216*) was fitted with the gun and interrupter gear and was successfully demonstrated at Doeberitz. At an early stage an adjustable head-rest was fitted as a means of ensuring that the pilot's head was in the correct position for sighting. This armed M.5K was designated M.5K/MG and was later given the military order number E.1/15.

A second M.5K (*Werke Nr. 258*) was armed with an LMG.08 gun, as were the two single-seat fighters E.2/15 and E.3/15 that Fokker took on a demonstration tour of operational units, starting on 23rd May 1915. A batch of the new Fokker fighters had been ordered with the military designation Fok. E I shortly after the first successful demonstration at Doeberitz. Fokker had been instructed to produce these aircraft with all possible speed, and his demonstration tour was intended to provide training for the pilots who were to fly the new fighters. By the time Fokker left Douai for Schwerin on 12th July 1915 eleven German pilots were flying Fok. E I monoplanes. One of these was Leutnant Oswald Boelcke, who took over E.3/15.

The production E I differed in detail from the M.5K/MG prototype. The engine was the 80-h.p. Oberursel and the bench-type seat was retained; a passenger could therefore squeeze in behind the pilot, as on the M.5, to the detriment of the aircraft's performance. The head-positioning rest that had been fitted to the M.5K/MG was retained on several of the production aircraft. To provide the pilot with a downward view an aperture was cut in the cockpit floor; it was covered by a flap that could be opened by means of a lever. Later aircraft had an additional petrol tank behind the cockpit and the fuel system underwent modifications.

In a letter dated 25th June 1915, Fähnrich Max

Immelmann, then an unknown pilot of *Fliegerabteilung* 62 at Douai, wrote:

"We have just got two small one-seater fighters from the Fokker factory. The Crown Prince of Bavaria visited our aerodrome to see these new fighting machines and inspected us and Section 20. Direktor Fokker, the constructor of this fighter, was presented to him. Fokker and a Leutnant Parschau gave demonstration flights for him and fired at ground targets from the air. Fokker amazed us with his ability.',

Immelmann was promoted to Leutnant with effect from 14th July 1915. On 31st July he flew a Fok. E I for the first time, and on the following day, apparently flying E.3/15, he shot down a British aircraft near Douai. The combat was quite a protracted and one-sided affair, for Immelmann's victim was a two-seater (probably a B.E.) that was being flown without an observer on a bombing mission and was therefore virtually defenceless. During the fight, if it can be so called, the Fokker's gun jammed three times. This was the first of many Allied aircraft that were to fall to Fokker monoplanes in the ensuing months.

As the Fokkers became more numerous their successes grew. Despite its poor performance and the several shortcomings of the armament installation, the Fokker proved to be a deadly instrument in the, hands of men like von Althaus, Boelcke, Buddecke, Immelmann, Parschau and Wintgens. A few E Is were used by the Austrian *Luftfahrttruppen*, but records of their activities are scanty.

The Fokker was not at first a wholly unqualified success in the Service, however. In July 1915 some of the production aircraft were sent to the flying school at Doeberitz for use as training aircraft. On 27th July one crashed fatally, and a second Fokker pilot was killed on the 31st. After a third Fokker fatality on 29th August the *IdFlieg* disbanded the Doeberitz Fokker unit, sent the aircraft back to Schwerin, and grounded the monoplanes as Service aircraft. However, the Fokkers' success at the front was so marked that the *IdFlieg* were compelled to allow the resumption of training, but they stipulated that it was to be done at the Fokker flying school at Schwerin. The first group of trainees were sent there from Doeberitz in October 1915.

Before and during the war several attempts were made to produce a more-or-less invisible aeroplane. In every case the normal fabric covering was replaced by a transparent material: all the experiments were unsuccessful because no material that was sufficiently

Fok. E I, 46/15.   (Photo: P. L. Gray)

transparent could be made strong enough or taut enough. The "invisible" Fok. E I was no exception. It was covered with a kind of cellulose sheeting, was flown once or twice, but was soon converted to a standard E I.

The Fok. E I was a somewhat makeshift aircraft, rushed into production without development or consideration of the need to refine details, and its engine and armament were alike unreliable. While the batch of E Is were going through the shops at Schwerin, Martin Kreutzer re-designed the aircraft to have the 100-h.p. Oberursel rotary engine. The revised design was given the Fokker type number M.14 and the military designation Fok. E II. A slightly taller undercarriage was fitted, the wheels being somewhat farther forward than on the E I; and a small triangular under-fin (more often removed than retained in service) was fitted immediately ahead of the rudder. The height of the cabane pylon was reduced but the struts were more substantial than those of the E.I.

A major difference between the Fok. E I and E II was the reduced area of the wings on the later type. This was cut down to about 14 sq. m. with the object of increasing the aircraft's speed, but in practice it made the E II more difficult to fly.

The prototype E II had to be flown with an 80-h.p. Oberursel because no example of the 100-h.p. engine was available. Enough engines had been made by the late summer of 1915 for deliveries of Fok. E II fighters to start in July, and eight were operational by October.

As the 14 sq. m. wings had failed to enhance the performance as had been hoped, new wings of 9·52 m. span were designed; the span of the E I had been 8·95 m. The type number of the modified aircraft remained as M.14, but the new military designation R III was allotted.

Oberleutnant Freiherr von Althaus with his Fok. E I.
(Photo: P. L. Gray)

Leutnant Max Immelmann in a Fok. E I, which bore a diagonal black and white stripe behind the cockpit.

The first Fok. E III went to the Western Front in August 1915. Thus the E I, E II and E III were operationally contemporary for a time. The E III was the best and most successful of the three, however, and was therefore the most numerous type. It was much sought after by the German fighter pilots once its qualities had been demonstrated. It retained the standard armament of one LMG·08 machine-gun. A few E IIIs had two guns, but this installation so reduced the aircraft's climbing performance that it found only limited use. Orders for substantial numbers of Fokker fighters were placed by the German army and navy and by the Austro-Hungarian government.

In general, airframes of the war period were simple structures that could be developed and produced much more quickly than contemporary aero-engines. Many aircraft could not be built in the numbers that were desired because suitable engines were not available in sufficient quantities. So it was with the Fok. E III, for the output of the Oberursel Motor Works could not match that of the Fokker factory.

Alternative engines were tried in the E III. At one time the prototype was flown with an 80-h.p. Le Rhône taken from a captured Nieuport 11. The maximum output of this excellent little French rotary was 92-h.p. at 1,300 r.p.m., which was better than the rather theoretical 100-h.p. of the unreliable Oberursel*; consequently the performance of the E III with the Le

---

* *The Oberursel of the Fok. E III that was tested at Central Flying School was found to deliver only 85 h.p.*

Rhône was considerably enhanced, particularly in its rate of climb and ceiling.

Apparently there was no thought of fitting production E IIIs with captured Le Rhônes, doubtless because too few fell into German hands in a usable condition at that early date. The other engines that were installed experimentally, the 100-h.p. Goebel Goe. I and 90-h.p. Siemens-Halske Sh. I, came too late. A Goe. I was fitted to the E III with *Werke Nr.* 520 in April 1916. The Sh. I came still later and little is known about its installation in an E III.

One E III was fitted with a completely circular engine cowling with a drain funnel let into its underside. This was apparently an attempt to recover some at least of the castor oil that was ejected by the engine: a tube ran from the apex of the funnel back and up into the fuselage. The date of this experiment is unknown, but it may have been quite late in the war, when Germany's supply of lubricating oils was beginning to run low. Alternatively, the oil may have been recovered for purposes of chemical analysis.

The first Fokker monoplane to fall intact into British hands was the E III No. 210/15 which, despite some seemingly conflicting records, must have been the Fokker that made a forced landing behind the British lines on 8th April 1916. Photographic evidence proves conclusively that 210/15 was the Fok. E III that was tested at Central Flying School, Upavon, on 30th May 1916; the official test report was No. M.48. The E III's speed was found to be only 83 m.p.h. at 6,500 ft., its service ceiling no more than 11,500 ft.

The E I that was covered with cellulose sheeting in an attempt to make it more or less invisible.

The forward fuselage of the prototype Fokker M.14, which was armed with a Parabellum gun.

This E III is almost certainly the aircraft that now hangs in the Science Museum, South Kensington.

It may also have been the Fokker that was pitted in mock combat against a Morane-Saulnier Type N at St Omer in the spring of 1916. The contest is best described in Cecil Lewis' words:*

". . . it was perfectly orthodox, and there remained only to put it up against a British scout to judge its performance. The Morane Bullet was chosen, and the two machines were run out on the aerodrome, side by side. All the General Staff assembled to watch the test. Both machines took off together, and it was immediately clear that the Morane was all over the Fokker. It climbed quicker, it was faster on the level, and when the two machines began a mock fight over the aerodrome, the Morane had everything its own way. A cheer went up from the ground. The bogey was laid. A description of the machine, its size, power, capabilities, was circulated at once to everyone in the Corps. It did a great deal to raise the morale and prepare the way for the Allied air supremacy later that year."

Last of the series was the Fok. E IV, of which the prototype emerged in November 1915. It represented an attempt to combine adequate performance with the twin-gun installation that had been unsuccessful in the E III. The Fok. E IV had a 160-h.p. Oberursel, a two-row rotary that required a fore- and aft mounting. The span was increased to 10 m., and there was a rudimentary top decking behind the cockpit. A new Fokker type number, M.15, was allotted to the E IV.

Immelmann wanted more fire power and suggested three guns. An installation was made in an E IV, for which Immelmann had requested the use of a captured 160-h.p. Le Rhône, another two-row rotary. While this engine was being prepared for the three-gun E IV a 100-h.p. Oberursel was fitted. With the Le Rhône installed, Immelmann took the aircraft over on 16th January 1916. Lack of spares for the big Le Rhône

* *Sagittarius Rising*, page 54.

later necessitated a change to the 160-h.p. Oberursel.

The triple-gun installation must have led to complications with the wholly mechanical interrupter gear. In March 1916 it malfunctioned and Immelmann shot away both blades of his airscrew. He recorded that he had scored at least three victories on his multi-gun E IV, but he came to dislike it and changed to a standard two-gun E IV (possibly E.127/16).

The favourable report on the E IV that Parschau had submitted in November 1915 was quickly proved to be over-optimistic. Brute force made the new type faster than its predecessors, but its manœuvrability was poor. In the event, the limited production of the 160-h.p. Oberursel restricted output of the E IV, and the type was reserved for use only by the best of the German fighter pilots.

By the standards of the 1914–18 war the Fokkers had a long operational life. Throughout the summer and autumn of 1915 and the winter of 1915–16 the German army generally followed much the same practice as the R.F.C., allotting one or two single-seat fighters to each *Feldfliegerabteilung* for the protection of the two-seaters that were the main equipment of these units. It was under this organisation that Max Immelmann and Oswald Boelcke scored their early victories as the Fokker pilots of Fl. Abt. 62.

Late in 1915 Major Stempel, Staff Officer for Aviation of the German Sixth Army, created three *Kampfeinsitzer-Kommandos* (single-seat fighter commands, abbreviated as KEK). The precise nature of these KEKs is hard to determine, but they do not seem to have replaced the basic Fl. Abt. organisation. KEK 2 was at Douai and included Immelmann, Boelcke and Mulzer; but Immelmann continued to regard himself as a member of Fl. Abt. 62. The KEK concept was probably a control arrangement to enable the army commander to call on all his single-seat fighters in a given area if the need arose.

Reports of the number of Fokkers in front-line service are conflicting. According to one source, the German Sixth Army had in August 1915 eight single-seat fighters, presumably Fokkers; by the following month the Third Army had three; and by the end of 1915 the total number of single-seat fighters in operational use on the Western and Eastern Fronts was only forty. On 20th February 1916 the Fifth Army was reported to have 147 aeroplanes, of which 21 were E-type aircraft. Between June 1915 and April 1916 the total deliveries of monoplane fighters to the Western Front were only 180; by 6th March 1916, when the German operations at Verdun were well advanced, the Fifth Army's strength of single-seat fighters had risen to 26. Another source states that 150 Fokkers, of which 110 were E IIIs, were in operational use on all fronts in April 1916.

In action the Fokker was not infallible. Its gun, the LMG.08, was not ideally suited to aviation use; its lubricating grease and the hemp ammunition belt

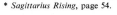

Fok. E II, No. 69/15, apparently photographed at Schwerin. (Photo: Imperial War Museum)

Leutnant Josef Jacobs with his Fok. E III.   (Photo: P. L. Gray)

would freeze. Similarly, the cold of winter or high altitude could cause the parts of the synchronising mechanism to contract sufficiently to cause it to malfunction. The gun could only be relied upon, all other things being favourable, when the engine (itself unreliable) was running at normal speed.

In spite of their faults and relatively small numbers the Fokkers were successful while they were virtually unopposed and had a tremendous influence on aerial combat during the winter of 1915–16, for the Allies did not at that time have an adequate counter-weapon. The combat advantage of the fixed forward-firing gun, when brought to bear on slow and unmanœuvrable two-seaters by an agile single-seater, was enormous. The Fokker gained a reputation that was out of all proportion to its quality as a military aeroplane.

Its depredations began in earnest in October 1915, and by mid-January 1916 the R.F.C. was so alarmed by its activities that special orders were issued, requiring an escort of at least three other aircraft for each reconnaissance two-seater that was to cross the lines.

The material success of the Fokker was augmented by the insidious psychological effect of the wildly over-dramatised outcry that was whipped up in Britain (more, it now seems, with a view to denigrating the Royal Aircraft Factory than to producing a remedy) and culminated in the Burbidge enquiry of 1916. These proceedings consumed a great deal of time and public money, did little more than reveal the ignorance of some of the accusers, and did not shoot down a single Fokker. That last task was left largely to the French Nieuport 11, the D.H.2, and the maligned Royal Aircraft Factory's F.E.2b—all of which had been designed and put into production long before the Burbidge enquiry began.

During the operations of the German Fifth Army against Verdun in March 1916 the French flying service began to make determined efforts to aid their cruelly pressed troops and succeeded in penetrating the German air defence. The failure of the German fighters to stop this penetration was attributed to the fact that their bases were too far from the front, and their fuel capacity was insufficient to permit long patrols.

This led to the first real concentration of German single-seat fighters. Hauptmann Wilhelm Haehnelt, Staff Officer for Aviation at Fifth Army Headquarters, gathered his fighter aircraft together at advanced bases at Avillers on the east bank of the River Meuse and Bantheville on the west bank. The units thus formed were known as *Kampfeinsitzer-Kommando Süd* and *KEK Nord* respectively. Boelcke sought and obtained permission to establish a third fighter flight at Sivry. This consisted of only two Fokkers, flown by himself and Lt. Notzke. These units were thus appreciably further east than KEK 1, 2 and 3 had been, and there was no operational connexion between the two groups of KEKs.

The Fokker's decline had begun as early as 5th January 1916, when the first Nieuport 11 was delivered to *Escadrille* N.3. Four and a half weeks later No. 24 Squadron, R.F.C. flew to France equipped throughout with D.H.2s. The first F.E.2a had gone to France as long before as 20th May 1915, but the handful of this type that saw limited operational use had no real opportunity to demonstrate the future qualities of the F.E.2b. The first all-F.E.2b squadron to go to France was No. 20, which arrived there on 23rd January 1916; three more squadrons (Nos. 25, 23 and 22, in that order) followed between 20th February and 1st April. The Fokker-beaters were gathering in strength.

Fok. E III, No. 210/15, photographed at Central Flying School, Upavon, May 1916.

(Photo: Aeromodeller)

A few E IIIs were used by the Austro-Hungarian Luftfahrttruppen. *One such was 03.43, which was armed with a single Schwarzlose machine-gun.*
(Photo: Peter M. Bowers)

Production: It is difficult to determine precisely how many Fokker monoplane fighters were built. According to some sources, a total of 625 Fokker monoplanes of the E I, E II, E III and E IV types were built. This figure does not withstand scrutiny, however. In 1915 and 1916, the total production of all German E-type aircraft was 647, a figure that must have included at least 150 (if not more nearly 200) monoplanes of designs other than Fokkers.

It seems that about 65 Fok. E Is and E IIs were built, and output of the E III was at least 258. It is possible that some airframes were never fitted with engines, and it seems that relatively few E IVs were used operationally.

Total production of all Fokker monoplane fighters is therefore likely to have been of the order of 450–475.

Service use: One or two Fokker monoplane fighters were on the strength of some *Feldfliegerabteilungen* from the summer of 1915 onwards. By the end of 1915 there were 82 such field avaiation sections and about 40 single-seat fighters in operational use on the Western and Eastern Fronts. In August 1916 only 48 German single-seat fighters of all types were serviceable on the Western Front.

Fokker fighters are known to have been used by the following units: *Feldfliegerabteilungen* 6b (Bavarian), 9 (Bavarian), 11, 23, 32, 37, 62 and 67. *German Fifth Army: Kampfeinsitzer-Kommando Nord* at Bantheville; KEK Süd at Avillers; fighter flight (Boelcke) at Sivry. *German Sixth Army: Kampfeinsitzer-Kommandos* 1, 2 and 3. At least one German naval defence squadron in Flanders had some Fok. E IIs. *Home Defence:* Interceptor flight at Freiburg; probably also used by *Kampfeinsitzer-Staffeln* at Trier and Mannheim.

Palestine: Fl. Abt. 300 at Beersheba. *Turkey:* E I and E III flown by Buddecke. *Austria-Hungary: Fliegerkompagnie* 10 at Aisovizza.

Pilots and known aircraft: F.l Abt. 6b: Leutnant Kurt Wintgens.

Leutnant Oswald Boelcke with his Fok. E IV, probably No. 174/16.

Fl. Abt. 9: Vizefeldwebel Eduard Böhme; E I 33/15 flown by Leutnant O. Kissenberth. Fl. Abt. 23: Lt Freiherr von Althaus; Lt Rudolf Berthold; E I 36/15 flown by Lt Hans Joachim Buddecke; Lt Carl Josef Jacobs. Fl. Abt. 32: E III 84/15 flown Lt Gustav Leffers; E III 400/15 by Lt Lehmann; E III 420/15 by Lt Diemer. Fl. Abt. 62: E Is 8/15, 13/15 and E II 37/15 flown by Lt Max Immelmann; E I 3/15 and E II 37/15 by Lt Oswald Boelcke; Lt Max Ritter von Mulzer; Lt Weber. Fl. Abt. 67: Lt Walter Höhndorf.

Turkey: E I 36/15 and E III 345/15 flown by Buddecke.

Weights and performance: (except where indicated the figures are from German sources).

Fok. E IV No. 189/16.

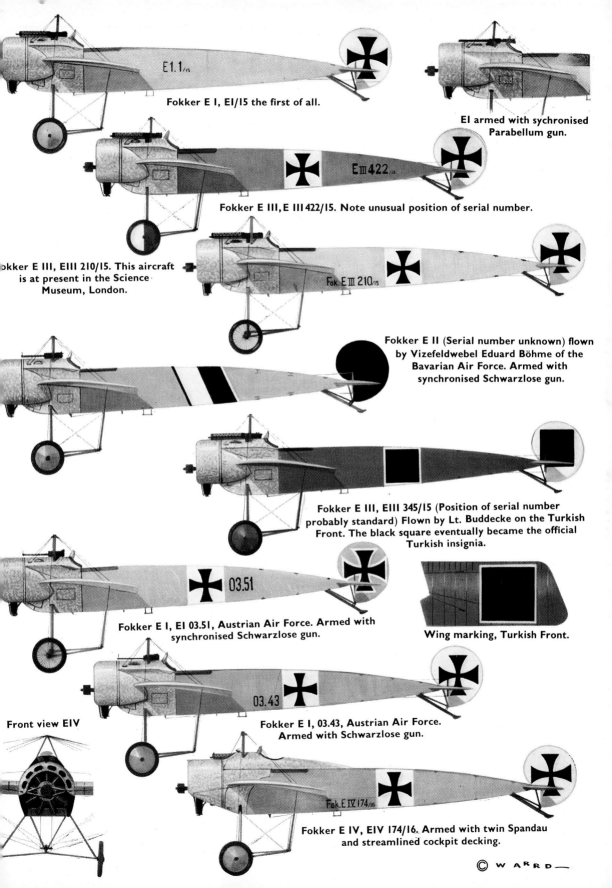

Fokker E I, EI/15 the first of all.

EI armed with sychronised Parabellum gun.

Fokker E III, E III 422/15. Note unusual position of serial number.

okker E III, EIII 210/15. This aircraft is at present in the Science Museum, London.

Fokker E II (Serial number unknown) flown by Vizefeldwebel Eduard Böhme of the Bavarian Air Force. Armed with synchronised Schwarzlose gun.

Fokker E III, EIII 345/15 (Position of serial number probably standard) Flown by Lt. Buddecke on the Turkish Front. The black square eventually became the official Turkish insignia.

Fokker E I, EI 03.51, Austrian Air Force. Armed with synchronised Schwarzlose gun.

Wing marking, Turkish Front.

Front view EIV

Fokker E I, 03.43, Austrian Air Force. Armed with Schwarzlose gun.

Fokker E IV, EIV 174/16. Armed with twin Spandau and streamlined cockpit decking.

© W A R D

In March 1916 Boelcke was reporting, of the Fok. E IV, that its climbing performance was so poor that Nieuports could escape from it. Other Fokker pilots were less fortunate: their monoplanes were unable to escape from the attentions of the Nieuports, D.H.2s and F.Es. The historian of No. 24 Squadron, R.F.C. wrote:

"Each flight frequently did three patrols of 1½ hours each per day. Results however, completely justified the effort, as the once dreaded Fokker monoplane was completely outclassed and defeated, being, indeed, literally hounded out of the sky."

On 18th June 1916 Immelmann's Fok. E III broke up in the air during a combat with an F.E.2b of No. 25 Squadron, R.F.C., flown by Lt. G. R. McCubbin with Cpl. J. H. Waller as his observer. The R.F.C. naturally claimed that Waller's shots had brought down the Eagle of Lille; the Germans, equally naturally, maintained that structural failure of the Fokker had followed the malfunctioning of the interrupter gear. Immelmann's death remains one of the classic mysteries of the first war in the air.

But it virtually marked the end of the Fokker monoplane's career. A few continued to be encountered for some weeks, and Fokkers remained in limited operational use on the Eastern Front and in the Middle East until the end of 1916. Thereafter the type was withdrawn for use at training units.

The special Fok. E IV, Werke Nr. 385, that was made to Max Immelmann's specification with three LMG.08 guns.
(Photo: Imperial War Museum)

SPECIFICATION

Power: **E I,** 80-h.p. Oberursel. **E II** (prototype and training version), 80-h.p. Oberursel; (production), 100-h.p. Oberursel U I. **E III,** 100-h.p. Oberursel U1; experimental installations of 80-h.p. Le Rhône, 100-h.p. Goebel Goe. I 90-h.p. Siemens-Halske Sh. I.
Dimensions: **E I.**—Span 29 ft. 3 in., length 22 ft. 1·7 in., height 10 ft. 5·4 in. **E II.**—Length 23 ft. 11·3 in., height 9 ft. 1·8 in. **E III.**—Span 30 ft. 10·4 in., length 23 ft. 11·3 in., height 9 ft. 1·8 in., chord 5 ft. 10·8 in., dihedral 0 deg., span of tail 9 ft. 6 in., airscrew diameter 8 ft. 3·5 in. **E IV.**—Span 32 ft. 9·6 in., length 24 ft. 7·2 in., height 10 ft. 1 in.
The wing area of the E I, E III and E IV is usually quoted as 16 sq. m. (172·2 sq. ft.), but this is probably an approximation. The wing area of the E II is believed to have been about 14 sq. m. (150·7 sq. ft.). The area of the elevators of the E III was 20 sq. ft.; of its rudder, 6·6 sq. ft.
Armament: The M.5K/MG was originally armed with a 7·92 mm. Parabellum MG.14 machine-gun, as was the prototype M.14. Standard armament of the Fok. E I and E II was one 7·92 mm. LMG.08 machine-gun; the E III could have two LMG.08 guns but more usually had only one; the E IV had two LMG.08. One special E IV for Max Immelmann had three LMG.08 guns. Some Austrian Fokkers had a single 8 mm. Schwarzlose machine-gun.

One or two Fokkers flew in Turkish markings, notably in the hands of Leutnant Hans Joachim Buddecke, who was sent to Turkey at the end of 1915 to assist the tiny air force of Germany's ally.

The R.F.C. also encountered Fokkers in Palestine, where several were added to the strength of Fl. Abt. 300 at Beersheba in 1916. In Mesopotamia, too, a few Fokkers were used by a German unit that was operating from an aerodrome at Shumran Bend in support of the Turks during the siege of Kut-al-Imara early in 1916.

With the arrival of the Albatros and Halberstadt biplane fighters the Fokkers were completely withdrawn from the Western Front in the late summer of 1916. A few lingered on on less active fronts—the last E II was still operational on the Eastern Front in December 1916—but by 1917 the Fokker monoplane was a rare bird. Fokker's star remained in eclipse until the Platz-designed triplane appeared at the front in the autumn of 1917.

© *J. M. Bruce, 1965*

Type	E I	E III	E III British test report	E IV
Weight empty (lb.)	787	878	920	1,025
Military load (lb.)	—	—	64	—
Crew (lb.)	—	—	180	—
Fuel and oil (lb.)	—	—	236	—
Weight loaded (lb.)	1,239	1,342	1,400	1,593
Max. speed (m.p.h.)				
at unspecified height	81	87·5	—	100
at 6,500 ft.	—	—	83	—
at 10,000 ft.	—	—	79	—
Climb to	m. s.	m. s.	m. s.	m. s.
3,280 ft.	7 00	5 00	— —	3 00
6,500 ft.	— —	— —	12 30	— —
6,560 ft.	20 00	15 00	— —	8 00
9,840 ft.	40 00	30 00	— —	15 00
10,000 ft.	— —	— —	28 00	— —
Service ceiling (ft.)	—	—	11,500	—
Endurance (hours)	1½	1½	2¾	1½

The author acknowledges his indebtedness to the researches of the late A. R. Weyl, especially his book Fokker: the creative years, *and to P. L. Gray for the loan of material.*

PRINTED IN ENGLAND. © Profile Publications Ltd., P.O. Box 26, Leatherhead, Surrey, England
by George Falkner & Sons Ltd., for McCorquodale City Printing Division London.

PROFILE
PUBLICATIONS

The
Supermarine
S.6B

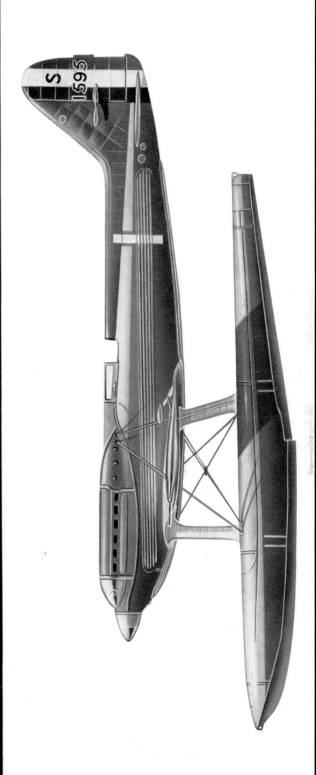

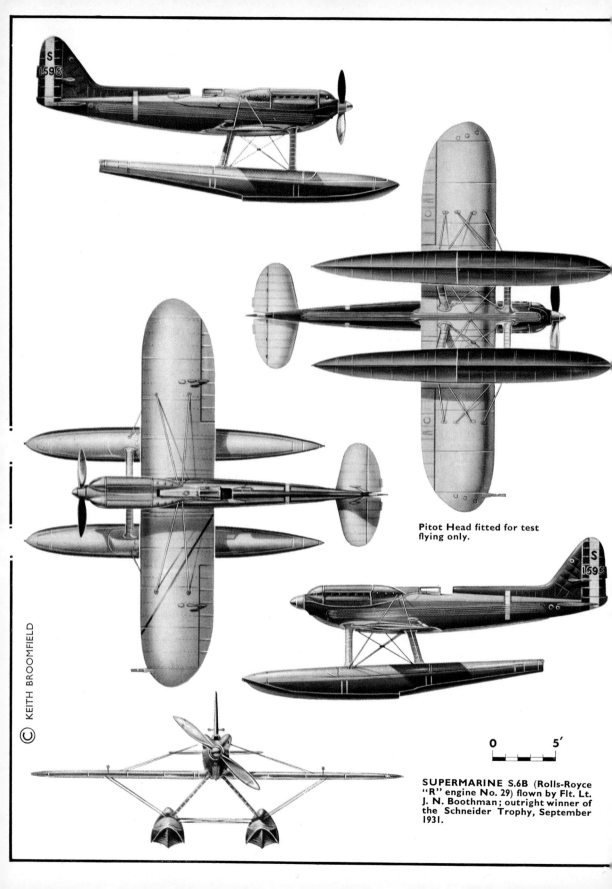

Pitot Head fitted for test
flying only.

© KEITH BROOMFIELD

0   5′

SUPERMARINE S.6B (Rolls-Royce
"R" engine No. 29) flown by Flt. Lt.
J. N. Boothman; outright winner of
the Schneider Trophy, September
1931.

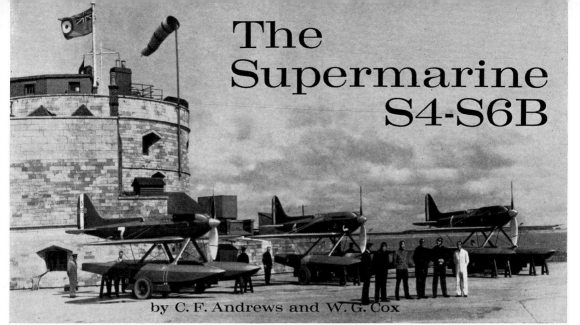

The Supermarine S4-S6B

by C. F. Andrews and W. G. Cox

The 1931 British team at Calshot R.A.F. Station. Left to right: S.6B S1596 reserve machine, S.6A N247 training machine converted from 1929 winner, S.6B S1595, outright winner of the Schneider Trophy for Britain.

The Schneider Trophy International Contest for Seaplanes was originally intended to encourage the development of aircraft which could use the sea as an aerodrome. At the first international meeting for seaplanes held at Monaco in 1912 it was evident that they were far behind contemporary landplanes in technical progress. To foster their progress M. Jacques Schneider donated a trophy bearing his name for a contest which included a speed trial over a closed circuit of several laps. The first Schneider Contest was held at Monaco in 1913 and, with breaks caused by W.W.I. and for other reasons, was held intermittently until 1931. In that year the Trophy was won outright by Great Britain, who had triumphed in three successive races. This triple success was achieved by the S series of Supermarine racing seaplanes designed by Reginald J. Mitchell, whose genius became even better known later as the originator of the Spitfire, immortalised in W.W.II. This *Profile* deals with the Supermarine S.4 of 1925, the S.5 which won the 1927 contest, the S.6 which was the 1929 winner and the S.6B, which wound up the whole series of Schneider Contests by capturing the Trophy for good in 1931.

Mitchell had indeed four Schneider winners to his credit, for the Supermarine Sea Lion II flying boat had gained a surprise victory in the 1922 Contest held at Naples, thus preventing the Italians from recording three wins in a row. The Italians likewise saved the Trophy in 1926 when de Bernadi scored a resounding win in the Macchi M.39, the Americans thus failing to capture the Trophy outright after two successive wins. The 1926 Contest, held at Hampton Roads, Newport, U.S.A., was remarkable in another way. For the first time since the first Contest in 1913 was won by Prevost on the Deperdussin racer, a monoplane provided the winner, all the intervening successful types being biplanes.

Mitchell had been the first designer to revive the

monoplane configuration in the racing seaplane, for his revolutionary S.4 entered for the 1925 Contest at Baltimore drew attention to the virtues of the type, especially aerodynamic, notably that of drag reduction. Actually Mitchell went a little beyond the state of structural knowledge at that time and the S.4, after setting up new speed records, crashed during the qualifying trials and was lost.

THE SUPERMARINE S.4

The design of the Supermarine S.4 was the direct result of the successful challenge of the Americans in the 1923 Contest held at Cowes, Isle of Wight, when two U.S. Navy Curtiss C.R.3 floatplanes filled the first and second places, beating by a wide margin the Supermarine Sea Lion III flying boat, a cleaned-up version of the 1922 winner at Naples. The Curtiss machines presented an exceptionally clean and compact design, innovations including wing surface-mounted radiators, an all-metal propeller and the new liquid-cooled Curtiss D.12 engine, installed in a carefully streamlined nose.

Mitchell realised that the small flying boat was obsolete for high speed conditions and began to devote a considerable amount of thought and time to the new problem confronting him, if he was to repeat his Naples success. The S.4 was his answer and it was as startling when it first appeared as the Curtiss C.R.3 had been. The feature that made the new Supermarine design so outstanding was that the wing, float chassis and tail unit were complete cantilevers. No bracing wires were used at all. The British Government supported the construction of the S.4 by agreeing to purchase the aircraft if the engine and airframe manufacturers shared the initial cost of building.

A decision was made by the Supermarine and Napier Companies to go ahead on the 18th March 1925 and the S.4 made its first flight on 25th August

The S.4 contender for the 1925 Contest showing its cantilever construction.

The monocoque fuselage of the S.4 under construction.

piloted by Henri Biard, Supermarine's chief test pilot. To design and build such an aircraft in five months was a great achievement and set the pattern for the Supermarine racers then to come.

The monoplane wing was made in one piece with normal front and rear spars of spruce flanges and plywood webs with a number of spanwise stringers re-butted into wing ribs, which had spruce flanges and ply webs. This structure was then covered top and bottom with plywood sheeting gradually increasing in thickness from the tips to the centre line of the wing. A trough was built on the undersurface of the wing to carry the water coolant pipe from the engine to the Lamblin type radiators located under the wing. These radiators were the only protuberances on the whole machine. An interconnected flap and aileron system was introduced, the ailerons being able to act independently or in conjunction with the flaps. Oddly enough, flaps were not used by Mitchell on any of his succeeding Schneider racers.

The fuselage was built in three sections; the engine mounting, the centre and the rear monocoque. Apart from steel fittings and the two "A" frames of steel tubing, which comprised the backbone of the centre body, the S.4 was constructed entirely in wood. It was interesting to note the resurrection of the monocoque fuselage after a lengthy gap in time, for the Deperdussin winner of 1913 also used that type of streamlined body. The floats were attached to the bottom of the two sloping "A" frames, the one-piece wing passing between the frames and were attached to them, while the engine mounting was attached to the forward frame.

A special version of the Napier Lion 12-cylinder,

water-cooled engine of the "broad arrow" configuration was developed to produce 700 h.p. for the short period of the race. This brief life, in fact, was a general characteristic of Schneider engines, particularly those that came later. The Lion had direct drive to the propeller and starting was by a Bristol gas starter unit. The propeller was an all-metal, Fairey-Reed type.

The floats, of the single-step type, were of wooden construction closely following the design of the Supermarine flying boats, that is, a fore-and-aft keel member along the bottom centre line with port and starboard chines, the three members forming the pronounced "Vee" underside of the floats. Double watertight bulkheads were provided and the whole structure was flexible enough to absorb a very considerable amount of punishment in rough water conditions.

Left: *The S.4 on the slipway works at Woolston, Southampton.* Right: *Capt. Biard leaving the primitive slipway at Baltimore for trials just before the S.4 crashed.*

The fuel and oil systems were conventional except that the petrol had to be carried in several tanks, there being insufficient room for a single unit. The oil cooler was located on the underside of the fuselage, only the cooling fins being exposed to the airstream.

Flying trials were conducted from Calshot air station, the Royal Air Force rendering invaluable help and making possible the expeditious conclusion of the test period, which included the setting up of new records. The S.4 was not a good aeroplane from the pilot's point of view, as the position of the wing in relation to his eyeline during take-off and alighting created a hazardous blind spot.

Before the S.4 was sent to the U.S.A. for the eighth Schneider Contest at Baltimore in 1925 a speed test was conducted over a straight course along Southampton Water during which it captured the World Air Speed Record for Seaplanes and the British Air Speed Record at 226.75 m.p.h.

The subsequent history of the S.4 and of the 1925 British Schneider team was one of misfortune. The liner carrying the team encountered severe storms and Capt. Henri Biard, the Supermarine pilot, slipped during one of these and sustained a sprained wrist. On arrival in the U.S. the British entries were housed in canvas hangars and during more bad weather one of the tent poles broke and fell across the tailplane of the S.4, causing damage. This was quickly repaired and

Head on view of S.5 disclosing offset starboard float and extremely small cross-sectional area of fuselage with faired engine banks.

S.5 N220 during mooring tests preceding the 1927 Contest at Venice. (Flight photo)

test flying began. It then confirmed what had in fact been suspected in England that the cantilever wing was subject to flutter, a phenomenon of which little was understood at that time.

This proved to be the undoing of the S.4 for during the mandatory taxiing and alighting trials the machine developed flutter when airborne. Capt. Biard lost control with the result that it fell into the sea and was wrecked, the pilot escaping without injury after being submerged. A hurried attempt to substitute the second Gloster III, to be flown by Bert Hinkler, also ended in disaster, the float chassis collapsing in a final attempt to pass the preliminary tests in bad conditions. This Contest was won by Lt. Jimmy Doolittle of the U.S. Army at 232·573 m.p.h., Hubert Broad being second on the Gloster III first string at 199 m.p.h.

THE SUPERMARINE S.5

The S.4 had been designed and built as an ideal. The S.5, its logical development, embodied all the hard lessons learned from the S.4 and other comparative aircraft. It could be fairly described as an exercise in aerodynamic efficiency.

F/Lt. Worseley on the S.5 with direct drive Lion racing neck and neck with F/O Kinkead on the geared Gloster IV during the 1927 Contest at the Venice Lido. The immense crowd in the foreground were very near the competing aircraft. (Flight photo)

F/Lt. Worseley's S.5 N219 under tow at Venice for the 1927 contest. (Flight photo)

Left: *The scoreboard at Venice in 1927 disclosing the better times of the British contestants.* (Flight photo)
Right: *F/Lt. Webster, R.A.F. crossing the finishing line at Venice in the S.5 thus winning the Schneider Trophy Contest of 1927.* (Flight photo)

Before the design of the S.5 could be put down as a paper project, an extensive programme of model research was carried out in the wind tunnels of the Royal Aircraft Establishment and the National Physical Laboratory. These tests were requested by the Air Ministry late in 1925 and were conducted on three-quarter scale models evolved from experience with the S.4 and the Gloster III.

The models comprised approximations of a standard fuselage, tail unit and floats, the main differences being in the wing and bracing arrangements. The first model had a low wing, braced by "W" formation struts and a tie strut between the floats. In the second model the two outer struts and tie strut were replaced by wire bracing. In the third model the high wing blended into the cylinder banks (like the contemporary Gloster IV) and braced in a similar manner to the first model. The object of the tests was to obtain data for estimating the performance of the S.5 and they were entirely successful, being within one per cent of the full scale figures ultimately achieved.

Pitching control problems of the proposed offset floats were also studied and these researches, with similar problems on the Gloster IV and the Short-Bristol Crusader, contributed a great deal to the technical achievements of the 1927 Schneider Contest. Model two suggested the most efficient system and this was incorporated in the design of the S.5, Mitchell having abandoned for the time being his cantilever wing.

While the model tests were proceeding, the High Speed Flight of the Royal Air Force had already been formed and were training at Felixstowe on the Gloster III and later on the Crusader. Meanwhile the Government order for seven Schneider aircraft had been confirmed, in the guise of fostering research into high speed flight, which later proved, more by accident than design, to have been an inspired decision when the end product was the winning of the Battle of Britain in 1940.

Experimental flying was intensified to investigate geared and ungeared engines, various propellers, cockpit fume problems and so on. All this testing, wind tunnel, model and full scale flying, proved extremely useful and the fact that the British Schneider entries for the 1927 race never required extensive modifications testified to the success of planning that went before.

The main lines of advancement in the S.5 were aerodynamic, as previously stated.

They comprised the following items:

1. The adoption of flush wing radiators for the water cooling of the engine; this provided the necessary cooling area and reduced drag.

2. The lowering of the wing, as compared with that of the S.4, to the bottom of the fuselage; this gave a better view to the pilot than that of the S.4 and a better angle to the bracing wires than a mid-wing arrangement.

3. The adoption of streamline wire bracing between floats, wing and fuselage.

4. Smaller cross-section of fuselage and floats to reduce drag.

5. An engine of greater power output, geared to give a more efficient propeller and therefore a better thrust/power factor.

To achieve these advantages a number of unusual

Left: *The metal semi-monocoque fuselage of the S.6 under construction.* Right: *The all radiator upper surface of the S.6 wing.*

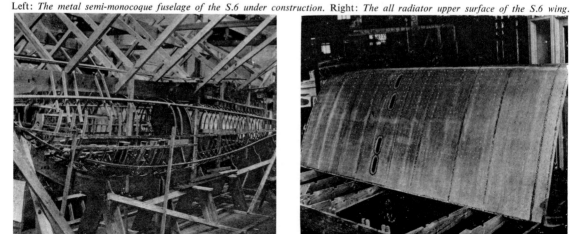

constructional features were incorporated in the design to meet the special conditions anticipated in this high-speed aeroplane.

S.5 CONSTRUCTION

The fuselage was built entirely of metal, mainly duralumin, and was of simple semi-monocoque form. It consisted of 32 closely spaced formers of flat "U"-shaped section with outward turned flanges to which the skin plating was attached, thus dispensing with longerons. The forward portion comprised a scoop-shaped engine mounting, stiffened by the engine bearers, with cross bracing between them. At the rear of this assembly, the main frame, which carried the supports for the wing spars, forward floats struts and wing bracing, isolated the engine compartment from the rest of the fuselage.

With this type of semi-monocoque structure it became possible to keep the cross-sectional area of the fuselage down to a minimum. The pilot sat on the floor and his shoulders touched the cockpit coaming so that the only space lost was the thickness of the skin. The fin was integral with the rear fuselage with slightly heavier frames for the rudder post and tail-plane spars. In the most heavily loaded areas the maximum of three thicknesses of 18g. plating was adequate.

Duralumin was also used in the construction of the floats, except the fuel tank, which was of tinned steel and was assembled as an integral part of the standard float. The floats, which were of the single-step type, followed the Supermarine system of hull construction for their flying boats, that is, with a central longitudinal keel member and chines with transverse frames stabilised fore and aft by stringers. The lower ends of the chassis struts were built rigidly into the floats and were reinforced where they left the floats, at which point they were subjected to heavy bending loads.

The wings of the S.5 were of conventional wooden construction, made in two halves on the normal two-spar principle, with ribs of three-ply spruce with wide flanges to secure the screw fixings of the wing radiators in addition to the three-ply wing covering, which was $\frac{3}{32}$ in. thick. From the wire bracing attachments on the rear spar a diagonal member ran outwards to the front spar to stiffen the wing against torsion, thus reducing the possibility of wing flutter. Wire bracing fork ends, etc., were entirely enclosed and flush fitting doors were provided top and bottom to give access for rigging and inspection.

Installing the Rolls-Royce "R" engine in the S.6 with R.J. Mitchell facing camera in foreground.

The wing radiators were placed over the wing skin and screwed to the three-ply covering. The engine cooling system was ingenious; the hot water passed from the engine into the header tank mounted behind the central cylinder block of the Napier engine. Piping then took the water along the rear edge of the radiators (located on the top and bottom wing surfaces) whence it flowed through them across the wings to the leading edge, where return piping took it back as cooled water to the engine.

The radiators were of 30g. copper sheet and covered almost the whole of the upper and lower wing surfaces. Each was built in sections $8\frac{1}{2}$ in. wide and consisted of two copper sheets rolled to the wing formation and sweated together. The outer sheet exposed to the air flow was smooth but the inner was corrugated to form the transverse water channels. Water troughs were sweated to the leading and trailing edges of each radiator to form the main flow and return channels and each radiator was detachable for repair without disturbing the rest of the system.

Oil cooling was provided by corrugated coolers of 26g. tinned steel 11 ft. long mounted along each side of the fuselage. Oil passed from the engine through one cooler into a filter, then into the oil tank (located behind the pilot) and thence back through the other cooler to the engine.

The tailplane, elevator and rudder were of orthodox wooden construction, covered with plywood. All control rods and levers (except aileron control) were enclosed for all moving surfaces and extreme care was

Left: *Launching the winning S.6 at Calshot for 1929 Contest tests.* (Flight photo)
Right: *Lighter-borne S.6 being taken out for trials in the Solent in 1929. The aircraft was slid into the water when reaching the starting line.*

N247, *the ultimate, taking off for trials in the 1929 Contest, held off Ryde, Isle of Wight.*

taken in the design to avoid any protuberances whatever. Even the cylinder block covers of the Lion engine were tailored to match the streamlining of the engine fairings and fuselage as can be seen in the head-on views of the S.5 photographs. The maximum cross-sectional area was 5·9 sq. ft. which was about as low as has ever been achieved in a racing aeroplane in this class.

Because of this small cross-sectional area and the C.G. requirements the problem of fuel storage was very difficult. It was finally overcome in a practical and simple manner by storing a part of the fuel in the starboard float. This arrangement brought bonuses by way of lowering the C.G. thus improving stability in the air and on the water and in balancing engine torque during take-off and to a certain extent in the air.

On the first S.5, N219, the starboard float containing the fuel tank was made longer than the port, but flying and taxiing tests proved that this extension was unnecessary for the two other S.5s. The starboard float was offset 8 in. farther from the aircraft centre line than the port on all three machines.

There was the usual race for the designers, pilots and engineers but on this occasion the British team went to Italy more confident and better prepared than in any previous Schneider contest. Most of all, the Government of the day had been right behind the enterprise, for as has already been said, the fruits of it were then unseen but made a great impact on the future in a more deadly contest.

In this *Profile* there is only space to describe the performance of the S.5s in the 1927 race, held over the Lido at Venice on a triangular course of seven laps, a total distance of 190 miles. In the event this turned out to be one of the finest air races ever held and certainly the most spectacular, for the aircraft roared low along the beach on each lap in full view of and close to the enormous crowd, estimated in many hundreds of thousands. Italian machines suffered one disaster after another leading to retirements from the race but the British entries, two S.5s and one Gloster IV, lapped consistently until the sixth lap when F/O Kinkead had to retire on the Gloster after losing his propeller spinner and experiencing engine vibration.

The two S.5s completed the course, F/O S. N. Webster being the winner on the S.5 N220 with the geared Lion engine at an average speed of 281·65 m.p.h. while F/Lt. Worseley was second on S.5 N219 with the direct drive Lion at 273·01 m.p.h. This victory was hailed by the whole of the British Press and re-established the supremacy of British aircraft design. Both the slower S.5 and the Gloster IV averaged 7 m.p.h. better than the best lap speed of the Italian Macchis and justified all the painstaking research, development and training that had preceded the actual event. It reflected great credit on the designers, and engineers, including the engine people, and on the Royal Air Force team of pilots and mechanics.

THE SUPERMARINE S.6 AND S.6B

Enthusiasm in official circles soon waned after the resounding British win in the 1927 contest but the Royal Aero Club, who were responsible for the British entries, managed by a remarkable piece of astute diplomacy to extend the period between races to two years, to the satisfaction of the *Federation Aeronautique Internationale* (the organising body) and the other competing countries. Everyone felt by that time that the original period of one year was inadequate to prepare suitable aircraft capable of beating existing times, as complexity in design and development was beginning to become painfully evident. In addition it gave the Club time to soften up Government opinion into agreeing to spend the money on a 1929 entry.

Consequently Italy, France and the U.S. were making strenuous efforts to recapture the Trophy and considerable improvements would be needed if Britain was to retain it. The Napier Lion was nearing the end of its development and R. J. Mitchell was looking for an engine of greater horsepower. Sir Henry Royce, after deliberation with his colleagues of Rolls-Royce, eventually guaranteed an engine of 1,500 h.p. and around this Mitchell started

F/O Waghorn, R.A.F. winning the 1929 Schneider Contest over the Spithead course on S.6 N247.

designing the Supermarine S.6. This was his first all-metal racer and was a logical development of the S.5.

The new Rolls-Royce "R" engine was a development of the 36 litres capacity "Buzzard" and the enormous power obtained with this unit was obtained by fitting racing superchargers, introducing a much higher compression ratio (made possible by using chemical fuels devised by F. Rodwell Banks of the Associated Ethyl Company) and greatly increased engine operating speeds. A convergent-divergent air flow into the carburettor facilitated a reduction in kinetic energy which produced a gain in the pressure energy of the mass air flow into the engine, which mass itself was enormous. All this technological advance produced a racing engine which gave 1,900 brake horse power at 2,900 r.p.m. and weighed only 1,530 lb., a remarkable achievement in piston engine development and, as it turned out, a world beater.

For the 1931 Contest the power was further increased of the "R" engine to the stupendous figure of 2,350 b.h.p. a result obtained by increasing the engine speed, the supercharger gear ratio and the size of the air intake. The engine speed at this power rating was 3,200 r.p.m. and the weight was 1,630 lb. or 11 oz. per horsepower.

Although the continued success of British machines in the two final Schneider contests was obviously due in great measure to the Rolls-Royce engine and the more sophisticated approach to the problem of greatly increasing power than that of the Italians or Americans (who tried to reach the same end by increasing cubic capacity), the aircraft designer had to make full use of the advantage conferred upon him.

As the Rolls-Royce engine was so much bigger and heavier than the Napier Lion the S.6 was also bigger than the S.5 and weighed fully loaded 5,771 lb. as against the 3,250 lb. of the S.5. Nevertheless the percentage weight of the wings and other components was reduced by careful design. The general concept of the S.6 was basically the same as the S.5, which in the light of aeronautical knowledge at that time, had proved right. The wings and all tail surfaces were metallised (almost wholly duralumin) but still retained the conventional two-wing spar construction and ribs comprised of diaphragm webs with large lightening holes and flanges of extruded angle section. The wing radiators were built up from 24g. duralumin sheets riveted together with spacers $\frac{1}{16}$ in. thick, which pro-

S/Ldr. Orlebar descending from the S.6 after capturing the World Air Speed Record.

vided the water cavity. The radiators were screwed to the wing structure and thus formed the wing surface.

Semi-monocoque construction was used for the S.6 fuselage as in the S.5 but there were 46 frames 6 or 7 in. apart. The only longitudinal members were the engine bearers which were of 14g. duralumin angle section and ran right back along the body following the fuselage contours. The whole fuselage with the fin was skinned with duralumin sheet.

With a thirsty engine like the Rolls-Royce "R" it became necessary in the S.6 to use centre portions of both floats as tanks. The float construction was similar in detail to the S.5. In the S.6, part of the front top surface of each float accommodated an additional radiator, but in the S.6B, so great was the area required for the dissipation of engine heat (some 40,000 B.T.U.s per minute), that all the top surfaces of the floats were used down to the chines. In the S.6B considerably more fuel was carried in the starboard float to balance the enormous engine torque.

To obtain the maximum efficiency with a fixed pitch propeller, the aeroplane required just sufficient excess thrust to overcome air and water resistance at take-off. Otherwise propeller efficiency at top speed suffered. For this reason the take-off of the S.6 had been difficult and, to improve this model, water tank tests were conducted on the S.6B floats, with the result that air resistance was greatly reduced as well as the "hump" water resistance. The stability of the floats on the water was also improved.

The special propeller of smaller diameter designed by the Fairey Aviation Company for the S.6B proved unsatisfactory as the aircraft refused to take off under full power, swinging violently to port under full opposite rudder. Eventually a compromise between

Left: *The Rolls-Royce "R" engine of 1929 and 1931.* (Science Museum photo)   Right: *Reginald J. Mitchell (left) and Sir Henry Royce—architects of the 1929 and 1931 Schneider victories.*

S.6B under construction and final assembly at Woolston in 1931.

Close-up of S1595 *at Calshot in 1931.*

S.6B S1595 *taking off in the Solent, 1931.*

the S.6 and S.6B propellers was arrived at which proved satisfactory. The method of take-off was to aim the nose several points out of wind and gradually turn into it as the speed picked up. The stick was held hard back into the pilot's stomach and kept there until the unstick when the S.6 and the S.6B became quite tractable aircraft at high speed.

A special oil cooling system had to be devised for the high power "R" engines, as engine temperature was critical. In fact, the races had to be flown at a maximum temperature and this was the deciding factor for the pilot in finding out how far he could open the throttle. The hot oil passed along the fuselage coolers (similar to S.5) to the top of the fin whence it ran down the insides of the fin skin via ribs and gutters to an integral tank with a filter and thence by the return cooler under the fuselage back to the engine. Small vanes placed in the cooler oilways kept the oil in contact with the outer surfaces and this method, arrived at after much experiment, increased the efficiency of the oil cooling system by 40 per cent.

Control surface flutter had been experienced with the S.5 and again with the S.6, so on the S.6B mass balances were added to control surfaces to eradicate this tendency. To avoid unwanted loading on the control column and rudder bar caused by small inaccuracies of construction, the elevators and rudder of the S.6B were fitted with small trim tabs to suit the characteristic of each individual aircraft.

The story of the S.6 and the S.6B in the Schneider Contests of 1929 and 1931 can be briefly told. F/O H. R. D. Waghorn won the 1929 Contest, held off Ryde, Isle of Wight, in the S.6 *N247* over a quadrilateral course of 50 milometres covered seven times, at an average speed of 328·63 mp.h. F/O R. L. R. Atcherley came in second on the other S.6, *N248*, at 325 m.p.h. but was disqualified for missing a turn. Two weeks later S/Ldr. A. H. Orlebar took the World

ENGINE DATA
(From Napier and Rolls-Royce Records)

Type and Designation	Napier Lion 12-cylinder Broad Arrow			Rolls-Royce "R" 12-cylinder Vee	
	VII (Direct Drive)	VIIA (Direct Drive)	VIIB (Geared)	(Geared and Supercharged)	
Year	1925	1927	1927	1929	1931
Bore	5·5 in.			6 in.	
Stroke	5·125 in.			6·6 in.	
Capacity	24 litres (1,476 cu. in.)			36·7 litres (2,240 cu. in.)	
Dry Weight (lb.) ...	750	850	930	1,539	1,640
B.H.P.	680	900	875	1,900	2,350
R.P.M.	2,600	3,300	3,300	2,900	3,200
Compression Ratio ...	8/1	10/1	10/1	6/1	6/1
Boost (lb./sq. in.) ...	Nil			13	18
B.M.E.P.	142 (estimated)	148 (estimated)	144 (estimated)	225	254
Fuel Consumption (pt./h.p./hr.) ...	·04	·046	·046	·6	·6
Oil Consumption (gall./hr.) ...	8	8	8	10	14
Engine Nos. ...	E.74	E.86	E.90	1, 3, 5, 7, 9, 11, 15	3, 5, 7, 9, 11, 15, 21, 23, 25, 27, 29, 31
Installation	S.4	S.5 (N219)	S.5 (N220, N221)	S.6 (N247, N248)	S.6B (S1595, S1596)

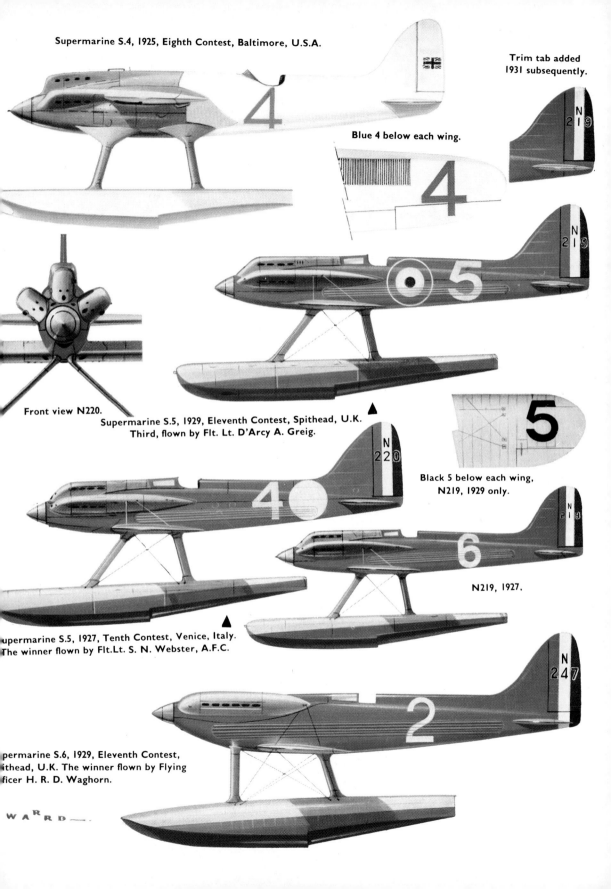

Supermarine S.4, 1925, Eighth Contest, Baltimore, U.S.A.

Trim tab added 1931 subsequently.

Blue 4 below each wing.

Front view N220.

Supermarine S.5, 1929, Eleventh Contest, Spithead, U.K. Third, flown by Flt. Lt. D'Arcy A. Greig.

Black 5 below each wing, N219, 1929 only.

N219, 1927.

Supermarine S.5, 1927, Tenth Contest, Venice, Italy. The winner flown by Flt.Lt. S. N. Webster, A.F.C.

Supermarine S.6, 1929, Eleventh Contest, Spithead, U.K. The winner flown by Flying Officer H. R. D. Waghorn.

WARD

S.6B S1595 with its R.A.F. handling crew at rest at Calshot in readiness for the 1931 Contest.

Air Speed Record in S.6 *N247* at 357·7 m.p.h.

In 1931 economic depression caused the Government to decline to finance a Schneider entry but Lady Houston stepped into the breach and provided the necessary funds. The existing S.6 design was adapted and developed as stated and F/Lt. J. N. Boothman flew over the triangular course in the Solent on S.6B *S1595* at an average speed of 340 m.p.h. and so, in the absence of foreign challengers at the starting line, won the Schneider Trophy outright for Britain. Later F/Lt. G. H. Stainforth raised the World Speed Record to 407·5 m.p.h. on S.6B *S1595*, fitted with a special "sprint" "R" engine. This historic aeroplane may be seen in the Science Museum in London. Near it is its illustrious descendant, a Spitfire of vintage 1940!

© *C. F. Andrews and W. G. Cox, 1965*

SPECIFICATIONS AND DATA

From official and company records. Any variations from figures sometimes published are due to differential loadings for test flight series.

Type	S.4	S.5	S.6	S.6B
Year	1925	1927	1929	1931
Serial and Racing Numbers	"4"	N219 "6" N220 "4" (winner) N221	N247 "2" (winner) N248 "8"	S1595 "I" (winner) S1596
Span	30 ft. 7½ in.	26 ft. 9 in.	30 ft. 0 in.	30 ft. 0 in.
Length (overall)	26 ft. 7¾ in.	24 ft. 3½ in.	26 ft. 10 in.	28 ft. 10 in.
Length (fuselage)	25 ft. 0 in.	22 ft. 0½ in.	25 ft. 3 in.	25 ft. 3 in.
Height	11 ft. 8½ in.	11 ft. 1 in.	12 ft. 3 in.	12 ft. 3 in.
Chord (M'plane)	6 ft. at root 4 ft. 3½ in. at tip	5 ft. 0 in.	5 ft. 8 in.	5 ft. 8 in.
Tailplane Span	8 ft. 2 in.	7 ft. 9 in.	8 ft. 1½ in.	8 ft. 1½ in.
Float Length	18 ft. 0 in.	18 ft. 6 in.	19 ft. 5 in.	24 ft. 0 in.
Float Track	7 ft. 6 in.	7 ft. 0 in.	7 ft. 6 in.	7 ft. 6 in.
Areas: Mainplane ...	139 sq. ft.	115 sq. ft.	145 sq. ft.	145 sq. ft.
Tailplane ...	15·8 sq. ft.	14 sq. ft.	15·8 sq. ft.	15 sq. ft.
Elevator ...	9·5 sq. ft.	5·8 sq. ft.	6 sq. ft.	6 sq. ft.
Fin	5·25 sq. ft.	4·50 sq. ft.	6 sq. ft.	6 sq. ft.
Rudder ...	6·625 sq. ft.	6·625 sq. ft.	7·5 sq. ft.	7·5 sq. ft.
Weight (empty) lb. ...	2,600	2,680 (N220)	4,471 (S.6A)	4,590
(loaded) lb. ...	3,191	3,242 (N220)	5,771 (S.6A)	6,086
Loading: (wing)	23 lb./sq. ft.	28 lb./sq. ft.	40 lb./sq. ft.	41 lb./sq. ft.
(power)	47 lb./h.p.	36 lb./h.p.	30·6 lb./h.p.	26 lb./h.p.
Aerofoil Section	Raf 30	Raf 30	Raf 27	Raf 27
Speed (maximum)	226·75 m.p.h. (world seaplane record)	319·57 m.p.h.	357·7 m.p.h. (world record)	407·5 m.p.h. (world record)
Speed "Landing"	85 m.p.h.	85 m.p.h.	95 m.p.h.	95 m.p.h.
Fuel (Imp. galls.)	40	50	106	135
Oil (Imp. galls.)	5	5	10	15
Water (Imp. galls.)... ...	10	15	20	25

PRINTED IN ENGLAND. © Profile Publications Ltd., P.O. Box 26, Leatherhead, Surrey, England, by George Falkner & Sons Ltd., for McCorquodale City Printing Division, London.

PROFILE
PUBLICATIONS

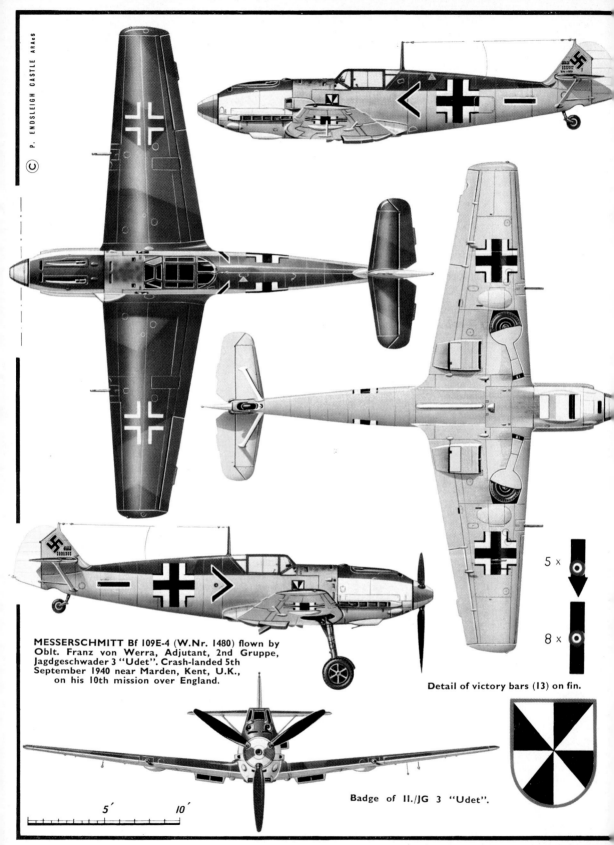

© P. ENDSLEIGH CASTLE ARAeS

MESSERSCHMITT Bf 109E-4 (W.Nr. 1480) flown by Oblt. Franz von Werra, Adjutant, 2nd Gruppe, Jagdgeschwader 3 "Udet". Crash-landed 5th September 1940 near Marden, Kent, U.K., on his 10th mission over England.

5 ×

8 ×

Detail of victory bars (13) on fin.

Badge of II./JG 3 "Udet".

5′   10′

It will be noted that the cowling panel immediately forward of the cockpit of the aircraft illustrated above is a replacement taken from an aircraft finished in a different camouflage scheme.

The Messerschmitt Bf 109E

by Martin C. Windrow

A Messerschmitt Bf 109E-4/N Trop of 2nd Staffel, JG 27 in flight over the Mediterranean. The tropical filter over the ram-air intake on the port side of the engine cowling is clearly visible. Note also the emblem of JG 27 on the nose and the white belly-band displayed by most Luftwaffe aircraft in North Africa. (Photo: R. Ward Collection)

The story of Willy Messerschmitt's Bf 109 fighter surely needs but little introduction. The best-known German military aircraft of W.W.II, it has probably monopolised more space in print than any other machine which took part in that great struggle. As the standard equipment of the German fighter force during the epic "Battle of Britain", the exploits of this aggressive little aircraft made its designer's name a household word throughout the civilised world; and it is a much-noised fact that more Bf 109s were built than any other combat aircraft of the war. As one of the two major production series the Bf 109E "Emil" represented the peak of more than four years' development; it was the equal of any contemporary fighter in squadron service anywhere in the world, and vastly superior to most.

The Bf 109 did not have an easy birth. Due to the long-standing feud between Secretary of State for Air General Erhard Milch and Willy Messerschmitt, the *Bayerische Flugzeugwerke* was in a precarious business position when in 1933 Messerschmitt and his joint manager Herr Kokothaki obtained a contract from a Romanian cartel to develop a new transport aircraft, a contract which saved B.F.W. from liquidation. Protests from officials of the *Reichsluftfahrtministerium* against Messerschmitt's acceptance of a foreign contract drew the retort that this step had been forced on B.F.W. by a total lack of home support for the company. Consequently, a fighter development contract was awarded to B.F.W. almost at once; similar contracts were awarded to the Heinkel, Arado and Focke-Wulf concerns and in view of Messerschmitt's lack of experience in high-speed combat design, B.F.W.'s chances in the scheduled competitive trials at Travemünde were extremely dubious.

Design work occupied Messerschmitt's team throughout the summer of 1934. The maximum use was made of features which had proved successful in the Bf 108 *Taifun* touring four-seater, such as leading edge slats, slotted flaps, and a completely enclosed

Oberleutnant Franz von Werra, pilot of the Bf 109E-4 depicted on the opposite page, escaped from captivity in Canada and returned to Germany via the U.S.A.; he was the only German officer to succeed in this feat. He is seen here posing by an SB-2 he destroyed on the Russian Front.

Above: *The Bf 109V14, which first flew in mid-1938.* Below: *The initial production variant Bf 109E-1 in factory finish.* (Photos: G. Heumann/Air Pictorial)

Bf 109E production line at Augsburg.

Scottie dog nose emblem on a Bf 109E-3 believed to have flown with JG 2 "Richthofen" in the Battle of Britain. The "Schnauzl" insignia was a personal rather than a unit motif.

A pilot of 8/JG 51 (previously 2/JG 20) boards his E-3 in a hurry. The aircraft bears the markings of the late 1939/early 1940 period, with black-green upper surfaces and narrow fuselage crosses.

Above: J-311, Bf 109E-3 W.Nr.2159, in the colourful fuselage markings of the Swiss Air Force. This machine was written off on 28th December 1949.   (Photo: Werner Gysin, Jr.)
Below: A Messerschmitt which crash-landed in Windsor Great Park on 30th September 1940 after misjudging an attack on two Avro Anson trainers. The numeral painted on the cowling was a marking not often employed as late as 1940.

cockpit. Despite the resultant poor vision during taxiing, a high ground angle was chosen in order to achieve the highest possible lift coefficient when landing. Messerschmitt was unable to obtain one of the new Junkers Jumo 210A engines of 610 h.p. for his prototype, so when the Bf 109VI was rolled out in September 1935 it was powered by a Rolls-Royce Kestrel V of 695 h.p. After a series of hurried flight tests by test pilot Knoetsch, the Bf 109VI (registration D-IABI, W.Nr. 758) was flown to the Rechlin Experimental Establishment, and suffered a collapsed undercarriage on arrival. Hasty repairs were effected, and the VI flew to Travemünde for the trials in late October. The other competitors were the Heinkel He 112VI, the Arado Ar 80VI and the Focke-Wulf Fw 159VI; and it was with considerable surprise that the German aviation world heard that Messerschmitt, although not the outright winner, had been awarded a contract for ten Bf 109s. (Heinkel obtained a similar contract, but the full story of the ill-fated He 112 would require a *Profile* of its own.) The Augsburg plant of B.F.W. had been working on further prototypes even before the results of the trials had been announced, and three more machines appeared during 1936.

The Bf 109V2 (D-IUDE, W.Nr. 809) and V3 (D-IHNY, W.Nr. 810) flew in January and June 1936 respectively, powered by Jumo 210A engines and with provision for two MG 17 machine guns in the upper nose decking; this was the armament envisaged for the production series Bf 109A. The Bf 109A in fact never appeared; international standards of fighter armament were being revised during this period, and in view of the rumoured four-gun armament of the Hawker Hurricane and Supermarine Spitfire it was decided to produce the Bf 109B with a battery of three rifle-calibre machine guns, the third firing through the airscrew spinner and being replaced by a 20-mm. MG FF/M cannon when deliveries of this weapon reached a practicable volume. The Bf 109V4 (D-IOQY, W.Nr. 878), carried three MG 17s initially, the cannon replacing the engine-mounted machine gun later. The V5, V6 and production prototype V7 flew early in 1937, and the first pre-production Bf 109B-0 machines for service testing approached final assembly in the same period.

The history of the Bf 109B, Bf 109C and Bf 109D has no place in the present article; suffice it to say that a steady trend of heavier armament, more powerful engines and more modern equipment can be traced through the successive series. Operational experience of great value was gained in Spain by the pilots and technical observers of the Bf 109B-1, B-2 and C-1 fighters which equipped the three *Staffeln* of *Jagdgruppe 88*, the fighter component of the *Legion Condor*. In their short but triumphant career in Spanish skies the Messerschmitt pilots laid the

Pre-flight briefing for the pilots of a Messerschmitt Staffel in France. The "triple chevron" marking was not a standard insignia and probably indicates that the Staffel was led by the Gruppe Kommandeur in person. (Photo: R. Ward Collection)

foundations for later victories; it was this hard core of veterans, led by men of the calibre of Werner Molders, who two years later came so close to forcing the R.A.F. to its knees.

The Bf 109E series stemmed from the prototype Bf 109V14, which flew for the first time in the summer of 1938. A major advance over previous variants was the installation of the 1,100-h.p. Daimler-Benz DB 601A engine, with direct fuel injection and improved supercharging. Armament comprised two MG 17s in the upper nose decking and two MG FF cannon in the wings. The V15 tested the engine-mounted cannon (which had reached an acceptable service status with the Bf 109D-0) but carried no wing armament; the ten pre-production Bf 109E-0 machines mounted two wing and two nose machine guns when they appeared late in 1938.

PRODUCTION BEGINS

The first Bf 109E-1s left the factory early the following year, and by the most stringent international standards they were formidable fighting machines. With two MG 17s above the nose (1,000 r.p.g.) and either two further machine guns or two MG FF cannon (60 r.p.g.) in the wings, the E-1 had a rate of fire of up to 290 lb. per minute. At 12,300 ft. a speed of 354 m.p.h. was attainable; a climb rate of 3,100 ft./min. and a service ceiling of 36,000 ft. put the first Emils in an altogether higher class than the obsolescent opponents which it would meet in the opening months of the war. The fighter-bomber variant, Bf 109E-1/B, was fitted with racks for four 110-lb. or one 550-lb. bombs; the Carl Zeiss *Revi* gunsight could be employed as a bombsight. (Recommended dive speeds for medium and high altitude bombing runs were 373 m.p.h. and 403 m.p.h. respectively.)

Fifteen Bf 109E-1s were sent to Spain in the late spring of 1939; two examples were coded 6.117 and 6.130. A third E-1 in the Spanish batch led a chequered career which ended only a few years before the time of writing; coded 6.106, Bf 109E-1, W.Nr. 790 was handed over to the Spanish Air Army by the homeward bound *Legion Condor* with only 25 flying hours on the log book. After no less than fifteen years service with various Spanish fighter units and training establishments it was finally handed to the Logrono Apprentice School in 1954 as an instructional airframe. Acquired in 1960 by the *Deutsche Museum* of Munich, the machine was re-conditioned by Hispano Aviacion of Seville and at the time of writing stands in the Munich museum, finished in the colours of JG 26 "*Schlageter*".

Production of the Bf 109 now moved from Augsburg to Regensburg, due to pressure of space brought about by the commencement of Bf 110 production. Massive sub-contract work was undertaken by the plants of Ago (Oschersleben), Arado (Warnemünde), Erla (Leipzig), and W N.F. (Delitzch and Wiener-Neustadt). Of the 1,540 machines delivered in 1939 less than 150 were actually manufactured by the Messerschmitt A.G. (as B.F.W. had been re-christened in July 1938).

When the Third Reich invaded Poland on 1st September 1939 the fighter strength of the *Luftwaffe* consisted of twelve *Gruppen* with a total establishment of 850 Bf 109E-1s and E-1/Bs. A thirteenth unit was equipped with the Arado Ar 68 and some 235 Bf 109D-1s were incorporated into the strength of the *Zerstörergeschwader*. The fighters did not operate in *Jagdgeschwader* at that time, but on paper they were

A Bf 109E-4/B in flight. This sub-type took part in many "hit-and-run" raids over Southern England in the late stages of the Battle of Britain. The aircraft illustrated served with 8/JG 1. (Photo: G. Heumann/Air Pictorial)

A Luftwaffe Oberfeldwebel supervises the loading of an SC 250 bomb on to a Bf 109E-4/B. Points of interest are the engine crank handle and the armour plate in the side-hinging canopy. This style of spinner decoration was known as "Kullerschnauze".

A Bf 109E-4 during flight trials displays standard 1941 colour scheme with radio call-sign codes. Note the flat-topped cockpit canopy, which offered improved armour protection over the earlier style of canopy employed on the E-3 variant.

organised into JGs 1, 2, 3, 26, 51, 52 and 53. One fighter *Gruppe* was also on the establishment of *Lehrgeschwader 1*, including a *Staffel* investigating the possibilities of searchlight-collaboration night fighting with the Bf 109E-1. The war in Poland was of such brief duration that the Fighter Arm was unable to gain a clear appreciation of its skill and organisation under combat conditions, the bulk of the operations falling to the light bomber and ground-attack formations.

WAR IN THE WEST

Probably the first occasion on which Bf 109s and Bf 110s exchanged shots with the Royal Air Force was a raid by 24 Wellington bombers of Nos. 9, 37 and 149 (B) Squadrons, R.A.F. on Wilhelmshaven on 18th December 1939. Bf 109Es of III/JG 77 engaged the formation with great success and twelve Wellingtons were shot down for the loss of two Messerschmitts, although several other fighters were severely mauled by the four-gun tail turrets of the British machines; these were the first examples of a realistic rear defence that the *Luftwaffe* encountered. A certain Leutnant Johannes Steinhoff, a *Staffelkapitan* in III/JG 77, shot down two bombers on this occasion; he was to serve near the end of the war as commander of the Me 262 unit *Jagdgeschwader 7*, with a score of 176 confirmed aerial victories.

The machines which participated in this action were Bf 109E-3s, improved sub-types which had reached the *Luftwaffe* late in 1939. With an armament of two MG 17s in the nose, two in the wings and one MG FF/M cannon firing through the spinner*, the E-3

was numerically the most important variant in the series; 1,868 machines were delivered during 1940. A number of export orders were filled; forty machines were supplied to Hungary, five to the U.S.S.R., two to Japan (where Kawasaki's planned licence production was eventually cancelled), seventy-three to Yugoslavia, nineteen to Bulgaria, sixteen to Slovakia, and no less than eighty to Switzerland. This latter batch were operated by *Fliegerkompagnie* 6, 15 and 21 with the Swiss Air Force coding J-311 to J-390. The *Dornier-Werke A.G.* of Altenrhein, Switzerland, also produced nine complete airframes, four pairs of wings and seven fuselage assemblies between April 1944 and March 1946. Swiss-built Bf 109-E-3s, coded J-391 to J-399, were distinguishable by their pointed airscrew spinners.

The next major action in which the Bf 109 played an active part was the *blitzkrieg* in the West; although thirty E-3s of I/JG 77 had taken part in the Norwegian campaign of April 1940, they saw little actual combat. During April and the first week of May 1940 *Luftflotten* 2 and 3, with a fighter strength of some 850 Bf 109E-3s (of JGs 3, 26, 27, 51, 52, 53 and 54) were mustered on the western borders of Germany. The *Armée de l'Air* at this time mustered some 530 fighters equipping twenty-three Groups; eleven Groups operated the Morane-Saulnier 406, four Groups the Curtiss Hawk 75A, and the remaining eight Groups the Dewoitine D.520, the Bloch 151 or the Bloch 152. A large number of these machines were destroyed on the ground during the dawn raids of 10th May, as were many of the Fokker D.XXIs of the Netherlands Air Force and the miscellaneous equipment of the Belgian Air Force. Holland was forced to capitulate on May 15th after a hopeless but gallant struggle; Belgium, thirteen days later. During the rest of May and early June the dwindling French squadrons fought back

Luftwaffe personnel in North Africa kill time with a game of "skat" on an upturned crate. Behind them stands a Bf 109E-4 Trop of 2/JG 27 in an unusual striped camouflage scheme.
(Photo: R. Ward Collection)

* *Although fitted, this weapon was ignored by some pilots, who complained of severe vibration when it was fired.*

A wrecked "Emil" of JG 27 abandoned at Daba, Egypt; of interest are the white wing-tips and the unusual marking of the aircraft's individual numeral on the fuselage band.
(Photo: D. F. Harris)

The Bf 109E-7 was essentially an improved E-4/N with shackles for a 66-Imp. gal. drop tank; the variant was widely used in the Middle East.   (Photo: G. Heumann/Air Pictorial)

with a bitterness and determination which could not save them from eventual defeat; nevertheless when the instrument of capitulation was signed at Compiègne on June 22nd, some 350 German aircraft had been destroyed. The Bf 109E had stood up creditably to the test of European warfare, acquitting itself well against the obsolescent French fighters and the Hurricanes of the B.E.F. Air Component; approximately 450 of the latter were lost during the campaign. The appearance of Spitfires over Dunkirk had evened the odds somewhat, but on the whole the Fighter Arm had no reason to look forward to the coming battles over the Channel with anything but confidence. One disquieting factor, largely outweighed by the *Luftwaffe's* numerical superiority, had been the number of Emils pinned down by lack of fuel during the rapid "airfield-hopping" advance to the coast. This shortness of range was to be the most serious shortcoming of the Bf 109E throughout its career.

THE GREAT TEST

Much has been written about the various "phases" of the Battle of Britain, and this mass of material based on conflicting interpretations of the same events has led to some confusion. Broadly, the pattern was as follows: attacks on shipping and coastal targets, followed by attacks on airfields and industrial targets, superseded by a daylight bombing campaign against London. In September 1940 the emphasis of the bombing switched to night raids, while the fighters undertook hit-and-run fighter-bomber sorties. The chronology of these stages of the campaign is open to a certain amount of dispute; but the attacks on Channel shipping by formations of about 50 aircraft occupied the month of July. R.A.F. Fighter Command was unable to extract the full benefit of the radar chain in these actions, but they provided both sides with a month's rehearsal for the later, more massive assaults.

Adler Tag (Eagle Day) was postponed several times and finally dawned on 13th August. The first large raid on the coast five days previously and the opening of attacks on the radar stations on 11th August had "stolen the thunder" of the Eagle Attack to some

extent; but two days later the heaviest fighting of the Battle took place, seventy-five German aircraft and thirty-four British were lost, and 15th August is significant in that it saw the massacre of the once-dreaded Junkers Ju 87 Stukas, and of an unescorted bomber force from Norwegian-based *Luftwaffe* units. For the next three weeks the *Luftwaffe* was engaged in heavy raids on Fighter Command stations and in drawing the Spitfires and Hurricanes into battles of attrition; one of the main objects of the whole campaign was, after all, simply the total destruction of Fighter Command. Several airfields were severely damaged, particularly Manston and Biggin Hill, and when the assault was switched to London on 7th September the *Luftwaffe* had come nearer than they realised to forcing the withdrawal of the South Coast squadrons to stations north of London, out of range of the Bf 109 escort fighters.

The attacks on London were mounted for several reasons; false German intelligence gave highly optimistic figures for the number of R.A.F. fighters already destroyed; it was thought that the remaining squadrons "resting" in the North would be drawn into the campaign if the capital was threatened; the recent bombing of Berlin demanded revenge raids; and the simple fact that London, as the nation's largest port and administrative centre, was an excellent military target. In fact the continuation of attacks on fighter bases would have reaped a better reward,

A Messerschmitt of 1/JG 27 demonstrates the almost uncanny effectiveness of its camouflage when flying low over the scrub-covered desert.
(Photo: R. Ward Collection)

Luftwaffe mechanics at work on the DB 601N powerplant of a machine of III/JG 27 during that Gruppe's service in the Balkans.
(Photo: R. Ward Collection)

although the first four or five days of the attacks on London were reasonably successful in terms of loss/victory figures. However, in the carefully planned attacks of 15th September the *Luftwaffe* lost 60 machines out of 1,790 as compared to 26 R.A.F. aircraft destroyed, and from this point on the size of German raids diminished; there were no longer large enough fighter formations available to protect the bombers to an acceptable ratio.

The Messerschmitt pilots fought with a skill, determination and courage throughout the Battle which can never be overshadowed by the distasteful necessities of propaganda. Sometimes frustrated by their rôle of nursemaids to the bomber formations, sometimes distracted by the necessity to protect the vulnerable Bf 110s and Ju 87s, and always handicapped by short range, the *Jagdgeschwader* came nearer than is generally appreciated to accomplishing the almost impossible task they had been set. The Bf 109Es were constantly in action during these months, flying several sorties each day in either the escort or the "free chase" rôle. The pilots were unjustly blamed for the heavy bomber losses; and their machines were abused

LUFTWAFFE FIGHTER UNITS WESTERN FRONT, 1st AUGUST 1940	
Luftflotte 2 (North France and Low Countries)	All units equipped with the Bf 109E-3.
JG 3 "Udet" Three Gruppen	"Paper" strength
JG 26 "Schlageter" Three Gruppen	1,171 a/c.
JG 51 Four Gruppen	1,118 pilots.
JG 52 Two Gruppen	Combat strength
JG 54 "Grunherz" Three Gruppen	878 a/c.
LG2 One Gruppe	869 pilots.
	At this time Royal Air
Luftflotte 3 (France)	Force Fighter Command
JG 2 "Richthofen" Three Gruppen	strength totalled 29
JG 27 One Gruppe	Hurricane squadrons
JG 53 "Pik As" Three Gruppen	with 527 a/c and 19
	Spitfire squadrons with
	321 a/c.

in September when each *Jagdgeschwader* was instructed to fit one *Staffel* with bomb racks. It is hardly surprising that the fighter pilots did not achieve significant results on these missions; many were only too anxious to get rid of their "eggs" on the first target which offered and reduce the dangerous handicap to their manœuvrability in unfriendly skies.

The Hurricane, usually committed to bomber-interception rather than fighter-versus-fighter combats, was in many respects inferior to the Bf 109E-3; but it gained many victories by virtue of its firepower, its extremely rugged construction, and the excellent gun-platform it offered. The Spitfire was committed to combat with escort formations of Emils on numerous occasions, and Mitchell's tight-turning thoroughbred soon earned the profound respect of the Messerschmitt pilots. The technical advantages and disadvantages largely cancelled each other out when the Bf 109E was pitted against the Spitfire; the outcome of any dog-fight depended to a great extent on the skill and determination of the pilots, but the *Luftwaffe* aircrew were constantly handicapped by the fact that fuel consumption allowed for only twenty minutes actual combat over Britain. The Battle of Britain cost both the British and German fighter squadrons their hard core of professional fliers; in the months and years to come the loss of men like Wick of JG 2 and Rhodes-Moorhouse of 601 Squadron R.A.F. was to be keenly felt.

LATER DEVELOPMENTS

Although the Battle of Britain was the Emil's greatest struggle, the stub-winged fighter saw action in several other theatres of operations before its replacement by the Bf 109F. During the Battle of Britain the E-4 variant reached the front line; with various improvements in the fields of armour protection and pilot vision, the E-4 differed from its predecessor mainly in armament. The engine-mounted cannon was discarded, and two MG FFs replaced the wing machine guns. The fighter-bomber E-4/B carried the bomb-rack layout pioneered on the E-1/B. The Bf 109E-4/N, powered by a DB 601N engine with improved fuel injection and supercharger coupling, was widely used in its tropical configuration in the Western Desert. This sub-type will always be closely associated with the exploits of JG 27 and JG 53, the two *Geschwader* which bore the brunt of the air war in North Africa. The next variants in the series were the E-5 and E-6, short-range reconnaissance fighters with no wing armament and a camera installed behind the pilot's seat; they differed only in powerplant, the E-5 having the DB 601A and the E-6 the 1,200-h.p. DB 601N. The campaigns in the Mediterranean and the Balkans provided an introduction to combat for the E-7 sub-type, essentially an E-4 with a jettisonable 66-Imp. gal. belly tank. This model was operated over Malta, and by III/JG 77 in Greece and the Balkans. (An ironic feature of the Balkan campaign were the

The Bf 109E was employed by at least two Luftwaffe units in the opening phases of the Russian campaign. Two examples of Russian-based Messerschmitts are illustrated here.
(Photos: R. Ward Collection)

combats which took place between German forces and Yugoslav pilots flying Bf 109E-3s of the original export batch.) The Bf 109E-7/U2 was a ground-attack variant extensively employed in North Africa, with additional armour protection for the engine and coolant radiators, and the E-7/Z was equipped with GM 1 boost, nitrous oxide being injected into the supercharger to provide additional oxygen and to act as an anti-detonant. The Bf 109E-8 was a variant which incorporated all the general modifications to previous models; and in the spring of 1941 the final production variant Bf 109E-9 appeared, a reconnaissance machine with no wing armament, an external 66-Imp. gal. tank, an Rb 50/30 camera, and powered, as was the E-8, by a 1,200-h.p. DB 601E engine.

The Bf 109E was being phased out of service when Germany invaded Russia in June 1941; but although some records indicate that the seven *Jagdgeschwader* which took part in Operation Barbarossa (JGs 1, 3, 51, 52, 53, 54 and 77) were equipped entirely with the Bf 109F-1 or F-2, there is evidence that the Emil was in fact used in Russia for several months. Two units known to have operated the Bf 109E in this theatre are JG 54 and SG 1.

The Bf 109F was born of Bf 109E, W.Nr. 5604, a test airframe fitted with a DB 601N engine in a new, streamlined cowling. The hybrid machine carried the codes V K + A B during a series of trials which opened on 10th July 1940 at Haunsletten. Many prominent *Luftwaffe* pilots felt that the reduced armament of the Bf 109F, which initially carried no wing armament, represented an extraordinary backward step in design. Major Walter Oesau's attitude may be regarded as typical of the distrust felt by many German veterans for the new type; the C.O. of JG 2 "*Richthofen*" after the death of Helmut Wick on 28th November 1940, Oesau refused to fly a Bf 109F while spares were available to keep his E-4 flying. Another pilot who found the cut-back in armament inexplicable was Major Adolph Galland, who commanded III/JG 26 "*Schlageter*" at Caffiers during the Battle of Britain and later became *Geschwader Kommodore* of this élite unit. A General at the age of 30, Galland rose to be Inspector-General of the Fighter Arm.

Another offspring of the Emil was the Bf 109T. The resumption of work on the projected German aircraft carrier *Graf Zeppelin* in July 1940 led to an order to Fieseler, the Messerschmitt sub-contractors, for ten "navalised" E-3 airframes, to be designated Bf 109T

A fitter wires up the firing button of a Bf 109E-4. The gun-sight head with reflector has not yet been installed, although the selector box can be seen at the top of the instrument panel.

(Träger = Carrier). The modifications comprised increasing the span of the manually-folding wings, the installation of catapult spools and arrester hooks, and the fitting of spoilers to the upper wing surfaces to steepen the glide and shorten the landing run. When work on the carrier was once more suspended, some fifty production T-1 airframes had been modified; and rather than re-convert the aircraft they were handed over to I/JG 77 after the actual deck equipment had been removed by Fieseler. This *Gruppe* operated from short Norwegian airstrips with frequent vicious cross-winds, and the locking tailwheel and increased span of the Bf 109T-1 was much appreciated by Lt.-Col. Seegert and his pilots. The machines were eventually handed over to a test unit based on Trondheim.

FLYING THE EMIL

Perhaps the principal feature governing the performance of the Bf 109E was the high wing loading of 32 lb. To compensate for the high loading, the result of Messerschmitt's deliberate marrying of the smallest practicable airframe with the most powerful engine

Bf 109E-4s of the Rumanian Air Force, with a Luftwaffe machine in the foreground. It is probable that the latter belonged to either JG 77 or I/JG 4, the last-mentioned unit being based at Mizil, Rumania, for much of the war as fighter defence for the Ploesti oil refineries.
(Photo: R. Ward Collection)

A captured E-4 under test by the R.A.F. Radiator flaps and balance horns are clearly visible. (Photo: Imperial War Museum)

available, various high-lift devices were incorporated. The long leading-edge slats, slotted flaps and ailerons demanded their own penalty in weight and drag, but on the whole the Bf 109E had an excellent aerodynamic finish.

The cockpit was cramped, with poor rear vision, and the awkward sideways-hinging canopy made open-cockpit take-offs impossible. On the other hand, the hinged panel in the forward left-hand side of the hood gave excellent foul-weather forward vision without draught. The dished seat was low and imposed a semi-reclining posture on the pilot; the instrument layout was good, flap wheel and throttle coming easily to hand. The steep ground angle drastically cut forward vision during taxiing; the heavy tailplane gave stability but turning took time and power. The throttle response was quick and clean, acceleration brisk, and the take-off short and steep. Skill was needed, however, to counteract the "heavy" port wing at the moment of unstick. (The weak, narrow under-carriage coupled with this incipient swing on take-off and landing caused the "write-off" of nearly five per cent of the Bf 109's total production of some 33,000.)

Once airborne and the aircraft cleaned-up, the two main characteristics of the Emil were immediately apparent; the first, perhaps disconcerting to an unfamiliar pilot, was the lack of trim available from within the cockpit. The other was the heaviness of control. Being unequipped with rudder trim control (save for a "ground-bent" metal tab on the rudder) heavy leg loads were needed at low speeds, these reversing when accelerating to high I.A.S. Longitudinal trim, however, was so effective that considerable strength was required in such actions as dive recovery, and this coupled with high natural stick loads demanded more pilot stamina than in, say, the Spitfire I and II.

As a fighter, flying in the medium-to-high speed regimes, the Emil flew accurately and steadily once the out-of-trim tendencies had been mastered. In combat the fighter was extremely stable and could be reefed round in high-g turns, only the banging-out of the leading-edge slats as the high-speed stall was approached perhaps causing gun aiming to be upset. Some Emil pilots, when attacked from a rear quarter, would resort to pushing the nose sharply down—by all text books disastrous in air combat—yet the Messerschmitt could at medium altitude out-dive most enemy contemporaries, and the direct fuel injection would enable the engine to continue running without falter (unlike the carburettor-equipped Merlins of the Spitfire and Hurricane).

At the other end of the speed range, the Emil was

kind to the pilot. As the stall was approached the aircraft was entirely stable until, at about 105 m.p.h. indicated airspeed, slight lateral unsteadiness was manifest and course use of rudder and aileron was necessary to maintain a level altitude. With wheels and flaps up, the stall occurred at about 95 I.A.S., and at about 12–15 m.p.h. less in the landing configuration with flap selected. Undoubtedly the wing slots contributed to this remarkable low speed stability. On the approach to land, forward visibility was poorer even than the Spitfire and Hurricane—the outcome of the pilot's semi-reclining posture and the high broad engine cowling. "Wheelers" were more customarily performed for this reason, and also for the fact that if speed *was* misjudged, complete airflow breakdown behind the slats invariably caused one wing, usually the port, to drop sharply.

On balance, pilots who flew Emils in comparison with contemporary Hurricanes and Spitfires considered that in terms of manœuvrability there was little to choose between the Bf 109E and the Spitfire I and II at altitudes between 12,000 and 17,000 ft., and that although one aircraft possessed some slight advantage in one regime, the other could outperform its adversary in another manœuvre. There can be little doubt, however, that above 20,000 ft. the Emil was the better machine. In comparison with the Bf 109E and the Spitfire, the Hurricane was at a disadvantage in that drag was higher than with either of its contemporaries, and the resulting lack of acceleration left the pilot in the Emil's sights too long for safety. In combat with the Bf 109E, the Hurricane was often called upon to display its magnificent robustness of structure to the full.

LUFTWAFFE UNITS AND MARKINGS

The basic *Luftwaffe* tactical unit was the *Geschwader*. The fighter *Geschwader* (*Jagdgeschwader or* JG) consisted of three or four *Gruppen*, each of which was in turn made up of three *Staffeln*. The sub-units were numbered independently; thus III/JG 77 (the third *Gruppe* of JG 77) was made up of 7/JG 77 (the seventh *Staffel* of JG/77), 8/JG 77 and 9/JG 77. Similarly, 1/JG 77, 2/JG 77 and 3/JG 77 together made up the strength of I/JG 77, and so on throughout the *Geschwader*. The operational strengths of these units varied considerably but an average *Staffel* mustered ten to sixteen aircraft, thus giving a *Geschwader* an establishment of between 90 and 150 machines—on paper. The "serviceable" figure was often much lower.

Jagdgeschwader and some *Schlachtgeschwader* (Ground-Attack Wings) employed the following identification markings. Each aircraft carried a large

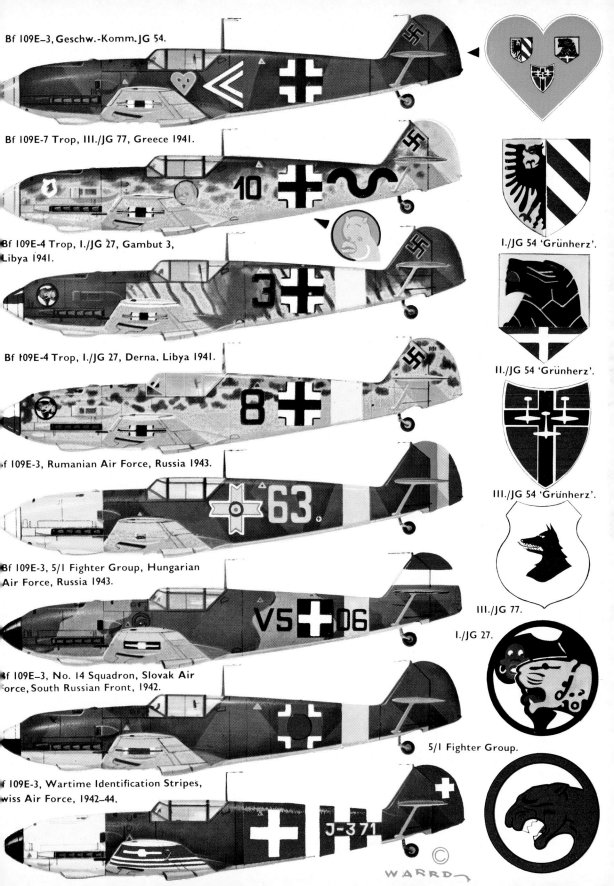

Bf 109E–3, Geschw.-Komm. JG 54.

Bf 109E–7 Trop, III./JG 77, Greece 1941.

Bf 109E–4 Trop, I./JG 27, Gambut 3, Libya 1941.

Bf 109E–4 Trop, I./JG 27, Derna, Libya 1941.

f 109E–3, Rumanian Air Force, Russia 1943.

Bf 109E–3, 5/1 Fighter Group, Hungarian Air Force, Russia 1943.

Bf 109E–3, No. 14 Squadron, Slovak Air Force, South Russian Front, 1942.

f 109E–3, Wartime Identification Stripes, wiss Air Force, 1942–44.

I./JG 54 'Grünherz'.

II./JG 54 'Grünherz'.

III./JG 54 'Grünherz'.

III./JG 77.

I./JG 27.

5/1 Fighter Group.

WARRD

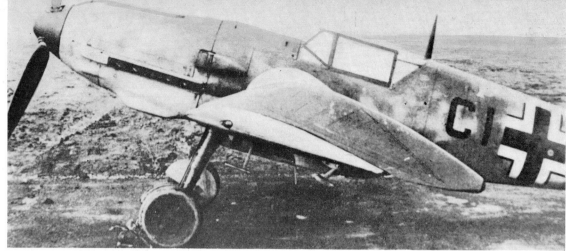

An unusual modification to a Bf 109E. Considerable research was carried out in Germany into the possibility of mounting over-wing slipper fuel tanks to Bf 109s and Fw 190s; this in turn led to the "para-capsule" project illustrated here. The upper forward section of the fuel tank was replaced by a transparency, and it was intended that a parachutist with full equipment should be accommodated in the housing. The operational potential was presumably fast low-level dropping of agents, or, conceivably, the evacuation of casualties.

numeral between one and sixteen (higher numerals usually indicated training establishments) painted in the *Staffel* colour (see table right) forward of the national marking on the fuselage sides. During the first 18 months of the war, "No. 1" was almost invariably the machine of the *Staffelkapitan*. In the case of Staff aircraft, a system of chevron-and-bar symbols replaced the numerals; for instance, a single forward-facing chevron indicated a *Gruppe* Adjutant (see painting on Page 2 of this *Profile*) and a double chevron, a *Gruppe Kommandeur*.

Behind the national marking on the fuselage sides appeared a system of symbols indicating the *Gruppe* within the *Geschwader*. No marking indicated I *Gruppe*; a horizontal bar, II *Gruppe* (see painting on Page 2 of this *Profile*); a wavy line, III *Gruppe* prior to the spring of 1941; a vertical bar, III *Gruppe* from this period until the end of the war. Where there was a fourth *Gruppe*, as in JG 51 "*Mölders*", the aircraft carried a small cross or solid circle behind the fuselage marking.

Considerable variation from this basic pattern was observed throughout the war. The identification markings were to some extent the responsibility of the individual unit or commander, and personal whims were sometimes indulged.

© *Martin C. Windrow, 1965*

The final stage of the Starr-Schlepp (rigid glider tug) research programme, forerunner of the Beethoven-Gerät composite weapon project, was the series of tests involving a Bf 109E-3 mounted on a DFS 230 troop glider; this combination was capable of independent performance throughout the flight pattern.

STRUCTURE OF THE GESCHWADER

Staffel Colour	I Gruppe	II Gr.	III Gr.	IV Gr.
White, black trim	I Stfl.	4 Stfl.	7 Stfl.	10 Stfl.
Red, white trim	2 Stfl.	5 Stfl.	8 Stfl.	11 Stfl.
Yellow, black or white trim	3 Stfl.	6 Stfl.	9 Stfl.	12 Stfl.

SPECIFICATION
Messerschmitt Bf 109E-4 Single-seat Day Fighter
Dimensions: Span 32 ft. 4½ in.; length 28 ft. 8 in.; height 11 ft. 2 in. (tail down, measurement from airscrew tip to ground line); wing area 174 sq. ft.
Powerplant: One Daimler-Benz DB 601Aa twelve-cylinder inverted-Vee liquid-cooled engine rated at 1,150 h.p. at 2,400 r.p.m. for take-off; V.D.M. electrically-operated controllable-pitch fully-feathering three-blade metal airscrew.
Armament: Two 7·9 mm. MG 17 machine guns with 1,000 r.p.g. mounted on engine crankcase, with muzzles protruding into blast troughs in upper nose decking, firing through airscrew arc. Two 20-mm. MG FF cannon with 60 r.p.g. mounted in wings and firing outside airscrew arc.
Weights: Empty 4,440 lb. Gross loaded 5,520 lb.
Fuel Tankage: 88 Imp. gal. in fuselage tank contoured behind and under pilot's seat.
Performance: Maximum speed 357 m.p.h. at 12,300 ft.; cruising speed 298 m.p.h. at 62·5 per cent rated power; stalling speed 75 m.p.h. in landing configuration with flaps down. Range, 412 miles at 62·5 per cent rated power at 16,400 ft. Initial climb rate 3,100 ft./min. Service ceiling 36,000 ft.

STRUCTURE
Fuselage: Oval section light metal monocoque, manufactured in two halves and joined longitudinally top and bottom. Each half constructed of longitudinal stringers and vertical panels; alternative panels had flanged edges to form Z-frames, holed to allow passage of stringers. Metal flush-riveted stressed skin covering.
Wings: Low wing cantilever monoplane. All-metal single-spar structure with metal flush-riveted stressed skin covering. Three fuselage attachment points on each wing, two on spar flanges, the third at the leading edge. Entire trailing edges were hinged, slotted ailerons outboard and slotted flaps inboard. Handley Page-type auto-slats on outboard leading edges. External mass balance horns on ailerons.
Tail Unit: Tailplane mounted on cantilever fin and braced to fuselage by a single strut on each side. Tailplane adjustable by hand wheel in cockpit. Balanced rudder and elevators. Metal frame; metal covering on fixed surfaces, fabric covering on movable surfaces.
Undercarriage: Retractable upward and outward by hydraulic jacks, with auxiliary hand-raising gear. Fixed tail wheel.

PRINTED IN ENGLAND. © Profile Publications Ltd., P.O. Box 26, Leatherhead, Surrey, England, by George Falkner & Sons Ltd., for McCorquodale City Printing Division London.

PROFILE
PUBLICATIONS

The
Supermarine
Spitfire
I & II

NUMBER

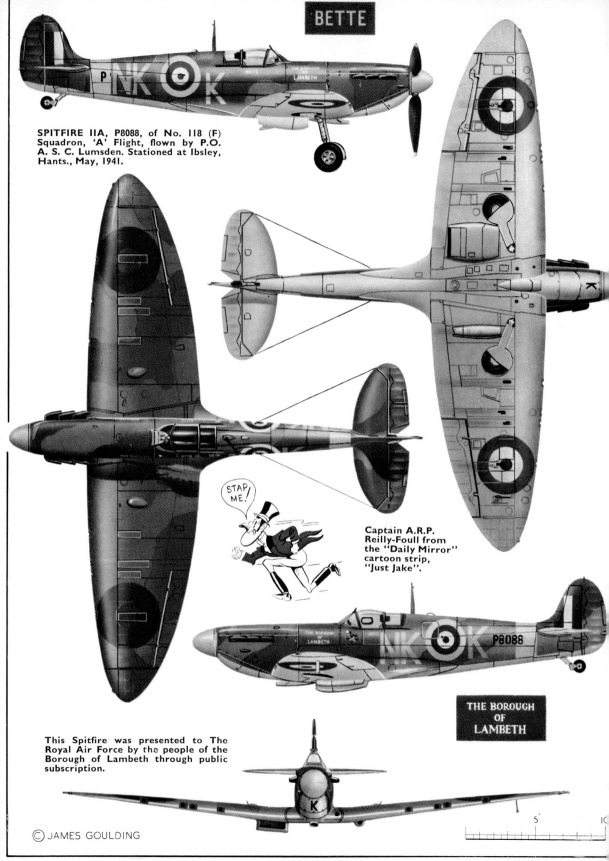

BETTE

SPITFIRE IIA, P8088, of No. 118 (F) Squadron, 'A' Flight, flown by P.O. A. S. C. Lumsden. Stationed at Ibsley, Hants., May, 1941.

STAP ME!

Captain A.R.P. Reilly-Foull from the "Daily Mirror" cartoon strip, "Just Jake".

P8088

THE BOROUGH OF LAMBETH

This Spitfire was presented to The Royal Air Force by the people of the Borough of Lambeth through public subscription.

© JAMES GOULDING

A H.F. wire aerial was originally fitted to spitfires, but later a V.H.F. aerial, utilising the existing mast only, was installed. P8088 had V.H.F. radio installed early in 1941.

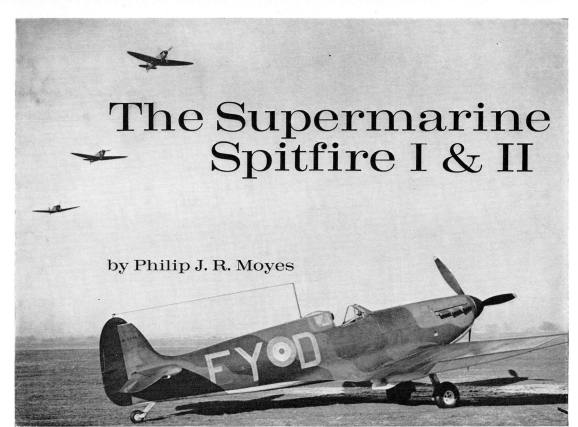

The Supermarine Spitfire I & II

by Philip J. R. Moyes

Spitfire Is of No. 611 Squadron at Digby, 11th January 1940. The aircraft on the ground is K9999, the serial being painted in minute figures on its fin.

The Spitfire was a fighter *par excellence*. It was a thoroughbred through and through, combining as it did sheer perfection of line with handling qualities that were second to none. It was a fighter pilot's dream plane—fast, deadly and docile.

The Spitfire obtained its first battle successes against the sporadic tip-and-run raiders in the "phoney" war, but the supreme trial of the "Spit." came during the Battle of Britain. Then it was that, alongside the more numerous Hurricanes, the Spitfire Is and IIs won, imperishable fame by smashing the awesome contrailing formations of *Luftwaffe* bombers and their fighter escorts until the onslaught faltered and ceased.

As the war progressed the Spitfire was continually modified and improved, and although the story of this development is outside the scope of this *Profile*, a few facts should, perhaps, be put on record. Most im-

portant of these are that the Spitfire remained a front-line fighter throughout the whole period of the war and, during that time, flew operationally on every front and took part in every major air action fought by the R.A.F. Other interesting facts concern production and performance: a total of 20,351 Spitfires was manufactured as well as 2,408 Seafires (the naval version of the Spitfire which was developed from the standard Mark VB Spitfire). From the advent of the prototype in 1936 to the Mark XXII in 1945, Spitfire speeds increased from 349·5 m.p.h. to 450 m.p.h., rate of climb from 2,500 feet per minute to 4,800 feet per minute and fire power from 4 lb. to 12 lb. per second.

ORIGIN

The Spitfire was the creation of that quiet, calm genius Reginald J Mitchell who, beginning in 1925, had evolved a series of high-speed seaplanes as contenders in the Schneider Trophy Races,* culminating in the superb S6B* which, in 1931, won the trophy outright for Great Britain at an average speed of 340·8 m.p.h. (and which, two weeks later, raised the world's speed record to 407 m.p.h.). The immediate predecessor of the Spitfire, in so far as actual hardware was concerned, was the Supermarine Type 224 (*K2890*), a single-seat monoplane fighter built to meet the requirements of Air Ministry specification F.7/30, and having a cranked (inverted gull) wing, an open cockpit, a fixed "trousered" undercarriage, and a 600-h.p. Rolls-Royce Goshawk steam-cooled engine. The Type 224 was not a success, mainly because the

The Supermarine F.7/30, unofficially named "Spitfire".

*See Profile *Number 39.*

3

specification was too tightly drawn and consequently gave Mitchell very little scope.

Even before it flew Mitchell was dissatisfied with the Type 224 and started work on a new design as a private venture. The original basic design, although incorporating an enclosed cockpit and a retractable undercarriage, envisaged the use of the Goshawk engine, but two further developments resulted in extensive redesign; first came the advent of the sensational Rolls-Royce PV-12 liquid-cooled engine (later to become famous as the Merlin); and, secondly, the issue by the Air Ministry of specification F.5/34

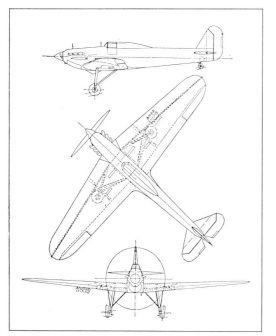

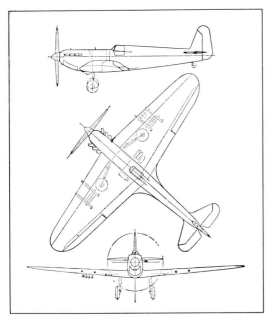

Above and below: Two of the many Supermarine F.7/30 development projects which preceded the Type 300 Spitfire. Both these projects had R-R Goshawk engines, four guns and carried four small bombs beneath the starboard wing.

calling for the installation of eight, instead of four, machine guns.

The Supermarine Type 300, as the final design was known, actually went far beyond F.5/34 and in January 1935, it was accepted by the Air Ministry for construction in prototype form to specification F.37/34, the latter being virtually written round the design for contractual purposes. The final mock-up conference was held at Woolston on 26th March 1935, and less than a year later (on 5th March 1936) the prototype Spitfire, *K5054*, powered by a 990-h.p. Rolls-Royce Merlin "C", took off on its maiden flight from Eastleigh airfield, Southampton, with J. "Mutt" Summers at the controls. Summers was chief test pilot for Vickers (Aviation) Ltd., which had acquired the entire share capital of the Supermarine Company in 1928.

STRUCTURE OF THE SPITFIRE

The Spitfire was in essence the smallest and neatest fighter which could be designed round the engine, pilot and eight-gun armament. An all-metal, stressed skin, low-wing, cantilever monoplane, it was characterised by its graceful elliptical wing (a design feature inspired by the similarly-shaped—but thicker in section—wing of the Heinkel He 70) the aerodynamic advantages of which far outweighed the production problems that it presented. The wing was thin (giving good high-speed handling qualities) and had, at 25 per cent of the chord, a single spar comprising tubular flanges and a plate web. Forward of the spar the wing was covered with heavy-gauge Alclad which formed, in conjunction with the spar web, a stiff strong, torsion box. Besides giving an excellent form to the nose portion of the wing this type of contruction had very good anti-flutter characteristics. Aft of the spar, the thinner gauge skin was supported by girder ribs and a false spar, to which latter the split flaps and fabric-covered ailerons were attached.

The fuselage was built in three sections. The forward part, which formed the engine mounting, was of tubular construction. Aft of this was a monocoque

The sleek Heinkel He 70 (actually the example used by R-R as a Merlin test-bed) and (below) the prototype Type 300 Spitfire whose design the German aircraft greatly influenced.

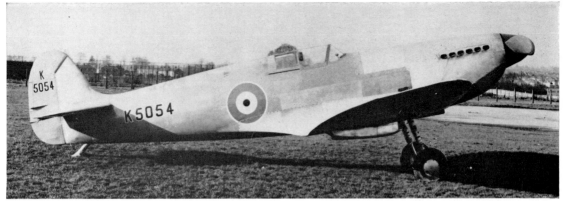

Above and below: *The prototype Type 300 Spitfire* (K5054) *with original fin and rudder. This aircraft was unpainted when first flown but was subsequently finished in a high-gloss pale blue—not cream or grey as has often been reported elsewhere.*

(Photos: Imperial War Museum)

F.16/36 was drawn up to cover the further development and production of the fighter. On 3rd June 1936 (shortly after the name Spitfire had been officially adopted) the Air Ministry placed an intial order for 310 Spitfires. This presented Supermarine with a colossal task; they had never before received such a large order. However no time was lost in reorganising the Woolston Works on a production basis; the design and construction of jigs and tools in hitherto unheard of quantities was rapidly proceeded with, and the labour force expanded with men and women of all trade.

Production proper began in March 1937, and at first Supermarine undertook the construction of fuselages only, together with the assembly and testing of the aircraft. Later they built wings too. The rest of the construction was widely sub-contracted, the main sub-

section built up on transverse frames, the longitudinals being intercostal except for the four main longerons. The foremost frame of this portion formed a fireproof bulkhead and built into it was the centre portion of the main wing spar (there was no conventional wing centre-section, for the wings butted on to the fuselage side). The tail portion of the fuselage was likewise of monocoque construction and incorporated the fin. This whole section was detachable.

The tailplane was an all-metal structure while the elevator and rudder were metal framed with fabric covering.

PRODUCTION AND EARLY SERVICE

From the outset of its official trials at Martlesham Heath the Spitfire proved a winner and specification

Above right and below: K5054 *seen after its fin and rudder had been redesigned.*　　　(Photo: Imperial War Museum)

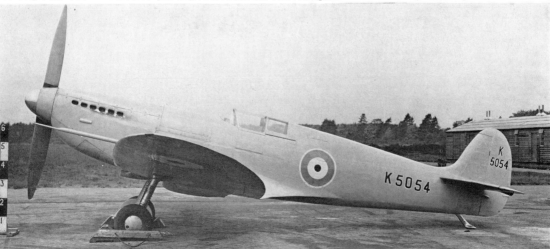

The ninth production Spitfire I, photographed while serving with No. 19 Squadron before the war.

(Photo: Imperial War Museum)

contractors in the early days (they were later joined by many other well-known firms) being General Aircraft Ltd. and Pobjoy Airmotors and Aircraft Ltd. (wings), Aero Engines Ltd. (ailerons and elevators), Singer Motors Ltd. (engine mounting), Folland Aircraft Ltd. (tail end), General Electric (wing tips), J. Samuel White & Co. Ltd. (fuselage frames), The Pressed Steel Co. Ltd. (wing leading-edge section), G Beaton & Son Ltd. and Westland Aircraft Ltd. (wing ribs).

The initial Spitfire production contract was due for completion in March 1939, but early manufacturing problems delayed this until August. Meanwhile, in 1937 the original contract was followed by an order for a further 200 machines. Also in that year Reginald Mitchell, who had been seriously ill for many months, died at the early age of 42. He was succeeded as chief designer at Supermarine by Joseph Smith who was subsequently to be responsible for the development of the Spitfire through numerous marks and variants.

On 12th April 1938, the Nuffield Organisation was contracted to build 1,000 Spitfires at a new "shadow" factory planned for erection at Castle Bromwich, near Birmingham. In the following year further contracts

were placed with Supermarine—on 29th April for 183 Spitfires, and on 9th August for 450—so that at the outbreak of war 2,143 Spitfires were already on order.

The first production Spitfire, *K9787*, was completed in July 1938, and both it and the second machine were retained for extensive handling trials. The third, *K9789*, was delivered on 4th August to No. 19 Squadron at Duxford, other Spitfires following at intervals until 19th December by which time the unit (which had previously flown Gauntlets) was completely re-equipped. With a view to obviating teething troubles, arrangements were made at Duxford for a programme of intensive flying to be done on *K9789*. Some 300 hours flying was completed within an extremely short period, and corrective action taken on a number of defects which came to light.

As production got into its stride, more squadrons were issued with Spitfires, and at the outbreak of war in September 1939, nine squadrons of the R.A.F.,[†] Nos. 19, 41, 54, 65, 66, 72, 74, 602 and 611 were fully armed with Spitfires and two more, Nos. 603 and 609, were in the process of conversion.

On 16th October 1939, Spitfires of Nos. 602 and 603 Squadrons engaged German bombers over the Firth of Forth and each squadron destroyed a Heinkel He 111, the honour of shooting down the first one going to No. 602. This was the first occasion when Spitfires fired their guns in action, and their victims (which fell into the sea) were the first enemy aircraft to be shot down over Great Britain since 1918. On 28th October 1939, Spitfires of the same two units shared in the destruction of a Heinkel He 111 which crash-landed close to the village of Humbie, on the Lammermuir Hills near Dalkeith. This was the first German aircraft to be brought down on British soil in W.W.II.

When the Battle of Britain began in early July 1940, there were 19 Spitfire squadrons in Fighter Command's order of battle and a list of these appears on page 12.

In outline, the early production Spitfire Is were similar to the prototype as originally completed,[‡] but there were many detail differences. For example the semi-circular wheel fairing doors hinged to the bottom of the undercarriage leg fairings were deleted, the flush exhausts replaced by triple ejector exhausts and the tailskid replaced by a castoring tailwheel. A Merlin II rated at 1,030 h.p. was installed in the first 174 aircraft (*K9787–K9960*), and the Airscrew Company's Weybridge two-blade, fixed-pitch wooden airscrew (which was similar to the prototype's de Havilland two-blader) gave place, from the 78th aircraft onwards, to

†*Until 1st September when they had been embodied in the R.A.F. some—those in the 600 series—had been Aux. A.F.*

‡*This qualification is necessary because the prototype was eventually brought up to Mk. I standard (and comouflaged).*

K5054 after being brought up to Mk. I standard, seen during pre-war night-flying trials. Because of its narrow-track under-carriage the Spitfire proved unsuitable for night operations except in bright moonlight.

The first Spitfire in service, K9789, undergoing maintenance at Duxford in 1938.

a three-blade, two-speed de Havilland airscrew; the latter increased the maximum speed by 5 m.p.h.—from 362 to 367 m.p.h. A domed cockpit hood was introduced during early 1939 and examples of both types of hood can be seen side-by-side in the 19-Squadron line-up below. Three somewhat later modifications were the introduction of (a) a redesigned aerial mast, (b) a bulletproof windscreen (made by fixing externally to the front of the windscreen a 1½-in thick bulletproof panel), and (c) 6 mm, armour plate behind the pilot's head.

Standard armament of the Spitfire in what became known as the type "A" wing was eight ·303-in. Browning guns with 300 rounds per gun. Although this was good for its time, the need for greater hitting power soon became apparent and towards this end, in June 1939, an early production Spitfire (*L1007*) was experimentally fitted with two 20 mm. Hispano can-

non, with 60 rounds each in drum-type magazines, in place of the four inboard Brownings. This aircraft became the prototype for the Spitfire IB (the "B" suffix indicated what eventually became known as the type "B" wing—the wing carrying four Browning guns and two Hispano cannon), 30 of which were delivered in the summer of 1940 to No. 19 Squadron for operational trials. In service the IBs were disliked owing to persistent cannon stoppages caused by unreliable feed and ejector mechanisms, and soon the aircraft were withdrawn.

From the 175th Spitfire I onwards, the Merlin III was installed. This powerplant, although of similar output to the Merlin II, had a standardised shaft for de Havilland or Rotol three-blade airscrews. The latter (two-position, metal) became available late in 1939 and 22 aircraft in the "N" serial range were specially fitted on the production line at Woolston for No. 19 Squadron which received the first of them on 1st November. By the end of the year these aircraft had been transferred to No. 54 Squadron. Between late June and early August 1940, all de Havilland airscrews on Spitfire Is at fighter stations were converted to constant speed units by de Havilland service engineers (except in the case of cannon-armed aircraft which received C.S. airscrews on production). The reason for this was that although the two-position airscrews fulfilled their original purpose of improving take-off, they were inadequate for climb and ceiling. The resulting improvement in performance did much to help smash the massive attacks of the *Luftwaffe* in the Battle of Britain.

A total of 1,583 Spitfire Is was built, including 50 by Westland. Before the outbreak of war several foreign governments planned to buy Spitfires, and export versions were designed for Estonia (Type 332), Greece (Type 335), Portugal (Type 336) and Turkey (Type 341). Foreign Office sanction to export these aircraft was withdrawn when war became imminent and only three were exported. They were *P9566*, *P9567* and *L1066*. They all went to Turkey, the last one having been originally consigned to Poland and diverted to Turkey after the Polish collapse.

Several experimental variants of the Spitfire I were produced and one which can be singled out for mention here was *R6722*, first of the Spitfire floatplanes. Originally a standard Spitfire airframe, *R6722* was

Trial installation of de Havilland three-blade V.P. airscrew on K9793 early in 1939. (Photo: Imperial War Museum)

Spitfire Is of No. 19 Squadron at Duxford during a Press visit on 4th May 1939. (Photo: "The Aeroplane")

P9450, the 601st Spitfire on acceptance trials in the spring of 1940, flown by Supermarine test pilot George Pickering.

hurriedly fitted with a pair of Blackburn Roc floats during the Norwegian campaign; however it was never flown in this form (which was known as the Type 342) and after the Norwegian campaign it was reconverted to standard.

The 48th Spitfire airframe from the initial Supermarine batch, *K9834*, was completed to a special standard (Type 323) and renumbered N.17 for an attempt on the world air speed record in 1938. The windscreen was specially streamlined, wing span reduced by 3 ft. 2 in. to 33 ft. 8in., flush riveting was used and a high-gloss finish applied. Further modifications were a larger radiator and oil cooler, and the replacement of the tailwheel by a skid. Powerplant was a strengthened Merlin III using 100-octane fuel, giving 2,160 h.p. and driving an Airscrew Company four-blade, fixed-pitch airscrew. It was hoped that N.17 or the Speed Spitfire as it became known would achieve 420 m.p.h., but before any attempt could be made, the world air speed record was raised to 463·92 m.p.h. by the Heinkel He 100 V8, this record being further increased very soon afterwards to

The Speed Spitfire, N17, seen at Eastleigh in 1939. This aircraft had a flush-riveted skin and a superfine blue and gold high-gloss finish.

Another view of the Speed Spitfire. During the war N.17 was converted to a P.R. aircraft and on D-Day Air-Cdre. J. N. Boothman flew it over the Normandy beaches.

469·22 m.p.h. by the Me 209 V1. Further work on N.17 as a potential record-breaker was abandoned and later, after being converted to approximately Mk. II standard, it became one of the first photographic-reconnaissance Spitfires.

SPITFIRE II

The Spitfire Mk. II (Type 329) was basically a Mk. I built exclusively at Castle Bromwich and powered by a 1,175-h.p. Merlin XII (fitted with a Coffman starter and running on 100-octane fuel) driving a Jablo Rotol three-blade C.S. airscrew. It incorporated Mk. I

refinements from initial production in the first half of 1940 and whereas the Mk. I had armour plating added in service, the Mk II. had it installed on production. There was 73 lb. of armour in all, some of it providing protection behind the pilot's seat and head, and the rest providing forward protection for the glycol header tank and the top fuel tank.

Deliveries of Spitfire IIs to the R.A.F. began in June 1940 (beginning with *P7260* on 6th June) in time for the Battle of Britain, but it was not until the following winter that re-equipment of the squadrons flying the Mk. I began in earnest. By 1st April 1941, 650 Mk. IIs had left the Castle Bromwich factory and the change-over was complete, most of the Mk. Is being relegated to a training rôle at O.T.U.s.

The Spitfire II was used in Fighter Command's early offensive sweeps (*Rhubarbs*) over Europe, the first of these missions being flown by two aircraft of No. 66 Squadron operating from Biggin Hill on 20th December 1940.

The Spitfire was, of course, designed as home defence interceptor fighter. Its fuel capacity of 85 gallons only allowed for take-off, a climb to altitude, 1·65 hours cruising and 15 minutes combat at full bore. In an effort to increase its operational range and give it a distinctly offensive capability a number of experiments were conducted. One of these experiments—using a Spitfire IA—introduced an overload

Right and below: *Spitfire IIA P8088 of No. 118 Squadron, Ibsley, May 1941, Named "The Borough of Lambeth" after its donors, this aircraft is the subject of the five-view drawing on page 2.*
(Photos: Alec Lumsden).

A Spitfire IIA—believed P7665—of No. 65 (East India) Squadron which was euqipped with Spitfires financed by the East Indian Fund for British War Services. (Photo: Imperial War Museum)

fuel tank under one wing and an oil tank under the other. The tanks were fitted flush-up against the wings just outboard of the undercarriage wheel wells between the inboard and three outboard machine guns in a fashion similar to that later employed for the long-range tanks on the Mosquito. Other experiments involving the installation of overload tanks were conducted with the Spitfire IIA, and in 1941/42 a few IIAs, each fitted with a 40-gallon long-range fuel tank under

Spitfire IIA P9565 with a 40-gallon long-range fuel tank under the port wing (Type 343).

the port wing (Type 343), served with Nos. 66, 118 and 152 Squadrons.

Production of the Spitfire II totalled 920 aircraft—all within the "P" serial range—of which 750 were built as Mk. IIA, and 170 as Mk. IIBs. A few surplus or salvaged Merlin XII engines were fitted to Mk. I airframes, thereby coverting them to Mk. IIs. Before production of the Mk. II began Merlin XIIs were tested in Mk. Is *K9788* and *K9830* which, in effect, became prototypes of the Mk. II.

During 1942 a service modification of the Spitfire II to meet a requirement in an air-sea-rescue rôle appeared as the Spitfire IIC. This version was fitted with a small rack for two smoke bombs under the port wing inboard of the oil cooler and two flare chutes in the fuselage just aft of the cockpit, housing a small dinghy and a metal food container. The designation "C" was adopted because the "C" or universal wing, although then in general use (on the Spitfire VC), had not been fitted to Mk. II Spitfires and "C" was the logical means of distinguishing it from the existing

Below: *Spitfire IIB P8649 "Bermuda III", one of four Spitfire IIBs presented to the R.A.F. by the Bermuda War Fund.* (Photo: Imperial War Museum)

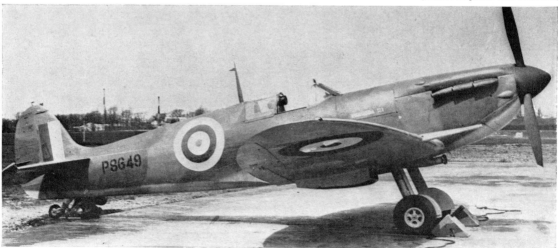

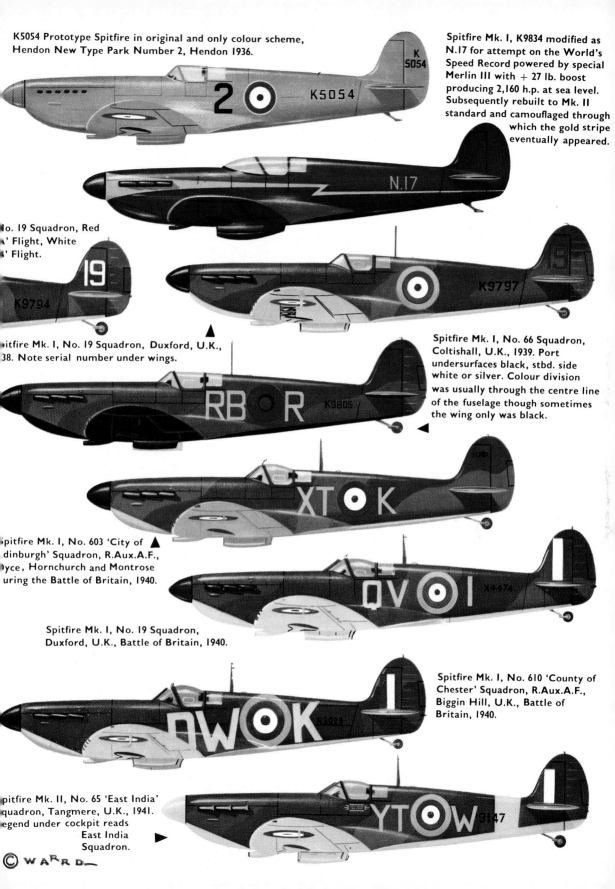

K5054 Prototype Spitfire in original and only colour scheme, Hendon New Type Park Number 2, Hendon 1936.

Spitfire Mk. I, K9834 modified as N.17 for attempt on the World's Speed Record powered by special Merlin III with + 27 lb. boost producing 2,160 h.p. at sea level. Subsequently rebuilt to Mk. II standard and camouflaged through which the gold stripe eventually appeared.

No. 19 Squadron, Red 'A' Flight, White 'B' Flight.

Spitfire Mk. I, No. 19 Squadron, Duxford, U.K., 1938. Note serial number under wings.

Spitfire Mk. I, No. 66 Squadron, Coltishall, U.K., 1939. Port undersurfaces black, stbd. side white or silver. Colour division was usually through the centre line of the fuselage though sometimes the wing only was black.

Spitfire Mk. I, No. 603 'City of Edinburgh' Squadron, R.Aux.A.F., Dyce, Hornchurch and Montrose during the Battle of Britain, 1940.

Spitfire Mk. I, No. 19 Squadron, Duxford, U.K., Battle of Britain, 1940.

Spitfire Mk. I, No. 610 'County of Chester' Squadron, R.Aux.A.F., Biggin Hill, U.K., Battle of Britain, 1940.

Spitfire Mk. II, No. 65 'East India' Squadron, Tangmere, U.K., 1941. Legend under cockpit reads East India Squadron.

© WARRD

P8131, *a converted Spitfire IIA, redesignated IIC. No. 276 Squadron.* (Photo: "The Aeroplane")

Mk. IIA and IIB versions with their "A" and "B" armament. Later, when rôle prefixes were introduced, Mk. IIC became A.S.R.II. About 50 Spitfire IIs were converted to IICs and the type served in the six A.S.R. squadrons controlled by Fighter Command, viz., Nos. 275, 276, 277, 278, 281 and 282.

Not long after re-equipment of the squadrons of Fighter Command with Spitfire IIs had been completed re-equipment with Mk. Vs began. Following their withdrawal from the squadrons, Mk. IIs continued to serve in various units chiefly at home and, at first, mainly in O.T.U.s. Late in the war Mk IIs could be found in such units at the Central Gunnery School and Technical Training Command Communication Flight. Others were used by the Air Fighting Development Unit to form "Circuses" (i.e. instructional teams in air-fighting techniques) which were attached to various Groups of Bomber and Coastal Commands and also to 2nd T.A.F.

SPITFIRE HANDLING NOTES

In the air the Spitfire I, in comparison with other types of the period, was incredibly "light" in every way, as well as being exceptionally fast—so fast that, on a cross-country flight, the maps were, so to speak, left behind, the pilot arriving at a destination at least ten minutes before any mentally-calculated E.T.A. War-

time ferry and test pilot, Mr. H. A. Taylor, writing of the Spitfire under the nom-de-plume "Indicator" in *Flight* in 1946 recalled that early production models of the Spitfire I had no engine-driven hydraulic pump and the undercarriage was operated by means of a long hand pump on the right. "Not only had one to change hands in order to select 'up' after take-off," he wrote, "but while flying with the left hand, this pump had to be worked vigorously and, with no previous experience of the type's very sensitive elevator control, departure was made in a series of fore-and-aft overcorrective pitchings. Later on, pilots learned to be very ambidextrous and to be in good control of muscular reflexes, so that the inevitable 'hunt' could be reduced to an amount which, at least, did not give them away to any watchers on the ground." Taylor went on to explain that in the early marks the throttle damper was not very effective unless tightened with a pair of pliers, it being necessary sometimes to stop pumping the undercarriage while changing hands yet again in order to deal with "the sudden extraordinary silence as the ivory-handled throttle vibrated quietly back".

Another little difficulty which occurred with many of the early Spitfires concerned the way in which the undercarriage selector would occasionally jam irrevocably in the half-way position when selecting "down". For one reason or another the "up lock" pins had become immovable, and it was necessary to take the weight off the retracted legs if any further landing progress was to be made. Since, of course, the only way of doing this was to invert the aircraft, Spitfires might occasionally be seen on their backs during the circuit. An alternative method of freeing the selector was to push the nose down violently, while, at the same time, giving the lever a sharp tug.

© *P. J. R. Moyes, 1965.*

Spitfire I cockpit. (Photo: Imperial War Museum)

SPECIFICATION

(Relates to Spitfire IA, figures in brackets relating to Mk.IIA).

Powerplant: One 1,030 (1,175)-h.p. Rolls-Royce Merlin III (XII) 12-cylinder 60° Vee liquid-cooled engine.
Dimensions: Span 36 ft. 10 in.; length (thrust line horizontal) 29ft. 11 in.; height 8 ft. 10 in. (12 ft. 3 in. over airscrew disc); wing area (gross) 242 sq. ft.
Weight: Normal loaded 6,200 lb. (6,275 lb.).
Performance: Max. speed 362 m.p.h. (370 m.p.h.); rate of climb 2,530 ft./min. (2,600 ft./min.); combat range 395 mls.; ceiling 31,900 ft. (32,800 ft.).
Armament: Eight 0·303-in. Browning machine guns with 300 (350) r.p.g.

SPITFIRE SQUADRONS IN FIGHTER COMMAND
ORDER OF BATTLE, 7th JULY 1940

No. 11 Group (H.Q. Uxbridge)
54 Sqdn. Rochford.
64 Sqdn. Kenley.
65 Sqdn. Hornchurch.
74 Sqdn. Hornchurch.
92 Sqdn. Pembrey.
234 Sqdn. St. Eval (1 section at Hullavington).
609 Sqdn. Warmwell.
610 Sqdn. Biggin Hill.

No. 12 Group (H.Q. Watnall)
19 Sqdn. Duxford.
66 Sqdn. Coltishall.
222 Sqdn. (converting) Kirton-in-Lindsey
266 Sqdn. Digby.
611 Sqdn. Digby.

No. 13 Group (H.Q. Newcastle)
41 Sqdn. Catterick.
72 Sqdn. Acklington.
152 Sqdn. Acklington.
602 Sqdn. Drem.
603 Sqdn. Dyce ("B" Flt. det. to Montrose).
616 Sqdn. Leconfield.

PRINTED IN ENGLAND. © Profile Publications Ltd., P.O. Box 26, Leatherhead, Surrey, England, by George Falkner & Sons Ltd. for McCorquodale City Printing Division London.

PROFILE
PUBLICATIONS

The
North
American
FJ Fury

NUMBER

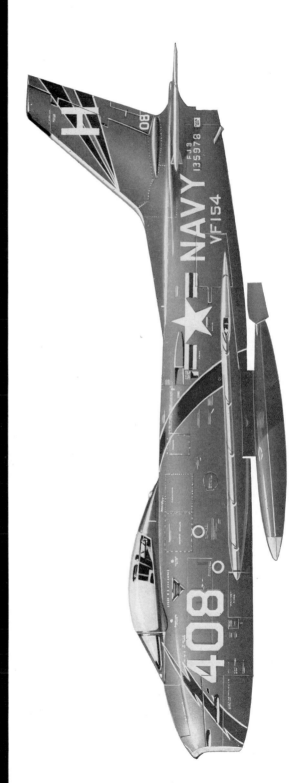

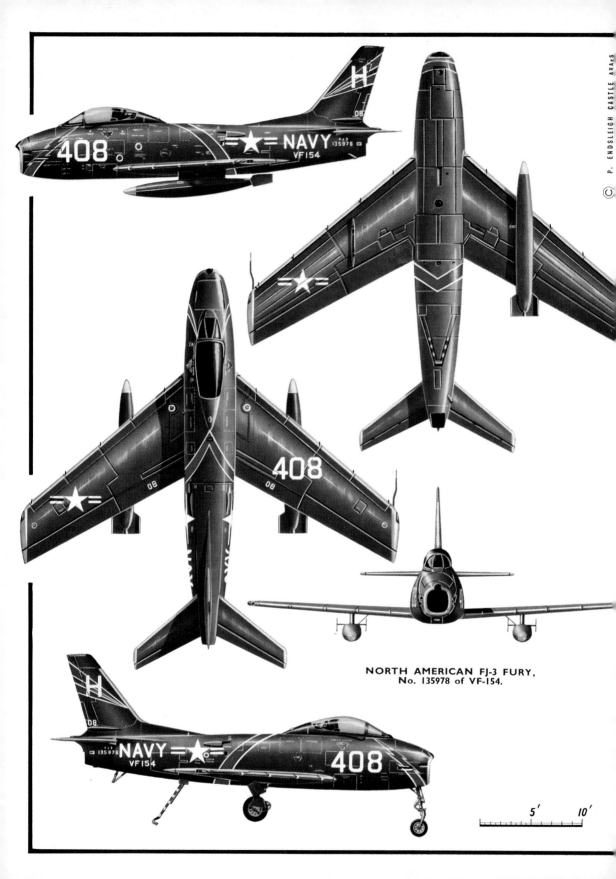

NAVY
VF154

408

NORTH AMERICAN FJ-3 FURY,
No. 135978 of VF-154.

5'   10'

The North American FJ Fury by Francis K. Mason

North American FJ-3M of VF-142 from U.S.S. Hornet. *Note the four-station wing, refuelling probe and wing fences. Photo taken over Japan, 22nd January 1957.*
(Photo: U.S. Navy)

The evolution of naval aircraft has for more than fifty years been a particularly exacting exercise, a commitment rendered infinitely more difficult by the economics of relatively small production orders. Thus by force of circumstances it has been found more expedient to adapt an existing or projected land-based aircraft design for the task of deck operation, with the result that with so much paraphernalia appended the naval combat aircraft has commenced life with an inbred inferiority when compared with its dry-footed contemporaries. Only in the years following W.W.II have high performance combat aircraft been evolved with deck operation of first importance in the Operational Requirement; this has undoubtedly followed the trend of uprating the fleet carrier to capital ship status.

One of the first examples of putting "the horse before the cart" was the North American FJ-Series of naval jet fighters. Of course the world recognises the excellence of the well-known F–86 Sabre (see *Profile* No. 2), yet it is perhaps an obscure fact that the NA–140 (XP–86) design stemmed from the NA–134, designed to a U.S. Navy requirement of 1945.

The North American NA–134 project designation covered the design and construction of three straight-winged fighter prototypes, ordered by the U.S. Navy on 1st January 1945. Developed from this was the NA–140 for an Air Force fighter, originally intended to have straight wings but, following intensive examination of sequestrated German research data on swept wings, was destined to materialise as the famous F–86 Sabre.

Deck landing speeds required by Navy fighters eliminated the consideration of a swept wing on the NA–134 design at that time and the project went ahead with straight wings, to become the North American XFJ–1. Unlike current fighters (e.g. P–59 and P–80) in service with or in production for the U.S.A.F., the new naval aircraft was designed around the axial flow General Electric J–35 which made possible the straight-through airflow from nose to tail without complications of wing-root or other lateral types of intakes.

Thus while efforts continued to develop an efficient swept wing for the XP–86 and extend its "on board" time, the Navy XFJ–1s commenced manufacture early in 1946 and first flew on 27th November that year—about ten months ahead of the XP–86.

With 3,820 pounds thrust from the J35–GE–2 engine, the first of the three prototypes (*39053–39055*) achieved a maximum speed of 542 m.p.h. at 16,000 feet, a service ceiling of 47,400 feet and an initial climb rate of 4,690 feet/minute. As a matter of passing interest these figures were extremely close to those of the British de Havilland Vampire I which had performed the world's first deck landing by a jet aircraft in late 1945 and which entered naval service during 1948.

Flight trials on the three XFJ–1s continued for almost a year, being accepted by the U.S. Navy during September 1947. Production had by then already started, the Navy having placed a contract for 100 FJ–1s as far back as 28th May 1945. Deliveries under this contract commenced in early autumn 1947 from the Los Angeles plant and passed to Navy Squadron VF–5A at San Diego on 18th November that year. In the course of two months this squadron, under Commander Evan ("Pete") Aurand, completed about 200

The unarmed first prototype XFJ-1, 39053.
(Photo: Courtesy North American Aviation Inc.)

3

dummy deck landings on a runway marked up to deck size, and on 10th March 1948 the Commander landed an FJ–1 on U.S.S. *Boxer*—the first jet landing on a carrier at sea under operational conditions. Landings and take-offs by other members of VF–5A followed and much initial experience was quickly gained in jet operations from a carrier deck. Slower acceleration by jets during take-off led to catapulting becoming standard practice, while the jets' greatly increased fuel consumption demanded larger fuel storage aboard carriers.

The FJ–1s, of which only 30 (*130342–130371*) came to be built—all at Los Angeles—were powered by Allison-built J35–A–4 engines; with 4,000 pounds thrust, top speed was 547 m.p.h. at 9,000 feet, and with two 165-gallon wing-tip tanks supplementing the 465 gallons of internal fuel the ferry range was 1,500 miles.

Throughout 1948 VF–5A remained the only U.S. Navy squadron jet-equipped, but when this unit was re-numbered VF–51 and took delivery of Grumman F9F–2s, the FJ–1s were delivered to reserve units ashore.

SWEPT WINGS

Successful development of the swept wing on the XP–86 had been continuing apace during 1947 under the design leadership of A. F. "Tony" Weissenberger

Resplendent in Naval Air Reserve colours, this FJ-1, 120368, flew from Oakland N.A.S., California, in 1950.
(Photo: William T. Larkins)

and Art C. Patch, and F–86As joined squadrons of the U.S.A.F. in 1948. By 1951, with events taking a more serious turn in Korea, the U.S. Navy had realised that swept-wing deck fighters were entirely feasible and, having studied a North American design proposal (NA–181) for a navalised F–86E, issued a letter contract on 10th February 1951 for development of prototypes. Commander Aurand, of VF–5A fame, was appointed Navy Project Officer.

Three prototypes were ordered from the Los Angeles plant. *133754* and *133755* (under NA–179) were essentially navalised F–86Es with vee-frame arrester hooks, lengthened nosewheel legs and catapult points. The third prototype, *133756*, under NA–181, was the first XFJ–2 flown, piloted by Robert

Above: *The first NA-179 prototype, 133754.* (Photo: Manufacturers.) Below: *Marine FJ-2 in natural metal finish. Note wing slats and two-store wings.*
(Photo: via John W. R. Taylor)

Hoover on 27th December 1951. *133756* carried the designation XFJ–2B, the B denoting a special armament modification for this machine carried four 20 mm. guns in place of the hitherto standard six 0·50-cal. machine guns.

As would be expected, these radical swept-wing prototypes underwent intensive trials. The two XFJ–2s, with J47–GE–13 engines, were delivered to Patuxent River for Service trials in 1952, and armament trials were undertaken at Inyokern on *133756*. Acceptance by the Navy of the prototypes was effected in June, July and December respectively, and carrier qualification trials were performed aboard U.S.S. *Coral Sea* in December 1952.

Production of FJ–2s was undertaken at North American's newly-opened Columbus, Ohio, plant in 1952. The original contract for 300 aircraft was reduced to 200 owing to the running down of the Korean War and the first aircraft was delivered in October 1952. Production continued until September 1954.

The FJ–2 Fury was, in effect, the U.S. Navy equivalent of the F–86F. Powered by a 6,000 pound thrust J47–GE–2 (Navy version of the J47–GE–27), the FJ–2 was equipped with folding wings and all-flying tail, and was armed with four 20 mm. guns with 600 rounds, aimed by a Mark 16 Model 2 sight and

Above: *An early FJ-3, 135810, with VC-3 during the Fleet Introduction Programme, at Patuxent River, Maryland, 1954.* (Photo: William T. Larkins). Below: *With retro-modified wings, FJ-3D2, 135809, served as a missile control aircraft and Navy Utility Squadron 3.*
(Photo: Ray Wagner)

FJ-3 of VF-51, 136008.　　(Photo: William T. Larkins)

FJ-3 of VF-154, 136978, at Moffett Field.
　　　　　　　　　　　　(Photo: William T. Larkins)

Navy/Marine markings on FJ-3, 135812, at Willow Grove in
June 1960.　　　　　　(Photo: William T. Larkins)

AN/APG–30 radar. Naval equipment raised the take-off weight to 18,791 pounds compared with 17,797 pounds for the F–86F–10; top speed was 676 m.p.h. at sea-level and 602 m.p.h. at the tropopause.

Although first production FJ-2s were delivered to the Navy in dark blue finish, most went to U.S. Marine Corps squadrons in natural metal finish. Korean War demands resulted in most of the Columbus effort being spent on Air Force F–86Fs, and FJ–2 production was slow during 1952, only five being completed during that year, and 25 by the end of 1953.

First squadron to receive FJ–2 was Marine VMF–122 at Cherry Point, North Carolina, in January 1954, being followed five months later by VMF–235 aboard U.S.S. *Hancock*, a newly-modified carrier equipped with C–11 steam catapults. By 1955 FJ–2s equipped six Marine squadrons, three—VMF–122, 232 and 312—with the Atlantic Fleet, and three—VMF–235, 334 and 451—with the Pacific Fleet. It was averred that the Grumman F9F–6 Cougar possessed a marginally better deck performance over the FJ–2 and it was the Cougar that gained Navy preference while the Fury remained with Marine units.

SAPPHIRE ENGINES

Perhaps as much on account of this failure to secure prime Navy contracts for the FJ–2 as for the successful development of late-series F–86s, North American commenced on March 3rd 1952 the design of the FJ–3 Fury* using the Wright J65–W–2 Sapphire engine of 7,700 pounds thrust, built under licence from Armstrong-Siddeley Motors Ltd., in England. The first Sapphire-powered Fury was the fifth production FJ–2, *131931*, this being used as a trial installation aircraft and thus became the prototype FJ–3 (though no XFJ–3 was officially recognised).

The first production FJ–3, *135774*, was completed

*Though contemporary designations are used for the FJ Fury series throughout this Profile, they were changed to conform to a standard U.S.A.F./U.S.N. designation system late in 1962. Under the new system the new designations were as follows: (FJ–3) F–1C; (FJ–3D) DF–1C; (FJ–3M) MF–1C; (FJ–3D2) DF–1D; (FJ–4) F–1E; (FJ–4B) AF–1E.

Below: *FJ-3, 136144, at Quonset Point, Rhode Island, June 1960.* Above, left: *Port side fuselage insignia of this aircraft.*
　　　　　　　　　　　　(Photos: R. W. Harrison)

Deck view of a VF-73 FJ-3M, 141435, aboard U.S.S. Randolph *on 22nd March 1957, during Carrier Qualification Trials.*
(Photo: U.S. Navy)

141478, an FJ-4B on external store trials. (Photo: William T. Larkins)

FJ-4B, 143569, of Navy Squadron VA-216. (Photo: William T. Larkins)

Fleet Air Gunnery Unit markings on FJ-4B, 139552. (Photo: William T. Larkins)

at Columbus on 11th December 1953 and was first flown by William Ingram. Differing from *131931*, the production FJ–3s were powered by J65–W–4s with enlarged air intakes. Slatted wings and flying tail were retained but ammunition for the four 20 mm. guns was increased by 48 rounds.

The FJ–3 succeeded where the FJ–3 had failed and altogether twelve Navy squadrons were thus equipped. By July 1954 twenty-four aircraft had been accepted and VC–3 and VF–173 performed the Fleet Intro-duction Programme at Patuxent River in the record time of 29 days, completing 703 flying hours. Two aircraft were written off, though through no fault of the design; one aircraft suffered an explosion after debris had been ingested during ground running, and another was ditched in the Patuxent River when the pilot became lost and ran out of fuel.

VF–173 was the first U.S. Navy squadron to land on a carrier when it joined U.S.S. *Bennington* of the Atlantic Fleet on 8th May 1955. A Fury of VX–3, flown by Commander R. G. Dose on 22nd August 1955, was the first American aircraft to use the mirror landing system, a system that became standard throughout American carriers. Another Fury squad-ron, VF–21, was the first squadron—in January 1956 —to land on U.S.S. *Forrestal*, the giant carrier designed expressly for jet aircraft operation.

Furies had, during 1955, undergone a number of alterations; in July the U.S. Navy abandoned the all-blue finish in favour of dull grey upper and white under surfaces. Wing slats were replaced by extended leading edges in which were accommodated 124 gallons of additional fuel. Underwing store points

Above: *FJ-4, 139474, with missile control electronics in under-wing store.* Below: *Shooting Star insignia on FJ-4B of VA-151.*
(Photos: William T. Larkins)

were increased from two to six making possible the carriage of 500 or 1,000 pound bombs, rocket packs or additional drop tanks. Sidewinder infra-red-seeking missiles, first fired at Inyokern in 1952, were fitted on the Fury from the 345th aircraft onwards. Sidewinder-equipped Furies, now designated FJ–3M, first joined the U.S. Pacific Fleet when U.S.S. *Bon Homme*, with VF–211 embarked, set sail from the West Coast for the Far East.

By the end of FJ–3M production in August 1956, the U.S. Navy and Marines were operating twenty-three Fury squadrons, a total which remained until

Below: *Striking in-flight view of an FJ-4B with three ASM-N-7 Bullpup missiles, missile guidance pod and two drop tanks.*
(Photo: U.S.Navy)

Above: *Late-standard FJ-4B, 143633*. Below: *FJ-4B of VA-216*.
(Photos: William T. Larkins)

the end of that year although one of the Marine units, VMF–451, replaced its FJ–2s with a new, long-range Fury—the FJ–4.

LONG RANGE ATTACK

Design of the FJ–4 had commenced at Columbus in February 1953 under the direction of Frank Compton. In June that year the project was established under NA–208 for two prototypes and NA–209 for production, and by July the following year the Navy had placed contracts for a total of 177 aircraft.

The new design was indentified fundamentally by a considerable increase in range, the fuel capacity being increased by 50%. To offset any loss of performance, the entire airframe was revised: a thinner wing of greater area and span, using integral skin/stringers and multi-spar construction, was milled from solid aluminium plate; mid-span wing control surfaces and high-lift flaps were incorporated, as were thinner tail surfaces—also with mid-span controls. A revised levered-suspension undercarriage was fitted to give an increased track of 11 ft. 7 in. Entirely new fuselage contours with a dorsal spine from cockpit to fin probably provided the most readily recognisable identification feature.

The first FJ–4, *139279*, was flown by Richard Wenzell on 28th October 1954, and was powered by the Wright J65–W–4 of the FJ–3; production machines however had the 7,700 pound J65–W–16A. Classified as long-range attack fighters, the FJ–4 carried additional armour in the nose, space being provided by reduction of ammunition for the 20 mm. guns. Four store wings could carry drop tanks, bombs and/or Sidewinders, but the "M" designation was not used. Performance included a top speed of 680 m.p.h. at sea-level and 631 m.p.h. at the tropopause, comparable with that of the Hawker Hunter 6, a British land-based contemporary.

As already mentioned, the first FJ–4s to enter service joined Marine squadron VMF–451 in 1956, and by March 1957 152 aircraft had been accepted by the Military. On 4th December 1956, however, a new variant—the FJ–4B—had flown. This version used a strengthened wing providing six attack-store strong-

Below: *Sidewinder-equipped FJ-3M, 141367, Nose boom was for flight trial intrumentation purposes.*   (Photo: U.S. Navy)

On flight trial at China Lake, this FJ-4 was equipped with four underwing launchers each with four ZUNI rockets. (Photo: U.S. Navy)

points. Equivalent to the U.S. Air Force's F–86H, the FJ–4B was fully equipped for low-altitude attack and, apart from the additional store capacity, was fitted with a LABS installation for the tactical delivery of a nuclear weapon. Additional speed brakes were fitted under the rear fuselage to allow more precise control of speed at low level.

The Fleet Introduction Programme of the FJ–4B was performed by VA–126 and VMA–223 on the Pacific Coast, particular emphasis being laid upon loft-bombing procedures, When the "Bravo Fury" entered service it introduced a number of new flight techniques with the Navy and Marines. Like some FJ–3s, the FJ–4B carried in-flight refuelling probes under the port wing, and in June 1957 "Buddy" refuelling was introduced with the addtion of underwing fuel packs. Thus a Fury fighter could take on an additional 3,163 pounds of fuel from another aircraft of the same type to extend its combat radius by about 50%.

In-flight refuelling was undertaken by Marine squadrons VMA–212 and 214 to enable them to complete the first trans-Pacific crossing by single-seat naval aircraft in October 1958.

Late development of the FJ–4 continued until the end of the nineteen-fifties. Martin Bullpup air-to-ground missiles, of which five (plus an equipment pack) could be carried, were added, and the first

overseas deployment of these weapons came about when VA–212 sailed aboard U.S.S. *Lexington* to join the U.S. Seventh Fleet in the Western Pacific in April 1959.

By the early nineteen-sixties Furies were being phased out of combat units and supplied to Reserve and shore units. All told, North American's Columbus plant delivered 1,112 aircraft to the Military between

Close up detail of XFJ-2 20 mm. gun installation.

SERVICE DEPLOYMENT OF FJ FURIES
(A) denotes U.S. Atlantic Fleet
(P) denotes U.S. Pacific Fleet

Aircraft	U.S. Navy	U.S. Marine Corps
FJ–1	VF–5A	
FJ–2		VMF–122 (A) VMF–232 (A) VMF–235 (P) VMF–312 (A) VMF–334 (P) VMF–451 (P)
FJ–3	VC–3 (A) VF–24 (P) VF–33 (A) VF–91 (P) VF–154 (P) VF–191 (P) VF–173 (A) VF–211 (P)	VMF–122 (A) VMF–312 (A) VMF–333 VMF–511
FJ–3M	VA–172 (A) VF–12 (A) VF–21 (P) VF–51 (P) VF–62 (A) VF–73 (A) VF–84 (A) VF–121 (P) VF–142 (P) VF–143 (P) VF–173 (A) VF–211 (P)	VMF–235 (P) VMF–334 (A)
FJ–4		VMF–232 (P) VMF–235 (P) VMF–451 (P)
FJ–4B	VA–55 (P) VA–56 (P) VA–63 (P) VA–116 (P) VA–126 (P) VA–146 (P) VA–151 (P) VA–192 (P) VA–212 (P) VA–216 (P)	VMA–212 (P) VMA–214 (P) VMA–223 (P)

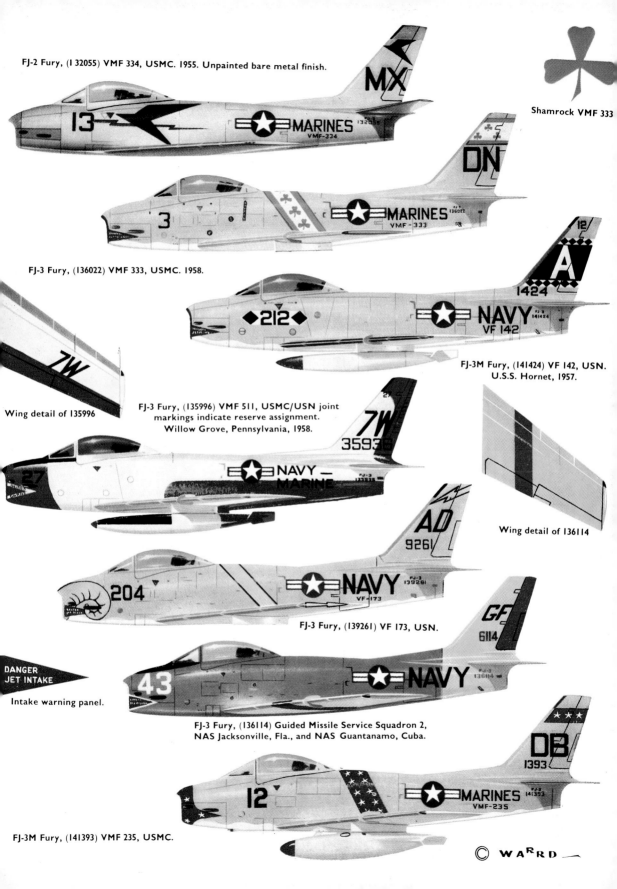

FJ-2 Fury, (132055) VMF 334, USMC. 1955. Unpainted bare metal finish.

Shamrock VMF 333

FJ-3 Fury, (136022) VMF 333, USMC. 1958.

FJ-3M Fury, (141424) VF 142, USN.
U.S.S. Hornet, 1957.

Wing detail of 135996

FJ-3 Fury, (135996) VMF 511, USMC/USN joint
markings indicate reserve assignment.
Willow Grove, Pennsylvania, 1958.

Wing detail of 136114

DANGER
JET INTAKE

Intake warning panel.

FJ-3 Fury, (139261) VF 173, USN.

FJ-3 Fury, (136114) Guided Missile Service Squadron 2,
NAS Jacksonville, Fla., and NAS Guantanamo, Cuba.

FJ-3M Fury, (141393) VMF 235, USMC.

© WARRD

FJ-4B with six ZUNI rocket launchers.
(Photo: via John W. R. Taylor)

FJ-4B, 143603, of VA-126 with underwing in-flight refuelling pack.
(Photo: Ray Wagner)

November 1952 and May 1958, perhaps a remarkable figure when it is remembered that Navy contracts were seldom regarded by manufacturers as prolific, and that during the same period Grumman, McDonnell, Chance-Vought (LTV) and Douglas were also building Navy fighters.

© F. K. Mason, 1965

FURY PRODUCTION FJ-1 TO FJ-4B

NORTH AMERICAN XFJ-1. Three NA-134 aircraft, serials *39053* to *39055*, ordered under Contract NOa(s) 5311, dated 1st January 1945. First flown on 27th November 1946. All three accepted, September 1947. Powered by a J35-GE-2. Six ·50 calibre guns.

NORTH AMERICAN FJ-1 FURY. Thirty production NA-141, serials *120342* to *120371* built at Los Angeles under Contract NOa(s) 6911, 28th May 1945. Accepted with J35-A-4 from October 1947 to April 1948.

NORTH AMERICAN XFJ-2 FURY. Three prototypes, serials *133754* to *133756*, Contract NOa(s) 51–756, 8th March 1951. As XFJ-2B (NA-185), 133756 was first flown 27th December 1951, at Los Angeles, while *133754* (NA-179) flew 19th February 1952. Powered by J47-GE-13, and accepted June, July, and November 1952. Last Navy Fury aircraft built at Los Angeles.

NORTH AMERICAN FJ-2 FURY. Production order for 300 NA-181 reduced to 200, serials *131927* to *132126* to Contract NOa(s) 51–642, 10th February 1951. First aircraft accepted at Columbus, October 1952, remainder from January 1953 to September 1954. Had J47-GE-2 and four 20-mm. guns, but *131931* had J65-W-2 as FJ-3 prototype.

NORTH AMERICAN FJ-3/FJ-3M FURY. The first production order was for 389 NA-194, *135774* to *136162*, on Contract NOa(s) 52–978, 18th April 1952. First aircraft flown 11th December 1953 at Columbus with Wright J65-W-4 and four 20-mm. guns. Remainder accepted from January 1954 to February 1956. After delivery, many redesignated FJ-3M with GAR-8 provisions.

Second production batch was originally for 214 NA-215, on Contract NOa(s) 54–322, 15th March 1954, 80 aircraft added by NOa(s) 55–174, and 145 cancelled. Total completed as FJ-3/FJ-3M was 149; *139210* to *139278*, and *141364* to *141443*. Accepted from December 1955 to August 1956.

NORTH AMERICAN FJ-4 FURY. Two NA-208 prototypes, *139279* and *139280*, and 150 NA-209 aircraft, *139281* to *139323*, and *139424* to *139530*, on Contract NOa(s) 54–323, 16th October 1953. First aircraft flown at Columbus on 28th October 1954 with Wright J65-W-4, accepted same week, and second production accepted in December. Remaining aircraft had J65-W-16A and were completed by March 1957. Two aircraft, *139282* and *139284* modified to FJ-4F.

NORTH AMERICAN FJ-4B FURY. First production batch of 25 aircraft, *139531* to *139555* from NA-209s on NOa(s) 54–323, as amended 26th July 1954, plus 46 FJ-4Bs, *141444* to *141489* (formerly NA-229), added 2nd November 1954. First aircraft, *139531*, flown 4th December 1956, and Contract completed in August 1957.

Second production order was for 184 NA-244, reduced to 151 FJ-4B, *143493* to *143643*, on NOa(s) 56–121, 5th April 1956. Aircraft accepted between July 1957 and May 1958.

The author wishes to acknowledge the considerable assistance given by Jay Frank Dial, William T. Larkins, Charles Thompson and Ray Wagner in the preparation of this Profile.

NORTH AMERICAN FURY SPECIFICATION

	FJ-1	FJ-2	FJ-3	FJ-4
Powerplant	4,000 lb. thrust Allison J35-A-2	6,000 lb. thrust General Electric J47-GE-2	7,650 lb. thrust Wright J65-W-48	7,700 lb. thrust Wright J65-W-16A
Dimensions:				
Span	38 ft. 2 in.	37 ft. 1 in.	37 ft. 1 in.	39 ft. 1 in.
Length	34 ft. 5 in.	37 ft. 7 in.	37 ft. 7 in.	36 ft. 4 in.
Height	14 ft. 10 in.	13 ft. 7 in.	13 ft. 8 in.	13 ft. 11 in.
Span folded ...	—	22 ft. 7 in.	22 ft. 6 in.	27 ft. 6 in.
Wing area	221 sq. ft.	287·9 sq. ft.	302·3 sq. ft.	338·66 sq. ft.
Weights:				
Empty	8,843 lb.	11,802 lb.	12,205 lb.	13,210 lb.
Loaded	15,115 lb. (clean)	16,482 lb. (clean)	17,189 lb. (clean)	20,130 lb. (clean)
Landing	—	14,125 lb.	14,165 lb.	15,333 lb.
Wing loading ...	68·3 lb./sq. ft. (clean)	65·3 lb./sq. ft. (clean)	56·9 lb./sq. ft. (clean)	59·5 lb./sq. ft. (clean)
Performance:				
Max. speeds (clean)	547 m.p.h. at 9,000 ft.	676 m.p.h. at sea-level 602 m.p.h. at 35,000 ft.	681 m.p.h. at sea-level 623 m.p.h. at 35,000 ft.	680 m.p.h. at sea-level 631 m.p.h. at 35,000 ft.
Initial climb rate ...	3,300 ft./min.	7,230 ft./min.	8,450 ft./min.	7,660 ft./min.
Max. range	1,496 miles (ferry)	990 miles (combat)	1,784 miles (ferry)	1,485 miles (combat)
Service ceiling ...	32,000 ft.	41,700 ft.	49,000 ft.	46,800 ft.
Stalling speed (all down)	121 m.p.h.	132 m.p.h.	133 m.p.h.	—
Source of material ...	U.S. Navy S.A.C. Chart dated 1/5/49	U.S. Navy S.A.C. Chart dated 1/10/55	U.S. Navy S.A.C. Chart dated 30/4/58	U.S. Navy S.A.C. Chart dated 30/8/58

PRINTED IN ENGLAND. © Profile Publications Ltd., P.O. Box 26, Leatherhead, Surrey, England
by George Falkner & Sons Ltd. for McCorquodale City Printing Division, London.

PROFILE
PUBLICATIONS

The
Pfalz
D III

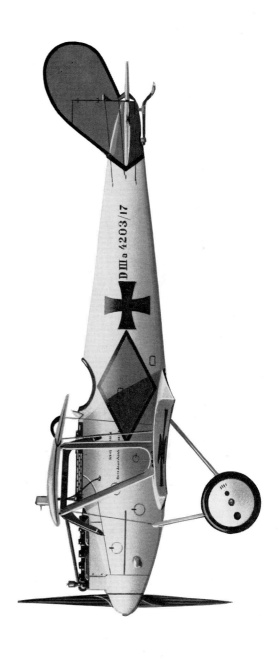

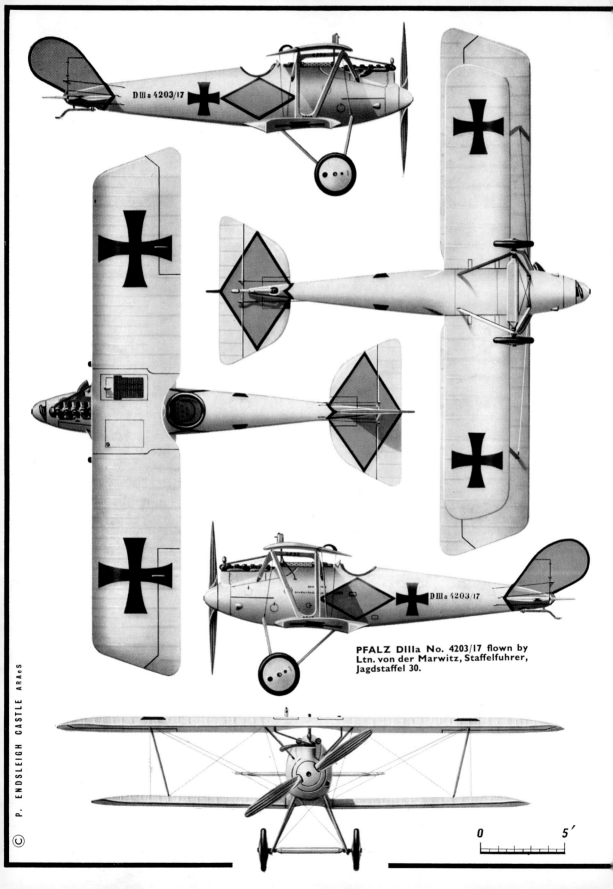

DIIIa 4203/17

PFALZ DIIIa No. 4203/17 flown by
Ltn. von der Marwitz, Staffelfuhrer,
Jagdstaffel 30.

© P. ENDSLEIGH CASTLE ARAeS

0   5´

The Pfalz D.III

by Peter L. Gray

Pfalz D IIIa with painted nose and inspection discs. Capt. F. G. Quigley is sitting in cockpit. This aircraft is fitted with the "saxophone" type of exhaust manifold.
(Photo: Canadian War Archives)

A slim silver biplane with angularly-raked wings lifted swiftly from the grass airfield, the early ground mist swirling in the vigour of its slipstream. Clear of the boundary hedge the machine rose no higher but set a westerly course for the lines, seemingly pursuing its own fleeting shadow cast before it by the morning sun, slowly rising astern. A grim-faced figure hunched over the control stick, concentrating on skilfully directing his roaring mount at roof-top height, towards the distant image of an Allied observation balloon swinging at the end of its cable.

In a trice he had traversed the brief section of "no-man's-land" which separated the trenches, and was way beyond the support lines almost before their unfortunate inhabitants had realised he was abroad. His intention was to reach and destroy the balloon before it could be hauled down by its high-speed winch, and so to avoid the maelstrom of fire its ground defences would hurl upon him. To screen his approach to the utmost he swung on to a road lined with poplars, bringing his aircraft below the level of the tree tops, which now rushed by scant inches from his wing-tips.

However, the ground defence crew of the balloon section were already alert and on morning "stand-to" —hearing the roar of his rapid approach they swung their L.M.G.s to cover their charge, whilst the winch

crew started the haul down with all speed. Seeing the gas bag quickly descending the German pilot realised his attack would not be the surprise he had anticipated. Undaunted, however, he decided to press on, easing back on the stick to intercept the balloon with a steeply-angled no-deflection shot. Oblivious of the ground defences he watched the target as it grew in his sights, then pressed the twin triggers to see his tracers lancing viciously into the balloon. He caught a momentary impression as the observer took to his parachute, an observer who, within seconds, was being followed by the flaming mass which had so lately supported him.

The pilot's exultation was short-lived, however, as he now flew into the hail of fire flung at him by the avenging ground crew, who had so accurately anticipated his course. His violent evasive manœuvres were to no avail; flames licking from the ruptured fuel tank, almost instantly engulfed the fighter which flicked on to its back and then plunged to the earth.

The little, shark-like fighter in which this courageous pilot flew comet-like to his death, had begun its life in the Pfalz factory of the Eversbusch brothers in the Bavarian township of Speyer on the River Rhine, near Mannheim. Although founded before the war it was not until 1917 that the firm produced a machine which was completely their own design. Very soon after

Left: *Pfalz D III 4185/17 Justa 5, with red and white fuselage bands photographed at Boistrancourt.* (Photo: von Hippel). Right: *Early production Pfalz D III in standard ex-works aluminium finish, showing clearly style and location of patee crosses and fuselage serial number. Also to be noted—the black datum on fuselage centre-line extending back from nose.* Photo: Egon Krueger)

3

Pfalz D IIIa 8143/17 displays straight-sided Balkankreuz of April/May 1918 period; overpainting of the earlier patee crosses on the wings is apparent. The decor is somewhat crudely marked, colours are not known but may have been deep yellow and pale blue.　　　　　　　　(Photo: P. M. Grosz)

Another view of D III 4158 at Boistrancourt.
(Photo: von Hippel)

hostilities ceased the company discontinued the manufacture of aircraft, unlike its more well-known Fokker and Albatros counterparts, and this probably accounts for its dropping into a considerable degree of obscurity, notwithstanding its having contributed a considerable number of machines to the German flying services.

It was in July 1913 that the three Eversbusch brothers, Alfred, Walter and Ernst, established a new factory at Speyer. It was largely financed through the Bavarian Government which wished to ensure it retained some degree of control over the equipment its flying services would use. Due to an insufficiency of reserve capital, the Pfalz company's original hope of acquiring a licence to manufacture Albatros aircraft came to naught. As an alternative the firm obtained a licence to build the Otto pusher biplane, Gustav Otto assisting in both a financial and advisory capacity. However, the astute Alfred Eversbusch quickly realised that the Otto machine was inferior to contemporary French aircraft, and negotiated with the Morane-Saulnier company the right to produce their two most successful designs; the Type H shoulder-wing monoplane and Type L parasol. Walter Evers-

busch, the youngest of the brothers, learned to fly at the Morane-Saulnier school and was awarded his pilot's certificate in July 1914, from which date he became the Pfalz test pilot until his untimely death in a crash on 1st June 1916.

LICENCE PRODUCTION

Production of the Morane-Saulnier monoplanes was slow and only three parasols had been constructed by the outbreak of war in August 1914. With the subsequent increase in demand, larger numbers came from the factory, but relatively few saw active service. The parasols were classified Pfalz A I on the introduction of military designations and were fitted with 80-h.p. Oberursel (Gnôme licence) engines. The majority saw service with the Bavarian flying schools but a few were used on active service in an unarmed reconnaissance capacity. The shoulder-wing monoplane, with the advent of the synchronised machine gun, was developed into the Pfalz E I to E IV series, which was used on the Western Front in 1915 and to an even later date in the Middle East theatre.

With the completion of the monoplane orders in 1916, the stronger and more agile biplane fighter had come into its own. Pfalz had brought out a biplane prototype, the D 4, a far from elegant development of the E IV monoplane and singularly unsuccessful. In consequence, with the necessary production facilities available, the Pfalz factory was awarded a licence to manufacture the L.F.G. Roland D I single-seat fighter, which began to emerge from the Speyer works early in 1917. Later in the year it was superseded by the Roland D II and D IIa which L.F.G. had developed. The Pfalz designers and technicians learned a lot from the manufacture of these, for the period, excellent fighters, and began to formulate their own ideas for a single-seat fighter design.

THE D III IS BORN

During 1916 the French Nieuport "chasers" had achieved a considerable advantage over their German adversaries on the Western Front, with their superior manœuvrability and performance in general. Captured Nieuports were made available to various of the German factories, including Pfalz. Certainly a little of the Nieuport was incorporated into the Pfalz fighter by the chief engineer Rudolph Gegringer (an Austrian citizen born in 1891), who was assisted by designers Geldmacher and Paulus. The prototype was wheeled from the workshops in the spring of 1917 and was seen to have utilised, in modified form, the Nieuport wing layout, with the lower wing of much narrower chord than the upper, to give a greater degree of visibility from the cockpit. The inherent weakness of the Nieuport lower wing, i.e. its single spar which developed a tendency to twist and break off in a prolonged dive, was avoided in the Pfalz aircraft which had a twin spar wing. The Albatros designers

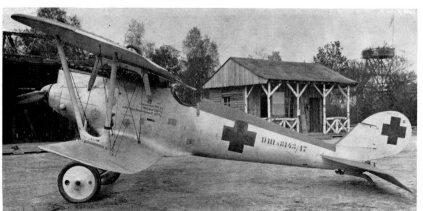

Side view of D IIIa 8143/17. Note the more pointed extremities of the interplane and centre-section struts compared with the earlier D IIIs.
(Photo: P. M. Grosz)

had followed the Nieuport arrangement more closely and had likewise developed the same weakness in their D III and D V machines.

CONSTRUCTION DETAILS

The prototype Pfalz was quite a successful and efficient aeroplane and was found to require little modification before going into production as the Pfalz D III. Horn-balanced ailerons replaced the plain ailerons of the prototype and imparted a livelier lateral control; also a more rounded rudder was fitted to the production machine. Power unit of the decidedly shark-like fighter was the well-tried, and eminently reliable, 160-h.p. Mercedes D III. This was carefully cowled with metal panels extending right up to the inlet manifolds and along the whole length of the cylinder block. The boss of the laminated airscrew was enclosed in a small neat, spinner, the tip of which was a flat disc on the early machines. Of semi-monocoque construction, the fuselage itself was built on a light basic structure of oval plywood formers and spruce longerons which was skinned with a plywood shell. This consisted of two three-ply layers, each less than a millimetre thick, and these layers were unusually applied in the form of strips about 3¼ inches wide laid on at about forty-five degrees to the horizontal and at ninety degrees to each other. They were bonded together with cold water glue and reinforced at the edges with tape. One half of the fuselage was covered at a time and then the whole was additionally covered with a skin of doped fabric. This method of diagonal wrapping, together with the thin plywood used, facilitated the implementation of the neat wing root fairings as an integral part of the fuselage structure. Twin forward-firing Spandau machine guns were housed completely within the fuselage with just the muzzles projecting each side of the fifth cylinder. On the Pfalz D IIIa, which soon followed the D III into production, the guns were re-located on top of the decking immediately in front of the windscreen—accessibility for servicing and replacement was the main criteria, but it was subsequently claimed that more accurate sighting resulted. Also an integral part of the fuselage structure were the fin and a tailplane stub, likewise duo-ply-skinned and fabric covered. The tailplane and one-piece unbalanced elevator were an angular, trapezoidal shape; they were of wooden framing and fabric covered. The section was of inverse

Rare shot of one of the 1918 batch of Pfalz D IIIa's—1306/18 with dark-painted (? black) fuselage and lonzenge-painted fabric underneath wings. (Photo: P. M. Grosz)

camber which gave stability in a prolonged dive and considerably assisted recovery. In the D IIIa a more rounded tailplane of greater chord and area was fitted, and this feature together with the machine gun siting, was the only visual difference between the two types. The balanced rudder was of pleasantly rounded profile, constructed from fine gauge steel tube—the only control surface to use this medium—and was fabric covered.

Wing geometry of the Pfalz D III was angular, Although differing in span and chord both were basically the same shape, of constant chord and with sharply raked tips. At a later date the lower wings were modified to a more rounded tip profile and both D III and D IIIa types were to be found with this style of lower wing eventually. Wings were, in fact, completely interchangeable for both machines. The upper wing was a one-piece structure, without dihedral, and conventionally based on two box spars wire braced to compression members. A unique feature of the spar construction was the insertion of a diaphragm at each

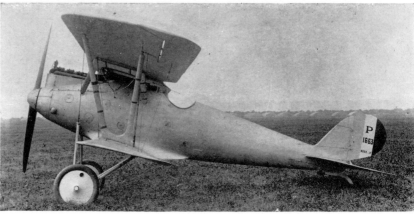

Above: *Factory-fresh in its aluminium dope D IIIa 4237/17 shows location of port side serial.* (Photo: P. M. Grosz)

Right: *Pfalz D IIIa 8033/17 captured by the French.* (Photo: P. M. Grosz)

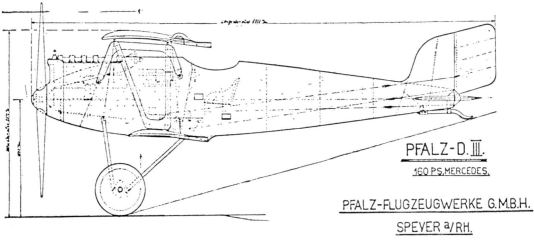

PFALZ-D.Ⅲ.

160 P.S.MERCEDES.

PFALZ-FLUGZEUGWERKE G.M.B.H.

SPEYER a/RH.

Pfalz factory drawing of prototype D III illustrates shape of the original fin and unbalanced rudder. (Courtesy: P. M. Grosz)

rib station, this was to transmit the sheer stresses across the spar and might, with advantage, have been a feature of all such box spars. Ribs were of three-ply fretted with lightening holes, softwood cappings strips were tacked to the perimeter. False ribs, spaced between the main ribs, extended as far back as the rear spar. The complete centre-section panel, with its shallow cut-out, was plywood covered.

A flush-fitted Teeves and Braun radiator was located in the starboard side, while the port side housed the service fuel tank to which the petrol was pumped from the main tank mounted on the spar roots of the lower wing. A sliding blanketing panel underneath the radiator could be adjusted by the pilot to vary the degree of cooling required. Horn-balanced ailerons, with characteristic German wash-out, were of wooden framing and operated by a curved crank lever, which in turn was actuated by cables running through the lower wing.

Bottom wing panels were attached to the carefully-fashioned root fairings and rigged with one degree dihedral: they followed the same style of construction as the upper wing. Centre-section and interplane struts were of inverted "U" and "Vee" pattern respectively. They were substantially built from several laminations of wood and in consequence it was possible to dispense with incidence bracing cables. The "Vee" interplane struts were made sufficiently wide at the base to join both spars of the lower wing. The shape of the strut extremities varied; in the early machines they were relatively blunt, in the later aircraft the tips were more pointed; attachment was by ball and socket joints.

The undercarriage structure was an orthodox "Vee" type chassis of streamlined steel tube with the axle and spreader bars neatly encased in a narrow streamlined fairing. Wheels were sprung with elastic shock cord, likewise the tailskid which was fashioned from ash to a peculiar "hockey-stick" shape. The undercarriage was cross-braced in the front bay only by stranded

wire cables, which medium was also used for the interplane bracing.

Up-rated Mercedes D IIIa engine with oversize pistons and higher compression ratios were fitted to

Oblt. Franz Hailer in dark-camouflaged D IIIa. The fuselage band is of blue and white diamonds. (Photo: Egon Krueger)

Above: *Cockpit and twin Spandau machine guns of D IIIa.* (Photo: Egon Krueger)

Below: *Pfalz D III in mint condition shows contrast between fabric-covered aluminium-doped fuselage skin and metal of nose panelling and inspection discs.* (Photo: Egon Kruger)

Rear view of Pfalz D III prototype, the original unbalanced ailerons may be noted. (Photo: Egon Krueger)

Another view of Pfalz D III 1366/17 photographed at Johannisthal, shows well the clean lines of this aircraft. (Photo: Egon Krueger)

the Pfalz D IIIa's and a modified exhaust manifold was usually fitted, of "saxophone" shape with the bell outlet against the first cylinder.

PRODUCTION AND SERVICE

Having passed its official acceptance test in June 1917 (*Typen-Prüfung*) production of the Pfalz D III soon got under way, but due to the complex fuselage construction it was not a machine that could be manufactured as speedily as the welded steel tube Fokker and simpler Albatros machines. It is recorded that only three D IIIs were in Front Line service by the end of August; numbers increased to 145 operational aircraft at 31st October and as many as 276 D IIIs and 114

Below: D IIIa 8052/17 with straight-sided Balkankreuz; fuselage cross is unusually outlined in white. The numerals "10" may also be seen underneath starboard lower wing in the original print; they were probably also repeated on port upper wing.
(Photo: Egon Krueger)

Pfalz D III of Jasta 10. Personnel from left: 1st Hptm. Schwarzenberger, 3rd Ltn. Klein, 5th E. Eversbusch, 6th Ltn. A. Heldmann. (Photo: Egon Krueger)

D IIIa's by the end of 1917. Thereafter the numbers of D IIIs decreased while those of the D IIIa went ahead; the position at 28th February 1918 was 182 D IIIs and 261 D IIIa machines—by the end of April the proportion was only 13 D IIIs to 433 D IIIa's. By the end of August only 3 D IIIs remained in Front Line service (coincidentally the same figure as that of a year before) while the number of D IIIa's was 166.

These figures, it must be remembered, do not represent the number of aircraft built but simply record the number that were still on the war establishment of Front Line units. The numbers actually built cannot be determined exactly—considerable research on this subject has been done by Peter Grosz and Ed. Ferko who conclude, tentatively, that production batches ran: *1350/17* to *1417/17, 4000/17* to *4399/17, 5880/17* to *6049/17, 8000/17* to *8339/17, 1234/18* to *1327/18,* totalling 874 machines, from which it may be surmised that probably about 1,000 Pfalz D IIIs and D IIIa's were built altogether.

First allocation of the Pfalz fighters, naturally enough seems to have been made to the Bavarian *Jasta* 16, 23, 32, 34 and 35, which had been transferred to the Bavarian Army on 4th July 1917. *Jasta* 76, 77, 78, 79 and 80 were also formed as Bavarian units during the winter of 1917–18 and received this equipment. Other *Jastas* which received Pfalz D IIIs and the later D IIIa's were: *Jasta* 5, 7, 8, 10, 11, 14, 15, 19, 20, 22, 24, 28, 29, 30, 36, 37, 40, 44, 46, 47, 48, 49, 51, 52, 53, 54, 56, 57, 58, 59, 61, 67, 69, and *Marine Feld Jagdstaffeln* I, II and III. Mainly the

Pfalz D III 4063/17 with dark-painted nose and complete tail assembly, unit unfortunately not identified.
(Photo: Egon Krueger)

Jadgstaffeln had an assorted complement of aircraft. The first Pfalz D IIIs operated in company with Roland D IIs and IIa's and later with Albatros D V and Va's and Fokker triplanes. Alex Imrie advises that from his intensive researches the only units to be equipped with the Pfalz D III and IIIa exclusively were *Jastas* 4, 10, 16, 20, 21, 24, 30, 32, 46, 61, 67 and *Marine Feld Jasta* II.

In service the Pfalz seems to have been a considerably maligned machine; many stories probably most of them apocryphal, circulating as to its unsuitability: "too slow", "does not climb", "too heavy", "won't recover from a spin", "fuselage weak", "not properly constructed", "tail weak and liable to break off", etc. In actual fact it was quite a good, rugged, aeroplane. Initially there was a tendency to failure of the upper wing-tips in combat—Ltn. Kroll, Commander *Jasta* 24 once had the misfortune to suffer this circumstance and nearly lost his ailerons—but stronger spars were ordered to rectify this. The Pfalz could dive a good deal faster than any other German fighter and with excellent stability, in consequence it provided a good gun platform. Its style of construction endowed it with an ability to absorb a fair degree of punishment.

There certainly was a tendency for the machine to get in a flat spin from which it was exceedingly difficult to recover—such an experienced pilot as von Linsingen of *Jasta* 11 spun into the ground on a Pfalz D IIIa. In an interview with Alex Imrie, Ltn. Kaus (of *Jasta* 30) stated he personally liked the Pfalz D IIIa very much and his favourite method of losing height was to spin down over the aerodrome!

In a report dated 25th October 1917, *Jasta* 24 expressed the following opinion on the Pfalz D III:

"It is slower than the Albatros D III; it is fast in a dive and is then faster than the Albatros D V. The climbing performance of Pfalz D III varies greatly, sometimes almost as good as the average Albatros D V but never better. It is not advisable for a unit to be equipped with both Pfalz D III and Albatros D V. However, Pfalz alone in one unit could be successful."

Whatever its real shortcomings may have been they were certainly not in the sphere of construction. Captured examples of both D III and D IIIa were critically examined and evaluated by Allied technicians and who were considerably impressed by the quality of the workmanship.

As the Pfalz machines were gradually withdrawn

D III 1386/17 used by Ltn. Lenz, Jasta 22, photographed at Mont aerodrome, August 1917. (Photo: Alex Imrie)

Pfalz D IIIa with Balkankreuz marks on fuselage and rudder, patee crosses were still displayed on wing surfaces.

(Photo: W. R. Puglisi)

from the *Jastas* in exchange for Albatros D Va's and later Fokker D VIIs, those that were considered to still be of use were reconditioned and sent to flying schools which specialised in the training of fighter pilots (*Jagdstaffelschulen*) although probably about a hundred D IIIa's were still soldering on with the combat units right up to the cessation of hostilities.

A particularly graphic account of a combat between a Pfalz D IIIa and, then, Capt Edward "Mickey" Mannock, Flight Commander 74 Squadron

Flugmaat Undiener with lattice-marked D IIIa 4215/17. Style and location of stencilling on fuselage may be noted.

(Photo: Alex Imrie)

R.A.F., flying an S.E.5a on 21st May 1918, is given by Ltn. Van Ira:

". . . the other Pfalz, a silver bird, and he had a fine set-to, while his patrol watched the master at work. It was a wonderful sight. First they waltzed around one another like a couple of turkey-cocks, Mick being tight on his adversary's tail. Then the Pfalz half rolled and fell a few hundred feet beneath him. Mick followed, firing as soon as he got into position. The Hun then looped—Mick looped too, coming out behind and above his opponent. The Pfalz then spun—Mick spun also, firing as he spun. This shooting appeared to me a waste of ammunition. The Hun eventually pulled out; Mick was fast on his tail—they were now down to 4,000 feet. The Pfalz now started twisting and turning which was a sure sign of 'wind-up'. After a sharp burst close up Mick administered the *coup de grâce*, and the poor old fellow went down headlong and crashed.

"This was a remarkable exhibition, a marvellous show. I felt sorry for the poor Pfalz pilot, for he put up a wonderful show of defensive fighting. Had he only kept spinning right down to the ground, I think he would have got away with it."

Of interest is the fact that Van Ira stated it was the

Nose close-up of crashed D IIIa 8282/17 shows air intake detail, inspection panels and machine guns to advantage. Also legend appertaining to weights may be noted.

(Photo: Imperial War Museum—Q12164)

Line-up of yellow-nosed Jasta 10 D IIIs near Courtrai. 3rd machine from right is Vzfw. Hecht's aircraft which was later captured.
(Photo: Alex Imrie)

first time he has seen a machine loop during a fight. Mannock said afterwards that he should not have followed through in a lop himself but made a steep climbing turn as the Pfalz looped, then half rolled to come back on his tail as he came out. Thereby he would have kept the machine in sight the whole time.

However, all combats did not end so disastrously for Pfalz pilots. That redoubtable exponent of the S.E. Capt. (later Major) J. B. McCudden reported on at least two occasions—6th September and 19th December 1917—when Pfalz D IIIs had eluded him. On the later date he, with two others of his patrol, manoeuvred for over half an hour with a Pfalz and an Albatros with no decision being reached. McCudden afterwards emphasised how splendidly the two German pilots co-operated and manoeuvred.

The mercurial Werner Voss was posted to command *Jagdstaffel* 10 at the end of July 1917 and used one of the first Pfalz D IIIs on which he recorded four victories before taking possession of a Fokker triplane. Another courageous German pilot who flew a Pfalz with great style, not to say precision, was Paul Bäumer of *Jasta* 2 (Boelcke) who was to score 43 victories. Von Hippel has remarked that when he (Bäumer) used to visit *Jasta* 5 at Boistrancourt he usually ran his wheels on the hanger roof to get them revolving before touching down!

COLOUR SCHEMES

In their final finish the Pfalz D III and D IIIa's were

Fuselage of Vzfw. Hecht's Pfalz D III 1370/17 after capture.
(Photo: Imperial War Museum—Q11898)

unique in leaving the Speyer factory painted all over with aluminium dope (*silbergrau*) which was a matt, or satin, silver finish. Interplane and centre-section struts were left in their natural wood finish protected by clear varnish. Serial numbers were painted in black in near Roman style letters and figures on the fuselage sides between the cross and the tailplane; these serials were also repeated in miniature on the apices of the struts and across the top of the rudder. The patee cross was standard national insignia until 15th April 1918 when the straight-sided Balkankreuz was introduced. On receipt of Pfalz D III some *Jastas* applied a drab camouflage to the upper and side surfaces but

Captured D IIIa 8284/17 marked with swastika motif. Wings appear to have been lozenge fabric covered and patee crosses on these surfaces were white outlined.

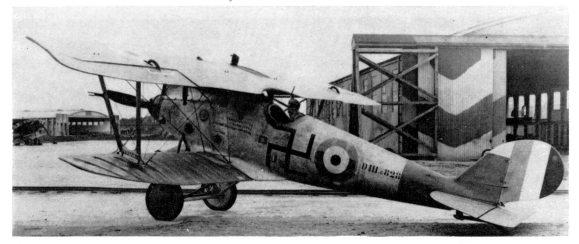

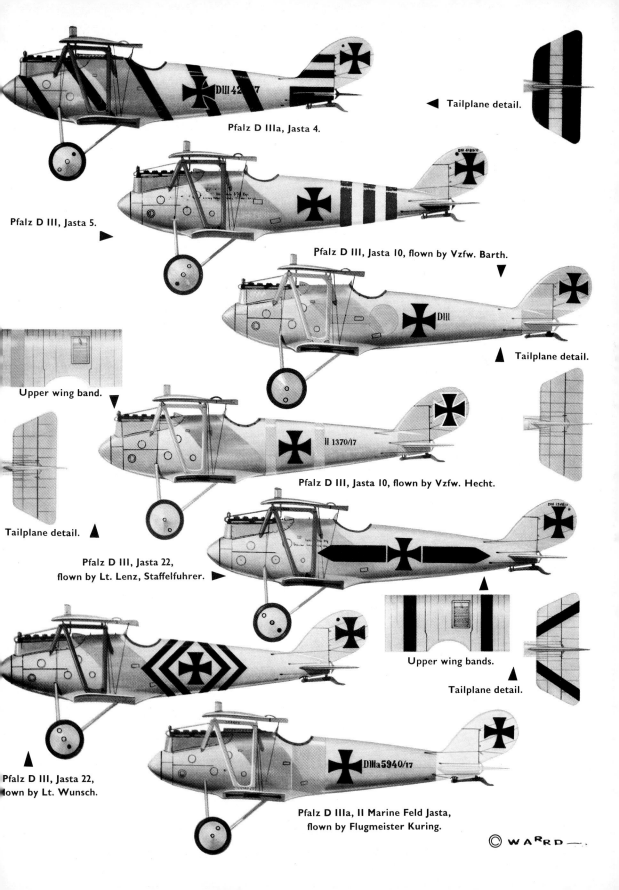

Tailplane detail. ◀

Pfalz D IIIa, Jasta 4.

Pfalz D III, Jasta 5. ▶

Pfalz D III, Jasta 10, flown by Vzfw. Barth. ▼

Upper wing band. ▼

Tailplane detail. ▲

Tailplane detail. ▲

Pfalz D III, Jasta 10, flown by Vzfw. Hecht.

Pfalz D III, Jasta 22,
flown by Lt. Lenz, Staffelfuhrer. ▶

Upper wing bands.

Tailplane detail. ▲

▲
Pfalz D III, Jasta 22,
flown by Lt. Wunsch.

Pfalz D IIIa, II Marine Feld Jasta,
flown by Flugmeister Kuring.

© WARRD

Another captured D III, 4184/14, orginal patee crosses overpainted with roundels. Tail and fuselage markings are reported as being chocolate brown.

D IIIa 6014/17 with ultimate style of narrow Balkankreuz. Non-standard style of serial marking is of special interest.
(Photo: Alex Imrie)

Pfalz D IIIA, 1306/18, landed at Schoondijke, 12th June 1918. In Dutch service until 1920. Note orange disc markings on fuselage and bottom of upper wing. Colour scheme was dark green, with pale blue or silver surfaces.
(Photo: G. H. Kamphuis)

D IIIa—4205/17 test pilot Wincziers killed 30th Oct. 1917; 4215/17 III Marine Feld Jasta; 4218/17 Js 24; 4223/17 Ltn. Linsingen Js 11; 4237 and 4256/17 Js 24; 4283/17 Ltn. Klein Js 10; 4285, 4287, 4289, 4291 and 4294/17 Js 24; 5888/17 Obltn. Bethge Js 30; 5922/17 Flzm. Zimpel III Marine Feld Jasta; 8033/17 captured by French; 8169/17 Ltn. Bellen Js 10; 8190/17 G. Wulf; 8282 and 8284 captured by British.

Courtesy E. Ferko and P. M. Grosz.

Dark-camouflaged Pfalz D III of Jasta 10. Fokker triplane in foreground is machine used by Werner Voss.
(Photo: W. R. Puglisi)

under surfaces were probably left aluminium. It has not been possible to confirm that they were painted the usual pale blue used underneath other types. More usually though, the aircraft were left in their basic "silver" dope, with the various unit and individual identities added as may be seen from the colour plate examples based on authentic information kindly supplied by Alex Imrie.

© *Peter L. Gray, 1965*

KNOWN SERIAL NUMBERS

D III—1370/17 Vzfw, Hecht. Js. 10; 1386/17 Ltn. Lenz Js 22; 1395/17 Ltn. A. Heldmann Js 10; 4005/17 Ltn. von Hippel (trainer); 4009/17 Ltn. Kroll Staffelführer Js 24; 4010/17 Js 24; 4023/17 I Marine Feld Jasta; 4042/17 Ltn. Skauradzum Js 4; 4049/17 Flg. Riensberg Js 10; 4062/17 Uffz Lingenfelden Js 16; 4074/17 I Marine Feld Jasta; 4075/17 I Marine Feld Jasta; 4094/17 Js 24; 4095/17 Js 24; 4096 and 4098/17 I Marine Feld Jasta; 4107/17 Js 24; 4111/17 I Marine Feld Jasta; 4117/17 Ltn. A. Heldmann Js 10; 4169/17 II Marine Feld Jasta; 4184/17 captured.

SPECIFICATION

Manufacturer: Pfalz Flugzeug-Werke G.m.b.H., Speyer am Rhein.
Powerplant: 160 h.p. Mercedes D. III and 175/180 h.p. Mercedes D IIIa.
Dimensions: Span 9·4 m. (30 ft. 10$\frac{1}{8}$ in.), length 6·95 m. (27 ft. 9$\frac{3}{4}$ in.); height 2·67 m. (8 ft. 9$\frac{1}{8}$ in.); area 22·17 sq. m. (237·75 sq. ft.).
Weights: Empty 695 kg. (1,529 lb.); loaded 865 kg. (1,903 lb.) D III 4125/17. Empty 695 kg. (1,529 lb.); loaded 915 kg. (2,013 lb.) D IIIa 8143/17. Empty 725 kg. (1,595 lb.); loaded 905 kg. (1,991 lb.) D IIIa 8282/17. (Taken from weights painted on actual aircraft.)
Performance: Max. speed at 10,000 ft. 102·5 m.p.h., at 15,000 ft. 91·5 m.p.h. Climb to 5,000 ft. in 6 min., to 15,000 ft. in 41 min. 20 sec. (Captured aircraft D III 4184/17.)
Max. speed 165 km. hr. (103·12 m.p.h.). Climb to 1,000 m. (3,280 ft.) in 3·25 min., to 2,000 m. (6,560 ft.) in 7·25 min., to 3,000 m. (9,840 ft.) in 11·75 min. (Comparative German figures.)
Pfalz D IIIa 5935/17 at a loaded weight of 911 kg. (2,004 lb.) made test climb to 5,000 m. (16,400 ft.) in 33 min. on 4th Feb. 1918.
Endurance: 2 to 2$\frac{1}{2}$ hours.
Armament: Twin fixed Spandau machine guns firing forward, each with 500 rounds of ammunition.

PRINTED IN ENGLAND. © Profile Publications Ltd., P.O. Box 26, Leatherhead, Surrey, England, by George Falkner & Sons Ltd., for McCorquodale City Printing Division, London.

PROFILE
PUBLICATIONS

The
Fairey
IIIF

NUMBER   131

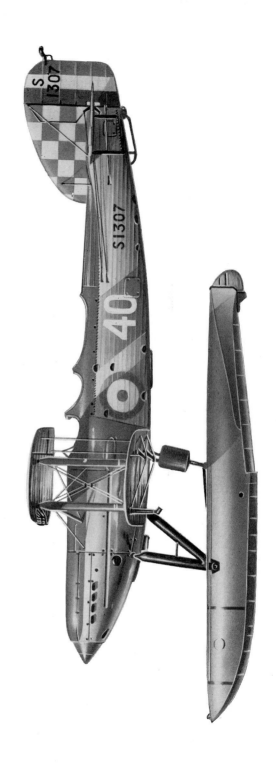

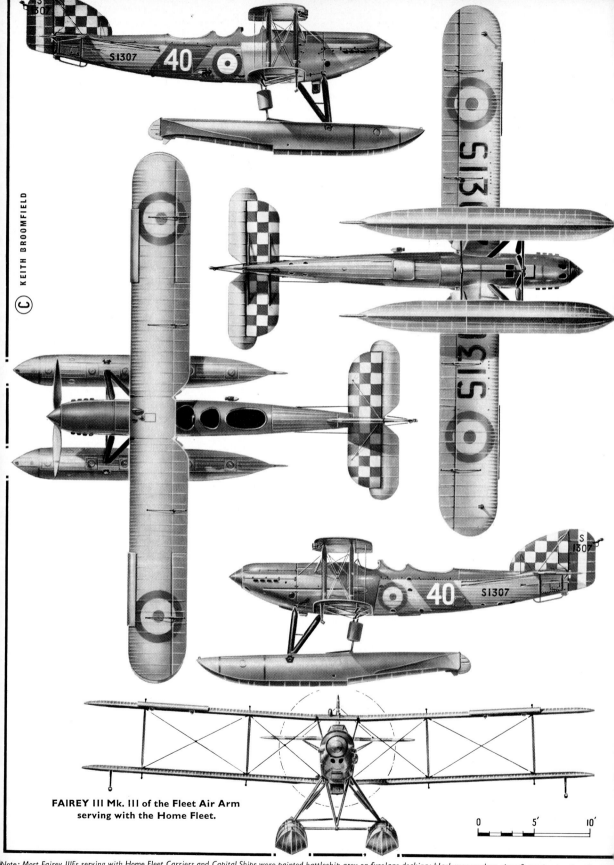

KEITH BROOMFIELD Ⓒ

**FAIREY III Mk. III of the Fleet Air Arm
serving with the Home Fleet.**

0   5′   10′

Note: Most Fairey IIIFs serving with Home Fleet Carriers and Capital Ships were painted battleship grey on fuselage decking: black was used on aircraft serving in other theatres

The Fairey IIIF

by Francis K. Mason

Fairey IIIF, Mk. III, of No. 824 Squadron, Fleet Air Arm.

"Och, but yon box o' bolts ha' gone fair since Kaiser Wullie's War" . . . immortal words attributed to an exasperated N.C.O. charged with the maintenance of a decrepit two-bay biplane struggling over the English countryside with an anti-aircraft target fluttering some 400 yards astern . . . in 1941.

The aircraft, *K1726*, was one of three Fairey IIIF Mk. IVBs still on Air Ministry Charge with No. 2 A.A.C.U. in February 1941, sole flying remnants of a basic design that had commenced way back, indeed, before the end of the Kaiser's War.

Developed as a landplane from the Fairey N.20 twin-float seaplane, the Fairey IIIA of 1917 was a two-bay equal-span biplane of wooden construction intended for fleet reconnaissance duties, operating from carrier decks. Fifty (*N2850–2899*) were built but few were delivered to the Home Fleet before the Armistice, and the type was withdrawn in 1919.

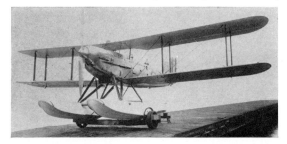

The first prototype IIIF, N198, as flown by Capt. Macmillan. Note the old horn-type arrester gear on the wheel axle.
(Photo: Ministry of Defence)

The first prototype at Hamble equipped with twin-float gear, and first flown with such on 20th April 1926.
(Photo: Capt. N. Macmillan)

The Fairey IIIB, like its precursor, was powered by a 260-h.p. Sunbeam Maori II but was a float-equipped bomber capable of carrying up to 250 pounds of bombs. Resorting to conventions of W.W.I. seaplane design, the IIIB was fitted with a top wing of considerably greater span than that of the lower. Thirty (*N2230–N2259*) were ordered and a small number was serving at Eastchurch and Felixstowe at the time of the Armistice.

Although built in far smaller numbers than the more famous Short floatplanes of the W.W.I. era, the Fairey seaplanes were very popular and it was through the medium of the Fairey Hamble Baby, the Campania and IIIs that Fairey Aviation embarked on a period of more than forty years of close association with the Admiralty and the continuous supply of aircraft to the Royal Naval Air Service and the Fleet Air Arm. By reason of the very exacting nature of shipboard duties and operation, Fairey aeroplanes have perhaps not been among the world's most exotic aerial creations, yet they came to be regarded with a touching affection by their many thousands of aircrew members down those forty years.

Reversion to equal span wings came in the Fairey IIIC, one example of which was delivered to the Great Yarmouth Royal Naval Air Station a few days before the Armistice. This was once again a three-float seaplane; that is to say that the aircraft was supported on the water by two main floats and a tail float. Sponson floats were attached under the lower wing tips for balancing during taxiing turns. Five aircraft were converted from IIIBs and a further thirty (*N9230–N9259*) were newly built during 1919 for active service with the North Russian Expeditionary Force. Carried to Archangel aboard H.M.S. *Pegasus*, IIICs carried out a number of raids on Bolshevik forces, but it is not known with what British unit they operated.

The IIIC was the first of the series to be powered by the Rolls-Royce Eagle, a 375-h.p. Mk. VIII being installed. The wing structure and planform of this aircraft remained essentially unaltered for fifteen years and was adopted by the next two variants, the IIID and IIIF. Bearing a marked resemblance to the IIIC, the prototype IIIC, *N9450*, was designed in 1919 and first flown by Col. Vincent Nicholl in August 1920 at

Hamble. It was at that time referred to as a IIIC (Improved), and the following 49 aircraft were delayed pending approval of a new Specification, 38/22. All told, 207 IIIDs were built for the Fleet Air Arm serving with the Home Fleet, the Mediterranean Fleet, on the China Station, and with No. 202 Squadron of the Royal Air Force. Later IIIDs were powered by the 450-h.p. Napier Lion IIB, V and VA, and many naval shore establishments possessed one or two wheel-equipped IIIDs. IIIDs also accompanied a task force sent to Shanghai aboard H.M.S. *Argus* in 1927 to safeguard British interests from the attentions of rebel Chinese forces.

Developments in deck operation during the mid 'twenties were slow in materialising. Up to 1926, aircraft were fitted with wheel axle hooks which engaged longitudinal deck wires. This system slowed the aircraft until it arrived at the lift—left "sunk" a few inches below deck level—on which it was lowered to the deck below. Another system used in conjunction with the longitudinal wires, incorporated wooden flaps, raised to halt the aircraft. As the result of countless broken undercarriages, both procedures were discontinued in 1926 and for several years decks were cleared for "unarrested" landings. New undercarriage design requirements were thus foreshadowed in 1925, by which time the Napier Lion engine had begun to display better compatibility with naval rigours and demands than the Eagle—prompting Faireys to set about a redesign of the IIID.

The new prototype *N198*—the IIIF—was first flown by Captain Norman Macmillan at Northolt on 19th March 1926. The flight, lasting 28 minutes, was carried out with ballast in lieu of second crew member, but the following day Capt. Macmillan took his wife with him—surely ample testimony to the pilot's satisfaction with the new design! This aircraft was the first British design to incorporate in the undercarriage a landing vertical descent rate of 12 ft/sec., for so many years the standard demanded for deck undercarriages. With finely cowled Lion engine and smoothly contoured fuselage the IIIF displayed a classic refinement of the old slab-sided IIID.

After 4 hr. 17 min. flying at Northolt, Macmillan delivered *N198* to Hamble, Avro's old airfield bordering Southampton Water, where the aircraft was converted to a seaplane by the addition of twin metal floats made by Fairey's. In this guise the prototype was again flown by Macmillan on 20th April 1926 from Hamble river.

Apart from the Hawker Hart variants, the Fairey IIIF was built in greater numbers than any other British military aircraft between the World Wars until the Hurricane was ordered in 1936. The IIIF Marks

Capt. Norman Macmillan, M.C., A.F.C., Chief Test Pilot, Fairey Aviation Co. Ltd., who tested the IIIF prototype landplane and floatplane. (Photo: Fairey Aviation Co. Ltd.)

I to III were three-seaters destined for the Fleet Air Arm, whereas the R.A.F.'s* version, the Mark IV was a two-seater. A total of 352 of the former and 243 of the latter was built for the British forces (in addition to a small number for export) between 1926 and 1932.

R.A.F. SERVICE

Anomalous within the Fairey IIIF designation, the R.A.F. Mark IV appeared in service *before* the naval versions. This was because the Air Ministry Specification 19/24 was in two parts, the first calling up a two-seat land-based general purpose aircraft to replace the Bristol Fighter in service with overseas R.A.F. Squadrons. Featuring composite construction, i.e. metal fuselage and wooden wings (the whole fabric-covered), the first IIIFs (*J9053–J9077*) to enter R.A.F. service were Mk. IVCs shipped to No. 47 (General Purpose) Squadron at Khartoum, replacing aged Brisfits. Station Commander at Khartoum was Air Commodore C. R. Samson, and this officer led the Squadron in the 1927 Cairo–Cape Town return training flight, a tradi-

* For ease of reference the terms R.A.F. and F.A.A. are used here to distinguish between the traditional land-based air force and the naval air arm of the Royal Navy, though of course throughout the period of Fairey IIIF's main service the Fleet Air Arm was manned and administered almost exclusively under the aegis of the Air Ministry by R.A.F. Officers and Other Ranks.

Early IIIF Mk. IVs of a home squadron (believed No. 35). Most of the aircraft display the angular fin and are ex-naval stock. (Photo: Ministry of Defence)

Early IIIFs of a Middle East Squadron flying over the desert. Note the black anti-glare decking adopted by overseas units.
(Photo: Ministry of Defence)

tional goodwill sortie undertaken in turn by R.A.F. squadrons based in the Middle East. No. 47 was among the few amphibious squadrons in the R.A.F. and in 1929 received a number of IIIF floatplanes which operated from the Nile at Khartoum.

With the transition to metal construction taking place in the R.A.F. in 1927, the next batch of 43 IIIFs consisted of an assortment of composite aircraft. Of these, *J9132–J9139* were referred to as IIIF Mark IVCM in which wooden fuselage stringers were added to the metal fuselage primary structure, and IIIF Mark IVM (*J9140–J9174*) in which the entire structure except the tail ribs was of metal. Most of these aircraft were delivered during 1928 to No. 207 (Bomber) Squadron at Eastchurch, though by then some aircraft (IIIF Mark Is) had been transferred from Fleet Air Arm stocks to make up unit establishment.

From mid-1928 to about 1930 the principal R.A.F. variant of the IIIF was the Mark IVM, though another sub-variant, the Mark IVM/A, appeared in

Showing the flag—literally. A photo taken in late 'thirties during a visit by an R.A.F. IIIF squadron to South Africa on a goodwill tour. This shows the Squadron Commander being met by a booted and spurred staff officer. Note the R.A.F. ensign aft of the cockpit and the coloured fin. (Photo: Ministry of Defence)

Another goodwill visit by No. 47 Squadron in the Middle East. Late series fins are fitted and the nearest aircraft (the Flight Leader's aeroplane) carries wing pennants.
(Photo: Ministry of Defence)

January 1930 with the entire structure of metal (including tail ribs).

The only other operational home-based IIIF-equipped R.A.F. squadron was No. 35 (Bomber) Squadron which was re-formed at Bircham Newton with D.H.9As in January 1929. In November that year these venerable aeroplanes were joined and eventually replaced by IIIF Mark IVM (GP)s. This squadron was among those that performed the annual set-piece "bombing" at the 1930 Hendon Air Display.

Overseas, however, IIIFs of the R.A.F. wrote themselves a fine piece of Imperial history, ranging across the Middle East and African skies on long training flights over scarcely-mapped desert. No. 47 Squadron again performed the 1928 and 1929 Cairo–Cape Town flights but in 1930 the flight was made by IIIFs of No. 14 (Bomber) Squadron based at Amman in Transjordan.

Three other overseas G.P. squadrons of the R.A.F. flew IIIFs; they were No. 8 Squadron at Khormaksar, Aden (whose aircraft were flown from Aden to Cairo and back in 1932, the flight being led by Sqdn. Ldr. Ralph Sorley); No. 45, who flew IIIFs between September 1929 and February 1936 from Helwan in Egypt, and No. 202 who operated IIIF floatplanes from Kalafrana, Malta.

A final R.A.F. G.P. variant of the IIIF appeared in the Hayes factory in 1930; this was the IIIF Mark IVB, commencing *K1697*, of which 62 examples were built. No precise definition of the IVB exists, and no hard and fast external distinction is made in contemporary handbooks. It was of all-metal construction, possessed naval landing-strength undercarriage mounting points, strongpoints for bomb rack attachments and was strengthened for catapulting. These and other variations were also, however, to be found in previous versions.

It may be of interest to mention briefly the process adopted in supplying IIIFs to the R.A.F. overseas. Most aircraft, on leaving Hayes, were taken on charge by the R.A.F. between 1927 and 1932 at No. 1 Aircraft Storage Unit at Henlow. Thence, if destined for Home Squadrons, the aircraft would be delivered to their bases; but if for overseas destination, the IIIFs were flown to the aircraft Despatch Unit at Sealand where they were crated up for shipment to the A.S.U. at Aboukir. Here they were assembled and either held for training with No. 4 A.F.S. or delivered to squadrons throughout the Middle East. Almost all repair work was carried out at Aboukir, as were the

IIIF Mk. IVs of No. 45 (Bomber) Squadron flying from their Egyptian base at Helwan in 1931. The diagonal fin stripe was vari-coloured according to flight allocation. The hazards of those policing duties are well suggested by the terrain shown in this photograph.
(Photo: Ministry of Defence)

considerable repair programmes. Many IIIFs came to be rebuilt at Aboukir as Fairey Gordons, the principal alterations being to the tail unit and the replacement of engine by a 525-h.p. Armstrong-Siddeley Panther IIA.

Many famous R.A.F. bomber pilots served on IIIF squadrons between the wars; perhaps the best-known, Sir Arthur Harris ("Bomber" Harris of W.W.II fame), as a Wing Commander, in 1932 led a long-range training flight of IIIFs from Heliopolis in Egypt down East Africa and back. H.R.H. the Prince of Wales used a IIIF on No. 24 (Communications) Squadron for many of his official excursions from Northolt, and was intercepted by Siskin fighters during the course of the 1930 Air Defence Exercises.

NAVAL SERVICE

It was undoubtedly in naval service that the IIIF provided the most significant contribution to British aviation history between the wars. Apart from serving with every British aircraft carrier of its day (namely H.M. Carriers *Glorious, Courageous, Eagle, Furious, Hermes* and *Argus*), it equipped the battleship *Valiant*, the battlecruiser *Hood*, and the cruisers

York, Exeter, Norfolk and *Dorsetshire*, and it served on every naval air station from Lee-on-Solent to the Shanghai racecourse.

Though the first IIIFs first entered R.A.F. squadron service in December 1927, deliveries into naval storage at Gosport commenced before the end of 1926. The aircraft carried a 3-man crew—R.A.F. pilot, naval observer and R.A.F. W/T operator/air gunner—and differed from the earlier IIID in having a "stepped" line to the top of the tail in place of the traditional straight line of previous Fairey aircraft. This outline, formed by the horn balance of the rudder, was retained in early IIIFs, but in late 1927 the familiar smooth elliptic curve was introduced. Some early machines were later retro-modified.

The first ten IIIFs built were in reality IIIDs adapted to meet the requirements of Spec. 19/24, though the later designation applied. These IIIFs (S1139–S1148) were delivered to Gosport during the winter of 1926–27 and were used for training purposes, some later being transferred to home-based R.A.F. units. S1147 was returned to Hayes for modification to two-seat layout and with this became the prototype for the R.A.F.'s General Purpose variant. S1148 was used for unarrested deck landing trials aboard H.M.S. *Furious* in 1927.

First true IIIFs were Mark Is, S1168–A1182, powered by Lion VA engines, the first of the batch being flown by Capt. Macmillan on 18th February 1927. Production of 32 Mark IIs at the Hayes factory got under way during the same year, these being

Illustrating the practice of identifying rebuilt aircraft, this IIIF was the fifth production aircraft (of the original naval contract), was rebuilt as a two-seater, issued to the R.A.F. and re-registered SR1143.
(Photo: Ministry of Defence)

Veteran of many itinerant demonstrations, G-AABY, was entered in the 1934 England–Australia race and flown by Fg. Off. C. D. Davies and Lt-Cdr. C. N. Hill. (Photo: John W. Caler collection)

With guns omitted, S1847 was converted from IIIF Mk. III standard to IIIF (DC) standard. Seen here at Martlesham Heath, this dual-control trainer was evaluated for the Fleet Air Arm—evidenced by the jury strut necessary for wing folding. Significance of the "H" on the fin is not known but may be a relic of a previous unit. Below: S1847, frontal view. (Photos: Ministry of Defence)

fitted with the Lion XI.

While these variants had been developed, the second prototype, *N225*, had undergone considerable modification, being built with all-metal structure thus becoming the Mark III prototype. Production changes to all-metal construction and adoption of the Lion XIA delayed the Mark III, the first production example of which did not fly until 26th March 1929. The Mark III was the most widely-used naval variant, 269 being built; two sub-variants, the IIIF Mark III (DC) dual-control trainer (10 built, *S1454–S1463*) and the Mk. IIIB (79 built, *S1474–S1552*) with strengthened fuselage for catapulting, were also produced.

Although stocks of IIIFs had grown at naval storage units during 1927, it was not until the following year that they entered operational service with the F.A.A. Between 1928 and 1932 IIIFs formed the equipment of twelve Flights, replacing IIIDs on No. 440, 441, 442, 443 and 444 Flights, Avro Bisons on Nos. 447 and 448, Blackburn Blackburns on Nos. 449 and 450, and Blackburn Ripons on No. 460 Flight aboard H.M.S. *Glorious* in the Mediterranean. IIIFs were also supplied to Nos. 445 and 446 Flights as initial equip-

ment. These Flights commenced merging from April 1933, No. 450 Flight becoming No. 820 Squadron; 442 and 449 merged to form No. 822 Squadron, 441 and 448 to become No. 823; 440 and 460 became 825. Of these squadrons, No. 822 in H.M.S. *Furious* kept its IIIFs longest—until 1936—and the IIIF Mark III was not declared obsolete until January 1940. At least one F.A.A. target tug was still airworthy at Hong Kong when the island was attacked by Japan on 8th December 1941. (Reference has been made in several books to IIIFs surviving in Ceylon, Madras, Aden and elsewhere in the Middle East well into W.W.II, but Admiralty and Air Ministry records suggest that the aircraft in question were Fairey Seals and Gordons—direct developments of the IIIF.)

No mention of naval IIIFs should be made without association with C. S. Staniland. Chris Staniland, with Norman Macmillan, performed almost all the manufacturers' development flying between 1928 and 1931; it was Staniland who first flew the IIIF Mark IIIB on 6th June 1930 and went on to do much of the rigorous catapult trials on this variant. Mark IIIBs were issued in seaplane form as well as with wheel undercarriage to the F.A.A., and served on Capital Ships of the Royal Navy until replaced by Hawker Ospreys during 1933. No fewer than eight IIIFs were

Above: *Launching a IIIF on the Nile at Khartoum, May 1930* (Photo: Capt. Norman Macmillan). Below: *Float-equipped IIIFs of No. 47 (Bomber) Squadron in flight during a visit to Malta during the early 'thirties.* (Photo: Ministry of Defence)

Above: *IIIF Mk. IVM floatplanes on the Nile. The second aircraft carries the flight colour on its fin. Note also the variations on float structure.* Below: *IIIF Mk. IVs at Khartoum. (In the picture the farthest aircraft is a Fairey Seal floatplane carrying flight leader's fin colours.)*

(Photos: Ministry of Defence)

J9061 *of No. 24* (Communications) *Squadron at Northolt. This aircraft was used to fly many V.I.P.s round R.A.F. units and featured a special two-seat cockpit layout.*
(Photo: Ministry of Defence)

allocated to H.M. Cruiser *York* and five to H.M.S. *Exeter* (later of River Plate fame).

An interesting development of the IIIF was the Fairie Queen. Three such aircraft were modified as radio-controlled aeroplanes with automatic pilot; one of these was shipped to Gibraltar where it served as a target for guns of the Mediterranean Fleet. Various R.N.A.S. at home and overseas also used target-towing IIIFs with windmill-winches on the port side.

Although as already stated, the IIIF was not declared obsolete with the F.A.A. until 1940, they were never considered to be as of "first line" combat effectiveness after the introduction of the Seal and Osprey. Being without arrester gear after the introduction of the transverse deck wires undoubtedly led to slower deck handling owing to the need to recover IIIFs from "all over the flight deck". Although a small number of IIIFs were fitted with arrester hooks, longeron strengthening was necessary and proved more trouble than it was worth.

S1317, *a IIIF Mk. III, was one of several examples used for catapult trials with the Catapult Flight at Leuchars.*
(Photo: Ministry of Defence)

Launching a IIIF seaplane on the slipway at Lee-on-Solent.
(Photo: via John W. Caler)

IIIFs IN MUFTI

Three IIIFs carried civil markings between 1928 and the mid 'thirties. The first, *G-AABY*, in common with the products of almost every manufacturer during the inter-war years, was a demonstration aircraft specially prepared by the Fairey Aviation Company in 1928–29. After having performed demonstration flights during the 1929 Olympia Aero Show it gave displays in Belgium, Austria, Yugoslavia and Greece in 1930; in the latter country it was converted to a seaplane for demonstration flights. Later it was shipped out to China for demonstration but was damaged and had to be returned home. Rebuilt at North Weald in 1934, it was entered in the handicap section of the MacRobertson Race to Australia, flown by Fg. Off. C. D. Davies and navigated by Lt.-Cdr. C. N. Hill. Trouble dogged the old biplane but, although retired from the Race, it arrived in Australia under its own power; thereafter it was sold (in 1935 as *VH-UTT*) and finally faded into obscurity in the New Guinea goldfields.

The two other civil IIIFs were *G-AASK* and *G-AATT*, powered by Armstrong-Siddeley Jaguar VIC radial engines, and were purchased by Air Survey Co., Ltd., for survey work in the Sudan. Both were delivered during 1930, but *G-ATTT* was written off before the end of the year. *G-AASK* survived until 1934 after having performed yeoman service in the unexciting task of aerial mapping.

FLYING THE IIIF

A number of pilots recall flying the IIIF as being a "gentlemanly pursuit", rather as one might talk of following hounds on horseback. Like the horse, the IIIF certainly outlived other modes of transport. It was immensely strong and though it lacked the power to allow tight turns without loss of height, there is no record of a IIIF's wings failing in the air. In fact, the extraordinary strength of the undercarriage was the undoing of many an unwary pilot who, perhaps used to "banging the thing down" on firm grass airfields at home, simply sank axle-deep in the desert airfield sand when trying the same expedient in the Middle East. The IIIF was unforgiving and simply executed a smart *tête-bêche* to the accompaniment of flying sand and much bending of propeller blades.

Perhaps the most oft-repeated remark among pilots' reflections was that relating to the feeling that

A IIIF (Intermediate) of a Fleet Air Arm home shore establishment in flight over the Tay Bridge. (Photo: Ministry of Defence)

one was in the middle of a very large aeroplane, remote from the engine, with wings and struts and things stretching a very long way away. In the F.A.A. the IIIF was a much-liked aeroplane, its very low deck-approach speed of 44 knots bestowing almost viceless landing-on characteristics; indeed when *Glorious* or *Courageous* steamed into a fifteen knot wind, they "took some catching up". Thus landing without arrester gear was scarcely the dangerous pursuit it may have sounded.

The unkindest task was unquestionably to fly the IIIF with a gunnery target in tow. Apart from the fact that the airspeed seldom achieved 80 m.p.h., target sorties usually dragged on for upwards of five hours, unless a lucky short attained its mark and removed the target. But the length of the IIIF's fuselage being buffeted by the slipstream of an over-revving Lion engine gave rise to what was known among staff pilots at Sutton Bridge as "Three-F Buttock", a painful affliction caused by correcting the interminable twitching of the fuselage in sympathy with a piece of canvas trailing a quarter-mile astern.

Infinitely more objective are Capt. Norman Macmillan's recollections of the IIIF:

". . . All her air controls were powerful, and although she had no stagger (to allow for ease of wing folding), her longitudinal stability was excellent owing to her

long fuselage moment with ample tail and elevator surfaces. She carried rudder in flight and this could not be trimmed as no trimmer was fitted; yet I had no difficulty in leaving Northolt one day in London fog and cloud, and climbing up through the murk without blind flying instruments.

"I liked the Lion V; it was freer from vibration than the later up-rated Lions, and it ran very smoothly with the Fairey-Reed metal propeller.

"She was very easy to fly as a floatplane, with excellent water stability and good control even in quite strong winds. Take-off from the water was easy, almost but not quite automatic from the hydroplaning condition, only a slight rear pressure on the controls needed to unstick.

"Aerobatically the IIIF landplane was surprisingly good. She looped with ease. She spun fast, with swift entry when deliberately stalled and ruddered, but she recovered quickly. Floatplane spins were different and at least 1,500 feet altitude above the sea were needed in which to recover level flight.

"When IIIFs were later fitted with Handley Page slots, I found that flight near the stall possessed improved lateral stability, but I also found that it was still possible to spin the landplane, although entry was more difficult. When she did spin, she spun even faster with slots and I found that she spun with one slot open and the other

In the twilight of its front-line life, the IIIF suffered the customary relegation to the indignity of target towing. S1836, seen here under trial at the Marine Aircraft Establishment, Felixstowe, is reported to have possessed a maximum towing speed of 68 knots (TAS) when equipped with floats! Just visible is the wind-driven winch on the port side of centre cockpit.
(Photo: Ministry of Defence)

A float-equipped Fairey IIIF Mk. IIIB—surely one of the most unwieldy designations ever applied to a military aeroplane!
(Photo: Ministry of Defence)

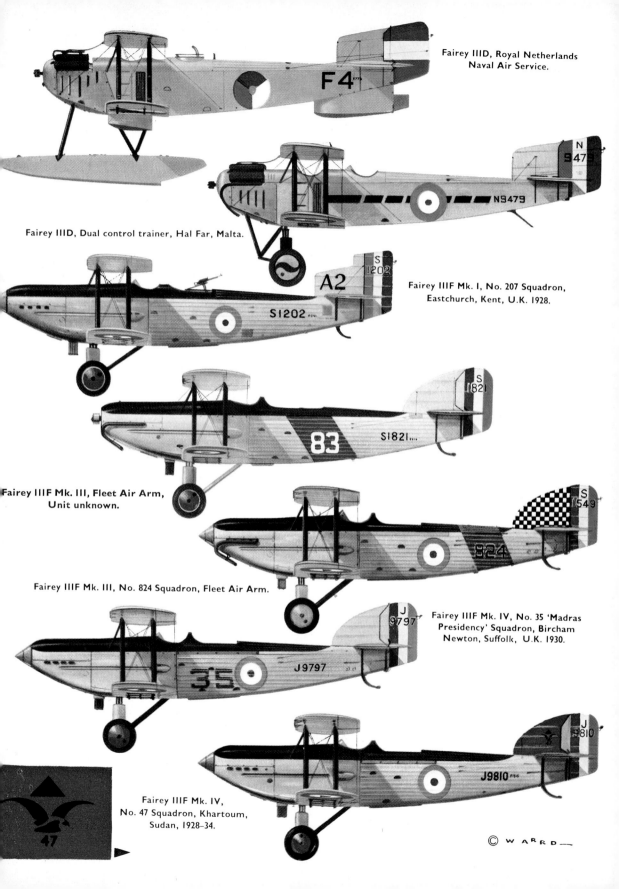

Fairey IIID, Royal Netherlands
Naval Air Service.

Fairey IIID, Dual control trainer, Hal Far, Malta.

Fairey IIIF Mk. I, No. 207 Squadron,
Eastchurch, Kent, U.K. 1928.

Fairey IIIF Mk. III, Fleet Air Arm,
Unit unknown.

Fairey IIIF Mk. III, No. 824 Squadron, Fleet Air Arm.

Fairey IIIF Mk. IV, No. 35 'Madras
Presidency' Squadron, Bircham
Newton, Suffolk, U.K. 1930.

Fairey IIIF Mk. IV,
No. 47 Squadron, Khartoum,
Sudan, 1928–34.

© W ARRD

Fairey IIIF Mk. III of the Fleet Air Arm serving with the Home Fleet.

Shown here at Calshot—the traditional Mecca of British sea-going aeroplanes—is the first production Fairey IIIF (DC) trainer equipped with floats. (Photo: Ministry of Defence)

closed. It was more difficult to recover from a spin when slots were fitted; more control had to be applied and the recovery was a good deal slower.

"Negative flap gave slightly faster speed when flying full out level, chiefly because it altered the fuselage angle slightly, and probably reduced the drag due to the open rear cockpits. Minus 2 degrees flap was best for top speed, plus 4 degrees for take-off and plus 8 for landing."

The IIIF was a memorable aeroplane, remembered with affection by many. One elderly senior R.A.F. Officer publicly attributed his long life and blameless service to the successive tours spent in flying "the ever-present, innocuous and entirely tractable IIIF". That great airman, Charles Lindbergh, on a visit to England in the late 'twenties when he flew a IIIF from Northolt, recorded otherwise, "A cavernous cockpit filled with nothing but smell and noise and me, supported by great shuddering wings strung together with random struts and wires and string. The engine sounded somehow as if it had been running since the beginning of time, but that it would go on until the end." *Sic transit gloria!*

© *Francis K. Mason, 1965.*

FAIREY IIIF PRODUCTION

Two prototypes built to Spec. 19/24, *N198* and *N225*.
Naval versions: S1139–S1148, 10 aircraft, IIIF early standard. S1168–S1207, 40 aircraft, IIIF Mark I; S1208–S1227, 20 aircraft, IIIF Mark II; S1250–S1262, 13 aircraft, IIIF Mark II; S1303–S1356, 54 aircraft, IIIF Mark III; S1370–S1408, 39 aircraft, IIIF (Intermediate); S1454–S1463, 10 aircraft, IIIF (DC) trainers; S1474–S1552, 79 aircraft, III Mark IIIB; S1779–S1865, 87 aircraft, IIIF Mark III, replacements. Total naval production, 352 aircraft.
R.A.F. versions: J9053–J9077, 25 aircraft, IIIF Mark IVM; J9132–J9174, 43 aircraft, IIIF Mark IVM (G.P.); J9637–J9681, 45 aircraft, IIIF Mark IVM; J9784–J9831, 48 aircraft, IIIF Mark IV (G.P.); K1115–K1121, 7 aircraft, IIIF Mark IV M/A; K1158–K1170, 13 aircraft, IIIF Mark IV M/A (G.P.); K1697–K1720, 24 aircraft, IIIF Mark IVB (G.P.); K1721–K1728, 8 aircraft, IIIF Mark IVB; K1749–K1778, 30 aircraft, IIIF Mark IVB, replacements. Total R.A.F. production, 243 aircraft.

SERVICE ALLOCATION AND OTHER NOTES

Representative allocation to R.A.F. units

No. 8 (Bomber) Squadron, Khormaksar, 1932–33—*J9143, J9664, J9665, K1119, K1121.*
No. 35 (Bomber) Squadron, Bircham Newton, 1930—*J9171, J9784, J9785, J9821, J9822.*
No. 45 (Bomber) Squadron, Helwan, Egypt, 1930–36—*J9640* (crashed 4/1/36), *J9658, J9659, J9660.*
No. 47 (Bomber) Squadron, Khartoum—*J9153, J9796, J9802, J9809.*
No. 207 (Bomber) Squadron, Eastchurch, 1929—*J9136, J9147, J9651, K1166, K1699.*
No. 1 F.T.S., 1963—*K1752, K1754.*
No. 2 F.T.S., 1933—*K1774.*
No. 4 F.T.S., 1934—*J9172,* 1936—*K1759;* 1941—*K1162.*
No. 14 Squadron, N.O.U.E. *—*J9812, J9813, J9819.*
Central Flying School, 1931—*K1168.*

Armament Practice Camp, Sutton Bridge, 1934—*K1774.*
Anti-Aircraft School, 1933—*J9681.*
Armament and Gunnery School, 1931—*K1159, K1163.*
No. 2 Anti-Aircraft Co-operation Unit, 1938—*K1726* (S.O.C. 10/3/41).
No. 603 (City of Edinburgh) Squadron, A.A.F., 1937—*K1752.*
Other Notes: Aircraft rebuilt as Gordons—*J9161, J9174, J9642* (crashed 3/2/36), *J9648, J9651, J9785, J9788, J9801, J9963, K1715* (sold to New Zealand, 1939); *J9154* referred to as IIIF Mark V, and thus Gordon prototype. *J9173* fitted with Rolls-Royce F.XI engine, 10/28.

*Not on Unit Establishment.

Naval Units equipped with IIIFs.

No. 440 Flight, H.M.S. *Hermes,* China Station.
No. 441 Flight, H.M.S. *Argus,* China Station; H.M.S. *Glorious,* Mediterranean Fleet.
No. 442 Flight H.M.S. *Furious,* Home Fleet, and R.N.A.S. Gosport.
No. 443 Flight, R.N.A.S. Lee-on-Solent; H.M.S. *Furious,* Home Fleet; Catapult Flight, West Indies and South Africa.
No. 444 Flight, R.N.A.S. Lee-on-Solent; Catapult Flight, Home Fleet (Capital Ships).
No. 445 Flight, H.M.S. *Courageous,* Mediterranean and Home Fleets.
No. 446 Flight, H.M.S. *Courageous,* Mediterranean and Home Fleets.
No. 447 Flight, H.M.S. *Furious,* Home Fleet; H.M.S. *Glorious,* Mediterranean Fleet; 1st Cruiser Squadron and Capital Ships, Mediterranean Fleet.
No. 448 Flight, H.M.S. *Eagle* and *Glorious,* Mediterranean Fleet.
No. 449 Flight, H.M.S. *Courageous* and *Furious,* Home Fleet.
No. 450 Flight, H.M.S. *Courageous,* Home Fleet.
No. 460 Flight, H.M.S. *Glorious,* Mediterranean Fleet.
No. 820 Squadron, H.M.S. *Courageous,* Home Fleet.
No. 822 Squadron, H.M.S. *Furious,* Home Fleet.
No. 823 Squadron, H.M.S. *Glorious,* Mediterranean Fleet.
No. 824 Squadron, H.M.S. *Eagle,* Mediterranean Fleet.
No. 825 Squadron, H.M.S. *Glorious.* Mediterranean Fleet.

SPECIFICATION

Fairey IIIF Mark IIIB and IV (in brackets)
General description: 3-seat naval spotter reconnaissance aircraft (2-seat General Purpose bomber).
Powerplant: 570-h.p. Napier Lion XIA (570-h.p. Napier Lion XIA) driving 2-blade Fairey Reed fixed-pitch metal propeller.
Dimensions: Span 45 ft. 9 in. (45 ft. 9 in.); length 34 ft. 4 in. (36 ft. 8⅝ in.); height 14 ft. 2¾ in. (14 ft. 2¾ in.); wing area 443·5 sq. ft. (438·5 sq. ft.).
Weights: Empty 3,923 lb. (3,790 lb.); loaded 6,301 lb. (6,041 lb.).
Performance: Maximum speed 120 m.p.h. (120 m.p.h.) at 10,000 ft.; climb 6·4 minutes (6·0 minutes) to 5,000 ft.
Armament: (same for both versions) one fixed forward-firing synchronised Vickers Mark 1 0·303-in. machine gun on port side of nose; provision for Lewis gun on Scarff ring or Fairey high-speed mounting on gunner's cockpit. Provision for up to 500 pounds of bombs under wings.

PRINTED IN ENGLAND. © Profile Publications Ltd., P.O. Box 26, Leatherhead, Surrey, England, by George Falkner & Sons Ltd., for McCorquodale City Printing Division, London.

PROFILE
PUBLICATIONS

The
Curtiss
Army
Hawks

NUMBER 45

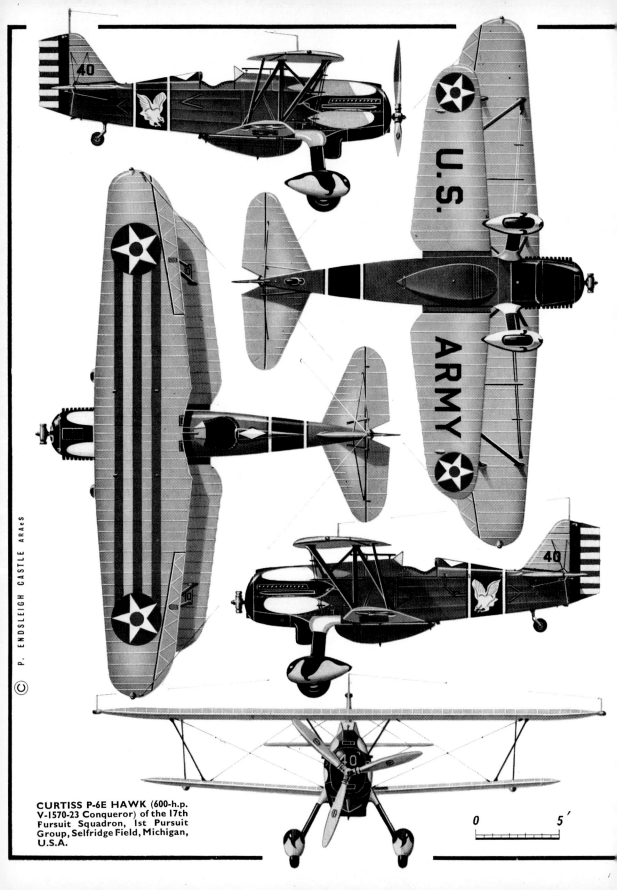

© P. ENDSLEIGH CASTLE ARAeS

CURTISS P-6E HAWK (600-h.p.
V-1570-23 Conqueror) of the 17th
Pursuit Squadron, 1st Pursuit
Group, Selfridge Field, Michigan,
U.S.A.

0   5'

The Curtiss Army Hawks

by Peter M. Bowers

P-6E of the 17th Pursuit Squadron, Selfridge Field, Michigan, showing the unique black and white "Snow Owl" markings

The Curtiss "Hawk", built by the Curtiss Aeroplane & Motor Company of Buffalo and Garden City, New York, is one of the most famous biplane fighter designs of the years between the two world wars. This graceful machine was in production for over a decade —a remarkably long life for a fighter of that period, and in its major production versions, P-1 and P-6, the "Hawk" was first-line equipment in the U.S. Army Air Service and the later Army Air Corps. Similar models served the U.S. Navy as F6C-1 to FC6-4 and considerably revised later models appeared in the fleet as F11C-2/BFC-2 and BF2C-1. Export models of all versions, some of which survived to the end of W.W.II, were sold abroad under a variety of factory-assigned "Hawk" designations. However, only the U.S. Army models are described in this *Profile*.

Because of the Army procurement policy of the time, under which the principal service aircraft types were procured from two different manufacturers, the "Hawks" did not enjoy a monopoly of the fighter rôle (this was called "Pursuit" from W.W.I until 1948, as shown in the "P-for-Pursuit" designation of the airplanes). They shared the limelight with their contemporaries, the Boeing PW-9s and P-12s, which outnumbered them slightly. However, due largely to their tapered wings and the refined fuselage and undercarriage details of the later models, the "Hawk" is the more memorable design and by far the favourite of the model builders.

ORIGIN OF THE DESIGN

The Curtiss "Hawk" fighter was developed directly from the line of specialised racing planes that Curtiss built for the Army and Navy between 1921 and 1925, which included two winners of the Schneider Trophy Cup. The common feature of all the Curtiss racers was the powerplant. This was a compact, water-cooled, direct-drive V-12 design that had been introduced in 1918 as the Curtiss-Kirkham K-12. In its post-war production version it had a displacement of 1,150 cubic inches and developed 435 h.p. The racing versions were of course operated at much higher power, but contributed much to the standard service versions. Later versions were the short-lived V-1400 model and the famous V-1570 "Conqueror", a 600-h.p. model that served the "Hawks" and other U.S. Army aircraft from 1927 to the beginning of W.W.II. At the time the "Hawk" was introduced, engines were known only by their manufacturer's given designation. Both U.S. military services adopted a type and size designation in the middle 1920's. The D-12 became the V-1150 because of its basic Vee design and its 1,150 cubic inch displacement. The letter "R" identified the air-cooled radial design.

Another feature of the Curtiss racers that was adopted for the new fighter model that led to the "Hawk" was the unique low-drag wing surface radi-

*Unless indicated, all the photographs appearing in this Profile are part of the Peter M. Bowers collection.

Left: *The fourth production PW-8, 24-204. This is the machine used by Lt. Russell Maughan in his famous "Dawn-to-Dusk" flight from coast to coast on 23 June 1924.* Right: *The XPW-8A with its original centre section radiator.* (Photo: U.S.A.F.)

The XPW-8A became XPW-8B when fitted with new tapered wings. The long boom is part of the test equipment installed during tests at McCook Field.

ator. Instead of the traditional honeycomb placed at right angles to the airflow on the nose or the side of the fuselage, the surface radiators consisted of longitudinal thin-wall tubes approximately one-quarter inch in diameter laid flat on the top surface of the upper wing. One feature of the Curtiss racers that was not passed on to the fighters was the heavy laminated wood veneer fuselage.

Following the trend of the times, Curtiss broke away from traditional wire-braced wood truss fuselage construction when it developed its new biplane fighter for the Army in 1923. Three prototypes, with welded steel tube fuselages and one of the first divided-axle undercarriages, were ordered on 27th April 1923. These were designated PW-8, for Pursuit, Watercooled, Model 8, under a designation series that had originated in 1920. The supplemental prefix letter "X" was applied retroactively to the PW-8 prototypes after the desirability of distinguishing between prototype and production versions of the same design became apparent in 1924. Air Service serial numbers for the proto-

types were *23-1201* to *23-1203*. The "23" indicated the fiscal year of the contract, 1923, while "1201" was the 1,201st airplane ordered in that fiscal year (1st July 1922 to 30th June 1923).

There were relatively minor differences between the first two XPW-8s, and the 25 production versions (*24-201* to *24-225*) were generally similar to the second prototype. The third prototype was held back at the factory for completion with entirely new wings and a new cooling system. It had been recognised, even before the production models were built, that the surface-type radiators were a liability on a combat machine. Their large area made them highly vulnerable to damage by gunfire, and the terrific total length of tubing created a serious leakage problem. The PW-8s were an interesting mixture of the old and the new, as might be expected in the first new fighter design produced in quantity since the end of W.W.I. While the fuselage and undercarriage were entirely new and of steel construction, the wings were not only all wood but were of thin section that required

Left: *The first P-1 after being fitted with an experimental inverted and air-cooled Liberty engine. The number on the fuselage is for racing.* Right: *The sixth P-1B, A.C. 27-68, photographed at the factory.*

Left: *P-1B 27-84 of the 43rd School Squadron.* Right: *P-10, 27-92, 43rd Squadron, Kelly Field, Texas. Group insignia appears on the fin.*

The first P-2, fitted with a turbo-supercharger and redesignated XP-2.

a second bay of interplane struts for stiffening. The PW-8s were the only post-war U.S. fighters to use double bay wings.

THE "HAWK" APPEARS

The configuration of the "Hawk" began to take shape with the appearance of the third XPW-8, which was designated XPW-8A. The wings were straight, as on the PW-8s, but the skin radiators were replaced by a core type built into the upper wing centre section somewhat in the manner of W.W.I German Albatros' and similar types. Heavier spars produced stiffer structure, so only a single bay of struts was required. By the time the XPW-8A was undergoing test at McCook Field, Dayton, Ohio, where the Army Engineering Division was located, a competitive design had made its appearance. This was the Boeing XPW-9, which incorporated some interesting new features, notably tapered wings and a "tunnel" radiator installation located beneath the engine. Neither of these

features was new, even on an American design, both having been seen on the Army's own XPW-1 design of 1920. Boeing, however, brought them to a degree of perfection that made them very attractive. Since the XPW-8A showed relatively little improvement over the Basic PW-8 with the same straight wing, the Army asked Curtiss to try the new features on it—first the tunnel radiator and then the tapered wing. The final configuration, designated XPW-8B and delivered in March 1925, was highly successful and became the prototype of the entire "Hawk" line, which started with an order for 15 P-1 "Hawks" placed by the Army in 1925. The "PW" designation was dropped when a new "P-for-Pursuit" designation was adopted in 1924. However, since Boeing PW-9s were in production at the time, the designation was retained for that one model until production ended in 1928.

THE "HAWK" DEVELOPS

The following descriptions of U.S. Army "Hawk" air-

Left: *The first XP-3A with the fuselage contours filled out to meet the lines of the experimental NACA engine cowling.* Right: *XP-3A No. 2, a standard P-3A also fitted with experimental cowling.* (Photo: U.S.A.F.)

Left: *P-3A fitted with Townend anti-drag ring. Insignia is of Technical Training Command, Chanute Field, Rantoul, Illinois.* Right: *P-5, essentially a P-1A with a turbo-supercharger.*

The XAT-4, a P-1A fitted with a 180-h.p. Wright-Hispano engine and tested as an advanced trainer. (Photo: Curtiss)

AT-5A, structurally similar to the P-1B but fitted with a 220-h.p. Wright J-5 radial engine for use as an advanced trainer. Later converted to P-1E. (Photo: U.S.A.F.)

The XP-6 was a P-2 fitted with the new 600-h.p. Curtiss V-1570 "Conqueror" engine. (Photo: U.S.A.F.)

planes are presented in number and letter sequence of model designation, with "X" models being listed before "Production" models. Some modifications of early airplanes received late designations while the production versions of high-number prototypes sometimes used much lower numbers.

P-1—The only noticeable external difference between the XPW-8B and the P-1 was the addition of aerodynamic balance area to the rudder of the P-1. Armament was the U.S. standard of the time, a pair of ·30 calibre Browning machine guns synchronised to fire through the propeller with alternate provision for a single ·30 and one ·50 calibre gun. Provision was made for interchangeable engine mounts that would permit use of the standard D-12 engine or an enlarged version, the Curtiss V-1400. As originally planned, the last five of fifteen P-1s ordered were to be delivered with the V-1400. The first P-1 was delivered in August 1925, and was used mainly as a test machine. After proving out the standard model, it was fitted with an inverted air-cooled "Liberty" engine modified by Allison and was entered in the 1926 National Air Races. Later, it was fitted with an experimental Curtiss V-1460 engine and redesignated XP-17. Only ten of the P-1s originally ordered were completed as such, with Air Service Serial numbers 25–410 to 25–419.

XP-1A—Not a prototype. Production P-1A 26–280 assigned experimental status for test work.

P-1A—Twenty-five improved P-1As were ordered in September 1925, with deliveries beginning in April 1926. Principal changes from the P-1 were use of the later D-12C engine, fuselage structure lengthened three inches, revised fuel system, and improved bomb release system. Serial numbers 26–276 to 26–300, inclusive. Only 23 P-1As were delivered as such, 26–296 being completed as XAT-4 and 26–300 as XP-3A, but three additional P-3As were created by installing D-12 engines in P-2 airplanes 25–421, 422 and 424.

XP-1B—Not a prototype. Production P-1B 27–71 used for test work.

P-1B—An additional 25 improved P-1s, structurally similar to P-1As but equipped with larger wheels, redesigned radiator and cowling, flares for night landings, and improved controls. By the time the P-1Bs were ordered in August 1926, the Army Air Service had become the Army Air Corps, so the P-1B serial numbers were written as A.C. 27–63 to 27–87 instead of using the former A.S. prefix.

XP-1C—Not a prototype. Production P-1C 29–238 temporarily assigned to test work.

P-1C—The last production P-1s were 33 P-1Cs, essentially P-1Bs fitted with 30-inch by 5-inch wheels with brakes. Ordered in October 1928, and delivery completed in April 1929. The last two were delivered with hydraulic shock absorbers instead of the rubber blocks used on earlier models. One was converted to XP-6B by engine change. P-1C serials 29–227 to 29–259.

P-1D—The 40 P-1Ds were not originally ordered as such. The Army reached the conclusion that standard fighter airframes fitted with lower-powered engines would make good advanced trainers. Industry was encouraged to develop the idea, so Boeing installed a surplus W.W.I Wright-Hispano "E" of 180 h.p. in a PW-9A to create the XAT-3 while Curtiss fitted the same engine to P-1A 26–296 to produce the XAT-4. The Curtiss design won the large production order. However, the disadvantage of the scheme soon became apparent. The weight of the P-1A airframe and its load factors were not reduced to be compatible with the lower power, so the performance of the airplane was disappointing. As a result, the Army ordered the first 35 AT-4s to undergo an engine change

P-6 (actually P-6A) 29–260 with fuselage contours filled out to match larger size of Curtiss "Conqueror" engine. (Photo: U.S.A.F.)

The first XP-6A was a P-1A fitted with XPW-8A wings and a "Conqueror" engine for the 1927 National Air Races. (Photo: Curtiss)

to the D-12 and redesignated them P-1D. The last five had the water-cooled "Hisso" engines replaced with air-cooled Wright J-5 radials and continued in the trainer rôle. P-1D serial numbers *27–88* to *27–97*, *27–213* to *27–237*.

P-1E—The last five AT-4s were completed as AT-5 with the new air-cooled Wright J-5 (R-790) radial engine of 220 h.p. that was considerably lighter than the Wright-Hispano. However, the disadvantages of low power in a highly-stressed fighter airframe were still the same, and the AT-5s were fitted with D-12 engines and redesignated P-1E. AT-5 serial numbers *27–238* to *27–232*.

P-1F—An additional 31 fighter-trainers with the J-5 engine were ordered as AT-5A. Their structural relationship to the AT-5 was the same as that of the P-1B to the P-1A, hence the difference in designation. Again, performance was disappointing, with a top speed of only 121·9 m.p.h. compared to 157·5 for the P-1B, which had a gross weight of 2,932 lb. compared to the 2,478 of the AT-5A. AT-5A serial numbers *28–42* to *28–72*. An additional P-1F resulted from installation of a D-12 engine in the second XP-21, *28–189*.

XP-2—Not a prototype. The first P-2, *25–420*, given an experimental designation after being fitted with a side-mounted turbo-supercharger.

P-2—The last five P-1s were completed with 600-h.p. Curtiss V-1400 engines and were redesignated P-2. The new engine did not prove to be a desirable article, so three of the P-2s (*25–421*, *422* and *424*) were converted to P-1As with D-12 engines and *25–423* became the XP-6 with the new Curtiss V-1570 "Conqueror" engine. Only the first one, *25–420*, remained a P-2.

XP-3—The last P1-A, *25–300*, was to have been completed at the factory with the new 390-h.p. Curtiss R-1454 air-cooled radial engine, but since this had already been tested in other aircraft and found unsatisfactory, a new Pratt & Whitney "Wasp" engine was ordered, installed before the XP-3 was completed.

XP-3A—The XP-3 completed with the new 410-h.p. Pratt & Whitney R-1340 "Wasp" engine in place of the Curtiss R-1454. Originally delivered with an

The last P-1C completed as XP-6B with "Conqueror" engine.
(Photo: Curtiss)

Chequered band is black and white. Above and Below: *P6Ds were P-6s and P-6As fitted with turbo-superchargers.*
(Photos: E. M. Sommerich and A. U. Schmidt)

uncowled engine, this airplane was used to test the early N.A.C.A. cowlings for radial engines, at which time the fuselage lines were filled out to fair to the cowling contours by adding formers and stringers to the fuselage. Later, when used to test the smaller Pratt & Whitney "Wasp Jr." engine, the XP-3A was redesignated XP-21.

XP-3A No. 2—Not a prototype. The first production P-3A, *28–189*, used for test work in connection with the N.A.C.A. cowling development. When fitted with a tight cowling and a large spinner, this airplane was entered in the 1929 National Air Races, the last time that the Army competed with civil aircraft in the races. Later, the second XP-3A joined the first in testing the "Wasp Jr." engine as XP-21.

P-3A—Five "Hawks" generally similar to the AT-5A used to service test the 410-h.p. "Wasp" radial engine in a fighter airframe. The Air Corps decided against the use of the radial in the "Hawk" although preferring it in the contemporary Boeing P-12 model. However, the liquid-cooled D-12s and "Conquerors" were at a decided disadvantage at altitude, and the Army conducted experiments with practically every different liquid-cooled "Hawk" model by installing turbo-superchargers to improve high-altitude performance. The Navy, however, switched from the D-12 in its equivalent F6C-1 to F6C-3 models to the "Wasp" in the F6C-4. The P-3As were originally delivered without engine cowlings, but narrow Townend rings were soon added. They did little, however, to increase the speed of the P-3As over the 154 m.p.h. maximum of the original uncowled XP-3A. P-3A serial numbers *28–189* to *28–193*.

P-6A with three-blade propeller and standard nose shape.

P-6A with modified nose and two-blade propeller.
(Photo: E. N. Sommerich)

XP-5—Not a prototype. The first P-5 assigned to test work.

P-5—Five "Hawks" similar to the P-1A but fitted with turbo-supercharged D-12F engines to service test the new engine. Gross weight increased to 3,421 lb. compared to 2,932 for the P-1B. Sea-level speed was only 142 m.p.h., but this increased to 166 at 25,000 feet. Service ceiling for the P-5 was 30,475 feet compared to the absolute ceiling of 21,350 feet for the P-1A. By the time the P-5s were delivered in 1928, the later "Conqueror" engine was in service and no further developments were undertaken with the D-12. P-5 serial numbers *27–327* to *27–331*.

XP-6—The fourth P-2 (*25–423*) was fitted with the new 600-h.p. Curtiss V-1570 "Conqueror" engine and redesignated XP-6. Used primarily as a test bed for the new engine, it was entered in the 1927 National Air Races and placed second to the XP-6A in the unlimited event with a top speed for the closed course of 189 m.p.h.

P-6—Originally 18 service test P-6s, sometimes referred to as YP-6s, were ordered with the "Conqueror" engine. These were to use Prestone (Ethylene Glycol) for cooling instead of water, but in order to get some machines into service as quickly as possible, nine were ordered completed with water-cooled engines. These were delivered in October 1929 as P-6, with serial numbers *29–269* to *29–273* and *29–236* to *29–366*. Two additional P-6s were created by completing two of three P-11s on order with the water-cooled "Conqueror" engine. Most of the P-6s were eventually converted to P-6D.

XP-6A No. 1—For its principal entry in the 1927 National Air Races, the Army ordered extensive modification of P-1A *26–295*. The old XPW-8A wings were installed after having been rebuilt to take the older PW-8 type surface radiator, the new V-1570 "Conqueror" engine was installed in a PW-8 nose cowling, and various minor refinements were undertaken. This machine won the unlimited race at a speed of 201 m.p.h. Useful only as a racer, the first XP-6A was destroyed shortly before the 1928 National Air Race.

XP-6A No. 2—Not a prototype. The fourth P-6A, *29–263*, temporarily assigned an experimental designation while being used for test work.

P-6A—The first nine machines of the original P-6 order completed with Prestone cooling systems. During the service test period, various minor changes in radiator shape were made and some of the machines were fitted with three-blade airscrews in place of the original two-bladers. One or more of the P-6As were

P-6E of 33rd Pursuit Squadron. Compare late style open wheel fairings (called "Pants") with closed style shown on page 3.
(Photo: A. U. Schmidt)

P-6E of 3rd Base H.Q. and Air Base Squadron, showing revised shape of elevators and inboard location of wing stars.

P-6E in camouflage paint for 1935 War Games.
(Photo: R. H. Lober)

converted to P-6D. P-1A serial numbers *29–260* to *29–268*.

XP-6B—The last P-1C, *29–259*, was completed with a "Conqueror" engine in place of the D-12 and was redesignated XP-6B. It was intended for a long-distance flight from New York to Alaska, to be accomplished by Captain Hoyt of the Army Air Corps. Because of this, the airplane was known at the factory as the "Hoyt Special". It crashed short of its goal and was shipped back to the United States for repair and subsequent test work.

P-6C—Designation not used. Originally intended to replace the Y1P-22 designation but cancelled when the new P-6E designation was assigned to the same airplanes.

XP-6D—The first P-6A, *29–260*, fitted experimentally with a turbo-supercharged V-1570C "Conqueror" engine in April 1931. Sea-level speed decreased slightly to 172 m.p.h. from the 178·6 of the P-6A, but top speed at 15,000 feet increased to 197 m.p.h.

P-6D—Following the successful test of the XP-6D,

The former YP-20 and XP-6E became XP-6F when fitted with a turbo-supercharger and enclosed cockpit.

XP-6F showing turbo-supercharger.
(Photo: Gordon S. Williams)

XP-6G was a standard P-6E fitted temporarily with a later model V-1570 "Conqueror" engine.

The XP-6H was the first production P-6E fitted with four wing-mounted ·30 calibre machine guns in addition to the normal pair of synchronised nose guns. (Photo: D. C. Cooke)

nine of the P-6s and an undetermined number of the P-6As were converted to P-6D between February and April 1932, by installing turbo-superchargers. The only outward difference from the XP-6D was the use of three-blade propellers instead of the two-bladers of the prototype.

XP-6E—This was a much-redesignated airplane, having been ordered originally as the third P-11, serial number *29–374*. It was completed as the YP-20 and was then fitted with the engine and landing gear of the XP-22 and redesignated XP-6E. Later, it became the XP-6F.

P-6E—Forty-six greatly improved "Hawks" were ordered under the service test designation of Y1P-22, since they were derived from the experimental XP-22 model. The designation was changed to P-6C to simplify book-keeping and the spare parts problem, since most of the major components were similar to those used on the existing P-6 models. However, this was changed to P-6E before delivery in late 1931 and early 1932. The most noticeable change was the use of a single-strut undercarriage and a completely revised nose with the radiator moved back to a position just ahead of the undercarriage, as developed on the XP-22.

The balance area of the rudder was decreased by raising the top rib of the fin while the elevators were enlarged by straightening out the previously tapered trailing edges. The armament installation was revised by mounting the machine guns at the sides of the fuselage instead of on top of it. Structural refinements brought the gross weight down to 2,760 lb. while the 700-h.p. V-1570C "Conqueror" engine permitted a top speed of 197·8 m.p.h. at sea-level. The last airplane on the P-6E contract was kept at the factory and converted to the XP-23. P-6E serial *32–233* to *278*.

XP-6F—In March 1932, the XP-6E was returned to the factory for conversion to XP-6F with a turbo-supercharged V-1570F "Conqueror" engine. Redelivery was made March 1933. Gross weight increased to 3,149 lb., 389 lb. over that of the P-6E. High speed at sea-level decreased to 194 m.p.h. but was a blazing 225 m.p.h. at 15,000 feet. Cooling difficulties precluded careful testing above that altitude. Other than the turbo-supercharger, the only distinguishing feature of the XP-6F was the use of a sliding canopy over the pilot's cockpit. The XP-6F had proved that as speeds exceeded 200 m.p.h., the traditional open cockpit was no longer satisfactory.

XP-6G—One P-6E, *32–254*, was used to test an unsupercharged V-1570F "Conqueror" engine. Later, the experimental prefix was dropped, the airplane becoming P-6G. Eventually, the standard V-1570C engine was reinstalled and the airplane reverted to P-6E.

XP-6H—The first production P-6E, *32–233*, returned to the factory and fitted with new wing panels containing ·30 calibre machine guns. Two were installed in the one-piece upper wing just outboard of the centre section struts and one was installed in each lower wing panel. All four fired outside of the propeller arc.

P-11—At the same time that the "Conqueror"-powered P-6s were ordered, three similar airframes were ordered with new 600-h.p. Curtiss H-1640 12-cylinder two-bank air-cooled engines under the designation of P-11. Before the machines were finished tests of the engine in other aircraft proved it unsatisfactory, so the first two P-11s were completed as P-6 while the third, fitted with a Wright "Cyclone" radial engine, became the YP-20. P-11 serial numbers *29–367, 368* and *374*.

XP-17—The first P-1, *25–410*, was used throughout its life as a test machine. While no designation change was made when the inverted air-cooled "Liberty" engine was installed, it became XP-17 when fitted with the experimental Curtiss V-1470, a 480-h.p. inverted

P-6E of 17th Pursuit Squadron on skis.

The first P-1 became XP-17 when fitted with Curtiss V-1460 engine. (Photo: U.S.A.F.)

air-cooled V-12 model. By the time the Curtiss engine was installed in 1930, the airplane was thoroughly obsolete. The experimental designation was to indicate the test status of the airframe and not a new experimental fighter prototype.

YP-20—The third P-11, *29–374*, was completed in October 1930, with a 575-h.p. Wright R-1820 "Cyclone" radial engine in place of the Curtiss H-1640 and was given the designation of YP-20. After test of the "Cyclone", the YP-20 was fitted with the nose-landing gear, and tail surfaces of the XP-22 and was redesignated XP-6E. After proving out the P-6E configuration, it was fitted with a turbo-supercharger and became the XP-6F.

XP-21—The first and second XP-3As, *26–300* and *28–189*, were fitted with the new Pratt & Whitney R-985 "Wasp Jr." engines in December 1930. As in the case of the XP-17, the new designation was assigned to identify a particular test configuration and not a new prototype. The new Pratt & Whitney engine delivered only 300 h.p. and service fighters of the time used nearly double that power. The first XP-21 became XP-21A with minor changes while the second was fitted with a D-12 engine and became a P-1F.

XP-22—The third P-6A, *29–262*, was extensively modified by installation of an entirely new nose and engine cooling system, gun installation, a single-strut undercarriage, a three-blade propeller, and revised tail surfaces. These items were removed and used on the YP-20, and the XP-22 reverted to a P-6A with its original equipment.

Y1P-22—Forty-six "Service Test" versions of the XP-22 were to be ordered under the designation of Y1P-22. This was unusual, since the normal service test order seldom exceeded 13 units. The airplanes were to have been redesignated P-6C before they were built, but were finally delivered as P-6Es.

XP-23—The last P-6E, *32–278*, was held at the factory and completed as the XP-23 with an entirely new monocoque aluminium fuselage, new tail surfaces, a new nose and landing gear, and a turbo-supercharged and geared G1V-1570-C engine. At a gross weight of 4,242 lb. the XP-23 had a top sea-level speed of 178 m.p.h. but reached 220 m.p.h. at 15,000 feet. The turbo-supercharger was later removed.

YP-23—The XP-23 redesignated when switched from "Experimental" to "Service Test" status. As YP-23 it flew with a two-blade propeller instead of the original three-blade model of the XP-23. In spite of the improved performance over the standard P-6E, there was no point in trying to extend the life of the biplane

The XP-22 was a P-6A fitted with new nose and landing gear and served as the prototype for the P-6E. (Photo: U.S.A.F.)

The XP-22 fitted with an experimental nose radiator during its test programme. (Photo: Curtiss)

fighter any further—the monoplanes were already beginning to take over, at least in the Army. The Navy, with its requirement for slow landing speed on aircraft carriers, kept the biplane in production for a few more years. The Curtiss P-6Es of 1931–32 and the Boeing P-12Fs of 1933 marked the end of biplane fighter procurement for the U.S. Army Air Corps.

ARMY "HAWK" COLOURING

From the original PW-8s up to the P-1Bs, the Army "Hawks" were painted in overall khaki brown, a colour which became increasingly dark over the years and eventually came to be called olive drab. In 1927,

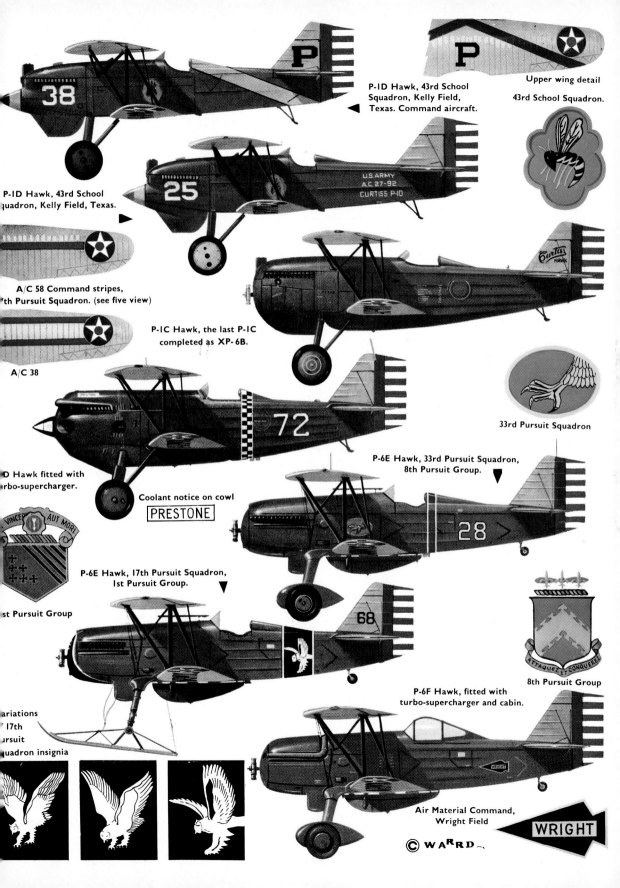

P-ID Hawk, 43rd School
Squadron, Kelly Field,
Texas. Command aircraft.

Upper wing detail

43rd School Squadron.

P-ID Hawk, 43rd School
Squadron, Kelly Field, Texas.

A/C 58 Command stripes,
8th Pursuit Squadron. (see five view)

P-IC Hawk, the last P-IC
completed as XP- 6B.

A/C 38

D Hawk fitted with
turbo-supercharger.

Coolant notice on cowl

PRESTONE

33rd Pursuit Squadron

P-6E Hawk, 33rd Pursuit Squadron,
8th Pursuit Group.

VINCERE AUT MORI

1st Pursuit Group

P-6E Hawk, 17th Pursuit Squadron,
1st Pursuit Group.

ATTAQUEZ ET CONQUERE

8th Pursuit Group

P-6F Hawk, fitted with
turbo-supercharger and cabin.

Variations
17th
Pursuit
Squadron insignia

Air Material Command,
Wright Field

WRIGHT

© WARRD

The XP-23 was the last P-6E completed with entirely new fuselage, nose, and tail surfaces.

After removal of the turbo-supercharger, the XP-23 was redesignated YP-23.
(Photo: U.S.A.F.)

the Army Air Corps abandoned the solid camouflage shade that had been in use since W.W.I and adopted high-visibility colouring in the interests of safety. All wings and horizontal and vertical tail surfaces were repainted in orange-yellow, also called chrome yellow, while fuselage, struts, and undercarriage remained olive drab. In 1935–36, the olive drab was replaced by a medium shade of greyish blue for fighters and other first-line combat types after some observation and training models had used it for several years. The Curtiss P-6Es retained this colouring until they were retired from service in 1939.

ARMY "HAWK" MARKINGS

When the PW-8s were introduced, the Air Service serial number was painted in large black figures on each side of the fuselage, as A.S. *23–1201* for the first XPW-8. The model designation and the name of the manufacturer were painted in three-inch black figures across the top of the rudder, as PW-8 CURTISS.

	P-1B	P-6A	P-6E
Wing Span	31 ft. 7 in.	31 ft. 6 in.	31 ft. 6 in.
Length	22 ft. 10 in.	23 ft. 7 in.	23 ft. 2 in.
Powerplant	Curtiss D-12D 435 h.p. at 2,300 r.p.m.	Curtiss V-1570A 600 h.p. at 2,400 r.p.m.	Curtiss V-1570C 700 h.p. at 2,400 r.p.m.
Empty Weight	2,104 lb.	2,389 lb.	2,068 lb.
Gross Weight	2,932 lb.	3,172 lb.	2,760 lb.
Speed (Sea level)	157·4 m.p.h.	178·6 m.p.h.	197·8 m.p.h.
Climb Sea level)	1,638 ft./min.	2,320 ft./min.	2,400 ft./min.
Service Ceiling	20,000 ft.	27,200 ft.	24,700 ft.
Absolute Ceiling	21,900 ft.	28,400 ft.	25,800 ft.

Machines under test at McCook Field had the airplane Project number painted on the rudder below the designation, as P 364 for the PW-8A. By late 1926, the size of the serial number on the fuselage was reduced, and the words U.S. ARMY were added above them, with the designation still appearing on the rudder. In 1928, all of the information was combined in a three-line legend on the aft portion of the fuselage, U.S. ARMY on the top line, then the manufacturer and model designation, and finally the Air Corps serial number. This lettering could be either black or white, but for the Curtiss "Hawks" was almost invariably white. In some cases, the last two lines were transposed.

The form and application of the U.S. national markings varied during the life of the "Hawks". Until the end of 1926, the star-in-circle marking was carried at the extreme wing tips and as large as possible. At the time the yellow colouring was adopted, the size of the circle was reduced to fit between the leading edge of the wing and the aileron spar, and the marking was moved inboard so that its outer edge was one diameter inboard from the wing tip. Throughout production of the P-1B, the tail marking consisted of three equal-width vertical stripes of blue-white, and red, with the red at the trailing edge in the manner of contemporary British and French designs. In November 1926, this was changed, retaining the vertical blue stripe but changing the red and white to thirteen alternating horizontal stripes in the style of the American flag. The change-over was not instantaneous, and some Army airplanes carried the old vertical stripes into 1928.

PRINTED IN ENGLAND. © Profile Publications Ltd., P.O. Box 26, Leatherhead, Surrey, England, by George Falkner & Sons Ltd., for McCorquodale City Printing Division, London.

PROFILE
PUBLICATIONS

The
Nakajima
Ki-43
Hayabusa

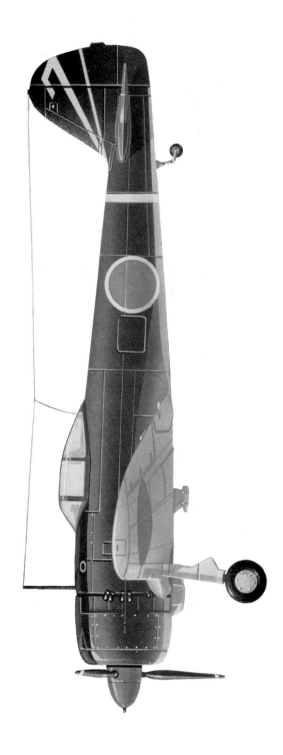

NUMBER

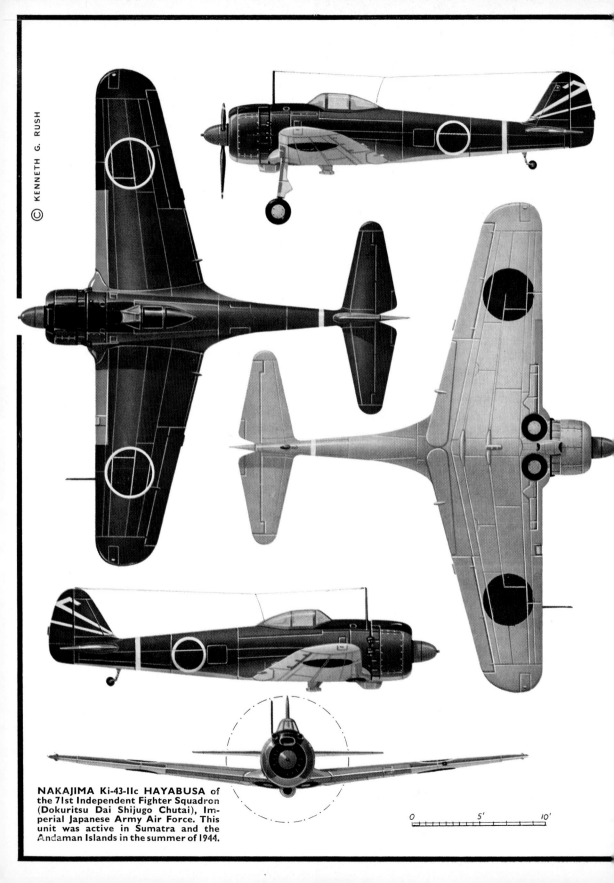

© KENNETH G. RUSH

NAKAJIMA Ki-43-IIc HAYABUSA of
the 71st Independent Fighter Squadron
(Dokuritsu Dai Shijugo Chutai), Imperial Japanese Army Air Force. This
unit was active in Sumatra and the
Andaman Islands in the summer of 1944.

0   5'   10'

The Nakajima Ki. 43 Hayabusa
by Martin C. Windrow and R. F. Francillon

A Nakajima Ki-43-IIa in flight. This aircraft is an early production model, with oil cooler incorporated in the intake under the cowling.
(Photo: via R. J. Francillon)

In April 1942 the armed forces of Imperial Japan were riding a wave of victory. Surprised, out-gunned, out-manœuvred, and vastly out-numbered, the Allied garrisons throughout the eastern land mass of S.E. Asia and the Indonesian archipelago were falling one by one in a series of bitter, unrecorded last stands. The largely inaccurate image of the Japanese soldier as a superman was beginning to seem unpleasantly substantial, and his victories were ensured by the complete air superiority gained in a matter of weeks by the air forces of the Imperial Army and Navy. The Navy had in the Mitsubishi Zero-Sen a fighter aircraft which captured the fearful imagination of half the world; but the name of the Zero's Army stablemate is even to this day virtually unknown outside specialist aviation circles. The Nakajima Hayabusa Type I fighter was an aircraft of great significance, bridging as it did the gap between two generations of fighting aeroplanes. In continuous production in one or other of its variant forms for six and a half years, it saw the Sun of Japan rise over China and Malaya and ended its career as a suicide aircraft as that sun finally set over the ravaged Home Islands.

In December 1937 the Japanese Army Air Force granted to the Nakajima Hikoki K.K., one of the most prominent of the nation's aircraft manufacturers, a development contract for a single-seat fighter designated Ki-43 to replace their own Type 97 Ki-27 fixed-undercarriage monoplane. The placing of this contract directly with a specific manufacturer was a precedent which indicated the Army Air Force's satisfaction with the Ki-27, the first truly indigenous Japanese design to achieve performance parity with leading foreign contemporaries. Encouraged by the success of this design the J.A.A.F. by-passed the usual process of comparative trials and awarded to Nakajima the contract for an even more competitive machine. The specification called for an interceptor/escort fighter with a top speed of at least 500 km/h.

(311 m.p.h.); a climb rate of 5 minutes to 5,000 m. (16,405 ft.); a range of 800 km. (500 miles); armament comprising two 7·7 mm. machine guns; and manœuvrability at least equal to that of the Ki-27.

The task undertaken by designer Hideo Itokawa was one of extreme difficulty. Each provision of the specification could be met, it seemed, only at the expense of one of the other requirements. The aircraft which emerged was a compromise and initially displayed all the weaknesses of a compromise. The powerplant was to be the new 950-h.p. two row fourteen cylinder radial Ha-25, the Nakajima-built counterpart of the famous *Sakae* (Prosperity) engine of the Mitsubishi A6M series. The Ki-43 design was the end product of a vigorous policy of weight- and drag-reduction, the former requirement aided by the fact that the original specification did not call for pilot or fuel cell protection, and finally emerged as an extremely slim, clean low-wing cantilever monoplane of all-metal construction. To minimise loadings the one-piece three-spar wing had substantial area, and an innovation in Army fighter design was represented by the fully retractable main undercarriage.

THE FIRST HAYABUSAS

The first prototype, *No. 4301*, was completed at Nakajima's Ota plant in the Gumma Prefecture on 12th December 1938, and flew for the first time early the following month from Ojima Airfield, Ota. *Nos. 4302* and *4303* were completed in February and March 1939 respectively and the three machines were handed over to J.A.A.F. test pilots after a brief programme of manufacturer's trials. These aircraft, painted light grey-green overall, were characterised by the lack of engine cowling gills, the metal panels in the rear of the cockpit hood, and the cockpit-mounted radio antenna mast. The reaction of service test pilots was unfavourable at this stage. To flyers accustomed to the extreme agility of the light fighters of the 1930s, the Ki-43 was sluggish and unresponsive;

3

A Ki-43-I of the 50th Fighter Sentai's 2nd Chutai, brought down almost intact near Chittagong in 1942.
(Photo: Imperial War Museum)

The Ki-43-Ic, first version to standardise the armament at two 12·7 mm. Type I machine guns, and major production variant of the Ki-43-I series.

and the Army pilots, to whom the skilful performance of the classic dog-fighting manœuvres was an article of faith bred into them from their earliest training days, were sceptical of the new design. Many were suspicious of the new features such as the enclosed cockpit and retractable landing gear and some felt that the weight of the retraction mechanism was an uneconomical luxury. It should be stated at this point, however, that at no time was any Ki-43 prototype fitted with a fixed, spatted undercarriage. This erroneous report appears to have been founded on wartime sources confusing the Ki-27 with the Ki-43; previously published drawings of the mythical fixed-undercarriage Hayabusa show landing gear members identical to those of the former aircraft. This point has now been verified by the recent translation of original Japanese documents.

Between November 1939 and September 1940 ten pre-production Ki-43-KAI machines were completed for service trials, numbered *4304* to *4313*. These differed in the following respects:

4304, 4306 to 4309 inclusive. Powered by Nakajima Ha-25 with single-speed supercharger driving a fixed-pitch two-blade wooden propeller. A new all-round-vision canopy was fitted and armament comprised two Type 89 7·7 mm. machine guns. Painted light grey-green overall.

4305. Identical to above except for the installation of an experimental Ha-105 engine with two-speed supercharger.

4310. Identical to *4309* except for an armament of two Ho-103 12·7 mm. machine guns.

4311. Basically similar to *4309*, but employed to test the new "butterfly" combat flaps. Probably the greatest single contribution to the Ki-43s success, these flaps could be extended in action with the result of increased control sensitivity, greater lift, and much tighter turning circle.

4312. An unpainted aircraft with alclad treated duralumin outer skin; cowling gills; radio mast on forward starboard fuselage side.

4313. Alclad duralumin outer skin; cowling gills; two Ho-103 12·7 mm. machine guns; "butterfly" flaps; smaller fuselage diameter and re-designed tail surfaces and wings similar to those adopted

on the production aircraft. Powered by Ha-105 engine with two-speed supercharger; radio mast on forward starboard fuselage side.

EARLY PRODUCTION

The new combat flaps made an extremely favourable impression on service pilots and earlier scepticism turned to enthusiasm. The initial production variant commenced construction at Ota in April 1941, and christened Hayabusa (Peregrine Falcon) the Ki-43-Ia began to reach fighter units some six months later. The Model Ia was similar in airframe to the pre-production machine *4313*; it was powered by an Ha-25 Type 99 engine rated at 980 h.p. for take-off, with a single-speed supercharger and driving a fixed-pitch two-blade wooden propeller on early production models and later a variable-pitch two-blade metal propeller.

Two Type 89 7·7 mm. machine guns were fired through the upper cowling, and two attachment points were located under the wing centre section behind and inboard of the main undercarriage attachment points. Top speed was 308 m.p.h. at 13,125 ft., and service ceiling was 38,500 ft. Climb rate was 5 minutes 30 seconds to 16,405 ft. When War broke out only forty machines had been delivered to combat units, and these were taken to the Malay Peninsula by the 59th and 64th Fighter Groups (see paragraphs on J.A.A.F. unit structure on p. 10 of this *Profile*).

Their first combat missions were escort sorties with Army Type 97 (Mitsubishi Ki-21) bombers attacking Hong Kong and strategic targets in Burma during the initial Japanese operations to isolate China. First interceptions by Allied aircraft were recorded by the American Volunteer Group's P-40 pilots and by the personnel of No. 67 (Fighter) Squadron, Royal Air Force, at that time equipped with Brewster Buffaloes. The 64th Group, led by Lt.-Col. Tateo Kato, became one of the most famous Japanese units to operate in South East Asia.

The Ki-43-Ia was soon supplanted on production lines by the -Ib variant, in which one of the 7·7 mm.

Model 1A Hayabusas in flight. (Photo: via R. J. Francillon)

A Ki-43-I in Chinese Nationalist hands.

weapons was replaced by a Type I Ho-103 12·7 mm. machine gun. The first mass-production variant was the Ki-43-Ic with two 12·7 mm. guns and capacity for two underwing 33 or 66 lb. bombs or two 44 Imp. gal. drop tanks.

Quickly replacing the Ki-27 as the standard first-line fighter of the J.A.A.F., the Hayabusa soon proved itself in action and became popular with Army pilots, many of whom gained their first taste of combat while flying the type. Admittedly their opponents in those early months were out-numbered, demoralised and generally equipped with obsolete machines, but there is no denying the effectiveness of the slim warplane which burst without warning on the British, Dutch, American and Chinese pilots in the grim months of Spring and Summer 1942.

THE Ki-43-II AND -III

In February 1942 the first of five prototypes of a new variant was completed. Designated Ki-43-IIa, the improved model entered production in the following autumn. From this time on production of the Model I was gradually run down, aircraft of this type being assigned to second-line duties at training establishments and a batch being supplied to the puppet "Royal Thai Air Force". (It is perhaps ironic to Western eyes that Hayabusas in service with this formation bore the insignia of the White Elephant.) The most obvious differences between the Ki-43-IIa and earlier sub-types included the improved Type 2 Ha-115 powerplant, rated at 1,130 h.p. for take-off, with a two-speed supercharger and driving a three-blade fixed-pitch metal propeller. The supercharger air intake was moved from under the cowling to its upper lip; other minor changes included the heightening of the windscreen and canopy, the fitting of a new reflector gunsight, and the strengthening of the wing attachment points to carry 250 kg. (551 lb.) of bombs. The omission of pilot armour and fuel protection in earlier models was now recognised to have been a mistake; 13 mm. head and back plates were fitted in the cockpit and self-sealing tanks were installed in the wings. The wing span was reduced by 60 cm. and wing area by ·6 sq. m.; this modification was not, as has been stated elsewhere, peculiar to the Ki-43-II KAI (Ki-43IIc) variant. Surprisingly, the armament remained standard at two Type I 12·7 mm. machine guns with 250 r.p.g., a battery decidedly inferior to contemporary Allied designs and one of the weakest points of the "Oscar", as the Hayabusa was known in Allied recognition-code parlance.

(Two code names were in fact allotted to the Ki-43. "Jim" was assigned by personnel in the China-Burma-India Theatre to a "Type I retractable gear fighter" thought to be a derivative of "Nate", the Nakajima Ki-27. The name "Oscar" was selected by Captain, later Col. Frank T. McCoy, Jr., U.S.A.A.F., and his staff, founders of the code-name system. A native of Tennessee, McCoy tended to select "hillbilly" names such as "Zeke", "Rufe", and "Nate"—short, simple, but unusual enough to stick in the memory.)

The mass production version of the Type I Model 2 was the Ki-43-IIb. Identical to the -IIa apart from minor equipment changes, the -IIb featured a deeper carburettor intake under the cowling incorporating a "honey-comb" oil cooler. Late production models

Close-up view of one of the Akeno Fighter Training School's Model 1B Hayabusas. Note airscrew decoration, fin emblem (see illustration on page 11 of this Profile) and early gunsight. (Photo: via R. J. Francillon)

A Ki-43-IIa being run up at Akeno. This machine displays to advantage the yellow strip carried on the wing leading edges of J.A.A.F. aircraft, indicated here by its appearance on the landing gear strut cover. (Photo: via Witold Liss)

had the oil cooler moved back to a position under the centre of the fuselage. Three prototypes of the Ki-43-II KAI were built between June and August 1942 and this version entered service in the summer of 1943. Further minor equipment changes were incorporated with an eye to ease of production and maintenance, but the main difference was the replacement of the exhaust collector ring by individual exhaust stacks which offered some measure of thrust augmentation. This variant, also known as the Ki-43-IIc (although this may be a "retrospective" designation introduced for clarity by Western sources) saw the wing attachment points moved outboard of the landing gear.

Development of the design continued until the end of the War despite the marked superiority displayed by the Allied types against which the Ki-43 was increasingly being committed. An improved sub-type designated Ki-43-IIIa appeared in May, 1944; powered by an Ha-115-II engine rated at 1,230 h.p. at 9,185 ft., the new version was similar in airframe and armament to the Ki-43-II KAI. It was manufactured mainly by Tachikawa (see production tables) and assigned principally to home defence units based around Tokyo and other large cities in the Home Islands, although the 13th Fighter Group is known to have flown the type in the final months of the War in Singapore and French Indo-China. It was also employed by *Taiatari* elements, the J.A.A.F. counterpart of the J.N.A.F.s *Kamikaze*

suicide corps. The final development of the Hayabusa was the Ki-43-IIb, a version of which only two prototypes had been completed before the Superfortress *Enola Gay* opened the last brief chapter of the Pacific war. Developed by Tachikawa, the -IIIb featured extensive modification of wing and fuselage structure and mounted two Ho-5 20 mm. cannon. This version was intended as a B-29 interceptor and was powered by a 1,250 h.p. Mitsubishi Ha-32/42 engine.

OPERATIONAL ASSESSMENT

The Japanese Army's Peregrine Falcon cannot be judged an outstanding machine by Western standards, but as the most extensively produced J.A.A.F. aircraft of the War it deserves recognition for the important place it occupied in the Imperial arsenal. When a complete aircraft was assembled at Brisbane, Australia, from components of several "write-offs" salvaged from Lae, New Guinea, in the autumn of 1943, Allied pilots who test-flew it were generous in their praise of the Hayabusas control response and manœuvrability. Take-off and landing characteristics were docile, and acceleration between 150 m.p.h. and 250 m.p.h. was extremely brisk. It could be "stunted" with complete safety at speeds of around 160 m.p.h./170 m.p.h., and turn and stall qualities were superior to those of any Allied fighter. It was a pilot's aeroplane, with no built-in vices. On the other side of the coin, it was hopelessly under-gunned,

Above and below: Two Ki-43-IIa's of the 2nd Chutai, 25th Fighter Sentai. This unit was active in China during 1944 and the first three months of 1945.

These flying studies of a Ki-43-II show to advantage the extreme slimness of the fuselage and general cleanliness of line which characterised the Hayabusa at all stages of its development. The streamlined, low-drag contours and light wing loadings combined with control sensitivity to make the Hayabusa a fighter pilot's delight from the point of view of manœuvrability; this was a prime consideration in Japanese aviation circles early in the war. The aircraft illustrated appears in these photographs to be finished in the night-fighter scheme of black and natural metal; but examination of the shade of the national insignia as reproduced here indicates that this effect may be simply the result of under-exposure of the original film.

The Model 2A appeared in the autumn of 1942. Among major innovations introduced with this version were reduced wing-span, armour protection for the pilot and self-sealing fuel tanks.

An unusual modification of the Ki-43-II KAI: a ski main undercarriage fitted for testing in Manchuria. Main gear legs were presumably locked down although this machine retains open wheel wells.

A Ki-43-IIa captured by United States forces. The marking style is of especial interest: note that the "bars" of the U.S. insignia have been added to the Japanese Hinomaro on the fuselage.

UNITS KNOWN TO HAVE OPERATED THE Ki-43 INCLUDE THE FOLLOWING:

Sentai	Period of Operations	Area of Operations
1st	1942–44	—
11th	1942?	Dutch East Indies
13th	August 1943–November 1944	New Guinea, Dutch East Indies (Ki-43-I and II)
	November 1944–February 1945	Singapore, French Indo-China (Ki-43-III)
17th	1942–43?	—
18th	1942–43?	—
19th	1942–43?	—
20th	December 1943–February 1945	Japan, Formosa
21st	1942	—
23rd	October 1944–August 1945	Japan
24th	March 1942–44	Dutch East Indies, New Guinea, Japan, Philippines, China
25th	1944–March 1945	China
26th	1942–August 1945	Manchuria, Philippines, Sumatra, New Guinea, Formosa
30th	June 1943–May 1945	—
31st	1942–45	—
33rd	1942–June 1945	China, French Indo-China, Dutch East Indies, New Guinea, Philippines, Sumatra
48th	Spring 1945–August 1945	China
50th	1942–44	China, Thailand Burma
54th	January 1943–August 1945	Japan, China, Formosa
59th	Summer 1941–43	Japan, China, Formosa, Burma, Malaya
63rd	1943–April 1944	Japan, New Guinea
64th	Summer 1941–August 1945	Japan, China, French Indo-China, Thailand, Malaya, Sumatra, Java, Burma
65th	1945	Japan?
71st	June 1944–45	—
72nd	May 1944–May 1945	—
73rd	June 1944–May 1945	—
77th	June 1943–April 1944	Manchuria, Burma, New Guinea
101st	November 1944–August 1945	—
102nd	November 1944–July 1945	—
103rd	November 1944–August 1945	—
104th	November 1944–August 1945	—
112th	July–August 1945	Japan
203rd	March 1942–August 1945	—
204th	January 1944–August 1945	Japan, Burma, French Indo-China, Formosa
248th	October 1942–August 1944	Japan

Dokuritsu Dai Shijugo Chutais (Independent or Direct Command Fighter Squadrons) which operated the Ki-43 Hayabusa are known to include:
1st, 2nd, 4th, 5th, 13th, 14th, 17th, 19th and 26th; dates and bases unknown.

Chutai	Date	Area of Operations
24th	March 1944–January 1945	Sumatra, Philippines
47th	—	Japan
71st	May 1944–August 1945	Sumatra, Andaman Islands, French Indo-China, Malaya

The Fighter Training Schools at Akeno and Hitachi also operated the Ki-43.

A wrecked "Oscar" in Burma, 1944. One of the many destroyed during the Imphal-Kohima battles which represented the last serious threat to Allied air superiority over the South East Asian mainland. (Photo: Imperial War Museum)

and often broke up under the heavier fire of less manœuvrable Allied aircraft. It was considerably slower than most British and American types, who could avoid combat at will. Granted a knowledge of the Oscar's weaknesses. Allied pilots could engage it with confidence even in the later marks of the P-40 series; and it was completely outclassed by the P-47, P-51, Spitfire and P-38.

The Hayabusa served on every front to which the Japanese Army Air Force was committed throughout the Pacific War; it fought over China, Malaya, Indonesia, New Guinea, the Philippines, the Home Islands, and the South Pacific islands. It played a considerable part in the Burma campaign of Spring 1944, and many fell to destruction around Thebaw, Kohima and Imphal. It was the loyal workhorse of an air force which shook the world, and as such it deserves more recognition than has been its lot over the past two decades.

With the exception of one squadron operating against the U.S. 14th Air Force in Southern China, the Ki-43s of the Royal Thai Air Force took an active part in the War. Other foreign formations to use the Hayabusa were the Indonesian People's Security Force, a Communist force which operated salvaged machines against the Dutch in 1946; and Groupes de Chasse 1/7 and II/7 of the French Air Army, who flew aircraft confiscated on their return to Indo-China against the Communist insurgents in that colony. The career of the Ki-43 in French hands was brief as Spitfire IXs were soon shipped from France to replace them. The only known surviving Ki-43 is a Model 2 (-IIa) at present mounted on a stand at Clark AFB in the Philippines.

© René J. Francillon and Martin C. Windrow, 1965.

(*The publishers wish to acknowledge their gratitude to Mr. d'E. C. Darby of New Zealand and to Aireview Magazine of Tokyo, Japan, for assistance in the preparation of some of the illustrations appearing in this Profile.*)

Underwing attachment points are clearly visible on this Ki-43-IIb of the Kumagaya Training School. This establishment's emblem appears on the fin in red.

A line-up of the 48th Sentai's Ki-43-IIs in China, Spring 1945.

The Ki-43-II KAI introduced individual exhaust stacks, which offered some thrust augmentation over the collector ring system employed on earlier variants.

J.A.A.F. Unit Structure

In the interests of clarity, the terms "Group" and "Squadron" have been used in place of the corresponding J.A.A.F. designations Sentai and Chutai. The Sentai was made up of three Chutais and an H.Q. section or Sentai Hombu. Each Chutai was made up of four Shotais or Flights of three aircraft. Thus the nominal strength of a Sentai was usually 40 aircraft, although some Sentais mustered more than three Chutais.

Some Chutais were not assigned to Sentais and were known as Dokuritsu Dai Shijugo Chutais or Independent Squadrons.

The next unit in the command chain was the Hiko-Dan or Air Brigade. Two or three fighter Sentais formed a Sentoki Sentai or Fighter Air Brigade, but more often a fighter Sentai was assigned to a Konsei Hiko-Dan or Mixed Air Brigade, together with a Keibaku Sentai (Light Bomber Group) and a Jubaku Sentai (Heavy Bomber Group). Two or three Hiko-Dans formed the Hiko-Shidan (Air Division) and the strategic Air Army or Koku-Gun grouped two or three Hiko-Shidans.

Key to J.A.A.F. Fin Markings illustrated opposite:

1. 1st Group, 2nd Squadron, 1943.
2. 1st Group, 1st Squadron, 1943.
3. 13th Group, 2nd Squadron, 1943.
4 and 5. Akeno Fighter Training School.
6. 23rd Group, 1944–45.
7. 63rd Group, 3rd Squadron, 1943–44.
8. 13th Group, 1944–45.
9. 64th Group, 1st Squadron, 1944.
10. 20th Group, 1944–45.
11. 24th Independent Squadron, 1944–45.
12. 77th Group, 1st Squadron, 1944.
13. 77th Group, 2nd Squadron.
14. 77th Group, 3rd Squadron.
15. 48th Group, 1945.
16. 77th Group, 1st Squadron, 1943–44.

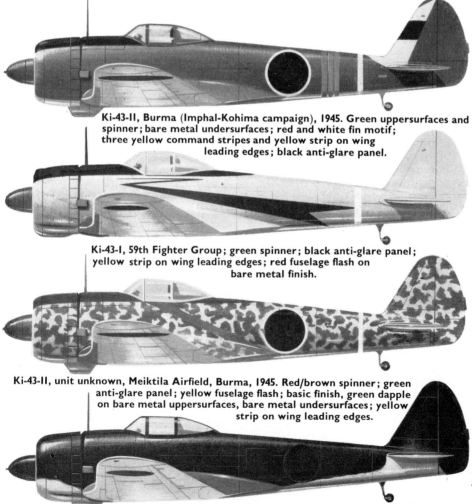

Ki-43-II, Burma (Imphal-Kohima campaign), 1945. Green uppersurfaces and spinner; bare metal undersurfaces; red and white fin motif; three yellow command stripes and yellow strip on wing leading edges; black anti-glare panel.

Ki-43-I, 59th Fighter Group; green spinner; black anti-glare panel; yellow strip on wing leading edges; red fuselage flash on bare metal finish.

Ki-43-II, unit unknown, Meiktila Airfield, Burma, 1945. Red/brown spinner; green anti-glare panel; yellow fuselage flash; basic finish, green dapple on bare metal uppersurfaces, bare metal undersurfaces; yellow strip on wing leading edges.

Ki-43-II in black and bare metal night-fighter finish; red spinner.

Ki-43-II, unit unknown; yellow fuselage band and fin motif outlined in red.

Ki-43-II, 68th Squadron; red fin motif outlined in white; white fuselage band.

Ki-43-II, unit unknown; fin motif *bare metal*; white fuselage band.

Aircraft above based on Alexishafen Airfield, New Guinea, 1945. All three finished in jungle green uppersurfaces, pale blue undersurfaces.

© WARRD

10

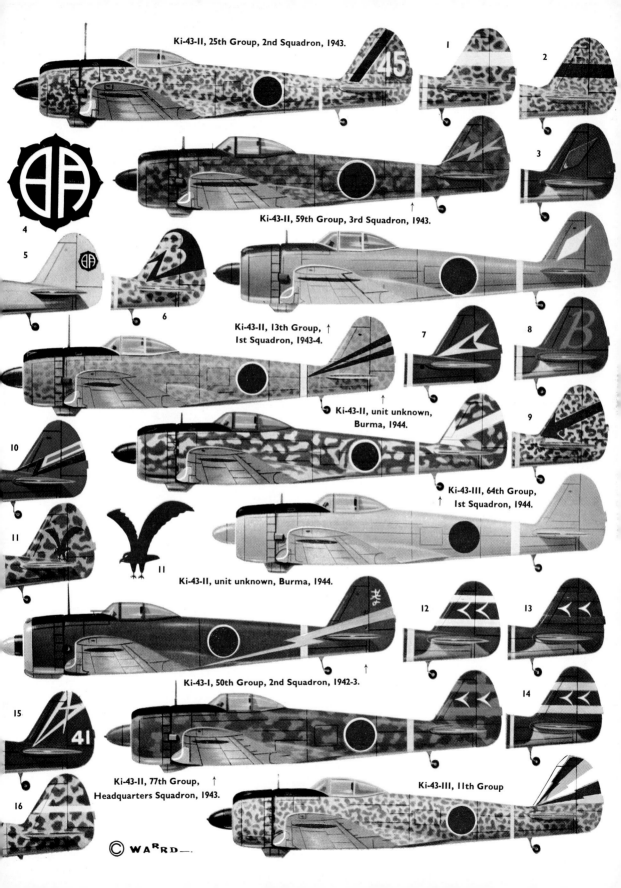

Ki-43-II, 25th Group, 2nd Squadron, 1943.

1

2

3

Ki-43-II, 59th Group, 3rd Squadron, 1943.

4

5

6

Ki-43-II, 13th Group, ↑
1st Squadron, 1943-4.

7

8

9

Ki-43-II, unit unknown,
Burma, 1944.

Ki-43-III, 64th Group,
↑ 1st Squadron, 1944.

10

11

11

Ki-43-II, unit unknown, Burma, 1944.

12

13

14

Ki-43-I, 50th Group, 2nd Squadron, 1942-3.

15

16

Ki-43-II, 77th Group, ↑
Headquarters Squadron, 1943.

Ki-43-III, 11th Group

© WARRD

Ki-43-IIa's on a Manchurian airfield, 1943. (Photo: via Witold Liss)

Ki-43 PRODUCTION

A total of 5,918 Ki-43s were manufactured between 1938 and 1945 by *Nakajima Hikoki K.K.*, in its main plant at Ota, Gumma Prefecture; at the First Army Air Arsenal (*Tachikawa Dai-ichi Rikugun Kokusho, or Rikugun* for short) at Tachikawa, Tokyo Prefecture; and at the plant of *Tachikawa Hikoki K.K.*, also at Tachikawa, Tokyo Prefecture. Production was broken down as follows.

Version	Nakajima		Rikugun		Tachikawa	
Ki-43 prototypes ...	3	December 1938–March 1939	—		—	
Ki-43 pre-production ...	10	November 1939–September 1940	—		—	
Ki-43-I Type 1 Model 1...	716	April 1941–February 1943	—		—	
Ki-43-II prototypes ...	5	February–May 1942	—		—	
Ki-43-II pre-production	3	June–August 1942	—		—	
Ki-43-II Type 1 Model 2	2,942	November 1942–September 1944	49	October 1942– November 1943	2,629	April 1943– August 1945
Ki-43-IIIa Type 1 Model 3	10	May 1944–August 1945	—			
Ki-43-IIIb	—		—		2	1945
Totals	**3,238**		**49**		**2,631**	

However, only some 5,751 Ki-43s were delivered and accepted by the J.A.A.F. as below:

Fiscal Year	Nakajima	Rikugun	Tachikawa
April 1941–March 1942	273	—	—
April 1942–March 1943	742		—
April 1943–March 1944	1,627		420
April 1944–March 1945	543	22	1,840
April 1945–August 1945 ...	—	—	284
Totals	**3,185**	**22**	**2,544**

SPECIFICATIONS
Nakajima Army Type 1 Fighter "Hayabusa" (Ki-43)

	Ki-43-Ia	Ki-43-IIa	Ki-43-IIIa
Span	37 ft. 6$\frac{5}{16}$ in.	35 ft. 6$\frac{11}{16}$ in.	35 ft. 6$\frac{11}{16}$ in.
Length	28 ft. 11$\frac{3}{4}$ in.	29 ft. 3$\frac{3}{16}$ in.	29 ft. 3$\frac{3}{16}$ in.
Height	10 ft. 8$\frac{3}{4}$ in.	10 ft. 8$\frac{3}{4}$ in.	10 ft. 8$\frac{3}{4}$ in.
Wing area	237 sq. ft.	228 sq. ft.	228 sq. ft.
Empty weight ...	3,483 lb.	4,211 lb.	4,233 lb.
Loaded weight...	4,515 lb.	5,710 lb.	5,620 lb.
Maximum weight	5,695 lb.	6,450 lb.	6,750 lb.
Fuel capacity	124 Imp. gal.+ 2 × 44 Imp. gal.	120 Imp. gal.+ 2 × 44 Imp. gal.	144 Imp. gal.+ 2 × 46 Imp. gal.
Engine	950 h.p. Type 99 (Ha-25)	1,150 h.p. Type 2 (Ha-115)	1,150 h.p. Type 2
Take-off rating ...	980 h.p.	1,130 h.p.	1,190 h.p.
Maximum rating ...	970 h.p. at 11,155 ft.	1,150 h.p. at 9,185 ft.	1,230 h.p. at 9,185 ft.
Airscrew diameter ...	9 ft. 6$\frac{3}{16}$ in.	9 ft. 2$\frac{1}{4}$ in.	9 ft. 2$\frac{1}{4}$ in..
Maximum speed ...	308 m.p.h. at 13,125 ft.	320 m.p.h. at 21,650 ft.	358 m.p.h. at 21,920 ft.
	—	329 m.p.h. at 13,125 ft.	312 m.p.h. at 9,190 ft.
	—	289 m.p.h. at S.L.	301 m.p.h. at S.L.
Cruise speed	199 m.p.h. at 8,200 ft.	273 m.p.h.	275 m.p.h.
Climbing speed ...	5 min. 30 sec. to 16,405 ft	5 min. 49 sec. to 16,405 ft.	5 min. 19 sec. to 16,405 ft.
Service ceiling	38,500 ft.	36,750 ft.	37,400 ft.
Range (normal/max). ...	745 miles/ —	1,095 miles/1,990 miles	1,320 miles/1,990 miles
Armament	2 × 7·7 mm. Type 89 2 × 33 lb. 66 lb. bombs	2 × 12·7 mm. Type 1 2 × 66 lb. or 551 lb. bombs	2 × 12·7 mm. Type 1 2 × 110 lb. or 220 lb. bombs

PRINTED IN ENGLAND. © Profile Publications Ltd., P.O. Box 26, Leatherhead, Surrey, England,
by George Falkner & Sons Ltd., for McCorquodale City Printing Division, London.

PROFILE
PUBLICATIONS

The
Chance
Vought
F4U-1
Corsair

NUMBER 47

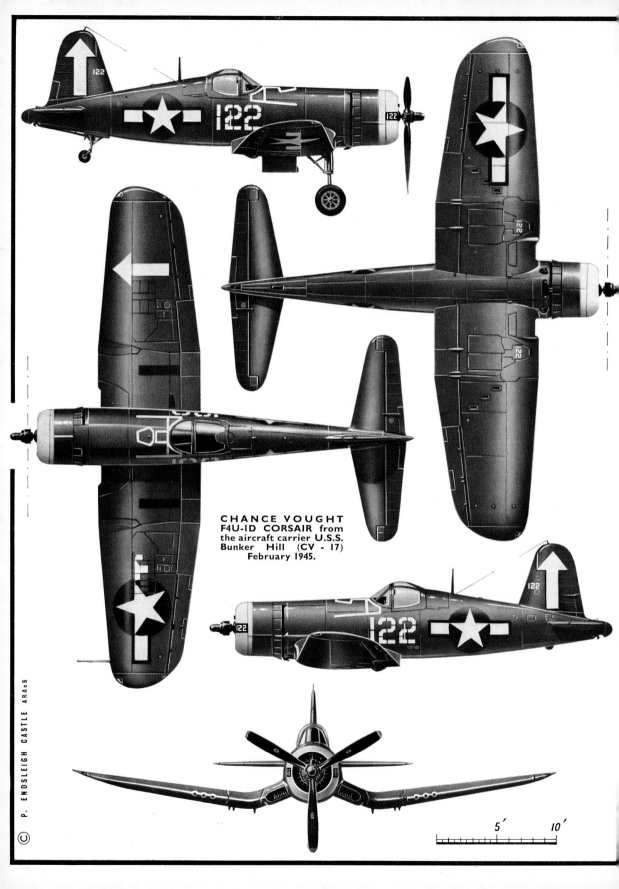

CHANCE VOUGHT
F4U-ID CORSAIR from
the aircraft carrier U.S.S.
Bunker Hill (CV - 17)
February 1945.

5´   10´

The Chance Vought F4U-1 Corsair

by J. F. Dial

A fine study of a U.S. Navy F4U-1 showing to advantage the three-shade camouflage scheme. (Photo: Vought)

To the ears of American G.I.s clawing their painful way off the bloody beaches of Okinawa in April 1945, the sweetest sound in the world was the whistling war-cry of a strangley-proportioned aircraft called the Corsair. In the shadow of their "Sweetheart's" cranked wings they found a brief respite from the danger that threatened them from every palm-grove and every scrub-covered ridge; but it is doubtful if any of them realised that the aeroplane which protected them had at one time been officially a "failure". The most important naval attack fighter of W.W.II, the Chance Vought Corsair remained in production for thirteen years, yet its first service trials had ended in failure in its chosen rôle.

The Corsair's most unique feature was the "bent" wing, the result of a marriage between the most powerful engine ever installed in a piston-engined fighter and one of the biggest propellers in the world. The inverted gull wing permitted the short, sturdy undercarriage required for carrier operations, allowed a low-drag, 90° wing-fuselage junction, gave the pilot better visibility over the wing and lowered the overall height of the folded wing. An added asset of the gull wing was a planing action during emergency water landings.

THE CORSAIR DESCRIBED

The fuselage structure was an all-aluminium monocoque of four main assemblies: engine section and forward, mid and aft fuselage sections. The engine section, ahead of Station 91¾, contained engine accessories, mounting and a Pratt and Whitney 18-cylinder twin-row R-2800-8 (-8W with water injection) Twin Wasp powerplant with two-stage supercharger and two-speed auxiliary geared 2/1. This latter operated only at High or Low blower settings. The Eclipse cartridge starter of early models was replaced by electric starters in the F4U-1D and fourth FG-1D. Hydraulically-operated cowl flaps opened to 35° for engine cooling; set full open they would remain at 35° until 105 knots I.A.S., when air pressure closed them until balanced by internal pressure. If blown closed they would re-open at lower airspeeds but if blown open, would remain open. Opening would

occur at approximately 350 knots when internal pressure over-rode the 750 lb./sq. in. actuator.

The Corsair's distinctive sound, which earned it among the Japanese the nick-name of "Whistling Death", was caused by the wing-root inlets for engine air. Placed in these inlets were the oil coolers which ejected hot air through adjustable doors under the wings just ahead of the spar.

For take-off and at low altitude air was fed directly into the carburettor and main stage blower via bypass doors on the intercoolers. With the auxiliary operating at high altitudes the air passed through the intercoolers; coolant air was ejected through a flap under the fuselage ahead of the centre-section spar.

The forward fuselage section, between Stations 91¾ and 186, contained the main fuel cell of self-sealing multi-ply rubber in a lined compartment free of dangerous projections. This compartment was ventilated and slightly pressurised by ram-air from a cut-out in the cockpit air duct. The tank was protected by an upper fuselage deck section of one-tenth inch aluminium.

The wing centre-section was an all-aluminium box-spar structure composed of main spar, inter-spar and leading and trailing edges; this was an integral part of the forward section.

The mid-section, between Stations 186 and 288, contained all radio and navigation equipment; fittings were included for the arrester gear dashpot and elevator controls as well as headrest and seat attachments. The aft section, between Stations 288 and 371½, carried fin and stabiliser attachment points and cut-outs and fittings for tail-wheel and fairing doors. The fuselage ended in a small tail cone containing the tail running light.

Wing structure consisted of the integral centre-section and hydraulically-folded outer panels of aluminium construction with fabric skin aft of the spar; jury struts locked the wings in the fully-folded position and could be unlocked and extended as the wings moved into the vertical position to permit refuelling and gun servicing. Wing airfoils were NACA 23000 section, 18% at root, 15% at fold and 9% at tip. Centre-section flaps were of aluminium structure

3

The XF4U-1 in flight. (Photo: Vought)

Another view of the prototype XF4U-1, showing the small bomb doors in the wing underside; these are indicated by the joint lines running through the national insignia. (Photo: Vought)

and aluminium covered, with a "flap gap" closure plate hinged to the outer flap and sliding into the inner to fill the aperture caused by the inverted gull wing. Outer panel flaps were of fabric-covered aluminium structure, and the ailerons were of plywood-skinned all-wood structure.

The fin was aluminium, off-set 2° to the right to counteract torque, with a fabric-covered rudder; both all-aluminium stabilisers and fabric-skinned elevators were interchangeable. In addition to normal trim tabs, ailerons and elevators had balance tabs to lighten control forces.

Fuel tankage consisted of a self-sealing cell of 237 gallons capacity (including a standpipe reserve of 50 gallons) and outer panel leading edge tanks of 63 gallons; the latter were equipped with carbon-dioxide vapour dilution to prevent detonation resulting from combat damage. A Duramold centre-line drop tank of 178 gallons capacity could be carried. F4U-1D models had no wing tankage and could carry two pylon drop tanks; these were either 154-gallon Navy Standards or 174-gallon Lockheed tanks.

The main landing gear legs rotated through 90° as they folded rearward to permit the wheels to lie flat in the wings. The rearward-folding tail-wheel, with the arrester hook attached to the strut, was self-centring, lockable and 360° swivelling with a $12\frac{1}{2} \times 4\frac{1}{2}$ in. pneumatic tyre; early models carried an $8\frac{1}{2} \times 4$ in. solid tyre.

Armament consisted of six ·5 in. Browning M2 machine guns, three in each outer wing panel, normally boresighted to converge at 300 yards. Inboard and intermediate guns carried 400 r.p.g. and outboard guns, limited by wing contours, carried 375 r.p.g. If desired the outboard guns, which most affected stability and flutter characteristics, could be removed.

THE FIRST OF THE LINE

The prototype XF4U-1 first flew on 29th March 1940 with Lyman A. Bullard at the controls, and its impressive speed of 405 m.p.h. gave the lie to the prevalent theories among Army Air Corps authorities that the future of high-speed fighter design lay in liquid-cooled engine projects. Pratt and Whitney were consequently permitted to cancel these latter projects.

In the specification for the XF4U-1 of 10th May 1938 the armament was set at two ·3 in. machine guns in the fuselage (500 r.p.g.), two ·5 in. guns in the wings (200 r.p.g.) with provision for replacement by two 23 mm. Madsen cannon, and internal bomb cells in the wings with a total capacity of 176 lb. In the prototype a "teardrop" aiming window was fitted below the centre-section, and some production aircraft had a rectangular transparency.

Ease and speed of mass production had not figured largely in the design as war was not considered imminent; thus a U.S. Navy request of 28th November

An early F4U-1 with "flat-top" canopy; points of interest are the rear-vision periscope just visible as a small protrusion on top of the windshield, the landing light, and the removable bomb rack under the outer wing panel. (Photo: A. G. Simmons)

"Flat-tops" of VF-17 in flight; the war-time censor has obscured the code "17" immediately forward of the fuselage star. (Photo: Imperial War Museum)

Armourers working on wing guns of an F4U-1 Corsair at Tutuila, Samoa. (Photo: A. G. Simmons)

An F4U-1 of VMF-214 "Blacksheep" on Turtle Bay airstrip, Espiritu Santo. Photographed in September 1943, this machine has had the arrester hook removed; many land-based Corsairs had hooks removed and wings locked down as an easily reversible "field mod". (Photo: A. G. Simmons)

1940 for production proposals led to a major programme of redesign to ease "producibility" and to bring the infant Corsair into line with changing military requirements. All armament was moved into the wings, and the main fuel cell was moved from the centre-section into the forward fuselage, thus necessitating the moving of the cockpit aft to the line of the trailing edge and opening a Pandora's box of visibility problems that were never satisfactorily solved during W.W.II. Armour totalling 170 lb. was added behind the seat, as side splash panels, and in the form of $1\frac{1}{2}$-in. laminated glass behind the windscreen; as previously stated, the fuel tankage was protected by a heavy aluminium plate.

A production contract was awarded to Chance Vought on 30th June 1941 and the first production

machine, Bureau of Aeronautics Number (BUNO) 02153 flew on 25th June 1942 with a top speed of 415 m.p.h., a sea-level climb rate of 3,120 ft./min. and a service ceiling of 37,000 ft. The first carrier trials were carried out on 25th September 1942 aboard the U.S.S. Sangamon (CVE-26) by Lt. Sam Porter in BUNO 02159, the seventh production machine. These trials drew attention to a number of problems which prevented the Corsair from going into carrier service with the U.S.N. for some years. The landing gear shock struts were too stiff; and there was a landing "kick" caused by local stall in the crank of the gull wing in the high three-point attitude. Experienced pilots learned to master this but accidents were numerous during training.* The individual actuators of each cowl flap leaked oil badly, as did the rocker-box, and this cut the already poor high-angle visibility. The early magnesium rockerbox covers of the R-2800 tended to warp; and when it was discovered that the R-1830s aluminium covers were interchangeable many Corsairs were modified with "borrowed" covers from Wildcats and Liberators. The cowl flap problem was finally solved by a modification in December 1942, using one actuator and a cable-and-roller mechanism.

The first Corsair squadron was formed at Camp Kearny, California, on 7th September 1942; this was Marine Fighting Squadron 124 (VMF-124) commanded by Maj. William Gise. October of that year saw the formation of the first Navy squadron, Fighting Squadron 12 (VF-12), at North Island under the command of Lt.-Cdr. Joe Clifton.

In order to avoid delaying aircraft on the production line a separate unit was set up to install combat

*Field units devised an extended tail-wheel strut, but CV frowned on the shifting of so much weight aft. Satisfactory results gained by a Goodyear "kit" for training units later led to production by CV; the addition of a spoiler to the starboard wing leading edge added further and also helped counteract torque at take-off.

Pilots "scrambling" from a Pacific combat base: the aircraft are F4U-1 "bubble-tops". (Photo: Vought)

The basic non-specular Pacific colour scheme is displayed by this F4U-1A with a Duramold centre-line tank of 178 galls. capacity. (Photo: Vought)

An F4U-1A with blown hood and centre-line bomb. (Photo: A. G. Simmonds)

modifications under the leadership of Col. S. Ridder-hoff, U.S.M.C., and Jack Hospers, Vought Field Service Manager throughout the entire Corsair pro-gramme. By the close of the year CV's Stratford, Connecticut plant had produced 178 F4U-1s and 66 had passed through the Hospers-Ridderhoff "com-mando" for 159 combat modifications. On 28th December, after three weeks of round-the-clock effort, 22 Corsairs were signed over to VMF-124 as "combat-ready"; and the first twelve machines arrived at Henderson Field on Guadalcanal on 12th February 1943.

INTO ACTION

On 13th February VMF-124 demonstrated their superiority over the Wildcat by escorting PB4Y-1 Liberators all the way to Bougainville. The following day they saw combat for the first time, and the inexperienced Corsair pilots were badly mauled by some 50 Mitsubishi Zeros. Two Corsairs, two Liberators, two P-40s and four P-38s were lost in this "Saint Valentine's Day Massacre", but the Corsairs soon gained an ascendancy over the Japanese which they never lost, VMF-124 being subsequently credited with 68 kills against a loss of four aircraft and three pilots. Within six months all Pacific-based Marine fighter squadrons had been re-equipped with the Corsair.

Top right: *The fume seal is clearly visible on this photo-graph of an F4U-1D taking off from the U.S.S.* Bunker Hill *for a raid on the Tokyo area early in 1945.*
(Photo: A. G. Simmons)

Above: *Corsair IV KD-244 (FG-1A Buno 14675) from 1842 Sqdn., H.M.S.* Formid-able, *on board U.S.S.* Shangri-La *(CV-38). The wing folding gap door is not closed, indica-ting that the wings are not yet locked down, or are about to be folded.*
(Photo: A. G. Simmons)

An F4U-1D Corsair aboard the U.S.S. Franklin *(CV-13).*
(Photo: A. G. Simmons)

The famous "Ole' 122", an F4U-1A of VMF-111 "Devil Dogs". This aircraft completed 100 dive-bombing missions against Japanese positions in the Marshall Islands, and had an official citation varnished into her cockpit. Note the 500-lb. bomb on a Brewster centre-line rack and the 100 mission markers under the cockpit. (Photo: Vought)

Since VF-12 had turned their machines over to Marines on Espirito Santo, VF-17 "Skull and Cross-bones" was the first Navy Corsair squadron to see action. Commanded by Tommy Blackburn, VF-17 became the first land-based fighter unit in the New Georgia area, and within 79 days of combat was credited with the destruction of 154 Japanese aircraft. This squadron has been called "the greatest Navy fighter squadron in history": it contained twelve aces (i.e. pilots credited with five or more victories) and

The F4U-1C, with four 20 mm. M-2 cannons. (Photo: Vought)

destroyed no less than 18 torpedo bombers in two passes while providing top cover for the carriers *Essex* and *Bunker Hill* during the first strike on Rabaul. When they ran low on fuel VF-17 became the first squadron to "operate" from a ship in combat.

The Corsair achieved a victory/loss ratio of 11·3/1; it proved "definitely superior" in trials with a captured Zero and gave favourable results in competitive manœuvres with a P-51, a P-47, a P-38 and a P-39. Above 12,000 ft. the Corsair outfought the Mustang and was considered evenly matched at lower altitudes. Against the F6F (even with Lt.-Cdr. "Butch" O'Hare at the controls of the Hellcat) the Corsair was more than a match for its opponent.

THE CORSAIR NIGHT FIGHTER

On 6th January 1942 CV submitted a proposal for the F4U-2 radar-equipped night fighter and the mock-up was ready for inspection by the Navy on 28th January. Pressure of normal production led to the cancellation of an initial order for 50; so "Project Affirm", the conversion of 12 standard F4U-1s, was initiated at Quonset Point, Rhode Island. Six machines were turned over to VF(N)-75 (Lt.-Cdr. G. Widhelm) and went into action from Munda Strip on New Georgia; Japanese night bombers had been carrying out nuisance raids in the area, but Widhelm's hand-picked

The 69th Corsair I, JT-168 (F4U-1 Buno 18190) at Bruns-wick, Maine.
(Photo: A. G. Simmons)

raised only $\frac{1}{2}$ in.; pilots thus adopted an almost "standing" posture when the seat was at full height, and this, coupled with the fact that the Corsair had no cockpit floorboards, gave one the impression of sitting on the edge of a deep pit with a yawning black chasm below. The pilot's posture was satisfactory for long flights but the more nervous felt a constant nagging fear that if they slipped they might just wind up somewhere in the mysterious depths of the fuselage bottom!

pilots soon rid the sky of these "Washing-machine Charlies". They claimed they shot down every enemy aircraft they saw; and a certain Lt. O'Neill startled himself by shooting down one he *didn't* see, a bomber which was in the way when he "tested guns" one night over Bougainville! The other 4FU-2s served with VF(N)-101 (Lt.-Cdr. R. E. Harmer) and went aboard the *Essex*. The night fighters were moved around considerably; at various times they flew from the *Hornet* and the *Intrepid* and served with VMF(N)-532.

GOODYEAR STARTS PRODUCTION

In November and December 1941, Brewster and Goodyear respectively had been appointed sub-contractors; and the first flights of the Brewster F3A-1 and Goodyear FG-1 had followed on 26th April and 25th February 1943. Goodyear, with a score of 4,014 machines, built almost as many of the initial model as the parent company. The first Goodyear aircraft were early flat-canopy versions but the majority were blown-hood types duplicating the F4U-1A and -1D. Due to what has been termed "poor management" Brewster had only turned out 735 Corsairs when the contract was terminated on 1st July 1944.

Very early production Corsairs were equipped with the Brownscope wide-angle rear-view periscope system, which was shortly replaced by a mirror in a small "bubble" in the sliding canopy.* The first aircraft to be fitted with the blown hood was BUNO *17456*, and the first production aircraft was accepted on 9th August 1943. The low cabin line and long nose of the early versions made accurate deflection shooting extremely difficult; the sight line was therefore raised 5 in. and the seat adjust increased to 9 in. Due to the urgency of production requirements the rudder pedals were moved aft but

COMMONWEALTH CORSAIRS

The first Corsairs for the Fleet Air Arm started to arrive in England in November 1943; these were designated Corsair I (Vought-built F4U-1), Corsair II (Vought-built F4U-1A and -1D), Corsair III (Brewster-built F3A-1), and Corsair IV (Goodyear-built FG-1). From the Corsair II onward 8 in. were clipped off each wing tip to allow storage in the lower headroom of British hangar decks; this modification resulted in a slightly higher stalling speed, but the stall was cleaner and easier to control. (The Royal Navy operated Corsairs from "Jeep" carriers long before the United States, and in some U.S.N. circles it was held that this might be a useful modification for American-flown Corsairs, although the majority opinion was that the sacrifice of wing area would be unjustifiable.) The Corsair equipped 19 Fleet Air Arm

There is no designation difference between these two versions. Indeed, there is no use of the designation "F4U-1A" for the blown-hood version in war-time CV documentation; this appears to be a post-war retroactive designation to bring terms into line with -1C and -1D designations.

Goodyear Aircraft flight-line at the company's Akron, Ohio, plant. Note folded wings of machines in background.
(Photo: Goodyear)

A R.N.Z.A.F. Corsair, serial NZ5218. (Photo: U.S.M.C. via Vought)

squadrons and formed the backbone of that service's Pacific fighter force. A total of 425 Corsairs were also supplied to the Royal New Zealand Air Force, deliveries commencing early in 1943. All from U.S. Navy contracts, they were delivered entirely out of sequence and may have been just "passing through" when assigned.

It was not until April 1944 that VF-301 completed the trials that finally permitted fleet service for the Corsair, and if a derogatory letter drafted by the Chief of Naval Air Operational Training, Jacksonville, Florida, had been sent through channels, the "bent-wing bird" might have been rejected a second time. In the hands of inexperienced pilots the F4U tended to bounce on deck landings; so "Programme Dog", the fourth modification programme, was initiated and completed in just ten days under the leadership of Jack Hospers. Modified oleo struts were free of "built-in-bounce" and VF-301 completed 113 deck landings on the *U.S.S. Gambier Bay* (CVE-73). After a series of comprehensive comparisons with the F6F-3 Hellcat, a Navy evaluation board stated on 16th May 1944 that:

". . . generally the F4U is a better fighter, a better bomber and equally suitable carrier airplane as compared with the F6F. . . . It is strongly recommended that the carrier fighter and/or bomber complements be shifted to the F4U type."

The threat of *Kamikaze* attacks necessitated a strengthening of carrier fighter units, and the Marines were called in to fill the gap. Thus, on 28th December

1944, VMF-123 (Maj. D. E. Marshall) and VMF-124 (Lt.-Col. Bill Millington) went aboard the Fast Carrier *Essex* in Ulithi Harbour. The first strike by U.S. carrier-based Corsairs was an attack on Okinawa on 3rd January 1945 by a formation of both squadrons under the command of Lt.-Col. Millington.

Cannon-armed Corsairs went into action for the first time on 7th April 1945, five pilots of VMF-311 blowing the wing off a Kawasaki *Lily*. The F4U-1C carried four 20 mm. M2 cannon with 120 r.p.g. and alternated on the production line with F4U-1Ds in batches varying from 3 to 43. (The F4U-1D carried normal six-gun armament and twin centre-section pylons for bombs or drop-tanks.) The last 266 Vought-built F4U-1Ds and FG-1Ds subsequent to the 295th machine were fitted with four fixed zero-length rocket-launching stubs under each wing. It was recommended that these were removed when not in use as they affected performance detrimentally.

Early production machines had attachment points for Mk. 41–2 bombracks under each outer wing panel, to carry a 100-lb. bomb; aircraft fitted with the centre-line drop tank installation could mount the Brewster bomb adaptor to carry either a 500 or a 1,000-lb. weapon. (There were instances of 2,000-lb. bombs being mounted. Charles A. Lindberg, a Technical Representative for United Aircraft, was pilot on the first occasion a 4,000-lb. load was carried, in an attack on Wotje Atoll.) March 1944 saw the first Corsair dive-bomber mission, an attack by VMF-111 ("The Devil Dogs") on Mille in the Marshalls group. In the

Goodyear FG-1s in flight.
(Photo: George J. Letzter)

seven weeks that followed, the Corsairs proceeded to drop 200,000 lb. of bombs on the enemy.

As the tempo of the war quickened, the Corsair played its part in bringing the wrath of the U.S. Navy to the Japanese Home Islands, and in support and cover missions during the invasions of Iwo Jima and Okinawa. Land-based Marine Corsairs flew 600 support missions on Okinawa from 7th to 30th April 1945. With the *Kamikazes* to contend with, VMF-411 shot down 17 enemy aircraft in one action, and the "Death Rattlers" destroyed 124 in a single Okinawa tour of duty. Major George Axtell, C.O. of the "Death Rattlers", said of the Corsair:

"It's the best fighter there is. It's rugged. It's a workhorse. You can use it for anything, including dive-bombing, and it's effective. You can shoot anything off or out of that plane and it still goes."

Vought terminated F4U-1 production on 2nd February 1945, with the delivery of the 4,996th machine. In air-to-air combat the Corsair had destroyed 2,140 aircraft for the loss of 189; in three years of battle she met the enemy wherever they appeared, and struck them down until there were no more. The first of a long line of fighting airplanes, the "Sweetheart of Okinawa" earned the affection of fighting men and earned it well.

New Zealand Corsair with centre-line and wing-root fuel tanks.

Left: *An F4U-1D of the U.S. Marine Corps on Okinawa.* Right: *FG-1D of the U.S. 2nd Marine Air Division.*   (Photos: U.S.M.C.)

Left: *F4U-2 radar-equipped night-fighters of VMF(N) 532 aboard the U.S.S.* Windham Bay *(CVE-92). Note that the aircraft facing the camera has only two guns in the starboard wing.* Right: *F4U-2s preparing to take off from the U.S.S.* Enterprise *for a mission over Truk.*   (Photos: A. G. Simmons)

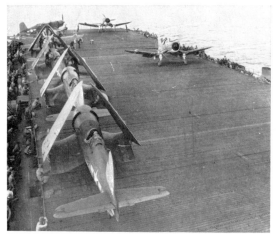
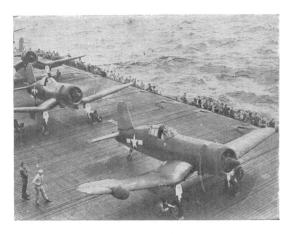

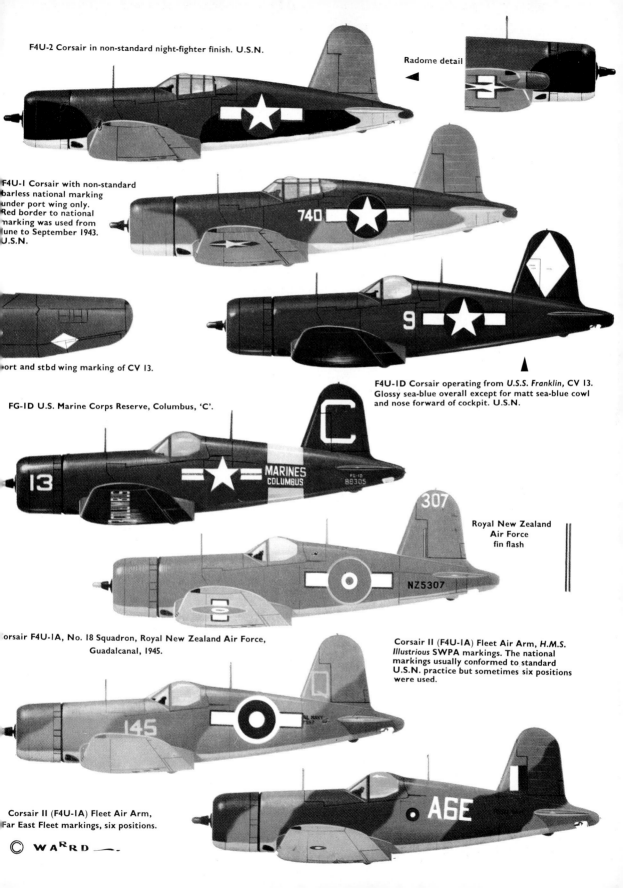

F4U-2 Corsair in non-standard night-fighter finish. U.S.N.

Radome detail

F4U-1 Corsair with non-standard barless national marking under port wing only. Red border to national marking was used from June to September 1943. U.S.N.

740

port and stbd wing marking of CV 13.

F4U-1D Corsair operating from *U.S.S. Franklin*, CV 13. Glossy sea-blue overall except for matt sea-blue cowl and nose forward of cockpit. U.S.N.

9

FG-1D U.S. Marine Corps Reserve, Columbus, 'C'.

C

13   MARINES COLUMBUS   FG-1D 88305

307

Royal New Zealand Air Force fin flash

NZ5307

Corsair F4U-1A, No. 18 Squadron, Royal New Zealand Air Force, Guadalcanal, 1945.

Corsair II (F4U-1A) Fleet Air Arm, *H.M.S. Illustrious* SWPA markings. The national markings usually conformed to standard U.S.N. practice but sometimes six positions were used.

145

Corsair II (F4U-1A) Fleet Air Arm, Far East Fleet markings, six positions.

A6E

© WARRD

Two fine illustrations of an F4U-1A with a 1,000-lb. bomb on a Brewster centre-line rack. The undersurface view shows the belly bomb-aiming window below the centre-section, immediately behind the bomb. (Photos: Vought)

PRODUCTION NOTES

Year	Chance Vought F4U-1, -1A, -1C and -1D	Goodyear FG-1A and -1D	Brewster F3A and -1A
1942	178	—	—
1943	1,780	377	136
1944	2,667	2,108	599
1945	74 (F4U-4 production commenced in 1944)	1,529	(Contract terminated July 1st 1944)
Total	4,669	4,014	735

Service Use	Type	U.S.N.	Royal Navy	R.N.Z.A.F.
	F4U-1	876*	95	—
	F4U-1A	1,232**	360	173
	F4U-1C	190	—	—
	F4U-1D	1,659***	150	192
	FG-1A	487†	99	—
	FG-1D	1,470****	843	60
	F3A-1A	305	430	—
	Totals	6,255*****	1,977	425

* = Includes 12 converted to F4U-2 standard.
** = Includes 173 to New Zealand.
*** = Includes 192 to New Zealand.
**** = Includes 60 to New Zealand.
***** = Includes 425 to New Zealand.
†Includes, reportedly, 2 "Flat-top" versions.

© *J. F. Dial*, 1965

Author and publishers gratefully acknowledge the assistance of the following in the preparation of this Profile: A. Schoeni, H. Cunningham, R. DeLeva, H. Hope, B. R. Winbourne, Richard Atkins and R. B. Brown, all of Ling-Temco-Vought; Jack Hospers, d' E. C. Darby and the N.Z.A.H.S., D. W. Brown of Goodyear Aerospace Corp. and Alan G. Simmons.

A blue-grey "bubble-top" Corsair taking off from the U.S.S. Core (CVE-13); probably an aircraft from the first Navy Corsair squadron, VF-12. (Photo: A. G. Simmons)

United States Corsair Units

U.S.M.C.: VMF-111 (Devil Dogs), VMF-112 (Wolf Pack), VMF-122, VMF-123, VMF-124, VMF-212, VMF-213, VMF-214 (Black-sheep), VMF-215 (Fighting Corsairs), VMF-216, VMF-221 (Flying Falcons), VMF-222 (Flying Duces), VMF-223, VMF-225, VMF-311, VMF-323 (Death Rattlers), VMF-411, VMF-422, VMF(N)-532.
U.S.N.: VF-12, VF-17 (Skull and Crossbones), VF(N)-75, VF-82, VF(N)-101, VF-301.
(The above list of units covers known Corsair squadrons, and is not necessarily complete.)

Corsair Aces:

Colonel Gregory M. "Pappy" Boyington, C.O. of VMF-124, 28 kills.
Major Joseph Foss, C.O. of VMF-422, 26 kills.
Lt. Robert M. Hanson, 25 kills, 20 of which were scored within 17 days.
Major Kenneth Walsh, 21 kills.
Major John L. Smith, 19 kills.
Lt. Ira Kepford of VF-17, 19 kills.
Major Marion Carl, 18½ kills.

SPECIFICATION

Dimensions: Wing span 40 ft. 11·7 in. Span (folded) 17 ft. 0·5 in. Length 33 ft 4·6 in. Height (taxi position) 15 ft. 0·07 in. Height (wing folded) 16 ft. 6 in. Max. height (wing vertical) 18 ft. 3·2 in. Wing area 314 sq. ft.
Weights: Empty 8,694·5 lb. Gross 11,092·8 lb. Useful load 2,398·2 lb. Wing loading 26·6 lb./sq. ft. Power loading 4·72 lb./h.p.
Powerplant: One Pratt and Whitney 18-cylinder twin-row R-2800-8(W) Twin Wasp B Series with two-speed super-charger.
Powerplant Ratings: Take-off 2,000 h.p. at 2,700 r.p.m. Military 2,000 h.p. at 2,700 r.p.m. *War Emergency 2,250 h.p. at 2,700 r.p.m. Max. Cruise 1,070 h.p. at 2,150 r.p.m. Economy Cruise 570 h.p. at 1,300 r.p.m.
Fuel Tankage: Internal 237 gallons. Normal Fighter 178 gallons. Overload Fighter 535 gallons.
Performance: Max. speed 415 m.p.h. at 20,000 ft. Stalling speed 79 m.p.h. at sea level. Initial climb 3,120 ft./min. Service ceiling (normal load) 37,000 ft. Take-off over 50 ft. obstacle (no wind) 1,430 ft. Landing over 50 ft. obstacle (no wind) 2,500 ft.

*This rating refers to the -8W powerplant with water-ethyl alcohol injection, fitted to F4U-1D and the fourth FG-1D. The injection of this mixture allowed the increase of power above Military rating by acting as an anti-detonant. 10·4 gallons were carried in three tanks with 40% alcohol used for anti-freeze protection. Initiated by the last ¾ in. of throttle movement, the device gave an extra 250 h.p.

PRINTED IN ENGLAND. © Profile Publications Ltd., P.O. Box 26, Leatherhead, Surrey, England, by George Falkner & Sons Ltd., for McCorquodale City Printing Division, London.

PROFILE
PUBLICATIONS

The
de Havilland
Vampire
Mk. 5 & 9

NUMBER 48

WA 432

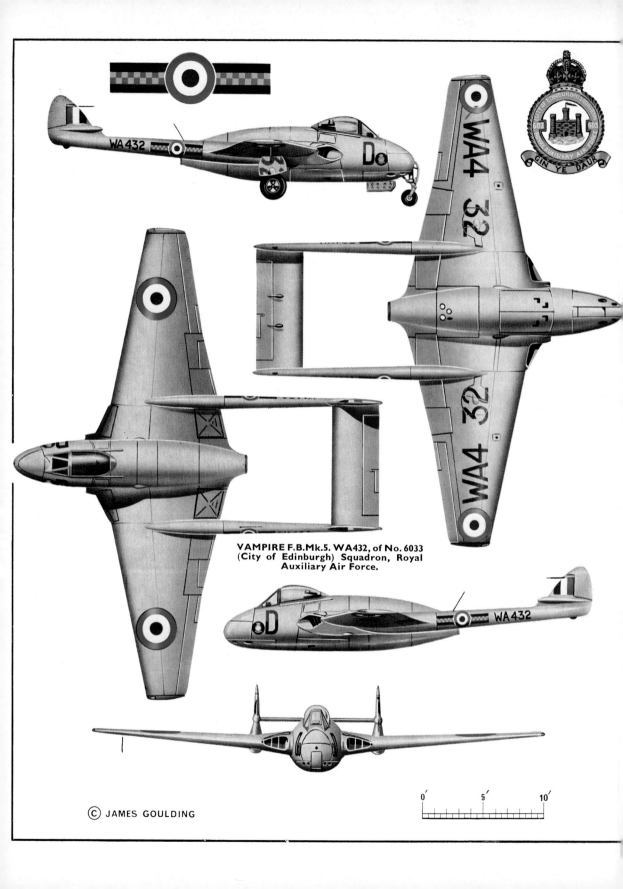

VAMPIRE F.B.Mk.5. WA432, of No. 6033
(City of Edinburgh) Squadron, Royal
Auxiliary Air Force.

GIN YE DAUR

© JAMES GOULDING

The de Havilland
Vampire Mk. 5 & 9

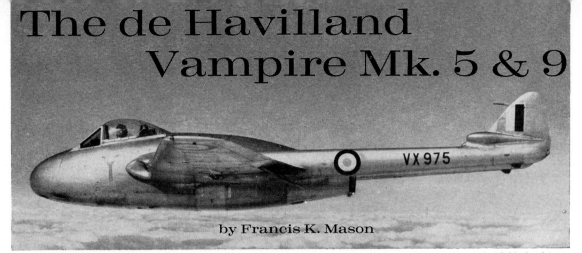

by Francis K. Mason

No. 247 (Fighter) Squadron Vampire F.B.5 flying from Odiham in May 1951. The unit letter on the nose was red with black edging—the Squadron colours.
(Photo: via R. Ward)

Fondly referred to by many post-war pilots as the "aerial kiddy car", the Vampire day fighter was certainly the last unsophisticated single-engine front-line aircraft to serve with Britain's Fighter Command. To qualify this distinction, one must first point out that all its flying controls were manually-operated without recourse to or necessity for power assistance. No radar was fitted and the fighter consisted of a simple airframe, "first generation" jet engine, and four 20-mm. Hispano guns aimed by a gyro gunsight. Only the twin boom layout set the Vampire aside as being unconventional among its contemporaries.

Detail design of the de Havilland D.H. 100 Vampire commenced early in 1942 after acceptance of proposals submitted to Air Ministry Specification E.6/41. Though this called for an experimental prototype, provision for gun armament was included in the design from the earliest days, the newly-established four 20-mm. Hispano gun battery being housed in the underside of the fuselage nacelle. Power was supplied by one D.H. Goblin I jet engine which employed a single-sided centrifugal compressor and produced 2,700 pounds thrust.

Construction was composite metal and balsa/ply, the fuselage nacelle continuing the wood application used in the successful Mosquito design which entered R.A.F. service in mid-1942. Three prototypes, *LZ548/G, LZ551/G* and *MP838/G* (characterised by tall triangular vertical surfaces generically similar to that of the Mosquito) led the way to a production order for 120 Mark Is being placed on 13th May 1944, and this was later increased to 300. Only about half-a-dozen production aircraft flew before the end of W.W.II, but, unlike so many other wartime British aircraft, production plans for the Vampire survived the post-war axe. Mark Is (with square-topped tail surfaces) entered R.A.F. service in 1946 as pure interceptors and also equipped squadrons of the Second Tactical Air Force in Germany, often replacing wartime generation fighters such as Typhoons, Mustangs and Tempests. On 3rd July 1948 they were the first jet aircraft to enter peacetime service with the Royal Auxiliary Air Force when they replaced Mosquitos on No. 605 (County of Warwick) Squadron.

Vampire Is were also supplied in various versions to Canada, Switzerland and Sweden, and thence by various routes to Austria and the Dominican Republic.

Vampire II was the designation applied to three experimental Nene-powered Vampires, *TG276, TG280* and *TX807*, identified by dorsal intakes demanded by the double-sided compressor of the Rolls-Royce engine. The latter aircraft was shipped out to Australia where (as *A78-2*) it performed much of the development work for the subsequent Nene-powered Vampire F.Mk.30.

The Vampire III represented an attempt to increase the effectiveness of the design in the environment of increased radar warning range, anticipated shortly after the end of the war. The first-generation jet fighter was widely characterised by a chronic lack of range, in the case of the Vampire I only about 700 statute miles. The early Vampires had used Mosquito-type underwing slipper tanks, but the Mark III introduced wing tankage and provision for 100- or 200-gallon drop tanks. Developed to Spec. F.3/47, the Vampire 3 (so designated after the change to arabic numerals) entered R.A.F. service late in 1947 and remained with the R. Aux. A.F. until well into the nineteen-fifties. The type was also characterised by alterations to the tail unit: the tailplane was lowered and the vertical surfaces were changed to conform more nearly to the well-known de Havilland outline.

The Vampire 3 made history when six aircraft of No. 54 (Fighter) Squadron became the first British jet aircraft to cross the Atlantic, refuelling in Iceland, Greenland and Labrador.

Re-design of the Vampire wing to accommodate pylon-mounted drop tanks inevitably led to the carriage of other stores and hence adaptation of the design for ground-attack duties. With low-level performance of prime importance, the wing span was reduced by two feet so that the wing tips were square cut (trials with this wing were carried out on Vampire I, *TG444*), and the provision of strongpoints for bombs and rockets was accompanied by greater strength factors and thicker wing skinning. The increased wing loading in turn resulted in greater sinking speeds on landing and this demanded undercarriage legs of increased travel. Thus was evolved the Vampire F.B.Mark 5.

THE VAMPIRE 5

The first production Vampire F.B.5 flew on 23rd June 1948 and by the end of the year was replacing Vampire 3s in Fighter Command. Next they started to replace Mosquitos in R.A.F. Squadrons in Germany and later joined Mark 3s in service with the

Air-to-air take-off view of an early Vampire 5; mainwheels are just commencing retraction, the nosewheel already locked up and covered.

R. Aux. A.F. It was however in Germany that the Vampire served in the largest numbers for, with the increased tension following the Berlin Airlift and with a war being fought in Korea, the R.A.F. faced increased responsibilities in Europe. By 1954 Vampire 5s had served with or were serving on Nos. 3, 4, 5, 11, 16, 20, 26, 67, 71, 93, 94, 118, 145, 234 and 266 (Fighter) Squadrons of the 2nd Tactical Air Force.

At home, Vampires served in Nos. 11 and 12 Groups in the south of England with Nos. 54 and 247 (Fighter) Squadrons at Odiham, and also Nos. 72 and 130 Squadrons. With the Auxiliaries, they served on Nos. 501, 502, 601, 602, 603, 604, 605, 607, 608, 609, 612, 613 and 614, and were still serving on these Squadrons when the R. Aux. A.F. was disbanded in 1957.

The Vampire 5 also served in the Middle and Far East, and it was in the latter area that their weapons were discharged in anger. No. 32 (Fighter) Squadron had operated Vampire 3s from Nicosia since 1949, and carried out tropical trials with the type; in January 1951 the Squadron moved to Shallufa and converted to Mark 5s. The month previously No. 60 Squadron, based at Tengah, Singapore, took delivery of Vampire 5s and very soon the new aircraft were in action against the terrorists at large in the jungle, using their rockets and bombs to good effect.

By 1953 the Vampire was becoming outdated in the Regular Air Force at home. (At the same time the Meteor 8 only managed to remain relatively effective by the addition of spring tabs and other minor improvements.) On being replaced by Meteor 8s, Vampire 5s were relegated to Flying Training Command, serving with Advanced Flying Schools Operational Conversion Units and the School of Air Armament.

One of many Vampire 5 formation teams, this group was flown by instructors from R.A.F. Swinderby during the mid 1950's.

(Photo: Ministry of Defence)

A No. 6 Squadron Vampire 5 raising the dust on take-off during air exercises in Jordan in 1950. No. 6 Squadron was at that time normally based in the Suez Canal Zone.

THE VAMPIRE 9

Experience with Vampire 3s and 5s in tropical climates during 1949-51 illustrated the need to provide the pilots with refrigeration equipment. The result was the inclusion of a Godfrey refrigerator unit in the starboard wing intake fillet, resulting in the fillet being extended about eight inches forward.

At the same time it had also been demonstrated that the performance of jet aircraft suffered in the high ambient temperatures of the tropics, and experience with Vampires exported to tropical countries had engendered the development of the uprated Goblin 3 which, with dual fuel booster pumps, developed 3,500 pounds thrust. This engine was also adopted in the Vampire F.B.Mk.9.

The first Vampire 9s to go into R.A.F. service overseas were ferried out by pilots of R.A.F. Transport Command to Nos. 28 and 60 Squadrons in the Far East during January 1952 where they gradually replaced F.B.5s.

Shortly afterwards Vampire 9s equipped the Middle East Squadrons, Nos. 6, 8, 32, 73, 213 and 249 based at Nicosia, Shallufa, Habbaniyah, Khormaksar and in the Suez Canal Zone. Aircraft of No. 8 Squadron,

based in Kenya, took part in the prolonged policing operations against the Mau Mau terrorists.

With the introduction of the Venom F.B.1 during 1954 and 1955, the Vampire 9s were brought home and joined earlier versions on training units.

In its day the Vampire was an excellent transitional training aircraft. In service with Operational Conversion Units at Valley in Anglesey, and Chivenor, North Devon, they were used to "convert" pilots from the North American Harvard to operational fighters such as the Gloster Meteor 8 and North American Sabre. They were also used to convert night fighter pilots from Mosquitos to the Vampire 10.

Among jet fighters, they were forgiving aeroplanes. During an air gunnery sortie from Chivenor a pilot returned to base with the target flag wedged in his starboard air intake. Another pilot, misjudging his approach to the Chivenor runway, undershot and rubbed the Vampire's belly on a threshold sand dune; realising his wheels were still retracted, he opened up and went round for a conventional landing. A more senior officer had a disconcerting experience during take-off when, just before unstick, the control column fouled his dinghy pack between his legs, causing the

The "weathercocking" action by 3-inch rockets well demonstrated by a Vampire 5 of the 2nd Tactical Air Force during air-to-ground firing practice.

A No. 8 Squadron Vampire 9 taking-off from R.A.F. Khormaksar, Aden.

dinghy to inflate; faced with rapidly diminishing living space, the pilot drew his revolver and blew a hole in the offending dinghy. Unfortunately he also holed his foot! Thereafter many R.A.F. pilots carried small knives sewn into the sleeves of their flying overalls.

Perhaps the luckiest escape from a Vampire 5 was that of Plt. Off. Roger Dimmock who, flying as No. 2 on a low-level flight over the Irish Sea, accidentally touched the water and immediately flamed-out. Performing the inevitable ditching was an act of instant self-preservation, but the aircraft promptly dived under the surface and came to rest on the sea bed about 30 feet down; quickly releasing his harness and hood, Dimmock shot to the surface in the cockpit air bubble.

THE VAMPIRE AT SEA

Ever since Lt.-Cdr. E. M. Brown, R.N.V.R., had performed the first-ever deck landings and take-offs by a pure-jet aircraft in the third Vampire prototype on H.M.S. *Ocean* on 3rd December 1945, the Admiralty maintained a close interest in the Vampire as a possible standard naval fighter. That this never

came about was not so much the fault of the aircraft as the opinion that carrier operations were not sufficiently flexible to allow combat application of jet aircraft at sea. On the one hand deck handling techniques did not lend themselves to the disruption caused by jet blasts, and on the other the critically short range and endurance of early jet fighters created a navigational burden upon the pilot such that the interceptor could only be regarded as "fleet top cover".

When the Air Ministry issued a specification covering the Vampire 5 with increased range in 1947, the Admiralty ordered 18 examples with which to intro-

Above: *A Vampire F.B.5, WA 332, of No. 7 F.T.S., based at Valley, Anglesey.*

Left: *This No. 60 Squadron Vampire 9 demonstrates the characteristic " torching " effect during engine flight at night.*

Echelon formation of No. 8 Squadron Vampire 9s in flight near Aden in 1954.

duce jet operating techniques to operational pilots and deck crews. Honours for the first British jet fighter to reach operational status however fell to the Supermarine Attacker.

First of the naval Vampires to fly—designated Sea Vampire F.20—was *VV136*, on 15th October 1948. Production machines were delivered to No. 700 Squadron at Ford and No. 702 Squadron at Culdrose, and also to No. 787 Squadron, replacing de Havilland Sea Hornets. During the course of deck trials Lieutenants G. Baldwin, D.S.C., and K. Shepherd of the Carrier Trials Unit performed more than two hundred landings at sea.

The Sea Vampire was distinguishable from the R.A.F. version in being equipped with a Vee-frame arrester hook installed *over* the engine jet pipe, so that when lowering it passed through the jet flow. Air brakes and landing flaps were enlarged to give better low speed control for the approach to the deck, and load factors were increased to cater for greater deck landing loads.

A development was the Sea Vampire F.21, of which three examples were produced, and this was used both at the Royal Aircraft Establishment, Farnborough, and on H.M.S. *Warrior* for undercarriage-less landings. With strengthened undersides the aircraft were flown on to rubberised deck surfaces with wheels retracted, the purpose being principally to accelerate deck handling simply by bodily manhandling the fighter out of the path of following aircraft.

VAMPIRES FOR EXPORT

Though not strictly akin to the Vampire 5, the Australian Nene-powered Vampire F.B.31 was developed from the Mark 3 through the Australian F.30 by modifications equivalent to those of the R.A.F.'s F.B.5. Eighty Vampire 30s were built, of which 29

No. 8 Squadron Vampire 9s on patrol over Mau Mau territory during the operations of the early 1950s.
(Photo: Ministry of Defence)

Fairey-built Vampire F.B.9, WR 264, *of the Royal Air Force College.*

became Mk. 31s. One other was converted to the Mark 32 which in effect corresponded to the R.A.F. Mk. 9 with cockpit conditioning added.

The principal export variant was the Vampire 6, powered by the Goblin 3. One hundred Mark 6s were licence built in Switzerland by a consortium comprising the Federal Aircraft Plant at Emmen, Pilatus and Flug und Fahrzeugwerke A.G.

Sweden ordered the Vampire F.B.50 based on the Mk. 5, while the Goblin 3-powered F.B.52 was sold to Finland, Norway, Egypt, Iraq, Lebanon and Venezuela, twelve standard Mark 5s were diverted to the Indian Air Force and 27 went to the South African Air Force. Overseas licence production included 80 F.B. Mk. 52As produced by Macchi and Fiat in Italy, and 67 standard Mark 5s assembled in France by S.N.C.A. du Sud-Est.

At the time of writing some Vampires are still airworthy in Venezuela, Finland and the Lebanon.

FLYING THE VAMPIRE

Undoubtedly the outstanding feature of the Vampire's handling characteristics was its incredible lightness and sensitivity of control. Ailerons were finely balanced and high rates of roll were possible though reversal was startling in its onset. The elevator was also highly effective and large accelerations resulted from relatively slight movements of the control column. On the other hand the rudders, on account of their small area, demanded coarse movement to be of much consequence.

Take-off. So simple were the Vampire's systems that only six take-off Vital Actions were necessary: trim neutral, high and low pressure fuel cocks "on", booster pump "on", flaps selected as required and air brakes "in". When flown clean, acceleration on take-off was sprightly and the aircraft could be lifted from the runway at about 110 knots. When carrying drop

Underwing 500-lb. bombs on Vampire F.B.9s of No. 60 Squadron, Tengah, Singapore.
(Photo: via D. Ward)

J28B Vampire of V.5 in natural metal finish. Numerals were painted black and panels were of orange-red dayglow. The Wings equipped with Vampires were F.8, F.9, F.15 and F.18.
(Photo: Bo Widfeldt)

Swedish Vampires allocated to F.5 of the Swedish Air Force (full unit markings not yet completed). (Photo: Bo Widfeldt)

tanks or bombs it was necessary to retract the wheels quickly otherwise the airflow between the stores and wheel fairings would build up and cause the doors to stay open. As no nosewheel brake was included, the still-rotating nosewheel entering its recess immediately below the pilot often caused so much noise and vibration that the uninitiated momentarily anticipated instant catastrophe.

In the air. Engine handling took some getting used to. Pilots experienced in piston engine handling had to learn to anticipate speed demands earlier as the power response from the Goblin was considerably slower, and any rapid throttle movement might cause engine surge, flame out or, at worst, a burst compressor.

Due to the relatively good power/weight ratio of the single-seat Vampire, the aeroplane was tremendously manoeuvrable within the 400-500 m.p.h. speed range. At lower speeds, however, steep turns required coarse use of rudder to maintain height, and it was uncomfortably simple to stall in relatively shallow turns. The stall was likely to be accompanied by quite sharp wing-drop, but a surprising amount of aileron control existed right down to the stall, albeit with marked control buffet. One was advised to recover quickly while use of the most effective elevator could be maintained. Though by no means dangerous, the spin could be embarrassing owing to blanking of the diminutive rudders and the necessity to use coarse elevator control resulted in the aircraft pointing at *terra firma* for an uncomfortable length of time while speed built up

Aerobatics in the Vampire were sheer joy and were strangely akin to those of light sporting aircraft, apart, of course, from the airspeed and amount of sky used. With judicious engine handling, the Vampire was the last British jet fighter to be capable of accurately precipitated hammer stalls, stall turns and wingovers.

At the upper end of the speed range, the Vampire behaved in singular fashion with the onset of compressibility, and from M = 0·71 up to 0·76 the aircraft displayed increasing porpoising and wing buffet until at M0·79 the aircraft would suddenly "break" up or down with the likelihood of a wing drop, giving the sensation of an "incipient" flick roll. Recovery from high Mach runs was simple with use of the air brakes, though below 250 knots these were of little real value.

Should a flame-out occur in flight, a forced landing was unavoidable as no re-light system was provided. Ditching was not recommended and, if over water, the pilot was advised to vacate his cockpit.

Landing. Landing vital actions, like those for take-off, were minimal: wheel brakes checked off, landing gear indicated down (three green lights), flaps fully down on final approach, and air brakes in. After turning on to the final approach at about 105 knots, speed was reduced so as to cross the runway threshold at about 95. Stall with gear down and power on would occur at little above 75 knots, so that touchdown would be aimed at about 10-15 knots above this when landing without stores. Owing to the sluggish engine response, power-on approaches were recommended in order to obtain quicker acceleration in the event of a go-round. The low landing weight meant that wheel locking could easily occur when using the brakes, and careful braking was necessary if constant tyre replacement was to be avoided! Anti-skid devices were not fitted.

The cockpit. By later standards, the cockpit was distinctly untidy. The fuel gauges were virtually invisible without moving the control column back! And then some mental arithmetic was required to tot up the fuel remaining in the various tanks. Although not required in flight (except in the event of a forced landing), movement of the low pressure fuel cock demanded double-jointed fingers as the lever was carefully concealed behind the throttle! Despite these shortcomings, view from the cockpit was superlative, and this together with the small size of the Vampire contributed to a feeling of being an integral part of a delightfully sensitive flying machine.

VAMPIRE 5 PRODUCTION

Manufacture by English Electric Co. Ltd., Samlesbury:
VV214–VV232,   VV443–VV490,   VV525–VV569,   VV600–VV611,
VV614–VV640,   VV655–VV700,   VV717–VV736; 220 aircraft, of which VV718, VV720–VV723, VV725–VV736 were diverted to the Indian Air Force.
VX461–VX464,   VX471–VX476,   VX950–VX990,   VZ105–VZ155,
VZ161–VZ197,   VZ206–VZ241,   VZ251–VZ290,   VZ300–VZ359;

Later production Vampire 5 of No. 614 Squadron, Royal Auxiliary Air Force.